THE MODERN HISTORY OF IRAQ

THIRD EDITION

THE MODERN HISTORY OF

IRAQ

PHEBE MARR

**WESTVIEW
PRESS**

A Member of the Perseus Books Group

Westview Press was founded in 1975 in Boulder, Colorado, by notable publisher and intellectual Fred Praeger. Westview Press continues to publish scholarly titles and high-quality undergraduate- and graduate-level textbooks in core social science disciplines. With books developed, written, and edited with the needs of serious nonfiction readers, professors, and students in mind, Westview Press honors its long history of publishing books that matter.

Find us on the World Wide Web at www.westviewpress.com.

Every effort has been made to secure required permissions for all text, images, maps, and other art reprinted in this volume.

Westview Press books are available at special discounts for bulk purchases in the United States by corporations, institutions, and other organizations. For more information, please contact the Special Markets Department at the Perseus Books Group, 2300 Chestnut Street, Suite 200, Philadelphia, PA 19103, or call (800) 810-4145, ext. 5000, or e-mail special.markets@perseusbooks.com.

Designed by Trish Wilkinson
Set in 11.5 point Adobe Garamond Pro

Library of Congress Cataloging-in-Publication Data

Marr, Phebe.
    The modern history of Iraq / Phebe Marr. — 3rd ed.
        p.   cm.
    Includes bibliographical references and index.
    ISBN 978-0-8133-4443-0 (pbk : alk. paper) — ISBN 978-0-8133-4521-5 (ebook)
1. Iraq—History—1921– I. Title.
DS79.65.M33 2011
956.704—dc23
2011021092

10   9   8   7   6   5   4   3   2   1

CONTENTS

PREFACE

Although Iraq is a comparatively new state—some ninety years old—of modest size, few countries have been the focus of such world attention or endured such domestic trauma in recent decades. Wars, sanctions, occupation, and brutal civil strife have brought abrupt, severe, and often disabling change to its historical trajectory, making it difficult to chart Iraq's future path and to relate these changes to Iraq's enduring continuities. Yet the continuities will remain. Iraq has had a remarkably rich and varied history. Even before recent headlines made Iraq a household word in the West, it was difficult to do justice to the complexity of Iraq's modern history and to explain the impact of rapid change and modernization on a society going back six millennia. Events since 2003, with their profound discontinuities and uncertainties, have now made this task more challenging, but new possibilities have also made it rewarding. Although much more is now known (but possibly misunderstood) about contemporary Iraq, even more remains opaque. This revision will not seek to provide answers to the future but rather to identify the forces at work since 2003, the trends and directions in evidence, and to relate them to Iraq's past history since its founding as a state in 1920.

This book is not meant to be an exhaustive and detailed history of modern Iraq. My aim instead has been to present a clear, readable one-volume account of the emergence of modern Iraq and the forces that shaped it. To understand how and why Iraq has reached this point in the context of a longer historical perspective, I have drawn extensively on many perceptive monographs and studies on modern Iraq. I have tried to include enough general interpretation of events to make the country and its people understandable and enough detail to give color to the events described. Above all, I have tried to be evenhanded in depicting the course of events and to avoid oversimplifying complex situations. Although the book is directed at the general reader, I hope that scholars and students of the Middle East as well as many of those now traveling and working in Iraq will find it useful.

The material has been grouped around several themes that, in my view, have dominated Iraq's history from 1920 to the present. The first is the creation and construction of a modern state within the boundaries bequeathed to Iraq by the British in the 1920s and the search by Iraq's leaders for a cultural and national identity capable of knitting together the country's various ethnic, religious, and social groups. This issue of identity and its impact on the Iraqi state is paramount today. A second theme is the process of economic and social development, a process that began at the end of the nineteenth century but greatly accelerated in the 1970s, although it has suffered a multitude of setbacks recently through war, sanctions, and social disruption. A third, and most essential, theme is the development of political institutions and ideologies and their interrelationship with domestic society and the world outside Iraq. The book seeks to show both changes and continuities in Iraq's political dynamics as well as to explain the results of a brutal totalitarian system, like that of Saddam Husain, on society, and the impact of foreign occupation on the political system emerging in Iraq today. A fourth theme is that of foreign domination and the interaction of the newly created state with the West, Iraq's neighbors, and the global environment. This theme has, of course, intensified with the occupation. Although Iraq's future is uncertain at the end of the first decade of this millennium, it is better understood through historical perspective.

In recent years a growing and valuable body of literature on Iraq written by Iraqis themselves has appeared, including memoirs, first-hand accounts, and studies. I have drawn on these whenever possible. Since 2003 a veritable flood of books and articles by journalists and practitioners has appeared in English about the occupation and its aftermath. Even though no one can read all of them, a number, especially those by Iraqis, have been very useful, and I have used them extensively.

As the Western side of this story can be readily accessed in these works, I have tried to focus in this book on Iraq. Freedom of the press and media in Iraq and the spread of the Internet to Iraqis have provided a multitude of new sources, such as blogs, which I have used selectively. Quantitative data and statistical reports from the United Nations, the World Bank, and international organizations, such as International Organization for Migration–Iraq, have also increased since 2003 and provide invaluable source material. The reader is warned, however, that statistics are still difficult to gather, are often subject to controversy, and should be treated with caution.

Acknowledgments

Traveling in Iraq and talking to people openly and freely were virtually impossible in Saddam's last decade. This changed in 2003 when the country opened up to Americans and others for a brief period of a year or two, but with increasing violence, traveling there subsequently became difficult and hazardous once again. Nonetheless, to supplement the published record, I have made extensive use of interviews with Iraqi political figures, educators, journalists, and ordinary men and women conducted during several trips to Iraq in 2004, 2005, 2006, and 2010. I would like to acknowledge their help, particularly Iraqi leaders in ISCI, Da'wa, Fadila, the IIP, and Iraqiyya, as well as various MPs, journalists, lawyers, tribal leaders, and civil society workers who gave generously of their time in attempting to explain what was happening in Iraq. In particular, I wish to thank Ibrahim al-Ja'fari, Abd al-Karim al-Musawi, Muwaffiq al-Ruba'i, Humam al-Hammudi, Saif al-Din Abd al-Rahman, and A. Heather Coyne for their help in arranging interviews and for the time they gave to my efforts. I am also indebted to Mas'ud Barzani, president of the KRG, and Jalal Talabani, president of Iraq, for their support and hospitality in making trips to Iraqi Kurdistan possible in the 1990s and to their staff for unfailing assistance and much valuable information.

I am also greatly indebted in this update of this book to the United States Institute of Peace for a fellowship grant for two years 2004–2006 to enable me to gather data on the newly emerging regime and its political figures. My time at the institute and the trips to Iraq it enabled me to make were indispensable. Above all, I wish to thank my intern during this period, Sam Parker, for his support, collaboration in research and writing, and fund of valuable ideas. He has contributed a great deal to the revision. I also thank Denise Natali for sponsorship of a trip to Kurdistan in 2010 and Jacob Passel and Sasha Gordon for help in preparing the manuscript.

My greatest gratitude goes to my husband, Louay Bahry, first, for his invaluable insights on Iraqi history as a former professor of political science at Baghdad University, and second, for his patience in putting up with my long hours in the library and at the computer.

Naturally the interpretations, as well as any historical errors in the manuscript, are my own.

NOTE ON TRANSLITERATION

Arabic words in this text have been transliterated according to the accepted system for written standard Arabic, with some modifications. The spellings reflect neither pronunciation, which may vary from place to place, nor accepted English spellings, which often reflect the way a word "sounds" in English rather than how it is spelled in Arabic. (It may be helpful to the English-speaking reader to note that Arabic uses only three vowels—a, i, and u; there is no e or o in Arabic spellings.) Hence, to the average reader the spellings of some words may be unfamiliar. For example, sheik appears as shaikh; the surname Hussein, as Husain.

However, I have simplified the standard transliteration to make Arabic spellings more accessible to ordinary readers and easier and less costly to print. These modifications need to be clarified:

- The subscript dots used to distinguish some Arabic consonants from others and the superscript lines used to indicate long vowels have been eliminated.
- The ta marbuta, which frequently appears at the end of words as an h, has been dropped except when used in a construct, where it appears as a t.
- The diphthongs "aw" and "ay" are represented as au and ai in the middle of words but not at the end.
- The letters ain and hamza, usually represented by an apostrophe, are omitted at the beginnings of words but are used to indicate either letter in the middle of a word; the ain is represented if it is the last letter in a word.

- The definite article al has also been omitted when a word stands alone but is used if the word is in a construct phrase. Hence al-'Iraq is simply Iraq.

These changes, though not satisfying to purists, should make the text easier to read.

Words of Persian, Turkish, or Kurdish origin that have become Arabized through usage in Iraq have been given their Arabic spelling. Exceptions have been made for a few names for which Kurdish or Persian spelling differs from Arabic. A few proper names have been spelled according to their common English usage, such as Gamal Abdul Nasser and Ahmad Chalabi. On occasion, well-known political figures, such as Nuri al-Sa'id and Saddam Husain, are referred to by their first names (Nuri and Saddam) because this is common Iraqi practice.

It may also be useful to explain the distinction between Shi'a and Shi'i, words referring to the same religious community in Islam. Shi'a is a noun, denoting the entire group, as for example, the Shi'a in Iraq; Shi'i is an adjective, the form used to modify a noun, as for example, Shi'i rituals.

This transliteration system has not been applied to the maps because of technical difficulties in changing the names on maps secured from outside sources. Hence, spellings on maps may differ from those in the text and from other maps. However, the map spellings are close enough to the transliteration system used in the text to make the place-names easily identifiable.

THE MODERN HISTORY OF IRAQ

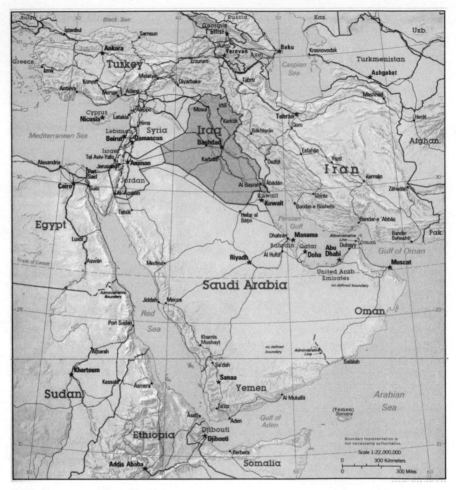

FIGURE 1.1 Middle East: Iraq

1

THE LAND AND PEOPLE OF MODERN IRAQ

The state of Iraq is a new, twentieth-century creation, brought into being by politicians and statesmen, but the area included within its borders is home to several of humankind's oldest and most creative civilizations. All have shaped Iraq's current identity. In the past, as today, diversity—of terrain, of resources, and, above all, of people—has been the chief characteristic of the territory and inhabitants that constitute contemporary Iraq. This diversity has been both a strength and a challenge. Harnessing Iraq's rich resources, whether its fertile river valleys or the black gold under its surface, and absorbing the medley of peoples living in these valleys has been the major preoccupation of Iraq's leaders, past and present. This is as true in the twenty-first century as in the fourth millennium BC.

Legacy of the Past

Iraq has a rich and variegated historical legacy on which to draw in shaping its national identity and its institutions. In fact, three elements of this past have been most important in forming the collective memory and consciousness of twenty-first-century Iraqis and shaping their institutions and practices: the civilization of ancient Mesopotamia, the Arab-Islamic heritage, and the legacy of the Ottoman Empire.

Ancient Mesopotamia

Ancient Mesopotamia's contributions to humankind's progress were many and varied, including the development of writing, the wheel, metal-working, literature, and science. Sumerians and their successors wrote poetry, created a mythology, and produced the world's first epic, the story of Gilgamesh. They built the first cities on the flood plains of the Tigris and Euphrates. Sumerian mathematicians used square roots and quadratic equations and created the first accurate calendars.[1]

But knowledge of this ancient civilization and its contributions was scant until the nineteenth century, when Mesopotamia's remains were unearthed by archaeologists. Until the midtwentieth century, ancient Mesopotamian civilization was taught in Iraq—if at all—mainly as a distant phenomenon almost unrelated to the modern country. This gradually changed in the second half of the twentieth century, however, when Iraqi artists and poets began to draw on this heritage in paintings and literature, while the government turned its attention to propagating the notion of a Mesopotamian heritage as an integral part of Iraqi tradition. But in the early decades of the modern state, Mesopotamia's civilization played a very small role.

The Arab-Islamic Civilization

In contrast, the Arab-Islamic conquest of the seventh century has been the decisive event in shaping current Iraqi identity. Arabic eventually became the predominant language of Mesopotamia, while Islam became the religion of almost all the country's inhabitants. It is mainly to the Islamic conquest of the seventh century that most Iraqis look for the source of their identity and the roots of their culture.

The decisive battle of Qadisiyya in 637 opened the rich territory of Mesopotamia, then under Persian control, to the invading Muslim army. However, the territory was only gradually absorbed and Islamized.

Many early Islamic political struggles were fought in Iraq. Husain, the Prophet's grandson, was killed near Karbala in 680, giving Shi'i Islam a martyr. Iraq acquired a reputation that it retains today of a country difficult to govern.

This changed for a time, beginning in 650 with the establishment of the Abbasid Caliphate, one of the great periods in Islamic history. Iraq came into its own as the center of a prosperous and expanding empire and an increasingly brilliant civilization that drew on the traditions of its immediate predecessors, the Greeks and Persians, in forming the emerging Arab-Islamic culture. The river valleys were now given the centralized control they needed; irrigation channels were extended, and agriculture flourished. So, too, did trade and urban life. By the tenth century, Baghdad, founded by the caliph Mansur in 762 as his capital, had a population estimated at 1.5 million and a luxury trade reaching from the Baltic Sea to China.[2] Baghdad also had a vigorous scientific and intellectual life, with centers for translations of Greek works and scientific experiments.

This period is remembered today with pride, but it did not last. By the middle of the ninth century, decline had set in that would last for almost a millennium. Gradually, the empire broke up. There were incursions from nomadic groups. A succession of dynasties governed parts of Iraqi territory with increasing indifference. The once great irrigation system deteriorated, and economic hardship followed. The Mongol attack on Baghdad in 1258 by Hulagu and another, even more devastating attack by Timur the Lame in 1401 delivered the final blows. Baghdad never recuperated.

This decline and its heritage of poverty, backwardness, and intellectual stagnation are the central facts of Iraq's modern history. Although the Abbasid Empire is remembered as part of a glorious past, it is the centuries of stagnation that followed that shaped the environment and character of the early period of the Iraqi state.

The Ottoman Empire

The Ottoman Empire governed Iraq for four centuries. In patterns of government, in law, and in the outlook and values of the urban classes, the Ottomans played a role in shaping modern Iraq second only to that of the Arab Islamic conquest.

The Ottoman conquest of Iraq began in 1514 as an outgrowth of a religious war between the Sunni Ottoman sultan and the Shi'i Safavid (Persian) shah. As the wars continued, the territory making up most of contemporary Iraq came under permanent Ottoman rule. When it first conquered Iraq, the Ottoman Empire was at the peak of its power and was able to give Iraq stable government and a uniform administration. Even though the Ottoman establishment was Sunni, it tolerated the Shi'a—at first. Unfortunately, the Ottoman-Persian conflict, which continued off and on until 1818, created in the minds of the Ottomans a suspicion and fear of the Shi'a of Iraq as prone to side with the Persians. Soon the Ottomans came to rely on the only element in the region they believed would support them—the urban Sunnis. During these long wars, the seeds of Sunni dominance in government were sown.

As the Sunnis tightened their grip on the reins of power, the Shi'a became alienated and strengthened their ties to Persia, especially in the holy cities of Najaf and Karbala. By the end of the nineteenth century, Persian influence in the holy cities and in much of southern Iraq was strong.[3]

A more important reason for Ottoman failure in Iraq was the weakness of the empire's own central government and its deteriorating control over its provinces. As the seventeenth century began, direct administration in the river valleys ceased, and Iraq faced another long period of stagnation and neglect. In the north, new Kurdish dynasties were established in the mountains and valleys. In the center and south, there were great tribal migrations from the Arabian Peninsula that reinforced tribalism.

The long cycle of decline finally halted with the rise of the Mamluks in the eighteenth century. Although alien in tongue and stock, these Ottoman "slave" administrators established dynastic rule in the Iraqi provinces, gradually extending their control from Basra to the Kurdish foothills, giving the Tigris and Euphrates valleys some stability, a modest economic and cultural revival, and some administrative cohesion. By the end of Mamluk rule in 1831, the outlines of the modern Iraqi state had begun to take shape. This trend was continued during the nineteenth century when the Iraqi provinces were gradually reincorporated into the

Ottoman Empire. In the south the Shi'i cities of Karbala and Najaf were brought under the authority of the Baghdad government. In the Kurdish countryside the local dynasties were broken up one by one and made to accept Turkish rule. Even more important were the reforms brought into Iraq by Ottoman administrators. The most outstanding reformer was Midhat Pasha, appointed to the governorship of Baghdad in 1869. His short tenure (1869–1872) marks the first concerted effort to build for the future.

Midhat's reforms fell into three general areas: administrative reorganization, settlement of the tribes, and establishment of secular education. First, Midhat introduced a new, centralized administrative system into the Iraqi provinces and extended it into the countryside, thus establishing the administrative framework of contemporary Iraq. Second, Midhat attempted to provide a regular system of land tenure with legally confirmed rights of ownership. Although urban speculators and merchants frequently bought up land at the expense of the peasants, the policy did enjoy some success. About one-fifth of the cultivable land of Iraq was given to those possessing new deeds of ownership.

Third, and most importantly, Midhat laid the groundwork for a secular education system in Iraq by founding a technical school, a middle-level school, and two secondary schools, one for the military and one for the civil service. Midhat's new schools brought striking innovations in two directions. They were public and free and hence offered a channel of mobility to children of all classes. They introduced a variety of new subjects, such as Western languages, math, and science, hitherto unavailable in religious schools. The three-year Law College was founded in 1908, providing the only higher education in the country. These schools represented the first and most important beachhead of modernization in the country.

These reforms helped create an economic revival. The telegraph and the steamship were introduced, and so was cash cropping. There was a striking change in the balance between the nomadic and settled populace. During the last half of the nineteenth century, the nomadic population declined from 35 to 17 percent while the settled rural population rose from 40 to 60 percent.[4] Contacts with the outside world also produced a revival of local learning and letters as well as new ideas. The development of a press helped spread all of these among the literate public. These intellectual and educational developments produced a new urban, literate class, a native Iraqi elite. Most members of this elite were the products of the secular schools established in the last quarter of the nineteenth century and the higher schooling in Istanbul, now available to Iraqis. Many went through the military academies, which were the chief vehicles of mobility for Iraq's lower-middle- and middle-class families.

By 1914 graduates of these schools were already staffing posts in the administration, army, new secular courts, and government schools. Although tiny in number, this group was immense in its influence. From its ranks came almost every Iraqi leader of any significance in the post– First World War period, and a number continued to dominate Iraqi politics until the revolution of 1958.

Nevertheless, the successes of the Ottoman reformers should not disguise the weaknesses of the Ottoman legacy. The Ottomans were foreign, and their reforms were aimed at recasting the population into an Ottoman mold. A native elite was being trained, but it was trained in an Ottoman pattern, that of authoritarian paternalism, in which the elite knew best how to govern and need not consult the governed.

Moreover, this native elite was drawn from only one segment of the population, the urban Sunnis. It was primarily the Sunnis, whether Arab or Kurd, who attended public schools and were given posts in the army and the bureaucracy. Not surprisingly, the Sunnis came to think of themselves as the country's natural elite and its only trustworthy leaders. Two important segments of the population, the rural tribal groups outside the reach of urban advantages and the Shi'a, were consequently excluded from participation in government. Little wonder that they should form the nucleus of opposition to the government in the early decades of the twentieth century.

The Land

The state of Iraq has existed only since 1920, when it was carved from three former provinces of the Ottoman Empire and created under British aegis as a mandate.[5] With a land area of 167,618 square miles (434,128 square kilometers) and a population of 31 million in 2011, Iraq is the largest of the Fertile Crescent countries rimming the northern edge of the Arabian Peninsula.[6] Lying between the plateau of northern Arabia and the mountain ridge of southwest Iran and eastern Turkey, Iraq forms a lowland corridor between Syria and the Persian/Arabian Gulf.[7] From its earliest history, Iraq has been a passageway between East and West. Its borders are for the most part artificial, reflecting the interests of the Great Powers during the First World War rather than the wishes of the local population. As a result, Iraq's present borders have been continually challenged by peoples living inside and outside the country. The southern section of the border with Iran, a contributory cause of the Iran-Iraq war of the 1980s, has not been finally settled, while a new, UN-demarcated border with Kuwait, agreed to by Iraq in 1993 under pressure, is still contentious.

The southeastern portion of the country lies at the head of the Gulf. Iraq controls a thirty-six-mile (58-kilometer) strip of Gulf territory barely sufficient to provide it with an outlet to the sea. From the Gulf, Iraq's border with Iran follows the Shatt al-Arab north, then skirts the Persian foothills as far north as the valley of the Diyala River, the first major tributary of the Tigris north of Baghdad. From here the border thrusts deep into the high Kurdish mountain ranges, following the Diyala River valley. Near Halabja it turns northward along the high mountain watersheds—incorporating within Iraq most of the headwaters of the major Tigris tributaries—until it reaches the Turkish border west of Lake Urmiyya. The mountainous boundary with Turkey ends at the Syrian border just west of Zakhu, Iraq's northernmost town. This northeastern region includes difficult and unmanageable mountain terrain and a substantial Kurdish population. The loss of control by the central government over substantial portions of this region in the 1990s made Iraq's northern borders with Turkey and Iran porous.

In the northwest the frontier separating Iraq from Syria meanders south across the Syrian desert from the Turkish border until it reaches the Euphrates near Qa'im. Here the borders make little pretense of following geography, jutting out into the adjacent desert and incorporating large areas of steppe. At the Euphrates the border turns west until it reaches Jordan, also a former British mandate, and then south a short distance to

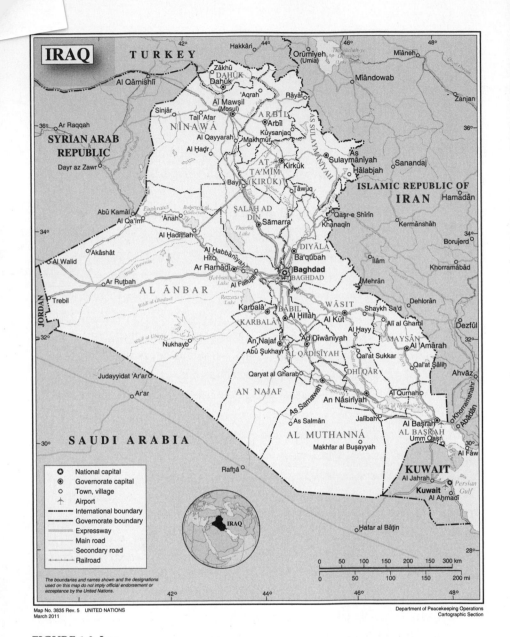

FIGURE 1.2 Iraq

the Saudi frontier. From this point the border follows a line of water wells separating Iraq from Saudi Arabia until it reaches the Kuwaiti border at Wadi al-Batin, at which point it turns north again, forming a common frontier with Kuwait, until it reaches Umm Qasr on the Khaur Abd Allah channel leading to the Gulf.

The terrain included within these boundaries is remarkably diverse, making Iraq a country of extreme contrasts. The Shatt al-Arab is a broad waterway with villages on its banks, lined with date groves. To the north of the Shatt lies swampland, traditionally inhabited along the Tigris by marsh dwellers living in reed houses built on stilts and raising water buffalo and along the Euphrates by rice-growing villagers. This natural wetland area, with high reeds and hidden waterways, has often functioned as a refuge for dissidents. A massive drainage system, constructed by the central government in the 1990s, progressively dried up much of this terrain, although some of it is gradually being restored. Between the marshlands and Baghdad is the delta, the most densely populated area of Iraq, once inhabited by the Sumerians and Babylonians of ancient Mesopotamia. It is a dry, flat area consisting almost entirely of irrigated farmland, with large villages and regional market towns hugging the riverbanks. North of Baghdad the two rivers diverge widely to form the Jazira (Island), the territory between the two. Although some irrigation farming is practiced here, it is mainly rain-fed territory—a land of gentle uplands sprinkled with smaller villages and provincial towns. Mosul, near the site of Ninawa, is the Jazira's major city and the center of its commercial life. To the north and east of the Jazira, the plains give way to foothills filled with settled villages and towns (mainly inhabited by a mixture of Turkish- and Kurdish-speaking people) and then to the high mountains, the home of the Kurds. These high mountain ranges, the heartland of Iraqi Kurdistan, constitute a remote and inaccessible area of deep gorges and rugged, snow-capped mountains rising to 12,000 feet (over 3,600 meters), broken only by the fertile valleys of the Tigris tributaries.

Within this diversity of territory the unifying feature of Iraq's geography is its twin river system. From the dawn of civilization, the rivers have provided the irrigation that made life possible for those inhabiting the flat, dry plains through which they flow, uniting the populations of the north and south and giving them a common interest in controlling the rivers and their tributaries. The rivers have also provided the arteries for trade and communication without which the cities that have made Mesopotamia famous could not have flourished.

The rivers are not an unmixed blessing, however. The Tigris has often delivered torrential floods in the spring, too late for the winter crop and too early for the summer. The south of the country has a poor natural drainage system, causing progressive salinization of the soil if irrigation is not controlled or the soil flushed. Without dams, barrages, and artificial drainage systems, the rivers cannot support continuous agriculture. Whenever such an organized system has existed, the country between the two rivers has flourished; when it has not, decline, unrest, and turmoil have often resulted.

Iraq today is a country rich in resources. With proper management, the river system can provide agricultural production to feed a good portion of the population, although dams built on the headwaters of the Tigris and Euphrates have reduced their flow in Iraq. Its agricultural potential, declining through overuse and, in recent years, neglect and abuse, is now dwarfed by petroleum. Iraq's proven oil reserves in 2010 were over 115 billion barrels, with another 100 billion of probable or possible reserves in areas not yet extensively explored. These reserves are the world's fourth largest, exceeded only by Saudi Arabia, Canada, and Iran.[8] With an estimated gross domestic product of over $91 billion in 2010, Iraq has ample sources of capital for development, if properly used and husbanded. Yet Iraq's problems in the twenty-first century resemble those of its past. The challenge is to organize the political and social environment in a way that will bring Iraq's considerable potential to fruition, give peace and prosperity to its people, and put an end to the repression, disruption, and conflict that have led, in recent decades, to conflict, disunity, and decay.

The People

Even if one can speak of an Iraqi state, it is not yet possible to speak of an Iraqi nation. Iraq's present borders incorporate a diverse medley of peoples who have not yet been welded into a single political community with a common sense of identity.[9] The search for this identity has been a shared, if elusive, project of all Iraqi governments and has become particularly acute since 2003. Considerable integration and assimilation have taken place since the inception of the mandate, but there have also been setbacks—especially in recent years—to the process of nation building, revealing the fragility of the demographic mosaic and even of the state itself.

The first and most serious demographic division is ethnic or, more properly speaking, linguistic. Arabic speakers constitute 75 to 80 percent of the population; Kurdish speakers, 15 to 20 percent. The Arabs

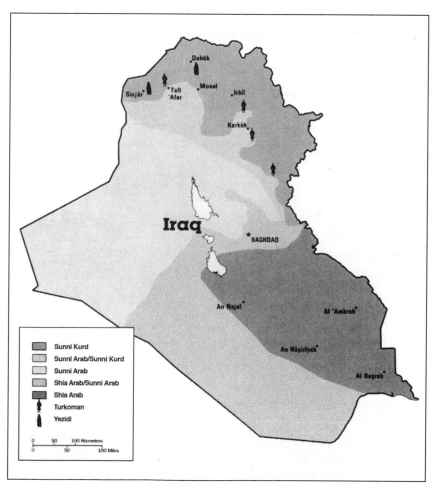

FIGURE 1.3 Ethnoreligious Groups in Iraq

dominate the western steppe and the Tigris and Euphrates valleys from Basra to the Mosul plain; the Kurds have their stronghold in the rugged mountain terrain of the north and east and the foothills that adjoin it. However, the Iraqi Kurds are only a portion of a larger Kurdish population with whom they identify on linguistic, cultural, and nationalistic grounds. In 2011 there were a little over 6 million Kurds in Iraq, about 13 million in Turkey (about 19 percent of the population), 9 million in Iran (13 percent of the population), and between 1 and 2 million in Syria (about 7 percent of the population). There are smaller numbers in Armenia, Azerbaijan, and Europe.[10]

A second major division in the population runs along religious lines between the two great sects of Islam, the Shi'a and the Sunni. Since the overwhelming majority of the Kurds are Sunni, this division affects mainly the Arabs, but the religious split has tended to segment Iraqi society into three distinct communities: the Arab Shi'a, the Arab Sunnis, and the Kurds.

The Arab Shi'a

The division of the Muslim community originated shortly after the Prophet's death in a political dispute over who should be selected caliph, or successor. The Sunnis, the majority, have accepted all caliphs who have held office, regardless of the method of selection, so long as they were able to make their claims effective. The Shi'a, the minority, took the side of the fourth caliph, Ali, cousin and son-in-law of the Prophet, claiming that the leadership of the community should have been his from the first and that only his heirs were legitimate successors. Eventually, the leadership of the Shi'i community devolved on religious scholars, called *mujtahids*. The fact that each individual Shi'a is expected to follow a leading *mujtahid* gives the Shi'i community stronger leadership and a greater sense of cohesion than its Sunni counterpart.

From the first, southern Iraq has been a stronghold of Shi'i Islam. As Arab tribes migrated from the Arabian Peninsula in the eighteenth and nineteenth centuries and settled in the river valleys, they were converted to Shi'i Islam by religious scholars and their emissaries. Today the Shi'a are the largest single religious community in Iraq, outnumbering the Arab Sunnis three to one and constituting a solid majority of the total population.

Under the Sunni Ottoman administration of Iraq, which began in the sixteenth century, Iraqi Shi'a were largely excluded from administrative positions, from the military, and from government-sponsored education institutions that trained for them. Not surprisingly, the Shi'a, so long excluded from government, came to be deeply alienated from it, although the Shi'a had their own educational institutions to train clerics (the *hawza*) and an independent source of finances (the *khums*— a fifth of net income required of followers).

The Arab Sunnis

In contrast to the Shi'a, the Arab Sunnis in Iraq tended to be more secular and, with the exception of some recently settled tribes, more urban in composition. As a result, their communal identity has been less developed. Unlike the Shi'a, the Sunnis do not accord special religious authority to their leaders—the scholars, jurists, and judges collectively known as *ulama* who define and uphold the rules that guide the community. Rather they follow the *sunna*, or customs of the Prophet (from which they take their name), and the *shari'a*, the body of Islamic doctrine, law, and ritual derived from the Quran and the *sunna*. It is to the *shari'a*, rather than to any particular leader, that the Sunni community owes adherence, a factor that has made it far more loosely structured than the Shi'i community.

Despite their minority status, the Arab Sunnis have traditionally dominated the political and social life of Iraq, originally owing to Ottoman support but later the result of the ability of Sunnis to maintain the command posts of power. Although no census has been taken that distinguishes among various Muslim groups, the Arab Sunnis probably represent about 15 to 20 percent of the population.[11] Geographically, they are concentrated in the northern part of the country, including the Arab tribal groups of the western steppe and the Arab villages and towns of the northern Tigris and Euphrates areas. The remainder of the

Arab Sunni community is almost wholly urban, situated in the cities and towns of the central and northern provinces. Substantial numbers of Sunnis also live in some cities of the south, especially Basra.

Although the collapse of the Ottoman Empire in the First World War removed Ottoman support for Sunni supremacy, it did not end Sunni dominance. That dominance has waxed and waned over time, especially socially and intellectually, but Sunni political control was more pronounced at the end of the twentieth century than at any time since the mandate. This political dominance and the resulting enjoyment of most of society's benefits have given the Sunni community a closer association with—and vested interest in—the emerging Iraqi state. Arab Sunnis have also had considerable affinity for the secular philosophies of Arab nationalism originating in neighboring (and largely Sunni) Arab countries. The displacement of the Sunnis by a new Shi'a leadership after 2003 has been a social and political change of major proportions.

The Kurds

The origin of the Kurds is still a matter of some historical dispute, with most Kurdish scholars claiming descent from the ancient Medes. However, because there was no written Kurdish literature until the tenth century, it is difficult to substantiate this identification.[12] Whatever their origins, the Kurds were almost completely converted to Islam. They became orthodox Sunnis, part of a vast Muslim empire and often its staunchest defenders. From time to time, particularly in the seventeenth and eighteenth centuries, Kurdish dynasties arose, but they lacked cohesion and were unable to maintain their autonomy.

The Kurds have proved the most difficult of Iraq's people to assimilate because of their numbers, geographic concentration, mountain inaccessibility, and cultural and linguistic identity. Language has been a major stumbling block. The Kurds speak an Indo-European language closely akin to Persian, although some also speak Arabic. Both Arabic and Kurdish are now official languages of the central government.

Even more important has been the sense of ethnic—even national—identity that the Kurds have developed. In the twentieth century, a sense of Kurdish identity based on language, close tribal ties, customs, and a shared history inspired Kurdish nationalist movements. Like their predecessors, however, these political groups lacked sufficient cohesion and coordination to achieve lasting results before the twentieth century.

The majority of Iraq's Kurdish population today is to be found in the mountains and foothills of the northeast, with Arbil as its political capital and Sulaimaniyya as its intellectual center. Until recently most Kurds were rural. However, the destruction of much of the Kurdish countryside, especially adjacent to Iran, and the forced migration of much of this population as a result of local wars and sometimes brutal actions taken by the Iraqi government under Saddam Husain have resulted in resettlement of large numbers of Kurds in cities and towns.

Other Minorities

Aside from these three major demographic groups, there are several smaller ethnic and religious communities in Iraq. In northern towns and cities along the old trade route that led from Anatolia along the foothills of the Zagros to Baghdad live members of a Turkish-speaking group known locally as the Turkmen. Comprising about 3 percent of the population and most numerous in the cities of Kirkuk and Arbil,[13] they are probably remnants of migrations of Turkish tribes dating from the Seljuk era of the twelfth century and of the Turkman tribal dynasties of the fourteenth and fifteenth centuries. The Turkmen, mainly Sunni and middle class, have for decades produced a disproportionate number of bureaucrats and have integrated well into modern Iraq.

In the south is a group of Shi'i Persian speakers with strong ties to Persia that have never been severed. Until the 1980s, they constituted 1.5 to 2 percent of the population, but in the wake of the Iran-Iraq war, this community was largely expelled from Iraq.[14] The Iraqi Persian speakers have frequently looked to Persian rulers to support their interests, causing them to be regarded with suspicion by the Ottoman Turks and more recently by Arab nationalist governments. Another Persian-speaking group distinct from these town dwellers is the Lurs, less than 1 percent of all Iraqis. Often called *faili* or Shi'i Kurds, they are almost all tribally organized villagers concentrated near the eastern frontiers of Iraq.[15]

Iraq also has a number of non-Muslim minorities—Christians, Jews, and a few other communities that predate Islam. Until 1951 non-Muslims made up about 6 percent of the Iraqi people,[16] and the Jews were the oldest and largest of these communities, tracing their origin to the Babylonian captivity of the sixth century BCE. Overwhelmingly urban, the bulk of the Jewish community lived in Baghdad, where Jews were often prosperous and influential merchants. The position of the community was radically changed by the impact of Zionism. With the establishment of Israel in 1948, the situation of Iraqi Jews became untenable, and their exodus in 1951 left only a handful. In subsequent years the community virtually disappeared.

Various Christian sects make up a little less than 3 percent of the population. Instability and attacks on the community after 2005 have led to a decline in their numbers. The largest denomination is the Chaldean Church, founded in the fifth century by the followers of the theologian Nestorius. In the sixteenth century they unified with Rome. Centered in Mosul and the surrounding plains, most Chaldeans speak Arabic, although some use a modified version of Syriac as a vernacular.[17]

Second in importance are the Assyrians, those Nestorians who did not unite with Rome. The British settled about 20,000 of them in the northern areas of Iraq around Zakhu and Dahuk following the First World War. The Assyrians, so called because they claim descent from the ancient Assyrians, proved to be one of the most unsettling elements in Iraq's modern history prior to the Second World War. Their uninvited intrusion into the country through the intervention of a foreign power was deeply resented by the Muslims and especially by the Kurds, in whose areas they were settled. In recent years the Assyrians have become more integrated.

Other Christian groups include the Armenian, Jacobite, Greek Orthodox, Greek Catholic, and Latin Catholic communities, but their numbers are small in comparison to those of other Christians. A small number of Protestants, almost wholly the result of the nineteenth-century Baptist and Congregational missions, live mainly in Baghdad and Basra.

Two other religious communities of obscure origin deserve mention. One is the Yazidis. Racially and linguistically Kurdish,[18] they are village dwellers located near Mosul. Their religion is a compound of several ancient and living religions, and its most notable element is a dualism most likely derived from Zoroastrianism. They have resisted attempts to integrate into the larger society. The second group, the Sabians or Mandeans, is a sect of ancient origin and diverse elements inhabiting portions of the southern delta. Their faith stresses baptism and contains elements of Manicheanism but not Islam.

Town and Tribe

To these ethnic and sectarian divisions, somewhat blurred since mandate days, must be added a third social distinction that has played a profound role in Iraq's modern history—the division between town and tribe. Though greatly softened in recent years by the growth of cities and the spread of education to the countryside, the legacy of tribalism is subtle but pervasive in Iraq.

The historical importance of the tribes in Iraq can scarcely be exaggerated. Nomadic, seminomadic, or settled, they surrounded the handful of cities and larger towns, controlled the country's communications system, and held nine-tenths of its land at the time of the mandate.[19] In 1933, a year after Iraqi independence, according to estimates there were 100,000 rifles in tribal hands and 15,000 in the possession of the government.[20] Although only a few of these tribes were nomadic, the bulk of the settled population of the country, whether Arab or Kurd, was tribally organized and retained tribal mores and customs.

The extension of tribal organization and institutions to rural Iraq has meant that much of the rural population failed to put down deep roots in the soil. The settled village community with its attachment to the land—the backbone of the social structure throughout most of the Middle East—has been a missing link in Iraq's social fabric. Instead of love of the land, loyalty to family and tribe has dominated Iraq's social and political life. Among the legacies of tribalism in Iraq are intense concern with family, clan, and tribe; devotion to personal honor; factionalism;

and, above all, difficulty cooperating across kinship lines—the underlying basis of modern civic society.

The only significant counterbalance to tribalism has been the economic and political power of the cities, but until modern times these were few in number and economically and culturally unintegrated with the rural hinterland. Aside from Basra, Baghdad, and Mosul, there were few cities worthy of the name at the end of the Ottoman era. Most were simply caravan stops like Zubair, fueling stations like Kut, or religious shrines like Karbala and Najaf, in which the benefits of law and order, trade and manufacture, were noticeable only against the background of poverty in the countryside. At the beginning of the nineteenth century, about a quarter of a population of a little over 2 million were urban; a quarter of these were concentrated in Baghdad.[21]

Rapid urbanization, the spread of education, and the extension of government into the countryside in the last half of the twentieth century greatly eroded tribalism and decisively shifted the balance of power to the cities. Nevertheless, although tribal organization is rapidly disappearing in the countryside, tribal customs and attitudes have left tangible influences. In political life, family, clan, and local ties often take precedence over national loyalties and broader ideologies.

2

THE BRITISH MANDATE,
1920–1932

The impact of British rule in shaping modern Iraq has been second only to that of Ottoman rule. In some respects the British left remarkably little behind; in others they made a more lasting impression. Before the British mandate, there was no Iraq; after it, a new state with the beginnings of a modern government had come into being. The British bequeathed Iraq its present boundaries and, as a result, potential minority problems and border problems with its neighbors.

Imposing British rule did not prove easy. Conquest took four years, and the first attempt at administration, the imposition of the Indian colonial model, failed after a nationalist revolt in 1920. Thereafter, Britain fell back on "indirect rule," using elements of the local population willing to work with them. To govern Iraq, Britain installed an array of state institutions: a monarchy to head the central government and symbolize Iraq's unity, an army and a bureaucracy to keep order and run the country, and a Western-style constitution providing for indirect elections and a parliament. A treaty with Britain regulated Britain's "advisory" and military support role. Britain also concluded an oil concession with the new Iraqi government, which kept control in foreign hands, but serious oil production did not begin until well after the mandate.

Much of this political structure—especially the monarchy and the Western-style parliamentary institutions—put down few roots and was swept away after 1958. This is not surprising because Britain's stay in Iraq was one of the shortest in its imperial career, and it spent few resources on Iraq. But the bureaucracy and the army, institutions predating the mandate, remained. So, too, did the Iraqi leaders placed in power by the British themselves—the Ottoman-educated Arab Sunni officers and bureaucrats. They and the traditions of government they brought with them would do more to shape modern Iraq than the British had.

The British Occupation and the Institutions of the Indian School

Despite Britain's long-standing interests in the Gulf, the British had no intention of occupying the Tigris and Euphrates valleys at the outbreak of the First World War. However, when it became apparent late in 1914 that Turkey, Britain's traditional ally, would enter the war on the side of the Central Powers and was mobilizing at the head of the Gulf, Britain decided to occupy Faw and Basra to protect its strategic interests and communications and its oil fields at the head of the Gulf. On 6 November 1914, British troops landed at Faw, and by 22 November they had moved up to Basra. In March 1917 they took Baghdad, and in 1918 they occupied Mosul.[1]

The administration initially imposed on Iraq was overwhelmingly the work of men seconded from the India Office and was modeled largely on Britain's imperial structure in India. The philosophy guiding the group was largely based on nineteenth-century ideas of the "white man's burden," a predilection for direct rule, and a distrust of local Arabs' capacity for self-government. These attitudes deterred the appointment of local Arabs to positions of responsibility. Meanwhile, the British dismantled and supplanted the Ottoman administration as rapidly as possible. A new civil and criminal code based on Anglo-Indian laws replaced the old Turkish laws, the Indian rupee became the medium of exchange, and the army and police force were increasingly staffed with Indians.

Reversing Turkish tribal policy, which had aimed at weakening tribal leaders and bringing the tribes under the control of the central government, the British now attempted to restore tribal cohesion, to make the paramount *shaikhs* responsible for law and order and the collection of revenue in their districts, and to tie them to the nascent British administration through grants and privileges. This policy was applied not only in the Arab areas but also to the Kurdish provinces as they were taken. Efficient and economical, this policy reduced the need for highly paid British staff in the countryside, but ultimately it strengthened the hold of the *shaikhs* over their tribesmen and their land. Entrenchment of a class of landlord-*shaikhs*, though not wholly a British invention, was certainly one of the most lasting and problematic legacies of the Indian school.[2]

It was not long before the policies of the Indian school generated opposition both in Britain and Iraq. In March 1917 the British government issued a memo making it clear that an indigenous Arab government under British guidance was to be substituted for direct administration. As a response to the memo, the Anglo-Indian civil code was replaced by a return to Turkish courts and laws. However, little else was changed. Local British bureaucrats continued to strengthen their hold on the country, appointing few Arabs to senior positions. The result was not long in coming.

The 1920 Revolt and Its Results

The 1920 revolt was sparked by an April 1920 announcement that the principal victors in the first World War, meeting at San Remo, had assigned a mandate for Iraq to Britain. Opposition to the British had already been growing for some time among Iraqi communities, inside and outside the country. Rising anti-British sentiment had been fanned by the nationalists in Baghdad, the Shi'i religious leaders of the holy cities, and disaffected mid-Euphrates tribal leaders.[3] Though the motives of these groups were mixed, all were united by a desire to be free of British rule. A chief feature of the movement was the unprecedented cooperation between the Sunni and Shi'i communities.

The revolt began on 30 June 1920, when a *shaikh* who had refused to repay an agricultural debt was placed in prison at Rumaitha. His incensed tribesmen rose up against the British, and they were soon joined by others. Anti-British sentiments were aroused, and the revolt spread. All in all, the insurgency lasted for about three months and affected about a third of the countryside; none of the major cities and few of the urban nationalists were affected.[4] The movement was disorganized, diverse, and localized, making it vulnerable to suppression by a determined central government.[5] However, the uprising was costly for the British—over four hundred lives and up to £40 million—and caused an outcry in the press at home and very nearly wrecked the British position entirely.[6] Although the revolt did not achieve Iraqi independence or turn real authority over to the Iraqis, it did succeed in discrediting the India Office policy thoroughly, and it assured a much larger measure of participation by the Iraqis in their first national government.

On 1 October 1920, Sir Percy Cox landed in Basra to assume his responsibilities as high commissioner in Iraq. The first decisive step in creating the institutions and structure of the new Iraqi state and the British role in it took place at the Cairo Conference of 1921. It was here that the three pillars of the Iraqi state were conceived: the monarchy, in the person of Faisal, the third son of the sharif of Mecca; the treaty, the legal basis for Britain's rule; and the constitution, designed to integrate elements of the population under a democratic formula. All three were intertwined.[7]

The Monarchy

On 27 August 1921, Faisal was installed as Iraq's first king. The founder of the Hashimite dynasty in Iraq was born in Mecca to a family that traced its lineage back to the Prophet. Firmly rooted by practice and conscience to the Arab nationalist cause, Faisal did not initially favor the Arab alliance with the British and became a supporter only by necessity. Faisal's subsequent career as head of the short-lived Syrian kingdom between 1918 and 1920, his fruitless efforts at the European peace conference on behalf of the Arabs, and his humiliating removal from power in Syria by the French served to sharpen his sense of realism and his ability to deal with a variety of people and groups.

Whereas some of his associates saw Faisal as weak, others saw him as a subtle politician, one of the few capable of manipulating and balancing various Iraqi forces. Whatever his style, it is clear that Faisal's position was weak. As a monarch imposed on Iraq by an alien, dominant power, Faisal was always conscious of the need to put down roots in Iraq and to appeal to its different ethnic and sectarian communities if the monarchy were to remain.

Once Faisal had been nominated, he needed to be elected. A well-managed plebiscite gave Faisal 96 percent of the vote; his real support was nowhere near that figure. Nevertheless, on 27 August 1921, Faisal was installed as king. With Faisal's accession the Iraqi nationalists who had served with him in the war and who had formed the backbone of his short-lived government in Syria returned to Iraq. Staunchly loyal to Faisal, Arab nationalist in outlook, yet willing to work within the limits of the British mandate, these repatriated Iraqis rapidly filled the high offices of state, giving Faisal the support he lacked elsewhere in the country. This handful of young, Ottoman-educated Arab lawyers, officers, and civil servants soon achieved a position in Iraqi politics second only to that of the British and Faisal, displacing the older notables originally installed by the British.

The intrusion of these Iraqis into the administration at all levels marked a first step in establishing Arab Sunni dominance in government. At the same time, it also had the effect of Arabizing the regime, a process intensified by the shift from Turkish to Arabic in the administration and the school system. Although the Ottoman civil code was retained and made the basis of its curriculum, the Law College, the institution responsible for training most bureaucrats, was put under Arab administration. The centralized education system in particular emphasized the Arabic language and Arab history, with an underlying thrust toward secularism and pan-Arabism; both had a long-lasting impact. This emphasis was mainly the handiwork not of the British but of Sati'-l-Husri, a strong Arab nationalist from Syria and chief education administrator in the early mandate.

However positive the contributions of the strong pan-Arab orientation, it thwarted the development of a more inward-looking, Iraq-centered patriotism while excluding and alienating large elements of the

Arab-speaking Shi'i population and the Kurds, who might have been more attracted to a distinctly Iraqi identity.[8]

The Cairo Conference also established a native Iraqi army. The lower ranks were drawn from tribal elements, often Shi'i, but the officer corps came almost solely from the ranks of former Ottoman army officers. Inevitably, these officers were Sunni, perpetuating Sunni dominance of the officers corps. Officers with pro-Turkish sentiments were soon weeded out, making the army officer corps primarily Arab in composition and orientation. Some Kurdish officers were eventually brought in as well.

The Treaty

The mandate awarded to Britain by the League of Nations had specified that Iraq should be prepared for self-government under British tutelage but left the means and mode to the mandatory power. The British decided to express the mandatory relationship by a treaty, deemed the most imaginative way to neutralize Iraqi opposition. Treaty negotiations with the Iraqis were begun shortly after Faisal was installed as king, and in October 1922 the Council of Ministers ratified the treaty.

The treaty was the backbone of Britain's indirect rule. It provided that the king would heed Britain's advice on all matters affecting British interests and on fiscal policy as long as Iraq was in debt to Britain. A subsequent financial agreement required Iraq to pay half the costs of the British residency and other costs, which not only placed Iraq in a state of economic dependence on Britain but also helped retard its development. The treaty also required Iraq to appoint British officials to specified posts in eighteen departments to act as advisers and inspectors.[9] It was with this network of intelligence and influence, supported by the provisions of the treaty and the option of military sanctions, that the British governed during the mandate. In return Britain promised to provide Iraq with various kinds of aid, including military aid, and to propose Iraq for membership in the League of Nations at the earliest possible moment. The duration of the treaty was to be twenty years.

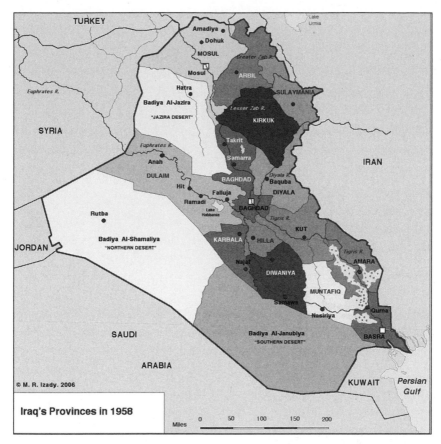

FIGURE 2.1 Iraq's Provinces, 1958

SOURCE: Authored by Dr. M. R. Izady and posted by the Gulf2000 project at Columbia University, New York, http://gulf2000.columbia.edu/maps.shtml.

The Constitution

The constitution was closely intertwined with the treaty. The first critical issue between the British and the Iraqis revolved around the powers of the king, whom the British hoped to make their instrument, and of parliament, which the Iraqi nationalists hoped to dominate. The proposed constitution gave Parliament sufficient power to bring down a cabinet but counterbalanced this power by granting the king the right to confirm all laws, to call for general elections, and to prorogue parliament.

This constitution was finally passed in 1924 by the Constituent Assembly after a long struggle with the opposition. With a few modifications, the constitution provided the country's political and legal structure under the monarchy until the revolution of 1958. It was an instrument well designed to foster Britain's indirect control. The monarch functioned partly as a symbol of unity but mainly as a means by which the high commissioner could bring his influence to bear in cases of conflict. Parliament soon became a stronghold of the tribal leaders whom the British had done so much to protect and strengthen. The constitution failed to take root, however—partly because Iraqis were never given real responsibility in the government and partly because they came to regard it as an instrument of foreign manipulation and control. As a result, Iraqi elites focused their energies not on developing constitutional institutions as a foothold of eventual control but rather on removing unwanted British influence.

The Kurdish Problem

European policymakers had originally expected that the Kurds, like the Armenians, would be given national autonomy or independence under a mandate. In fact, the abortive Treaty of Sevres, concluded in August 1920 with the Ottoman sultan, had provided for an autonomous Kurdish state and had stipulated that the Kurds of Turkey and Iraq could apply for admission to the League of Nations within a year. The problem lay in finding suitable Kurdish leaders to assume responsibility for such an administration.

The one British attempt in this direction had failed. In 1922 the British had appointed Shaikh Mahmud al-Barzinja as governor of Sulaimaniyya. Shaikh Mahmud was expected to establish a viable Kurdish entity there, yet remain compliant toward British influence. In short, Mahmud was to become a Kurdish Faisal. To aid him in the task, the British allowed a number of Ottoman-trained Kurdish army officers and administrators to join him. The hope was that they could infuse a sense of nationalism into an essentially tribal environment.

But Mahmud attempted to carve out an independent principality, sacrificed the loyalty of his Kurdish officers in appointing his relatives to high positions, and was also in touch with the Turks. These actions alienated any British support Mahmud might otherwise have acquired, and in February 1923 the British forced him out of power. By the summer of 1923, when elections for the Constituent Assembly were finally held, the Kurds were no longer offered a choice of joining the new Iraqi state or holding aloof. The Kurds were brought under the sovereignty of the new Iraqi state by fiat. The inclusion of the Kurdish minority into the Iraqi state was a fateful decision both for the Kurds and for the future stability and direction of the Iraqi state.[10] The border with Turkey was finally fixed by an international commission in March 1925.

Oil and the Slow Pace of Development

Negotiations between Britain and Iraq for an oil concession began later in 1923 and generated a protracted and acrimonious debate. The main sticking point was Iraq's demand for 20 percent ownership in the company, which would have given Iraqis a voice in management and some control over oil production. The company refused, and Iraqis, fearing the loss of the Mosul *wilaya* (province) to Turkey if they did not give in, signed the concession in March 1925. It was not until October 1927 that the new Iraq Petroleum Company brought in its first well north of Kirkuk. Although the oil concession and the revenue it eventually brought Iraq are among the most important legacies of the British mandate, the benefits from oil were slow to materialize. Only in the 1950s did substantial revenues from oil begin to accrue to Iraq.

During the entire mandate period, Iraq lacked the funds for development and penury was widespread. Continuing budget deficits were exacerbated by Iraq's obligation to pay its share of the Ottoman debt and to pay for the public facilities constructed by Britain. As a result, little was accomplished under the mandate in the way of economic or social development. Although there was some increase in agriculture, Iraq's resources were underdeveloped and a large proportion of its population remained illiterate.[11] The educational situation under the mandate was poor, owing partly to lack of funds and partly to the small numbers trained by the British, who were afraid of producing more graduates than the bureaucracy could absorb. In 1930 only 159 secondary students passed the public examination.[12] At the end of the mandate, much of Iraq's countryside—where 70 percent of the population lived—was still virtually untouched by modernization and modern industry had scarcely begun.

In the cities a small middle class of civil servants, retail merchants, and professionals had begun to emerge, but the bulk of the population—urban and rural—remained at or near the poverty level. Urban migration, although not as severe as in the 1930s, produced a group of uprooted people inhabiting urban slums. A small number of workers benefited from the start of the oil industry and the development of the port and the railroad system, but the lack of funds slowed the growth of industry and infrastructure. Meanwhile, local artisans and craftsmen were gradually undermined by foreign imports.

The Nationalist Movement:
Composition and Outlook

The early 1920s, which brought the creation of the state and its instrumentalities, also marked the beginnings of strident opposition to foreign control. Nationalist opposition was to dominate the political scene right up to the revolution of 1958. The opposition's dislike of the foreign connection came to include the parliamentary institutions established by the British and the groups they placed in power, contributing to the removal of both in 1958.

The period of opposition, despite its spasmodic and spontaneous nature, can be divided into three overlapping waves. The first wave was the 1920 revolt already discussed. Based mainly on tribal insurgents, urged on by Shi'i religious leaders and various urban elements, it was the first and only armed confrontation with the mandatory regime. In addition to its effects on British policy, the revolt's impact on Iraqis was profound. The decisiveness with which the tribes were defeated convinced many of the urban leaders that recourse to armed revolt would be futile while British troops remained on Iraqi soil and were not counterbalanced by an Iraqi force. They promptly turned their attention to the development of a regular army, which would replace the tribes as a military force and could ultimately be used as an instrument against the British. As for the tribal leaders, their power to influence events was greatly diminished after 1920, although not entirely eliminated.

The second wave of opposition accompanied the cabinet's treaty discussions in 1922 and the subsequent election of the Constituent Assembly that was to ratify the treaty. This opposition, led primarily by urban nationalists and expressed through political parties and the press, had a strong Shi'i component. In June 1923 a series of *fatwas* (religious decrees) against the election were issued by Shi'i religious leaders. When the king and the government, backed by the British, decided shortly thereafter to arrest the offenders, including a leading Shi'i cleric, a number of Shi'i *mujtahids* withdrew in protest to Persia, expecting this act to generate pressure on the cabinet from disaffected Shi'a and from the Persian government. It did not. In fact, the appeal of the *mujtahids* to a foreign power—Persia—alienated not only the British but the Sunni politicians as well. When the *mujtahids* were allowed to return much later, it was only on the condition that they formally renounce their political activities. The failure of this move dealt a decisive blow to Shi'i clerical participation in politics.[13]

The Arab Sunni opposition, though it shared the antiforeign sentiments of the Shi'a, disliked the prospects of Shi'i dominance even more. Many feared that Shi'i leadership of government would open the door to sectarianism and even to theocratic rule. To many Sunnis the creation of a secular state based on Arabism, even under temporary British control, seemed preferable. In any event, the suppression of the Shi'i militants left the leadership of the nationalist movement in the hands of Arab Sunni nationalists willing to cooperate with the British.

Arab Sunni nationalists led the third wave of opposition to the treaty, which began at the Constituent Assembly in 1924 and continued until the end of the mandate. The opposition attempted to strengthen the Chamber of Deputies at the expense of the cabinet and the king. In general, tribal groups joined the opposition in return for compensation in two areas: confirmation of their rights to land and a guarantee that their disputes would be settled according to tribal custom embodied in a separate

Tribal Disputes Code. On both counts they were successful. These compromises ultimately helped to bolster the position of the emerging tribal landlord class and to forge an alliance between the urban Sunni politicians and the Shi'i tribal leaders of the south, an alliance subsequently supported by legislation granting the *shaikhs* tax immunities and benefits.

Political and social dynamics soon took on a character that persisted right up to the revolution of 1958. Political life came to revolve around a tripartite balance of power. One element consisted of the king, a foreign monarch dependent on the British for his position but anxious to develop a more permanent power base among the local politicians. Another comprised the British, anxious to neutralize the opposition and to see their supporters in the offices of prime minister and minister of interior. A third component consisted of a shifting group of Arab Sunni politicians, some more anti-British than others but all willing to assume office. One feature of the period was political pluralism and sometimes-intense competition for power at the top. Nuri al-Sa'id, a staunch supporter of the Arab revolt and of Faisal, was a leading exponent of this group.[14] A few Kurds and Shi'a joined this contingent. Unused to political parties, the politicians formed parliamentary blocs, based mainly on personal ties and shifting political alliances.

Few of these politicians had roots in any large constituencies outside the halls of parliament, except for their links with tribal leaders. The failure to build broadly based political institutions or to reach out to groups beyond their personal or familial circles was a critical weakness of the nationalist movement. It allowed for manipulation by the British and the monarchy and prevented any one group from establishing sufficient power to move the country along in a particular direction.

The establishment of these urban Arab Sunnis in the political sphere was accompanied by developments in the economic sphere that gradually gave them an economic and social base as well: the growth of a new landed class, owing largely to the acquisition by private individuals of prescriptive rights over large tracts of land. Many of these investors were resident tribal *shaikhs* anxious to gain legal title to the land inhabited by their tribes, but most were urban investors and speculators who, profiting from the security introduced by the mandate, borrowed capital and bought up land. By 1930 the growth of a new oligarchy of landlords, urban entrepreneurs, and politicians was well under way.

Meanwhile, another development was under way—the buildup of the army and the security system under British aegis. These institutions soon became the real support base for the urban Arab Sunni nationalists in their struggle against the British, although the majority of army recruits came from the Shi'i south—the area the nationalists most desired to penetrate. The reach of the central government was extended, slowly but surely, into the countryside. One indication of this expansion was the increased effectiveness of tax collecting, which now reached groups and individuals who previously had been only marginally involved. By the end of the mandate, virtually all citizens of every class were liable for taxes.

The 1930 Treaty and the End of the Mandate

In June 1929 a newly elected labor government in Britain announced its intention to support Iraq's admission to the League of Nations in 1932 and negotiate a new treaty recognizing Iraq's independence. Nuri al-Sa'id became the new Iraqi prime minister. Although the British had some doubts about Nuri's ability to handle the situation, they were soon disabused of this idea. Nuri's firm hand was needed, for the government was faced with an opposition movement more broadly based and vocal than ever before. For the first time, Nuri used the tactics for which he later became famous. He silenced the opposition, muzzled the press, and insisted that the king prorogue parliament. Nuri's successful handling of the treaty issue and the internal opposition raised him to the position of Iraq's first politician in the eyes of the British, a position he was to hold thereafter.

In June 1930 a newly elected Iraqi parliament ratified the treaty that would take Iraq into the League of Nations. The treaty ended the mandate but retained British influence. Britain leased two bases and retained a right to all Iraqi military facilities; British "advisers and experts" remained. In return, Iraq was to receive military training, equipment, and assistance from Britain.[15]

Although suppressed by Nuri and tempered by subsequent events, opposition to the treaty and the foreign tie continued to surface in subsequent years, and even during periods of calm, suspicions of Britain's hidden hand remained. It is only in the light of this continued opposition to the treaty that the revolution of 1958 and the anti-Western sentiment since that date can be understood. Though unsuccessful in eliminating British influence, the nationalist agenda and the anti-imperialist orientation the opposition projected came to exercise profound sway over successive generations of educated Iraqis.

Although the nationalists opposed the treaty because it did not sever the British tie, Iraqi minorities—in particular the Christians and the Kurds—opposed the treaty because it weakened the tie. Fearful for their status, they began the agitation that was to plague the new state in the decade after independence. Through all of this, however, the king and Nuri stood firm, and in October 1932 Iraq was admitted to the League of Nations, the first mandated state to receive its independence.

As British advisers departed from Baghdad, their place was taken by just the constellation of forces the British had envisaged. The throne inherited most of their power, and cabinets continued to be controlled by pro-British former army officers and lawyers, led by Nuri al-Sa'id. A new opposition party, Ikha-l-Watani (National Brotherhood) was briefly allowed into the citadels of power. It was led by Arab Sunnis but included new elements, such as the Shi'a Ja'far Abu-l-Timman and a liberal, left-wing reformer, Kamil al-Chadirchi. However, the party soon split over the willingness of some members to collaborate with the British and accept the treaty. In the countryside tribal leaders, well contented with the privileges they had received for their support, remained for the moment quiescent. Although the Shi'a and the Kurds were mainly excluded from the emerging structure of power, their opposition had been neutralized by a few seats in the cabinet and by representation of their more moderate elements in parliament. The main weakness of the mandate and mandatory institutions was their narrow scope. They reached only the upper urban strata, scarcely affecting the rural areas and the lower urban classes.

Such a result in 1932 is not surprising. In retrospect, British tutelage had been short—a mere decade or so. Even though "liberal" institutions—a parliament, elections, an open press, and political parties—had been created in Iraq, their effective operation was hampered not only by British limits but also by the absence of Iraqi "liberals" and a homegrown liberal ideology. Indirect rule generated, instead, strong antiforeign sentiments and a national movement that, because of its leaders' Ottoman background and training, had deeper roots in the army and the bureaucratic structures of state than in the parliament or political parties. These cultural continuities would color much of Iraq's subsequent political history.

3

THE EROSION OF THE BRITISH LEGACY, 1932–1945

The end of the mandate ushered in a period of transition and of troubles for the new state and its leaders. The gradual withdrawal of the British advisers brought Iraqi politicians face-to-face with a variety of internal problems they had thus far avoided. One was the breakdown of Iraq's fragile unity. A number of religious and ethnic groups reasserted their claims to autonomy or a greater share of power in the central government. These problems were compounded by a resurgence of tribalism in the south, now mixed with Shi'i disaffection.

The withdrawal of the British and the diminution of their influence also led to a noticeable disillusion with the constitutional system and a search for new principles of social and political organization. The search was impelled by pressures for faster economic development and greater social justice in the distribution of wealth and privilege. Reinforcing these trends were new ideas from abroad that crystallized into two schools of thought that tended to divide the Iraqi intelligentsia between them.

On the one hand were the Arab nationalists, interested in building up the institutions of state and expanding Iraq's influence in the Arab world. They were drawn into Arab politics. On the other hand were the social reformers, moved by growing awareness of social discontent and discrepancies in wealth and opportunities. They were more focused on Iraq and had more appeal to minorities and the Shi'a.

Continued social disturbances and their manipulation by politicians gave the new army its first opportunity to intervene in politics. In 1936 Iraq underwent its first military coup, which very nearly brought about the collapse of the constitutional regime. However, the new government established by the coup was willing to work for social reform and to concentrate more on Iraq than on the Arab world. This reform attempt did not succeed. Instead, the military—and, more specifically, the sector of the military with strong Arab nationalist sentiments— came increasingly to dominate the political system.

British pressures to involve Iraq more deeply in the Second World War increased anti-British sentiments and polarized Iraq's politicians, who were unprepared to deal with such weighty matters. These events led in 1941 to a temporary unseating of the pro-British politicians, a counterinvasion by British forces, and a second British occupation of Iraq. This occupation was a decisive turning point in Iraq's history. The British restored the former pillars of the regime to a position from which they could not be dislodged except by revolution. Their intervention created considerable resentment not only of the occupation but also of the ruling group and its association with a foreign power. These sentiments were suppressed during the war, but they did not disappear.

An Era of Communal and Tribal Rebellion, 1932–1936

With the end of the mandate and the withdrawal of the British, Iraq attempted to create a strong government of national unity. King Faisal moved to propitiate the nationalist opposition by bringing some of its members into the government, but a series of problems threatening the national unity of the new state soon challenged this cabinet. The challenge began in the summer of 1933, when tensions with the newly settled Assyrian community exploded in a serious crisis.

The Assyrian Affair

To many outsiders the Assyrian affair was symptomatic of how Iraq would deal with a dissident minority. The settlement of the Assyrians in Iraq after the First World War and continued British protection of the group had long been resented by the Muslim population. The Assyrian community made claims to autonomy based on its previous status as a separate religious community under the Ottomans. Iraqi nationalists saw the Assyrians as a military and ideological challenge to Iraq's national unity. On the one hand, British reliance on the Levies, a British-trained force wholly recruited from Assyrians, was feared and resented by the fledgling Iraqi army, sensitive to its own weakness.[1] On the other hand, Iraqi independence and the shift in responsibility for internal defense to the Iraqi army worried the Assyrian community. The Levies threatened to resign en bloc and to regroup in the north with a view to forming an Assyrian enclave there.

The situation came to a head in August 1933 when fighting began between the Assyrians and the Iraqi army. Who fired the first shot has not been clearly established, but at the end of the battle thirty Iraqi soldiers and about half as many Assyrians were dead. A few of the remaining Assyrians managed to reach their villages, about five hundred crossed the border to Syria, and the rest were rounded up and shot by the army.

Anti-Assyrian and anti-British sentiment among the Iraqi population had reached an unprecedented pitch. Soon after the first affray, armed Kurdish irregulars massacred about a hundred Assyrian villagers at Dahuk and Zakhu. The worst act, however, occurred on 11 August in Sumayyil, when unarmed Assyrian villagers, clustered at the police station for protection, were killed by an army company, possibly under orders from Bakr Sidqi, the general in charge of the forces in the Mosul area. Whether or not Sidqi was responsible, 315 Assyrians perished at Sumayyil and at least forty villages were looted and partially destroyed.[2]

Apart from the human tragedy, the consequences of these acts were far-reaching. Iraq's capacity for self-government, and particularly its treatment of minorities, was challenged by many in the international community, and the reputation of its newly independent government was harmed. Inside Iraq distrust between minorities and the government would poison the political atmosphere for some time to come.

A less spectacular but more significant outcome was that the Assyrian affair brought the army into national prominence for the first time and showed its future political potential. The affair elevated Bakr Sidqi to the position of a national hero. Offers to serve in the army now poured in from tribesmen and Kurds, making possible the passage of a conscription bill. This legislation strengthened the military and the nationalists.

The Death of Faisal

In September 1933 Faisal died suddenly of a heart attack. His death removed one of the few men capable of moderating the differences among Iraq's diverse elements and destroyed the promising start he had made in incorporating opposition elements into a coalition government.

His twenty-one-year-old son, Ghazi, assumed the throne. Where Faisal had been at home among the townsmen and tribesmen and had taken to the interpersonal style of politics in Baghdad with zest, Ghazi cared little for the intricacies of Baghdad politics and often neglected his royal duties. On the positive side, however, his youth, his genuine nationalist feelings, and his closeness to the young army officers put him in tune with the emerging educated classes.[3]

Meanwhile, politicians in Baghdad continued to jockey for position, ignoring real problems. The resignation of Faisal's coalition cabinet led to a struggle for power within governing circles. The machinations of politicians would have been less serious had they not come on top of tribal dissatisfactions that had been smoldering for some time. These now provided the raw material for disruptions that politicians could—and did—manipulate.

Tribal Revolts

The political scene was dominated for the next two years by tribal revolts, which grew out of a complex of causes. At the root of this tribal unrest was the transition from a society based on tribal organization and values to one based on settled agriculture and the emergence of a state. A striking manifestation of this transition was the erosion of the power and authority of the *shaikh* within the tribe as the new state extended its bureaucracy into the countryside. The conscription law passed in January 1934 was a prime example.

Landholding was another. Throughout the 1930s attention was focused on fixing rights of land ownership and tenure to encourage investment in agriculture and expansion of cultivated land. The practice of modern agriculture and the need to encourage investment required fixed titles over specified territorial plots.[4] The welter of claims and counterclaims finally gave rise to the Land Settlement Law of 1932. Under this law a new form of tenure—*lazma*—could be granted by the settlement authorities to anyone who had enjoyed usufruct of the land for at least fifteen years, but land so granted could not be sold outside the tribe without the approval of the government.[5] The intent of the law had been to safeguard the tribesman against alienation of the land, but except in a few areas, it was in fact used by urban investors and tribal *shaikhs* to secure legal title and to reduce the tribesmen to the status of sharecropping tenants. Far from ameliorating the problem, the law spurred intense competition for land titles, which played a major role in stirring up tribal insurgence.

The scramble for the land was accompanied by the gradual dispossession of the peasant. In 1923 only an estimated one-tenth of the peasants could claim traditional personal rights in the land. The remainder was at the mercy of the newly established landlord-*shaikhs*. By 1930 the reduction in tribesmen's status had resulted in widespread migration to the cities. This migration gave rise to the notorious 1933 Law for the Rights and Duties of Cultivators, which stipulated that no peasant could be employed unless he was free from debt. Almost all peasants were indebted to their landlords.

These difficulties were further compounded by Shi'i grievances. The main grievances were the paucity of Shi'i representation in the central government and an inadequate share of the national resources. A number of religious Shi'a further believed that the government in Baghdad was illegitimate because it was secular, Sunni, and foreign dominated and that participation in the government was both unlawful and sinful. However, this attitude was challenged by a number of Arab Shi'a who, by the late 1920s, preferred to participate in politics and were willing to protest their underrepresentation.[6]

Attempts by Arab Sunni politicians to dissolve Shi'i particularism in a philosophy of secular Arab nationalism also created some animosity. Such an orientation expressed aspirations for eventual integration of Iraq into a greater Arab state that would, inevitably, be mainly Sunni. The alternative, focusing on an Iraqi state with its Shi'i majority, might require adjustments in the power structure and even a modified stance toward Persia, a prospect causing fear and anxiety among many Arab Sunni elites.[7] These Sunni sentiments were expressed in a book, *al-Uruba fi-l-Mizan* (Arabism in the Balance), published in June 1933, which was critical of the Shi'a's unwillingness to give their loyalty to the state and to pan-Arabism. The author was brought to trial and briefly imprisoned, but Shi'i hostility had already been aroused and turned against the government.[8]

These underlying factors would not of themselves have been sufficient to cause a tribal revolt, but after an outbreak of tribal rebellion in Daghghara on 15 March 1935, the king decided to install the opposition in a new cabinet. This cabinet was drawn almost exclusively from the strongest and most experienced of the inner circle of Arab Sunni nationalists and supporters of the pan-Arab orientation. It was headed by Yasin al-Hashimi, leader of the National Brotherhood Party. Members of the previous government and their tribal supporters were furious. The Shi'a took the opportunity to set forth even more stringent demands in a fascinating pamphlet, "Mithaq al-Sha'b" (The People's Pact). It was the clearest statement yet of Shi'i alternatives to the current government, demanding equal representation in the central government and more local rule in the south.[9] An election to the assembly, enlarged to make room for more Shi'i *shaikhs*, failed to satisfy the Shi'a or to prevent a resurgence of tribal rebellions.

There is little need to chronicle the various revolts here, which, with one exception, took place in the south. Disturbances began in May 1935 in Rumaitha and spread to Suq al-Shuyukh. They were followed by Yazidis in Sinjar rising up against conscription. A second rash of out-breaks began in Nasiriyya in 1936, followed by others in Rumaitha and Daghghara. Greed, tangled land claims, religious sentiment, and the weakening of tribal authority—especially symbolized by conscription—contributed in differing degrees.[10]

Dominance of the State and the Army

The cabinet acted with unexpected firmness in upholding the authority of the state and the central government, essentially ending tribal insurgence as a tool for political change. The initial rebellions were put down by Bakr Sidqi, who was lenient at first. When the rash of revolts continued in 1936, however, Sidqi became more ruthless. Military forces were sent to rebellious areas, and air force bombing took a heavy toll in lives. Summary executions were carried out under martial law. These measures were sufficient to bring peace to the tribal areas of the south.

At the same time, the cabinet fortified and expanded the army and the bureaucracy. By 1936 the number of men in the armed services had risen to about 23,000, double the figure for 1933, and the Royal Iraqi Air Force grew from a few planes to three squadrons.[11] A paramilitary training program with a nationalist orientation, known as *futuwwa* (named after a medieval brotherhood devoted to chivalry), was introduced into the school system. These policies were accompanied by a strong Arab nationalist campaign in the press.

What proved to be the government's undoing, however, was not the problem of the tribes but the increasingly authoritarian posture of the prime minister, Yasin al-Hashimi. Feeding opposition fears of a dictatorship, he began clamping down on open political activity and concentrating power in his own hands. He dissolved his party, the National Brotherhood, and then the opposition party, Wahda (Unity). Hashimi's repression of the press made Nuri's previous treatment seem mild by comparison. Hashimi was called the Bismarck of the Arabs, intimating his possible leadership of a greater Arab unity scheme.[12]

By 1936 Hashimi was beginning to hint at a prolonged tenure, claiming he hoped to be given the next ten years of his life to realize the aims desired by the country. The pronouncement caused immediate controversy. Whatever Hashimi's motives, his wish was soon dispelled. A carefully planned conspiracy had been afoot for some time, involving not unruly tribes but the instrument on which nationalist politicians had lavished so much attention—the army.

The Bakr Sidqi Coup, 1936

The coup revealed the mix of forces at work in Iraq, as well as the different directions the state might have taken. Although personal ambition surely played a role, so, too, did the impetus for reform. Although the coup was known by Bakr Sidqi's name, it was not initially the work of the general but of Hikmat Sulaiman. A member of a well-known Ottoman family, Sulaiman was interested not only in power but also in Iraq's more rapid economic and social development. He advocated a thoroughgoing secularism and modernization along Turkish lines. This attitude brought him into close communion with Sidqi and the army.

Sidqi's motives, like Sulaiman's, were mixed. He had reached the highest position open to him in the army and now found the way to advancement blocked by the prime minister's brother, who was chief of staff. But Sidqi also wanted the army expanded and modernized, which could not be achieved without removing the prime minister and his cabinet. Thus, when Sulaiman first broached the idea of a coup to Sidqi in the autumn of 1936, the suggestion fell on fertile ground.

The Political and Intellectual Climate

To understand the coup, however, one must also grasp the political and intellectual climate that enabled Sidqi and Sulaiman to mobilize enough support to carry out their conspiracy. New ideas were permeating Iraq during the 1930s, influencing Iraq's intelligentsia. Two schools of thought, in particular, dominated.

The first school was drawn from the rising dictatorships of Europe. As educated Iraqis traveled through Germany and Italy or read of these countries' spectacular economic and social advances, they began to identify progress and efficiency with authoritarian governments and social mobilization. A monolithic form of government seemed to offer a more effective means of unifying fragmented countries and modernizing backward societies than did constitutional democracy and the free enterprise system. More rapid development, political unity, and greater social discipline were the desiderata of this school of thought. Fascist Italy and Germany in the early days of Adolf Hitler were the models.[13]

The authoritarian regime that exerted the most powerful influence on Iraqis, however—especially on the older generation of nationalists—was that of Mustafa Kamal's Turkey. As an Islamic country with traditions and problems similar to Iraq's, Turkey offered a more attainable example than European regimes did. The use of the state to encourage the development of industry, agriculture, and education had wide appeal. Above all, Kamal's masterful handling of parliament and its fractious politicians seemed—particularly to the military—to set an example worth following.

The second school of thought to stir the Iraqi imagination was democratic socialism. Iraqis were inspired less by the example of the Soviet Union than by the British Labour movement. A need for social rather than merely political reform, an appreciation of the economic basis of power, and dissatisfaction with the policy of the ruling oligarchy of politicians and landowners were keenly felt by the younger generation of Iraqis, the first to receive a Western-style education. This school of thought emphasized social justice, a more equitable distribution of political power and wealth, and genuine economic reform. In the early 1930s, young reformers began to coalesce in a loosely knit organization known as the Ahali group.[14]

By 1935 Ahali had attracted several older and respected politicians, including Ja'far Abu-l-Timman and Hikmat Sulaiman. With the addition of these politicians, the group's emphasis shifted from intellectual matters to the achievement of political power. But the Ahali group did not become a political party. It was still new and lacking structure and organization, and with no grassroots support as yet, it was prone to exploitation.

The Unfolding of the Coup

The actual steps leading up to the Bakr Sidqi coup were kept secret. About a week before the coup, Sidqi approached the commander of the first division and secured his cooperation. When all appeared ready in the army, Sulaiman appealed to the Ahali group for support. Although some hesitated before committing themselves to a breach with the constitution, most joined the conspiracy, convinced that the group would have an unprecedented opportunity to put its ideas in practice.[15]

Events then marched to a swift conclusion.[16] On 29 October 1936 planes dropped leaflets over Baghdad demanding Hashimi's resignation and the appointment of Sulaiman as prime minister. Meanwhile, the army began a march on Baghdad under Sidqi's leadership. The king was anxious about his own future, but once it was clear that the coup was designed to replace the cabinet and not the king, Ghazi was willing to acquiesce. Meanwhile, bombs were dropped near the Council of Ministers' building. Shortly thereafter Hashimi resigned and Sulaiman was appointed prime minister. The following day Yasin al-Hashimi, Nuri al-Sa'id, and Rashid Ali al-Kailani, the minister of justice, left the country. Hashimi died of a heart attack in 1937, but Nuri and Rashid Ali returned later to play pivotal roles in their country's political life.

The coup was a major turning point in Iraqi history.[17] It made a critical breach in the constitution, already weakened by government politicians and their willingness to stir tribal rebellion, and opened the door to military involvement in politics. The coup also made a clean, if temporary, sweep of the old ruling group that had governed the country since its founding. Only one veteran politician, Sulaiman, found his way into the new government.

The change seemed to spell the gradual demise of the establishment. It also raised the possibility of a new direction in domestic politics. Much depended, however, on whether the new government could keep the army out of politics, restore constitutional procedure, and move ahead on some basic reforms.

Attempts to Liberalize and Their Failure

The cabinet Sulaiman appointed after the coup represented a mixture of coup participants. Sulaiman became prime minister, Sidqi became chief of staff, and the Ahali group received the lion's share of economic and social ministries. The new government brought new people to power, many of whom had been educated under the British rather than the Ottomans. Liberal, leftist reformers acquired power for the first time. They meant to bypass the established alliance of urban Sunni politicians and rural landlords, redistributing power and privilege and developing a broader-based constituency among the middle and lower classes. Had their program succeeded, Iraq's subsequent history might have been very different.

A less noticeable but more significant change was that the new government contained few Arab Sunnis and not a single advocate of the pan-Arab cause on which all previous governments had been founded. This configuration resulted in a more Iraq-centered foreign policy oriented toward better relations with Turkey and Iran instead of with the Arab countries. In 1937 the Sa'dabad Pact was concluded among Turkey, Iran, Iraq, and Afghanistan, a group that prefigured the later Baghdad Pact. Iraq also reached an agreement with Iran (mediated by Britain) that attempted to settle the boundary between Iran and Iraq on the Shatt al-Arab. The agreement gave freedom of navigation on the Shatt to Iran and increased the territory under Iran's jurisdiction, concessions that aroused some public opinion against the government.[18] Sulaiman's cabinet gave birth to the "Iraq First" policy of Iraq for the Iraqis and took cognizance of the need for good relations with Iraq's non-Arab neighbors. However, the cabinet's neglect of the Arab nationalist cause was soon to cause considerable trouble.

The new government began its work amid considerable popular support, but popular support could not for long mask the ultimate incompatibility of its two major components. Authoritarian by training and outlook, Sidqi was determined to make the army the main vehicle of power in the state; the liberal democratic reformers were bent on changing the social structure of the country. These differences, papered over in the common desire to overthrow the previous regime, soon generated conflict.

Initially, the reformers appeared to be strong. The new government promised an end to the suppression of liberty and advocated reforms in the educational system and the distribution of state lands. Its program called for an annulment of laws against the peasants, an encouragement of trade unions, and a spread of culture among the masses—a call for broad-based, rather than elite, education. This was, in short, a bold attack on privilege.[19]

However, it was not long before opposition began to surface from a number of sources. Chief among these were the landlord-*shaikhs*, who felt their authority to be threatened, and the Arab nationalists, who were unhappy over the Turkish orientation of the cabinet and over the agreement with Iran. Most important was opposition from Bakr and his supporters in the army.

A conflict between Sidqi and the Ahali group was probably inevitable. It came when tribal supporters of the previous cabinet rebelled and Sidqi and Sulaiman decided to crush them by force. Sulaiman's decision was made without his consulting the cabinet. When the three reform ministers heard of it, they resigned. The episode signaled a clear victory for Sidqi and his contingent. Sulaiman promised the dissolution of the newly elected parliament, and a second election was in fact held to remove leftist influence. Thus ended any attempt to tamper with Iraq's social structure until after the revolution of 1958.

These moves came too late to save the regime. Opposition to Sidqi had been growing, chiefly among the Arab nationalist politicians, who were in contact with a group of Arab nationalist army officers.[20] These officers resented Sidqi as a Kurd who had encouraged Kurds in the army, and they felt the policy of Sulaiman's government had been too pro-Turkish. The Shi'a detested Sidqi for his brutal suppression of the tribes. Above all, the opposition was aided and abetted by members of the previous cabinet. Nuri al-Sa'id, motivated partly by revenge and partly by opposition to the cabinet's policy, waged an incessant campaign from Egypt against the cabinet.[21] Once again the army, or a portion of it, intervened. On 11 August 1937, Bakr Sidqi was shot point-blank by a soldier under orders from the Arab nationalist officers.

Sidqi's assassination put Sulaiman and his regime in a critical position. It soon became clear that the bulk of the officer corps in Mosul sided with the plotters. When units in Baghdad also sided with these officers, civil war seemed possible. To avoid this contingency, the government resigned on 17 August 1937. The new regime, which had come to power with such great expectations of reform, had fallen within ten months.

The Bakr Sidqi coup and the collapse of the coalition government had far-reaching results. One was to remove the left from power. The reformers were unprepared for their task in terms of organization, ideological cohesion, and political experience and were no match for the army. Moreover, Sulaiman and the left grossly underestimated the strength of two other political forces in the country—the Arab nationalists and the conservative landowners.

With the weakening of the left, power gravitated into the hands of the conservative and nationalist elements at a critical time. Opening a door to a misuse of power by the military, the coup of 1936 was followed by a series of less overt but continual military interventions behind the scenes, which became the most marked feature of political life in the years between 1936 and 1941.

The Army in Politics, 1937–1941

In the years immediately following the assassination of Bakr Sidqi, three distinct strands developed in Iraqi politics. One was the return of the establishment politicians and their pursuit of business as usual. These politicians—especially Nuri—continued to wage their own power struggles and personal vendettas, neglecting pressing social issues and the threatening international situation brought about by the onset of the Second World War. Second was the reemergence of the Palestine problem and the resulting intensification of anti-British and Arab nationalist sentiment, especially among key groups such as the students, intelligentsia, and officer corps. Third were the increased intrusion of the army in politics and the continued erosion of the constitutional system established by the British. Previously, the politicians and the British had unquestionably manipulated parliament, but military dominance in politics was to prove even more damaging. The intertwining of these three strands gradually drew the young officers further into politics, intensified their pan-Arab feelings, isolated the pro-British politicians, and eventually precipitated the crisis of 1941.

The Return of the Establishment

In the wake of Sulaiman's resignation, Jamil al-Midfa'i, a former prime minister whose conciliatory policies were well known, was appointed prime minister. To heal old wounds, he adopted a policy of "dropping the curtain" on the past. This policy, backed by the moderates and the king, did not satisfy Nuri, who began to agitate for the removal of Midfa'i's cabinet and for punishment of Sulaiman and his supporters. On this issue, Nuri found common ground with the Arab nationalist officers who opposed Midfa'i's policy and who feared retribution for Sidqi's assassination should Sulaiman return to power. On 24 December the officers insisted on the resignation of the cabinet on the grounds that the army no longer had confidence in it. Nuri made clear that he fully supported the officers, and Midfa'i's resignation followed the same day. Nuri al-Sa'id became prime minister for the first time since 1932.

He then attempted to deal with Hikmat Sulaiman and his collaborators in the coup. An alleged plot against the life of the king was "discovered" in March 1939, and Sulaiman and a number of his group were implicated, brought to trial, and convicted. The evidence convinced no one. Only the intervention of the British ambassador got the sentences reduced and saved Sulaiman's life. This indicates the extent to which Nuri was willing to go to achieve retribution and the degree to which personal feelings were allowed to dominate politics.

The Death of Ghazi

No sooner had the trial been settled than the government was faced with an unexpected crisis. On 4 April 1939 the king, under the influence of alcohol, drove his car at high speed into an electric pole. He died of a fractured skull shortly thereafter. This official version of the king's death has always been suspected by Iraqis and particularly by the nationalists, who have claimed that Nuri and the British had a hand in it.[22] There is no hard evidence to support this conclusion, but there is little doubt that Ghazi's death came as a relief to Nuri and the British. Always in tune with the younger army officers, the young king had become an outspoken advocate of anti-British and nationalist sentiments.

Ghazi's death created a serious political vacuum at the center of power. The young king left an infant son, Faisal II, but no clear-cut provisions had been made for a regency. This was a delicate matter because the regent would exercise the power of the throne for the next fourteen years. Among the contenders was Abd al-Ilah, Ghazi's cousin. He was known to be pro-British and had good relations with Nuri and the officers who supported him. He was also young—twenty-six—and for that reason the politicians probably felt that they could control him. On 6 April 1939 Abd al-Ilah was appointed regent.[23]

Abd al-Ilah had been born and raised in the insulated environment of Mecca, had been educated at the British-run Victoria College in Egypt, and had come to Iraq only in 1926. He always seemed to feel an outsider in Iraq, more at home among the English than among Iraqis, a factor that later put him at a disadvantage. Nonetheless, Abd al-Ilah used his position to draw the establishment closer to the British than to the nationalists. As a result, the year following the king's death was one of relative stability. The calm was deceptive, however. Beneath the surface nationalist sentiment continued to mount, creating a climate of opinion that would eventually isolate the pro-British politicians and create irresistible pressures within the establishment.

The Rising Tide of Nationalism

These pressures were exacerbated by events outside Iraq that inexorably drew the country and its politicians deeper into regional and international affairs. By the end of the decade, two issues had come to a head. Both worked against the British connection. The first was the partition of Palestine and Britain's role in furthering that outcome. The second was the onset of the Second World War in Europe, in which Britain and its allies were challenged by the forces of fascism. The two issues were intertwined. The Palestine issue helped fuel indigenous anti-British feeling, while the divisions in Europe appeared to some to provide alternative sources of support.

Despite residual anti-British feelings among Iraqis, it is doubtful whether the Palestine struggle would have inflamed public opinion to the extent it did if not for the influence of Amin al-Husaini, the *mufti* (religious jurist) of Palestine. The resistance movement in Palestine, led by the *mufti*, had reached a peak between 1936 and 1939 with riots and armed resistance to the British. After the British crushed the resistance movement, the *mufti* took refuge in Baghdad, adding his voice to the mounting anti-British sentiment.

Meanwhile, the onset of the Second World War exacerbated social and economic problems in Iraq, leading to commercial disruptions, inflation, and a shortage of funds. The mass of the population in rural and urban areas continued to live in poverty, which was soon to be intensified by the shortages of the war. The slow pace of development and the disruption of a war thrust on Iraq by foreign powers increased the rancor of Iraqi politicians and fed the intense anti-British feeling that was shortly to engulf Iraq.

These sentiments were stoked by the growth of Arab nationalist ideology in the school system, particularly at the secondary and college levels, where the Arab nationalist seeds had taken root. By the 1930s the introduction of new texts, heavily oriented toward pan-Arabism, in history and the social sciences were having an impact. Pan-Arab sentiments were strongly influenced by German ideas of nationalism and were encouraged by Fritz Grobba, the German minister in Baghdad until 1939.

Intrusion of the Officers into Politics

A commitment to Arab nationalism was clearly shared by the younger generation of army officers; indeed, it was the main motive force behind their increased forays into the political arena. Politicization of the army officer corps had begun at least as early as 1930 when Taufiq Husain, a fiery lecturer at the Military College, advocated military intervention in politics on the model of Turkey and Iran. By 1934 there were at least seventy officers in his circle. It was not long, however, before a number of these broke away from Husain and formed their own group, oriented toward a more pan-Arab policy. Alienated by Bakr Sidqi's lack of interest in Arab affairs, this group had been behind Sidqi's assassination and the subsequent military action that had put Nuri back in power in 1938.[24] By 1940 the core of this group had narrowed down to four: Salah al-Din Sabbagh, Muhammad Fahmi Sa'id, Mahmud Salman, and Kamil Shabib. All were to be key participants in the events of 1941. One more individual, Yunis al-Sab'awi, a journalist, also played a key role in sharpening the Arab nationalist sentiments of the officers and encouraging their political activism.[25]

By 1940 all three strands of politics—personal fear, the pan-Arab issue, and the intrusion of the military in politics—came to a head once again. In February Nuri tried to resign. Personal dissension in the cabinet over his treatment of adversaries, as well as the general tensions brought about by the Palestine issue, had made his position untenable. The young officers, however, fearful of losing their positions, organized yet another quiet coup to keep him in power. Nuri stayed temporarily but used his time to retire several senior officers who favored ending the intrusion of the young officers in politics. This act secured their position and eased the situation temporarily. On 31 March 1940 Nuri was finally able to step down as prime minister. On his advice, former prime minister Rashid Ali al-Kailani formed a new cabinet. However, the damage had been done. The third coup had put the young nationalist officers in complete control of the country's armed forces. It would not be long before they would precipitate another crisis, one the civilian politicians were unable to handle.

The 1941 Coup

Much ink has been spilled on interpreting the events of 1940 and 1941 and the brief war that resulted in the second British occupation of Iraq.[26] The Anglophile party in Iraq has always regarded the movement labeled with Rashid Ali's name as an illegal one and as a breach in the constitutional system. This view prevailed for a time in Iraq with the victory of the regent and the pro-British forces. The nationalists, more closely tied to opinion inside Iraq and less attuned to foreign concerns, viewed the movement as a genuine assertion of Iraq's national rights, a further step in achieving Iraqi independence, and a blow struck for the Arab cause and the Palestinian struggle. In the long run, with the eventual domination of nationalist governments after 1958, this interpretation prevailed.

In May 1940 the fall of France put the Vichy government in control of neighboring Syria, threatening British communications in the Middle East. When Italy declared war on the Allies on 10 June 1940, the British asked Iraq to break off diplomatic relations with Italy, fearing that the Italian Embassy would be used as a center of espionage and propaganda for the Axis powers.

When Nuri, as foreign minister, asked the cabinet to comply, a rift in the government opened. One group, led by Nuri and supported by the regent, favored the British. The other faction, represented by Rashid Ali but led by the *mufti* and the officers, wished to remain neutral or to bargain support for reducing British influence in internal affairs. This group won out. In the summer of 1940 it tentatively explored the possibility of German support in case of an open conflict with Britain.

In the meantime, British patience had run out. In November 1940 the British forced the issue by delivering a virtual ultimatum to the government, giving Iraq two choices: It could keep Rashid Ali, or it could retain the friendship of Britain. A rapid succession of events followed. Rashid Ali resigned, and a new cabinet, headed by an army officer, Yasin al-Hashimi's brother, Taha, was formed. He tried to put the army officers back in the barracks and failed. Backed by the officers, Rashid Ali then returned as prime minister. The officers surrounded the palace with forces, but the regent managed to escape. Nuri and several other pro-British politicians left the country with him. The regent's departure made it necessary for the four officers and Rashid Ali to act outside the constitutional system. This came to be known as the Rashid Ali coup.

Rashid Ali and the officers now formed a new government, composed wholly of the nationalist party, an act accomplished in the midst of a high tide of nationalist sentiment. On 10 April they deposed Abd al-Ilah, appointing a distant relative in his place. Rashid Ali was deputized to form his third and last cabinet. Even with the crisis completely out of hand, Rashid Ali desperately tried to find a compromise. However, the British demanded that British troops be allowed to land in Iraq, presumably to be transported through the country in accordance with the treaty. Rashid Ali agreed, and on 17 and 18 April British troops landed at Basra.

From here on Rashid Ali lost whatever measure of control he had once held over the officers. Apparently blind to the probable consequences, the officers informed Rashid Ali that the British troops would have to leave the country in a few days. The British, who were attempting to evacuate women and children by plane from Habbaniyya, were told that if the plane left the ground, it would be fired upon. The British regarded this as an act of war, and on 2 May the local British commander decided to attack the Iraqi forces surrounding the base without warning. Within hours the Royal Air Force had destroyed twenty-five of Iraq's forty planes. The Iraqi army soon withdrew to Falluja. In the meantime, British reinforcements streamed in from Jordan. They captured Falluja on 19 May, and the way lay open to Baghdad.

The government that had precipitated the war collapsed shortly. On 29 May, as British columns approached Baghdad, the four officers escaped to Iran, where they were soon joined by Rashid Ali, Amin al-Husaini, and their followers. On 30 May a new mayor of Baghdad and a committee he formed signed an armistice with Britain. On 1 June Abd al-Ilah arrived in Baghdad with Nuri and others. They were entrusted with the formation of a government made up of the pro-British party alone. Thus ended the most serious attempt since the 1920 revolt to sever the British tie and to unseat the regime Britain had established. It ended, as previous attempts had, with a British victory. But events showed how thin the British influence was; without the second British occupation, it is doubtful how long that influence would have remained.

On the positive side, the victory bought the British and the regime they had established additional time—almost two decades—to put down roots and work on a better foundation. It restored a constitutional system to Iraq and buttressed Iraq's relations with the winning side and the dominant European powers. However, the crisis also had profound negative repercussions for the future; all the participants paid a price sooner or later.[27] Many supporters of Rashid Ali were executed or imprisoned; suspected sympathizers were dismissed or confined in camps. Those who were executed for precipitating the events of 1941 were regarded as martyrs by much of the army and the Iraqi population, generating a deep rift in Iraqi society. The young officers who overthrew the regime in 1958 believed they were but completing the task left unfinished in 1941.

The Second British Occupation and Its Legacy, 1941–1945

In June 1941 the first contingent of British forces reached Baghdad and began to requisition houses and buildings; the second British occupation of Iraq had begun. It was clearly recognized, however, that the situation was temporary and would lapse at the conclusion of the war with the withdrawal of British troops.

On 9 October, to no one's surprise, Nuri was asked to form a new cabinet. The second occupation indissolubly linked the ruling circles of Iraq, especially the regent and Nuri, to the British. The willingness of these politicians to act as mediators between the British and their own people and their pursuit to the death of the followers of Rashid Ali gradually cut the regime off from much of the articulate middle class, making them ever more dependent upon the British.

Internment, Trials, and Reorganization of the Government

Shortly thereafter preparations were made for the internment of those the regime considered dangerous. Although this category was supposed to include only Rashid Ali supporters and those with open Axis sympathies, personal motives were also at work in the arrests. The total of those interned during the war may have reached 700 to 1,000.[28]

Of far more significance than these internments were the trials and executions of the movement's leaders. Late in 1941 an Iraqi court-martial was established; on 6 January 1942 it handed down the severest possible sentences. Rashid Ali, three of the four colonels, Yunis al-Sab'awi, and one or two others were all sentenced to death in absentia; others received long sentences of imprisonment.

During a second trial, many of the original sentences were reduced. This did not hold true for the four officers involved in Rashid Ali's government. All four of the officers and Yunis al-Sab'awi were eventually captured and hanged. Of the leaders who had participated in the movement, only Rashid Ali and the *mufti* managed to escape. Many army officers in particular were bitter over the treatment accorded their colleagues, which created a vendetta and marked a point of no return in the attitude of many Iraqis toward the regime.

The regime turned next to the army and the education system. Throughout the remainder of the war, Nuri reduced both the size and influence of the army. In the spring of 1944 a British officer, Major General James Renton, was sent to Iraq to reorganize the military. He put the army in the shape it was to assume right up to the revolution of 1958. Ottoman-trained officers were replaced by younger men, mainly trained by the British.

The regime turned next to the Ministry of Education. The British rightly attributed much of the pro-Axis sentiment in the country to the spread of extreme nationalism in the curriculum and textbooks and among the teachers. Offending teachers were dismissed, and some of the most offensive texts removed.[29] Finally, the regime took steps to protect itself from a repetition of the events of 1941 through a constitutional amendment designed to buttress the throne. The king was given the right to dismiss the prime minister if necessary, a prerogative that would be exercised by Abd al-Ilah until the young king's maturity. The regent could thus legally remove an obstructive cabinet such as Rashid Ali's should it come to power.

The removal of so many nationalists had thinned the ranks of the Arab Sunnis from which the regime had usually drawn support. The remaining wartime cabinets drew far more heavily on the Shi'a and the Kurds, who for the first time equally balanced or together sometimes outnumbered the Arab Sunnis in the cabinet.[30] This circumstance provided an opportunity for the emergence of new political figures and a younger generation among the Shi'a and the Kurds.

This was accompanied by a political shift of far more significance for the future—encouragement of the left. The departure of the strong Arab nationalists opened the door to the liberal-leftist elements that had supported the Ahali group. At the same time, the regime itself began to take a more benign view of the leftists, giving the Communist Party and other left-wing movements an opportunity to organize and to establish roots in the schools and among the workers. The Communist Party achieved an important hold among the intelligentsia and the working class that it retained in spite of the persecution of the late 1940s and the 1950s.

The Wartime Economy

The war years marked a turning point in social and economic life as well. Spiraling wartime inflation and the shortage of goods (especially grains) created unprecedented opportunities for exploitation. The resulting scramble for wealth created some affluence but more often built breathtaking fortunes for a very few. Gradually the gap between the rich and the poor, and even between the wealthy and the merely well-to-do, widened, creating new social tensions and breaking down the old ties of family and community and the values that sustained them. What made the situation even more intolerable was the close tie between political power and wealth and the obvious corruption in high places. As a close-knit oligarchy of wealth and power evolved, the legitimacy of the regime was further eroded. Meanwhile, the middle class of civil servants, army officers, and teachers, caught on a treadmill of fixed salaries, saw their economic and social position worsen daily. The situation of the poor often became extreme, and bitterness against the government broke out in riots and strikes.

The first and most important factor in the postwar economy was inflation, produced partly by the descent of British troops on Iraq and partly by war shortages. Grain prices rose from an index of 100 in 1939 to 773 in the peak year of 1943.[31] Among those who profited most from these circumstances were the grain producers and dealers, who suddenly found an expanded market for their produce at higher prices.

But the grain trade, though the most lucrative, was not the only means of gaining wealth. Another profitable business was importing. All sorts of items were in short supply, and those who could corner the market on some item turned a nice profit. In fact, the government was forced to institute an import licensing policy, but import licenses then became a scarce commodity themselves. The profits made in the purchase and sale of valuable import licenses often exceeded the profitability of the import trade itself. So valuable were these licenses that ministers, senators, and almost all deputies registered as licensed importers, even though they did not engage in business themselves; they then sold the licenses to merchants.

Meanwhile, salaried employees working for the government suffered. While the cost of living rose five-, six-, and sevenfold,[32] employee salaries rose only 25 percent.[33] As for workers, their wages in 1939 were estimated at ID 3.38 a month, or ID 40 ($95) a year.[34] The war years were punctuated by bread strikes, especially in 1943, when shortages were greatest and prices reached a peak. The strikes were put down by the police, although police action was accompanied by attempts to supply bread to the masses.

The closing years of the war hastened the polarization of society and helped set the stage for the revolution of 1958. Economically, the war created an ever-more-visible oligarchy. Politically, it brought back a regime tied almost wholly to the British, the landlords, and the wealthy. The removal of the nationalists gave opportunity to other groups. The introduction of more Shi'a and Kurds into leadership posts alleviated ethnic and social tensions. But the regime, in the hands of old-school politicians like Nuri and a pro-British regent, failed to provide a new matching vision of Iraqi identity that would appeal to moderate nationalists. The demise of the nationalists also opened the door to the left. Some of these leftists were genuine liberals, interested in reforms and constitutional processes, but others were committed Marxists, who now worked to widen the gap between the regime and the people and to pave the way for the new social conditions of the postwar era.

4

THE END OF THE MONARCHY, 1946–1958

The last decade of the monarchy was a study in contrast. On the surface, political life appeared stable. The establishment politicians, supported by the landlord-*shaikhs*, the new urban wealthy, and the upper reaches of the army, seemed firmly entrenched in power. Beneath the surface, however, new social groups, motivated by different ideals and aspirations, emerged to challenge establishment values and policy. In country and city alike, poverty was widespread, even as new oil wealth was creating visible pockets of urban affluence and modernity. The regime recognized the need for change and attempted some modest reforms, but it tried to circumvent the established classes with a development program that avoided problems rather than addressing them.

Perhaps the most significant change occurred in the intellectual and cultural realm. Along with the spread of education and the press, increased contact with the West introduced new ideas and values that posed a sharp contrast with the past. The left demanded rapid social change, a more egalitarian society, and greater personal freedoms; the younger generation of Arab nationalists wanted faster movement on Arab unity and greater independence from the West. The regime did little to counteract these ideas or to put forth a social vision of its own.

Nowhere were these contradictions more apparent than in the area of foreign policy. While the regime clung to the British tie, bitterness over the events of 1941 and the wartime arrests and executions continued. These feelings were exacerbated by the Arab defeat in Palestine and the establishment of the Israeli state. In the 1950s the eruption of revolutionary movements in other Middle Eastern states—Muhammad Mussadiq in Iran, Gamal Abdul Nasser in Egypt—caused strong reverberations inside Iraq. Regional changes occurred against the backdrop of the Cold War and its intrusion into the Middle East. The Soviet Union's support for local Communist parties, aimed at disrupting or unseating pro-Western governments, was matched by the West's attempts to shore up its supporters; both efforts helped polarize political forces in the region and inside Iraq.

Foreign policy problems were matched by and intertwined with domestic difficulties. Aided by the spread of the press and radio and by an expanded educational system, new political parties proceeded to politicize the new socioeconomic groups, especially the educated middle class and the new working class. Their influence was increasingly evident in strikes, demonstrations, and riots that further undermined and weakened the establishment.

In the face of these difficulties, the regime failed to shift the locus of its support or to develop the political institutions capable of moderating conflict. Instead it continued to rely on the police to put down disturbances and on the manipulation of elections to assure compliant parliaments. Neither was the opposition up to the challenge. The only common ground on which the opposition could unite was anti-imperialism and a severing of the regime's foreign tie. In the end, domestic discontent and foreign policy issues coalesced to overwhelm the regime and remove most vestiges of the British legacy.

Further Attempts at Liberalization

In the aftermath of the war and the Rashid Ali coup, the regent set forth a liberalization policy in a speech on 27 December 1945, promising permission for political parties, a new electoral law, measures to improve social security and unemployment, and some redistribution of wealth. He also suggested a modification of the treaty with Britain. His most important step was a decision to license five new political parties. Although three of the five proved to be short-lived, the remaining two, the Istiqlal (Independence) Party and the National Democratic Party, survived to play a critical role in the postwar period and in the early part of the revolutionary era. Both helped to shape the mentality of the emerging middle class, and between them they captured the minds and hearts of the younger generation of educated Iraqis.

The Istiqlal Party was anti-British and pan-Arab. It called for the elimination of remaining British influence in Iraq, espoused independence for Muhammara (now Khuzistan, a province with a majority of Arabic speakers) in Iran, and championed the Palestinian cause. The Istiqlal came down heavily on the side of secular pan-Arabism and against the development of a separate Iraqi identity, although it did demand progressive social reforms. It drew its support mainly from the Sunni Arab population, although it was headed by a Shi'a, Muhammad Mahdi Kubba, and some Shi'a joined. There were no Kurds in Istiqlal.[1]

The National Democratic Party, led by Kamil al-Chadirchi, was an outgrowth of the older Ahali movement. It stood for political freedoms, land reform, abolition of monopolies, and a more equitable distribution of wealth to be achieved mainly through tax measures. Because of an emphasis on domestic policy and reform and a lack of interest in pan-Arab schemes, the National Democratic Party appealed to minorities and the Shi'a as well as to the liberal and left-leaning elements of the educated middle class.[2]

Both parties were opposed to the Western alliance. Both the Istiqlal and the National Democratic Party appealed almost wholly to the urban literate classes. Neither had a widespread or tightly knit organization, but the two parties dominated the legal opposition and helped to create and spread a climate of hostility to the establishment and its foreign tie.

Although the Iraq Communist Party was not among the licensed parties, it functioned underground and had roots going back to the 1930s. Its real impetus came in 1941 when Yusif Salman, a Chaldean and a self-educated worker known as Comrade Fahd, took over the party leadership.

He put together a central committee whose membership consisted primarily of journalists, teachers, and lawyers.[3] Almost half of the members were Jews, Christians, or Shi'a, indicating the appeal of the party to the minorities and to Shi'a still resentful of their small share of power and privilege. By 1946 the Communist Party was the best-organized political group in the country. The party's support was drawn partly from the literate intelligentsia—especially students, bureaucrats, and teachers—at the lower end of the middle-class pay scale and partly from workers, particularly those in the vital oil, port, and railway sectors. The Communists had little influence in rural areas among the peasants. Another weakness was their lack of concern for Arab nationalism, including the Palestine issue.

Despite the flowering of new political parties, the liberalization program was short-lived. The activities of the newly licensed parties and especially of the unlicensed Communist Party soon confirmed the opponents of reform in their belief that an open political system would lead only to an overthrow of the regime itself. There is little doubt that the Communist Party had a hand in fomenting a strike by oil workers in Kirkuk. On 12 July 1946 workers clashed with police; eight workers were killed, and scores were wounded when police fired into the crowd.

The incident, dubbed the Kirkuk Massacre by the opposition, clearly worried the regime. On 16 November the cabinet resigned. The main casualty of the affair, however, was not the cabinet but the reform program. With matters out of hand, the regent turned to Nuri to conduct an election. A new cabinet was formed under Salih Jabr, the first Shi'i prime minister in Iraq's history, and a member of the younger generation educated under the mandate. But despite progressive views on some issues, Jabr proved even less liberal than his predecessors. Within six months of taking office he had banned two left-wing parties.

The Portsmouth Treaty and the *Wathba*

The regent now turned to revision of the 1930 treaty with Britain, which he hoped would meet the objections of the opposition. In this he was misguided. The treaty had always been a divisive issue in Iraqi politics, and the opposition wanted it eliminated, not modified. The British were also skeptical of revision, fearing negotiations would open a Pandora's box.

Nevertheless, in May 1947 negotiations with the British began in Baghdad. The major issue was who would have control over the air bases. By December a preliminary agreement had been reached on Iraqi control. An Iraqi delegation left for London to complete the negotiations. There the two sides quickly reached agreement and signed the treaty at the Portsmouth naval base on 15 January 1948.

The Portsmouth Treaty provided for the removal of British troops from Iraqi soil and gave Iraq sovereignty over the bases, but it still tied Iraq to Britain in terms of supplies and military training, and the agreement to surrender the bases to Britain in time of war negated any possibility of future neutrality. However, the treaty's actual provisions were not at stake; what was at stake was the continuation of a treaty at all and the whole issue of the British tie.

While the British and Iraqi delegations were exchanging congratulatory speeches in Portsmouth, events in Iraq were reaching the crisis that has come to be known as the *wathba* (rising).[4] On 16 January 1948, during a student demonstration against the treaty, police fired on the crowd, killing four people and wounding more. An uproar ensued. By the end of January, virtually every articulate element in the country—the parliament, students, professors, and the lower classes—had come out against the treaty. For a time a real atmosphere of civil war prevailed in Baghdad.

The *wathba* showed that by 1948 the urban population at least had been thoroughly won over by the opposition, which was able to mobilize large crowds. The *wathba* inaugurated a period in which "the street" played an increasing role in political dynamics. On 27 January, the day after Jabr returned from England, there was another clash between demonstrators and police. According to official sources, at least seventy-seven were killed; several hundred wounded. Jabr resigned. Although it remained for the succeeding cabinet to repudiate the Portsmouth Treaty, the opposition had clearly achieved its main aims: cancellation of the treaty and the fall of Jabr's cabinet.

The *wathba* illustrated the depth and breadth of resentment, from both left and right, against the regime and its foreign connection. Though the British were silently outraged, the rejection of the Portsmouth Treaty made little real difference to them: They merely fell back on the old 1930 treaty. Inside Iraq the *wathba* gave the opposition more confidence and encouraged it to challenge the establishment more aggressively.

The Portsmouth Treaty and the *wathba* illustrated the strong tie between domestic and foreign affairs, as well as the difficulties in opening the system and managing social change. A new cycle of politics ensued. When faced with a crisis, the regent would attempt to arrange the return of Nuri and his colleagues as the only ones strong enough to protect the throne. The appointment of these politicians, especially Nuri, would trigger the eruption of opposition. This would be followed by attempts to appease the opposition by bringing in new men or known moderates and temporarily removing Nuri. The opposition would seize this opportunity to push for more drastic changes in domestic and foreign policy, the situation would deteriorate, and Nuri and his cohorts would be brought back to deal with it. At each turn of the wheel the same methods were tried—street violence by the opposition and police action by the regime. In the process, no strong center group emerged to mediate differences between the regime and its opposition.

War in Palestine

The British treaty was not the only foreign policy problem facing Iraq. All through the Portsmouth crisis, the Palestine problem had been a gathering storm. The Palestine problem was the one issue that could unite the Iraqi population, Sunni and Shi'i, religious and secular, rich and poor. By the outbreak of the first Arab-Israeli war in May 1948, Iraqi passions were thoroughly aroused.

In May 1948 Iraqi troops were dispatched to Palestine, where a swift victory was expected back home. In fact, the troops expected orders to advance, but none came, which later gave rise to accusations of betrayal on the part of Arab regimes. These circumstances came amid a ceasefire, concluded under pressure from the United Nations at the end of May, that worked to the advantage of the Jewish forces. When fighting resumed, the tide turned in their favor, an advantage they retained until their final victory.[5]

The poor Arab showing in the war focused attention on the economic, social, and political conditions at home and strengthened the position of those who had been calling for greater Arab unity. These sentiments were particularly acute among the younger members of the officer corps who had fought on the front and who felt cheated out of victory.

Meanwhile, the large and well-established Jewish community in Iraq had come under attack, and its position became increasingly untenable. In 1951 the Iraqi government decided that Jews should be allowed to leave if they wished, thinking that only a few thousand would do so. To the government's surprise, the number exceeded 100,000, almost the entire community.[6]

The withdrawal of the Jewish community left a large gap in the economy and the professions, in which Jewish expertise and foreign contacts had contributed much to Iraqi society. The vacuum left by the Jewish exodus was soon filled by enterprising Shi'a and Christians, providing both communities with a new channel of mobility. The younger generation of Shi'a, educated in technical and professional subjects, moved into positions in medicine, law, and finance. Some used the capital acquired by an older generation of Shi'i landlords and merchants to become entrepreneurs, creating the backbone of a new Shi'i middle class.

Oil and Economic Development

Despite these roiling political events, the 1950s were a decade of economic and social change, beginning in the oil sphere but spreading to other areas as well. These developments began to change Iraq in some fundamental ways. The first step in this direction was increasing Iraq's oil revenue and then turning it toward long-term development. One problem here lay in negotiating a new agreement with the Iraq Petroleum Company (IPC), a consortium owned by several major international oil companies (British, American, French, and Dutch) with competing interests

TABLE 4.1 Iraqi Oil Fields, 1960

Field	Discovery Date	Daily Average, in Barrels
Naft Khana	1923	3,300
Kirkuk	1927	643,087
Ain Zala	1939	18,425
Zubair	1949	72,936
Butma	1952	8,516
Bay Hasan	1953	33,387
Rumaila	1953	172,648
Jambur	1954	11,033
Total		963,332

SOURCE: Reprinted by permission from Charles Issawi and Mohammed Yeganeh, *The Economics of Middle Eastern Oil* (New York: Praeger, 1962), p. 93.

in other Middle East oil countries.[7] As a result, by the early 1950s oil production began to be a major factor in Iraq's economy. Between 1952 and 1958 output and revenues doubled, raising Iraq's oil income to ID 84.6 million ($237.7 million) in 1958.[8] Large new fields were developed—in Zubair in 1949 and Rumaila in 1953; both were in the south near Basra (see Table 4.1). Iraq now took the first steps toward a phenomenon that would become more pronounced in later decades—increased dependence on the export of a single resource controlled by a foreign-owned company and subject to international market conditions beyond Iraq's control. In short, Iraq became a "rentier" state, dependent for its livelihood not on its productive sectors but on "rents" from oil. By 1959 oil revenues contributed some 60 percent of the government budget.[9]

Oil revenues enabled Iraq to make a sustained effort at long-term development for the first time. The development program was Nuri's answer to social and political unrest. Seventy percent of oil revenue was now set aside for development, and a development board, independent of the government, was established to spend the funds. Emphasis was put on long-term investment in the country's natural resources and development of infrastructure.

The first priority went to agriculture, which received 33 to 45 percent of total allocations. The bulk of this went toward large-scale flood control and irrigation schemes. By 1958 a number of these projects had been completed or were near completion, including the Tharthar Dam (opened in 1956), which prevented the flooding of Baghdad, and the Habbaniyya scheme north of Ramadi, which provided a water storage facility and a dam on the Euphrates. Two large dams were also built in Kurdish territory—the Dukan Dam on the Lesser Zab and the Darbandikhan Dam on the Diyala.

The second priority was transportation and communications. Here, too, large-scale projects—roads, railroads, ports, and airports—were stressed. By 1958 2,000 kilometers (1,243 miles) of main roads, 1,500 kilometers (932 miles) of local roads, and twenty bridges had been built, while the Basra port was enlarged and a new airport was constructed in Baghdad.[10] The Development Board constructed five electric power plants, the Daura refinery, and light industries such as cement and textile plants.

One study concluded that the area used for grain production increased 50 percent over pre–Second World War levels, while grain production increased 56 percent.[11] Despite population growth, by 1958 Iraq was self-sufficient in wheat and rice and produced enough barley to export 25 percent of its crop.[12] Most of the agricultural growth in this period, however, took place in the private sector and was due to individual investments in pumps and tractors, not the development program.

Though these advances were considerable, most agriculture was still practiced by primitive methods. By 1958 70 percent of the population still earned a living in agriculture, but they produced only 30 percent of Iraq's income.[13] The government attempted to skirt the problem of land reform by appropriating development funds for the distribution of uncultivated state lands to peasants. However, these projects were too small in scope to relax the grip of the large landholders on the rural economy. In 1958 some 3 percent of large and very large landholders controlled almost 70 percent of the land (see Table A.5).

TABLE 4.2 Size of Industrial Establishments, 1954

Number of Workers in Establishments	Number of Establishments	Percentage of Total	Total Number of Workers	Percentage of Total
1	10,157	45.2	10,157	11.2
2	5,651	25.2	11.302	12.5
3	2,805	12.5	8,415	9.3
4	1,383	6.1	5,532	6.1
5	804	3.6	4,020	4.5
6–9	933	4.2	6,455	7.2
10–19	433	1.9	5,718	6.3
20–99	199	0.9	8,185	9.1
Over 100	95	0.4	30,507	33.8
Total	22,460	100.0	90,291	100.0

SOURCE: Adapted from Kathleen Langeley, *The Industrialization of Iraq* (Cambridge, MA: Harvard University Press, 1961), p. 90. Taken from the Industrial Census of Iraq, 1954.

Meanwhile, there was little industrial development to employ the rural population flowing into the cities. According to estimates, in 1950 of the 60,000 people engaged in industry other than oil, almost all were working in small undertakings where work was done mainly by hand (see Table 4.2).

Whereas these shortcomings were structural, more serious politically was underspending in the social sphere, the origin of the regime's main problems. Little was spent on short-term projects that would have raised living standards, particularly among the volatile urban population, whose expectations increased as more oil funds were generated. In 1950 only 23 percent of the school-age population was in school; illiteracy was estimated at nearly 90 percent. By 1958 Iraq's institutions of higher education were turning out only a little over a thousand graduates a year (see Tables 4.3 and A.4). Despite progress in health services, which had reduced epidemics, endemic diseases such as malaria and trachoma were still widespread. Only 40 percent of municipalities had safe water supplies, most had no electricity, and sewage was almost totally neglected, even in Baghdad.[14]

TABLE 4.3 College Graduates, 1958

College	Graduates
Law	164
Education	213
Engineering	82
Tahrir (women)	102
Commerce	104
Arts and Sciences	148
Medical	75
Pharmacy	29
Police	20
Divinity	58
Agriculture	44
Nonacademic Institutions	88
Total	1,127

SOURCE: Iraq, Ministry of Planning, *Report on Education in Iraq for 1957–1958* (Baghdad: Government Press, 1959), pp. 16, 26.

The Uprising of 1952

These economic and social shortcomings help explain the periodic out-breaks of violence and the emergence of the street as a factor in Iraq's political life. Demonstrations by students, workers, and others, often organized by the left and the ICP, would get out of control, leading to violence. This was the case with the so-called *intifada* (uprising) of 1952, the most serious outbreak of violence since the *wathba*. The unrest was sparked by events in neighboring Middle Eastern countries that created a new political climate in the area hostile to established regimes and their collaboration with the West. The rise of Mussadiq in Iran and the Iranian nationalization of the Anglo-Iranian Oil Company in 1951 inspired demands from the opposition in Iraq for nationalization of IPC. In Egypt a new group of young officers successfully overthrew the monarchy on 23 July 1952, and installed themselves as rulers.

More important for Iraq, however, was a strike of port workers in Basra on 23 August 1952. Generated by a dispute over pay between workers and the government, the strike soon escalated under the leadership of the Communists. They even managed to take over Basra's generator, temporarily cutting off water and electricity in the city. Police moved in, the inevitable clash took place, and once again injury and death were the result.[15]

On 26 October students at the College of Pharmacy struck over an amendment to the rules governing their examinations. By this time strikes had become a way of life among the student population. Before long the localized strike turned into riots, spreading throughout other cities as well. By mid-November most of the urban centers of Iraq were in disorder. The American Information Office was included in the attacks, indicating that the United States was associated in the public mind with the British as an unwanted power.

On 23 November the regent appointed a government under the control of the chief of staff of the army, now prime minister. Martial law was announced, all political parties were banned, a number of newspapers were suspended, and a curfew was declared. Wholesale arrests of rioters and politicians—including some former ministers and deputies—ensued. This ended the *intifada* but marked another turning point for the regime. Although the opposition was insufficiently organized to unseat the regime, the widespread alienation of critical sectors of the population was clear.

The Accession of Faisal II

On 24 May 1953 Faisal II reached his majority and became king of Iraq. His enthronement should have initiated a new era. He was young (eighteen) and Western educated, and he had democratic ideas. However, having been educated mostly by British tutors, Faisal was out of touch with Iraqi popular opinion. Of far more importance, Crown Prince Abd al-Ilah had no intention of relinquishing real power to the young king, even after 1953. He was also seeking ways to isolate Nuri and pursue his own policy. After consulting with a number of politicians, Abd al-Ilah decided on the dissolution of parliament and a new election.

The Elections of 1954

The election of June 1954 has rightly been regarded as the freest under the monarchy. All licensed parties participated, and when it was over, Nuri's party, though obtaining the largest single bloc of seats (fifty-one) fell below a controlling majority. The National Democratic Party returned six members, including Kamil al-Chadirchi; Istiqlal returned two. Even a known Communist sympathizer was elected. To all appearances the stage was set for the revival of legal opposition and possibly some reform. This was not to be. And once again the culprit was foreign affairs.

The Anglo-Iraq Treaty of 1930 was due to expire in 1957; for the security tie with Britain and the West to be maintained, Iraq had to negotiate a new one. For any new treaty to be negotiated and a repetition of the *wathba* avoided, most establishment politicians believed that Nuri was essential. However, Nuri laid down several conditions for his return to power—among them the dismissal of parliament and a new election.[16] This sealed the fate of the newly elected chamber and, as it would turn out, any chances for political reform.

Nuri began a systematic suppression of all political activity that surpassed any previously undertaken. A series of decrees designed to uproot the left permitted the Council of Ministers to deport persons convicted of advocating communism or anarchism or working for a foreign government and to strip them of Iraqi citizenship. As a fitting climax to these activities, in September 1954 a new election produced what has been called "the unopposed parliament." So tightly was it controlled that before the election was held over one hundred delegates were returned unopposed, with only twenty-two seats contested.[17]

The election and the decrees effectively put an end to any open political activity for the next four years, and Iraq settled down to rule maintained by the police and the army. There is little doubt that this suppression produced short-term stability, but it put almost complete power in the hands of a man increasingly unable to come to terms with the new forces about to shake the Arab world. The opposition, deprived of any hope of change, was driven from the halls of parliament underground, where it inevitably became more revolutionary.

The Baghdad Pact

At the time that the renegotiation of the Anglo-Iraq Treaty began, the defense posture of the Middle East and its relations with the West were still in a fluid stage. A younger generation of Arabs wanted complete independence from the West. The older politicians, still in control in Iraq, understood the inherent weaknesses of the regime and the state and the need for some kind of support from outside.

One possibility was to join Turkey, Iran, and Pakistan in a collective defense arrangement then beginning to take shape under the guidance of US Secretary of State John Foster Dulles. This arrangement was based on loose bilateral agreements that could later be joined by other countries, including Arab states. Nuri liked the shape of this arrangement, but an alliance of Iraq, Turkey, and Iran was a connection that the Arab nationalists in Iraq had always opposed because Turkey and Iran were non-Arab and firmly allied with the West. The most serious problem was posed by Egypt. Owing to strong anti-British political forces in Egypt, Nasser felt the need to distance himself from Western alliances. Aware of the need to consult with Nasser, Nuri went to Cairo to discuss matters with him. According to those present, there may have been some misunderstanding on both sides. Nasser asked Nuri to wait but told Nuri he was free to do what he thought was best. Nuri seems to have left with the dangerously erroneous impression that he had secured Nasser's agreement to pursue a treaty of alliance with Britain and the other non-Arab countries.

Nasser issued a warning against Arabs joining the new pro-Western bloc. Nonetheless, Nuri went forward, and on 24 February 1955, an Iraqi-Turkish agreement was signed. England joined the agreement, placing the two bases at Habbaniyya and Shu'aiba under Iraqi management in return for the right of air passage in Iraq and the use of the bases for refueling. In case of attack on Iraq, Britain would come to Iraq's aid, and the British would continue to equip, supply, and help train Iraq's military forces. In fact, a main Iraqi motive behind joining the pact was to revise the Anglo-Iraq Treaty in a way that would neutralize domestic opposition; adhering to a regional security agreement seemed to accomplish that purpose. On 23 September Iran joined the agreement; on 3 November Pakistan followed suit. Baghdad became the headquarters of this new alliance system—known as the Baghdad Pact. The United States, which had originated the idea, did not officially join the pact, but it became a member of the pact's various committees and cooperated fully with it.

Egypt's rejection of the pact was immediate. There was no secret made of Iraq's intention to induce the other Arab countries to follow its lead. If this had been achieved, Iraq would have led the way into a new security arrangement, forming the cornerstone of a new alliance system tying the Arab countries to the West. This prospect threw down a challenge to Nasser that he could not fail to take up. Arab unity, independence from the West, and the struggle for leadership of the Arab world were at stake.

The consequences of the pact for Iraq's subsequent history cannot be exaggerated. On the positive side, the pact unquestionably strengthened Iraq's internal defenses and helped build up the state's infrastructure. Good relations with Turkey and Iran also paid internal dividends in continued peace with the Kurds and the Shi'a, an important factor neglected in subsequent regimes. But the pact's disadvantages were overwhelming. It split the Arab world into two camps—those favoring a Western alliance and those favoring neutrality or even joining the USSR. It brought the Cold War to the Middle East and embroiled Iraq in a constant succession of foreign policy problems at a time when it needed to concentrate on the home front. It revived a heated anti-Western campaign in the area that Iraq, with its anti-Western opposition, did not need. The challenge to Nasser's leadership initiated a cold war between Egypt and Iraq aimed at the elimination of either Nasser or Nuri. The intensity of this struggle swept all other issues aside for the next four years.

The first and ultimately most damaging manifestation of this cold war was the propaganda campaign broadcast by the Voice of the Arabs in Cairo, vilifying Nuri and the regime that had signed the pact. The Voice of the Arabs penetrated the village, the field, the barracks, and the dormitory. Gradually its message spread hostility—previously limited mainly to the urban groups—among rural areas as well, swelling the numbers of those opposed to the regime.

The Suez Crisis

In the midst of this situation, Nasser precipitated the Suez crisis. His successful nationalization of the Suez Canal in 1956 and the resulting tripartite attack on Egypt by Britain, France, and Israel had profound repercussions throughout the Middle East. In Iraq the actions of the British in Suez undercut the regime's entire position. The Suez disaster confronted Nuri with a crisis almost as severe as the *wathba*. Throughout the remainder of 1956, the country was in an uproar. Strikes spread to Najaf and the four northern provinces, threatening to destabilize Shi'a and Kurdish areas. In November 1956 the IPC pipeline through Syria was blown up by hostile forces, thereby drastically cutting back Iraq's oil revenues and its development program. Even though the disturbances tended to subside by 1957, many saw Nuri and the regime in a race against time that he appeared to be losing.

The UAR and the Federation

Before long Iraq was faced with another foreign policy crisis. On 1 February 1958, Egypt and Syria announced the formation of the United Arab Republic (UAR). This relatively short-lived experiment was launched largely to avoid further Communist penetration in Syria, but it created immediate fears in Jordan and Iraq that the next step would be the overthrow of their own regimes by forces favorable to the union. King Husain of Jordan now took the initiative. He invited the Iraqis to Jordan and proposed, as a joint reply to the new UAR, an Iraqi-Jordanian federation. Very little discussion appears to have taken place on the merits and demerits of the federation. Like the UAR, it was formed in haste and as a reaction to external events.

The federation was negotiated in Amman between 11 and 14 February 1958. Nuri was the only one to voice skepticism from within the

Iraqi establishment. He felt the federation was unnecessary and would be a burden on Iraq's finances, and events proved him correct. The constitution of the federation provided that each country was to retain its political system and gave Jordan an escape clause that absolved it from joining the Baghdad Pact. Significantly, Iraq was to supply 80 percent of the federation's budget.[18]

The tale of the federation is soon told. One of Nuri's first acts as the federation prime minister was to invite Kuwait to join the federation, a move that would have made the federation more palatable to Iraqis. Kuwait could have shared the expenses, and many Iraqis regarded Kuwait as a part of Iraq, detached from the Ottoman Empire by the British. However, for Kuwait to join the federation, Britain would first have to recognize Kuwait's independence. The federation idea was unenthusiastically received in Kuwait, which did not want its territory or its oil resources swallowed up by Iraq and Jordan, and by Britain, which was not ready to relinquish control over Kuwait.

Opposition and the Establishment

While the regime was involved in federation affairs, the opposition, now underground, was coalescing into a united front. This process had begun as early as September 1953 when the Istiqlal began to cooperate with the National Democratic Party. In 1957 the Istiqlal and the National Democratic Party turned to the more radical elements in the political spectrum, forming the United National Front, which included the Communist Party and a relative newcomer to the Iraqi scene, the Ba'th (Renaissance) Party. The Arab Ba'th Socialist Party, as it was officially known, had originated in Syria in the early postwar years. Its program combined the two strands of political thought that had dominated the intelligentsia since the 1930s—pan-Arabism and radical social change. Led by Fu'ad al-Rikabi, a Shi'a from the south, the Iraqi Ba'th, in this period, was nonsectarian and appealed to both Shi'a and Sunni Arabs.

Far more serious for the regime was disaffection in the army. Troubles in the officer corps had come to light as early as 1956, when a plot to overthrow the regime had been discovered. Though the leaders had been dispersed, intelligence sources in 1958 revealed new conspiracies.[19] Lulled into a false sense of security by his repressive tactics, Nuri evidently dismissed these signs. In May 1958 civil war broke out in Lebanon. Fearing that it might spread, King Husain asked that Iraqi troops be sent to Jordan to protect its frontiers, and this event sealed the fate of the monarchy in Iraq. Ordered to march to Jordan, the troops marched instead on Baghdad. A swiftly executed coup ended the Hashimite monarchy and Nuri's regime in the early morning hours of 14 July. At the time few mourned their passing.

The Hashimite Monarchy in Retrospect

The monarchy has been much maligned by successor regimes, which have often conveniently forgotten its real accomplishments. Among these were the creation of a professional army and bureaucracy of impressive proportions and an economic development program that would sustain revolutionary regimes for some time to come. Consciously or otherwise, the monarchical regime did much to create the modern Iraqi state and the structural underpinnings of an Iraqi national identity. Despite considerable progress, however, the regime's economic achievements were not sufficient to stem the tide of opposition or to prevent the regime's overthrow.

One of the most serious of the regime's weaknesses was its continual involvement in foreign affairs at the expense of domestic problems. Nuri's declining years were spent with the Baghdad Pact, the Suez crisis, and, finally, the federation, while lesser men were left to deal with domestic issues. By 1956 the foreign pillar on which the regime largely rested—its alliance with Britain—had also become more of a liability than an asset in the aftermath of Britain's inept handling of the Suez crisis.

The regime's greatest weakness was its failure to build viable political institutions to support its rule. Leaders relied on the army and bureaucracy as the mainstay of the state and on martial law rather than political bargaining. The monarchy refused to shift its basis of support from the rural class of tribal leaders and landlords (now augmented by the urban wealthy) to the new urban middle class. Urbanites, particularly from the middle and lower-middle classes, remained underrepresented in the political structure, and they rapidly came under the influence of the opposition.

The old regime allowed the opposition to dominate cultural and ideological discourse in Iraq, failing to articulate an ideology of its own that might have appealed to a broader spectrum of Iraqis. It vacillated between a policy of Iraq for Iraqis and pan-Arab nationalism. Perhaps the greatest disservice to the country was the regime's refusal to deal with the opposition in parliament, where opposition leaders could have achieved a measure of responsibility and experience. Instead their steady exclusion from power reinforced their isolation and their radicalism. There was some integration of Shi'a and Kurds into the organs of state, but little was done to foster a distinct Iraqi identity that would have encouraged this trend.

5

THE QASIM ERA, 1958-1963

The "revolution" of 1958, designed to reform and modernize Iraq, instead brought a decade of instability and military dictatorship. The Western-style political institutions that, fragile as they were, had begun to take root were gutted. Progress in knitting ethnic and sectarian communities together in the new state also unraveled, though more slowly.

Revolutionary regimes did make substantial changes in a number of directions—some badly needed. They ended the grip of the landed class and the urban wealthy over the political system and placed the new middle class firmly in power. Initially, civilian opposition politicians, particularly reformers and leftists, played a role in government. They introduced policies of egalitarianism, a spread of economic development to poorer areas, and greater social mobility for the dispossessed. But it was not long before these civilians were displaced by their military colleagues and Iraq settled into a pattern of military dictatorship.

The main problem for new regimes that subsequently came to power was an absence of political structures for governance and an inability to mobilize wide enough constituencies to rule. The result was a constant attempt to overthrow the government in power—from within and from without. Between 1958 and 1968, there were four changes of regime and countless failed coups. Qasim's regime, which made a genuine attempt at reform, was too left leaning for the Arab nationalists and was overthrown by the conspiratorial Ba'th Party in 1963. Its authoritarian rule, far more oppressive than Qasim's, ended in a short nine months. A "palace coup" brought Abd al-Salam Arif and then his brother, Abd al-Rahman, to government until 1968. Even though they were more moderate, they also relied mainly on the military to govern. The Arif regime was finally overthrown in 1968 by another combination of disgruntled military and the Ba'th, anxious for a turn at power.

With this level of instability, little could be accomplished in the realm of economic and social development. Ruling elites were badly split in ideology and in political orientation. The left wanted concentration on Iraq and radical social change; the Arab nationalists wanted union with other Arab states. The Kurds, whose movement was now revitalized, demanded autonomy and more separation. The absence of a common agenda helped unravel the consensus underlying the state.

New regimes also realigned Iraq in foreign policy. Ties with Britain and the West were loosened and, indeed, often became acrimonious. A bitter struggle ensued with Britain over oil, with detrimental effects on Iraq's oil revenues. Closer ties, and an arms import relationship, with the Soviet Union gradually drew Iraq into the orbit of the Soviet bloc.

The Qasim era began this revolutionary process. It was most notable for its Iraq First orientation and its attempt at social reform. But like its historical predecessor, the Bakr Sidqi regime of 1936, which had tried to marry the military with leftist reformers, the experiment ended with the dominance of the military. The Qasim regime ushered in an era of change. But it also opened the door for a domestic struggle for dominance of the state that ended by destroying more than it could create.

The Military Revolt of 1958

The military coup that finally overthrew the monarchy and inaugurated a new era in Iraqi history succeeded more because of luck and audacity than of good planning or organization. Although the coup unquestionably reflected deep-seated discontent in the military, the Free Officers, as their movement came to be called, gave far more thought to the overthrow of the existing regime than to what would replace it. As a result, they were unprepared for the responsibilities thrust upon them. Like their civilian counterparts in the opposition, they were riddled with internal disagreements and jealousies, as well as profound differences on the direction and orientation the country should take.

The Free Officers Movement

The military had remained aloof from politics in the early postwar years, but trouble in the officer corps began again in 1952. That year's riots against the regime played a role in crystalizing discontent among the officers, but what really set them thinking about a coup was the successful military revolt on the Nile. Officers and civilians alike had been increasingly impressed with Nasser's social reforms in Egypt and his nonalignment movement.

The first revolutionary cell in the officer corps was apparently organized as early as September 1952. The movement gained momentum in the autumn of 1956 under the impetus of the Suez crisis. Several new groups were formed, some apparently influenced by the liberal democratic program of the National Democratic Party (NDP) and others by the communists. Most, however, were pan-Arab in orientation. A number of these groups gradually coalesced and by 1957 had formed the Baghdad Organization, the nucleus of the Free Officers executive committee. Brigadier General Abd al-Karim Qasim became head of the group because of his seniority in rank.

The fourteen members of the central committee may be taken as fairly representative of the movement.[1] The overwhelming majority were Arab Sunni. There were only two Shi'a, reflecting the weakness of Shi'a in the officer corps, and no Kurds, although a few joined the movement to represent Kurdish views. Most came from the middle or lower-middle class, although three—Qasim and the two Arif brothers, Abd al-Salam and Abd al-Rahman—came from poor families. Five had studied in England, but they were a distinct minority.

This committee functioned as the executive and planning arm of the Free Officers, but there was apparently little cohesion of aims and policy among its members. According to one member of the group, a general program was drawn up. The program called for, among other things, (1) a struggle against imperialism and an end to pacts and foreign bases; (2) a removal of feudalism and freedom of the peasants from exploitation; (3) an end to the monarchy, together with the announcement of a republic; (4) a constitution and establishment of a democratic regime; (5) complete recognition of the national rights of the Kurds and other minorities within the framework of national unity; (6) cooperation with all Arab countries; (7) Arab unity; and (8) a return of Palestine to its people.[2] The program was primarily concerned with foreign policy. Some kind of land reform was contemplated, but beyond the call for social justice, economic and social goals were vague in the extreme. An eventual return to civilian democratic rule was expected, but little thought was given to constitutional processes or procedures.

The 14 July Coup

When the coup finally came on 14 July, it was the work not of the Baghdad Organization but rather of two men, Abd al-Karim Qasim and Abd al-Salam Arif, who found themselves in a position to carry it out and seized the opportunity. The coup was triggered by the unexpected revolt in Lebanon against the pro-Western regime of President Kamil Sham'un and the resulting fear in Baghdad and Amman that the revolt might spread to Jordan. The Twentieth Brigade, in which Arif headed a battalion, received orders to proceed to Jordan to strengthen King Husain's forces. Arif and Qasim, the latter in charge of the Nineteenth Brigade, decided to act. Arif was to move on Baghdad, and Qasim was to remain with his brigade at Jalaula as a backup force in case resistance was encountered and then move slowly to the city later on.

In the early hours of 14 July, Arif occupied the broadcasting station that became his headquarters. He personally made the first announcement of the revolution on the radio. He denounced imperialism and the clique in office, proclaimed a new republic and the end of the old regime, and promised a future election for a new president.

Meanwhile, two detachments of his own battalion were dispatched, one to the Rihab Palace to deal with the king and the crown prince and the other to Nuri al-Sa'id's residence. The crown prince, partly because he lacked the will and partly because he wished to save his own life and that of the king, ordered no resistance. This sealed his fate and that of the royal family. At about 8:00 AM, the king, the crown prince, and the rest of the family left the palace and assembled in the courtyard. There a young captain opened fire. Others joined in, and the family was killed.[3] This ended any hope of restoring the Hashimite dynasty in Iraq.

The force that went to Nuri's house was less successful. Nuri had managed to escape, but on 15 July he was recognized on a street and shot dead on the spot.

About noon on 14 July, Qasim arrived in Baghdad with his forces and set up his headquarters in the Ministry of Defense. Even with his arrival, the officers were still in a precarious situation. Key officers who could offer resistance decided to wait and see what would happen. Iraq's allies were in the same quandary. King Husain, who had tried to warn the chief of staff of the Free Officers movement some two weeks earlier, wanted to intervene, but he, too, hesitated because of his own internal situation and because of lack of support from Western allies.[4] Thus a coup organized by a small group of officers acting on an ad hoc basis succeeded.

For most of the early hours of the revolution, Arif, an impetuous man, was in control. The first pronouncements of the revolution, promising freedom and an election, had inspired confidence, but Arif soon urged the liquidation of traitors. Uncontrollable mobs surged through Baghdad. The body of Abd al-Ilah was dragged through the streets and hung at the gate of the Ministry of Defense. The day after Nuri's burial, his body was disinterred by the mob and also dragged through the streets. Several Jordanian ministers and US businessmen staying at the Baghdad Hotel fell into the hands of the mob and were killed. The overwhelming majority of Iraqis regarded these deeds with horror and disgust. They caused irreparable damage to Iraq's international reputation and marred the revolution's image in the minds of many of its own people.

The Coup Government

The new government, agreed on by Qasim and Arif himself, had at its head a three-man sovereignty council designed to appease Iraq's three major communities, the Shi'a, the Kurds, and the Arab Sunnis. Muhammad Mahdi Kubba, the Shi'i, was the former head of the Istiqlal Party; Khalid al-Naqshabandi, the Kurd, was a former officer; Najib al-Rubai'i, the Arab Sunni, was an officer and a tacit supporter of the Free Officers movement.

A cabinet, remarkable for the spectrum of opposition it included, was also announced. It comprised two National Democratic Party representatives, one member of the Istiqlal, one Ba'th representative, and one Marxist. It also included a strong representative of the Kurds and a liberal Arab nationalist.[5] Aside from Qasim and Arif, only one Free Officer, Naji Talib, was given a cabinet post (social affairs).

The cabinet was a masterstroke that showed considerable consultation with the politicians. It propitiated the entire opposition movement and lent the regime a legitimacy and respect that would have been difficult to achieve as a mere army movement. Included in the cabinet were liberals, Marxists, Arab nationalists, and Kurds committed to greater Kurdish autonomy. All, however, agreed on ending Western political and economic control over the country, represented by the Baghdad Pact, foreign bases, and the Iraq Petroleum Company (IPC), while supporting a reorientation in foreign policy toward the Soviet Union.

Though less evident, the cabinet and the sovereignty council were also fairly representative of Iraq's ethnic and sectarian communities. Together they comprised six Arab Sunnis, five Arab Shi'a, four Kurds, and one person (Qasim) of mixed Sunni-Shi'i parentage. In particular, the Kurds were propitiated by recognition as equal partners in the state. More importantly, the new government symbolized empowerment of the new, educated middle class, which saw itself replacing an upper class of landlords and the urban wealthy.

However, control by Qasim and Arif of key military and security functions left little doubt about where real power lay. As a sign of future problems, the lion's share of power went to Qasim, who became prime minister and minister of defense while retaining his position as commander in chief of the armed forces; Arif became deputy prime minister and minister of interior, as well as deputy commander in chief.

The Temporary Constitution

Thirteen days after the revolution, a temporary constitution was announced. According to this document, the state was a republic, Iraq was part of the Arab nation, and Islam was the religion of state. The Council of Sovereignty was to carry out the powers of the presidency, and the powers of legislation were vested in the Council of Ministers, with the approval of the Council of Sovereignty. The executive function was also vested in the Council of Ministers. There was no separation made between executive and legislative powers.

The constitution was most important for what it left unsaid. There was no mention of a new representative assembly or an election. Nothing was said, for example, about how the Council of Ministers would be appointed and dismissed. The constitution merely masked the real power structure that was emerging—joint rule by two military men behind a cabinet of respected political leaders who did not yet suspect what was in store for them.

One potential source of problems was that many Free Officers who had expected to participate in the new government through a revolutionary command council (RCC) or a similar mechanism were excluded or put in subordinate positions. The disaffection of the Free Officers sowed the seeds of much future discord, but this was not the cause of the first rift in the revolutionary front. A struggle for power between the two main protagonists of the coup began no less than five days after the stunning revolt that had put the country in their hands.

The Struggle for Power

The struggle must be seen in the context of the ideological conflict that now emerged in Baghdad. On the one hand were opposition forces whose main thrust had been Arab nationalist and who saw the revolution as the first step toward greater Arab union. On the other hand were those less interested in unity than in Iraqi independence from the West and thorough political and social reform at home. In this struggle the "moderate middle," lacking organization or a vision, was soon left weak and disabled, subordinated to a struggle for power between two men wishing to control the state.

Qasim Versus Arif

The struggle between Qasim and Arif was initiated over a key policy question—union with Egypt. Arif, encouraged by the Ba'th and the Arab nationalists, favored prompt union; Qasim was more cautious in his approach to this issue. In a widely publicized tour of the provinces, Arif made ill-considered speeches strongly advocating union with the United Arab Republic (UAR). He referred frequently to Nasser, while scarcely mentioning Qasim. There is no evidence that Qasim was opposed to better relations with other Arab countries, but Arif's challenge to his leadership and the precipitous and untimely drive for unity, particularly under Nasser's leadership rather than Qasim's, forced Qasim into action.

Qasim's patient and clever manipulation of affairs behind the scenes assured his success in the ensuing power struggle. He found opponents of unity among the Communists, who organized demonstrations in favor of Qasim and against immediate union. In September, after Arif had made another bid for leadership by reviving the idea of the RCC in a public speech (an appeal to other Free Officers), Qasim moved to retire Arif from his posts. On 30 September he was retired as deputy prime minister and minister of interior and sent off to Bonn as ambassador, but he soon returned to Baghdad. Finally, on 5 November, amid rumors of an attempted coup against the regime, Arif was arrested on charges of attempting to assassinate Qasim and of trying to overthrow the government. A month later he was sentenced to death. The sentence was commuted to life imprisonment on the recommendation of the court.

Ideological Issues

In one respect, the struggle was over Iraq's new identity. Would the revolution focus on an Iraqi state in which various communities had a greater share of power or on merging Iraq into a larger Arab entity with greater collective power to challenge the West? In another respect, it was also a struggle over how far to go in restructuring society. How much emphasis should be put on social justice, perhaps creating a state on the socialist model, and how much on liberal democratic ideals more along Western lines of parliamentary democracy? Right from the beginning, the very intensity of the struggle eroded the unity of the new regime and its prospects for eventual political stability.

The chief participants can easily be identified. On the nationalist side were two main groups. A loose coalition of Arab nationalists who favored the ideal of pan-Arabism continued the tradition of the older Istiqlal Party but drew their inspiration primarily from the Egyptian revolution and often looked to Nasser for leadership. Closely allied with the Arab nationalists and drawing on much of the same support was the Ba'th Party. The major impetus for the Ba'th Party's growth came after the 1958 coup, when it utilized a surge of pan-Arab sentiment to organize and gain adherents. Nasser was not their hero, however. The Ba'th Party looked instead toward Syria, where the party had originated and where its firmest base lay. Its leadership was youthful and zealously committed. Its strong organization and its ideology made it a much more effective competitor in the struggle for power than the amorphous Arab nationalist group.

The leading group on the left was clearly the Communist Party. The Communists continued to make inroads among the dispossessed, the Shi'a, the Kurds, and the intelligentsia. The other main contender on the left was the National Democratic Party, the main group standing both for socialist reform and liberal democratic institutions and procedures. Unfortunately, the NDP was no better organized than it had been in Nuri's day, and it soon split between those supporting and those opposing Qasim.

These four groups vied with one another for the dominant position in the state. The struggle perpetuated the old polarization of the intelligentsia between the Arab nationalists and the leftists, but this time with a difference. The older opposition groups had been rooted in liberal traditions favoring elections and an open political system; the Ba'th and the Communists were both clandestine, highly organized groups committed to a total monopoly of power, by ruthless means if necessary.

The fierce struggle of the next year and a half was precipitated by nationalist efforts to dominate the power struggle by removing Qasim and, in part, by a growing fear of Communist ascendancy. Qasim's increased reliance on the left was a response to this challenge. The struggle generated a fear of chaos on the part of successive governments that soon ended any hope of a return to a democratic system. It polarized the ruling elite between nationalists and leftists, and it left a legacy of escalating violence and ruthlessness that worsened as time went on.

The Challenge of the Nationalists

The nationalist forces soon put forth a succession of challenges to Qasim. The first, and most easily deflected, came from an unlikely candidate, Rashid Ali al-Kailani, who had returned to Baghdad after seventeen years of exile. Accused of planning a coup, Kailani and a few of his supporters were arrested and tried. On testimony that he had been working for a union with Nasser, Kailani was sentenced to death but never executed.[6] This sentence persuaded the Arab nationalist politicians in the cabinet to resign in February 1959. Their place was quickly filled by leftists supported by Qasim.

Outside the government, the Communists moved into the breach. They sent cables to Qasim urging death for Arif and other traitors and addressing him as Qasim, the "Sole Leader." They infiltrated key organizations, including the broadcasting station, the press, and the proliferating professional associations. The officer corps remained a nationalist stronghold, although the Communists made inroads there as well. To compensate for their weakness in the military, the Communists attempted to capture the Popular Resistance Force, a civil militia.

The Mosul Revolt

This rising tide of Communist influence and the Communists' radical rhetoric, which Qasim appeared to support, provoked the next—and the most serious—nationalist challenge, the Mosul revolt. Led by Arab nationalists, the revolt was actually inspired by a mixture of motives. It was as much anti-Communist as it was pro-nationalist. The main leader of the revolt was Abd al-Wahhab al-Shawwaf, commander of the Mosul garrison. He and other officers who supported him came from conservative, well-known Arab Sunni families with little to gain from communism.[7] As members of the Free Officers movement, they resented the fact that they had been shunted aside to less important posts.

Although tentative plans for a coup had been laid by these officers, their hand was forced prematurely by the leftists and Qasim. The Peace Partisans, a leftist organization, announced that it would commemorate its founding in Mosul on 6 March 1959, with a huge rally. Peace Partisans and its Communist supporters poured into Mosul from all over Iraq, and by 6 March they numbered about 250,000. The nationalist officers decided to act. Plans had already been made for the cooperation of two other groups outside the army: the Shammar tribe surrounding Mosul and the UAR, now openly hostile to Qasim. Although the Peace Partisans rally passed without a major outbreak, on the following day demonstrations, attacks, and counterattacks escalated between the Communists and the nationalists, now reinforced by Shammar tribesmen. On 8 March the revolt was proclaimed and fighting broke out in earnest.

From the start the revolt suffered from haste and poor planning. Only two units from outside Mosul joined Shawwaf. The support from Egypt was also mishandled; the radio transmitter from the UAR did not arrive in time. An attempt to bomb the broadcasting station in Baghdad on 8 March failed. On 9 March Qasim sent airplanes to bomb Shawwaf's headquarters. Shawwaf was wounded in the attack and killed in the hospital where he went for treatment. Shortly thereafter the movement collapsed.[8]

For Mosul the aftermath of the revolt was far worse than the rebellion itself. As the Shammar tribes faded into the desert, Kurds looted the city and attacked the populace. The Communists and the Peace Partisans massacred the nationalists and some of the well-to-do Mosul families, looting their houses. All kinds of animosities festering beneath the surface erupted. Christians killed Muslims, Kurds attacked Arabs, and the poor looted the rich. The chaos that ensued provided a stark glimpse of what might be in store for a "new" Iraq if order were not restored with a firm hand. That was averted with swift, if brutal, action. Leaders of the revolt were taken into custody by Qasim, brought to trial, and executed.

The Ba'th Attempt

The failure of the Mosul rebellion, the execution of its perpetrators, and the apparent tide of communism had convinced the Ba'th Party that the only way out was to eliminate Qasim himself. In the spring of 1959, a group of young Ba'thists, including Saddam Husain, plotted to shoot Qasim as he passed through Rashid Street in his car on 7 October. In fact, the attempt was botched and failed in its objective.[9]

The group did succeed in wounding Qasim, but he recovered. Some of the Ba'thists managed to escape to Syria, including Husain, but seventy-eight others were rounded up and taken to court, where they brazenly defended their acts.[10] Indeed, it was the trial and the testimony of the participants that first brought the Ba'th national attention. Some of the conspirators were acquitted; others were given the death sentence and imprisoned. None of the death sentences was carried out.

The Challenge of the Communists

The collapse of the nationalist attempts against the Qasim regime left the Communist Party as the most powerful and influential political force in the country.[11] Well before the Ba'th attempt on Qasim, the Communists had moved to consolidate their already impressive position. Leftist officers had replaced the commanders responsible for the revolt in the north. On 13 July several Communists or Communist supporters were appointed as ministers, thereby shifting the cabinet toward the radical left.

Not surprisingly, the domination by the left was reflected in the regime's foreign policy and its domestic social agenda, aimed at ameliorating conditions for the poor.

Foreign policy was decisively reoriented. On 24 March 1959, two weeks after the Mosul revolt, Qasim announced Iraq's withdrawal from the Baghdad Pact, a move that had long been expected. Ties were formed with the Soviet Union, which had been permitted to reopen its embassy in Baghdad immediately following the overthrow of the old regime. These steps were followed by extensive economic, military, and cultural agreements with the USSR.

The regime also took its first steps toward social reform. Among the first of several measures were those designed to help the urban lower classes. Rent ceilings were lowered, and eviction by a landlord was made more difficult.[12] Price controls on foodstuffs were instituted, trade unions were now permitted, and income taxes were reduced for lower-income groups. Many former slum dwellers were resettled in simple, sanitary brick houses, which partially replaced the Bund (Dike), the festering ghetto area that had surrounded the east side of Baghdad. The area was named Madinat al-Thaura, "City of the Revolution."

The Kirkuk Eruption

Despite these early victories, the Iraq Communist Party recognized how precarious its position was. The hostility of the nationalists, though temporarily sidelined, was clear. Even within the reform movement, the party faced some opposition. The Communists were interested in moving toward the Soviet model of state control over the economy and society and the development of mass organizations that they could control. Their competitors, the more moderate NDP, wanted redistribution of income to the middle and lower classes, political liberties and elections, and reinstitution of a more responsive and representative parliament. The issue of Communist control of the state was stirring even greater animosity from conservative elements in society. Some in the party reckoned that they would need to move fast to consolidate their gains or the regime might turn on them as had happened in the past.

The Communists announced that on 14 July 1959, the first anniversary of the revolution, they would hold a rally in Kirkuk designed to show mass support for the party. Kirkuk, the Communists reckoned, would be an ideal location for the intimidation of their adversaries. The leading families in the city were Turkman. They formed a well-educated, relatively conservative group of upper and middle-class bureaucrats, merchants, landowners, and businessmen. The town was also inhabited by a substantial number of Kurds, many of whom had migrated there to work for the oil company as laborers. A number of Kurds had joined the Communist Party; others belonged to the Kurdistan Democratic Party (KDP), which was allied with the Communist Party. Kirkuk also had a large concentration of oil workers, who could be mobilized by the Communists.

Unfortunately, matters got out of hand. As in the Mosul revolt, traditional animosities between the Kurds and the Turkmen erupted. A bloody battle followed in which at least thirty were killed and over a hundred injured.[13] The Kurds were responsible for most of the deaths.

The Decline of the Communists

In Baghdad Communist Party leaders denounced these criminal acts and Qasim condemned the episode as barbaric, but for the Communists the damage had been done. Qasim now moved to clip the wings of the extreme left. The Communist press was gradually extinguished, and the Communist newspaper was banned for nine months and soon disappeared. Communists and their supporters were dismissed from the cabinet. Despite these setbacks, the Communists still supported Qasim. They remained his main support until the end of his regime, and a number of Communists retained their high posts.

The wave of Communist activity has raised questions about whether the party actually could have captured the government. In retrospect this seems unlikely. Although there was a groundswell of new Communist members in 1959 (20,000 to 25,000), the hard core of the party was much smaller. In the mid-1950s it had only about 500 registered members.[14] The Communists were largely helped into power by Qasim to counteract the nationalist threat; to the end, they remained dependent upon him, and he had no intention of relinquishing power. Even if the party had wished to take over the government, it would not have been able to accomplish this without the backing of its ally the Soviet Union, and the Soviet Union was opposed to a takeover. The Soviets did not wish to risk retaliation from the West or to assume economic responsibility for Iraq if the Western powers used oil as a weapon against the regime. Above all, they were unwilling to risk their newly won position in Egypt for an as-yet-unknown regime in Iraq.[15]

Attempts to Liberalize and Their Failure

The negative effect of Kirkuk did not prevent an attempt at some liberalization. Partly in response to pressure from the Communists and partly to generate popular support for himself, Qasim announced on the anniversary of the revolution in 1959 that a permanent constitution would be drawn up and political parties licensed by January 1960. The constitution never materialized, but the political parties did. However, Qasim soon showed that he was not interested in the creation of any parties that could possibly challenge his leadership.

Formation of Political Parties

Among the first to apply for licenses were two parties, both calling themselves Communist. One represented the Iraq Communist Party and its central committee; the other, unquestionably instigated by Qasim, was headed by a dissident Communist Party member. The latter party was quickly granted a license, whereas the real Communist Party, despite its willingness to make concessions on its programs, was refused. The National Democratic Party was also divided over the issue of whether to support Qasim. Nonetheless, the NDP was awarded a license.

The Kurdistan Democratic Party (KDP) received a license because of its favorable attitude toward Qasim, but it was soon harassed when it took a position of opposition. Two Muslim-oriented parties came into the field: the Islamic Party and the Tahrir (Liberation) Party. Both were

refused licenses, but the former, which had the backing of the powerful
Shi'i *mujtahid* Muhsin al-Hakim, appealed to the Court of Cassation
and won its case. The Islamic Party took a decidedly anti-Communist
line and was increasingly hostile to Qasim. Its license was withdrawn in
1961 and some of its leaders jailed. For obvious reasons, no Arab nationalist parties applied for licenses.

The parties initially issued programs and engaged in political activities. With the Communists and the Arab nationalists sidelined, most
parties were essentially Iraq First in orientation and relatively moderate
in their demands. In time they should have been able to take root, but
it soon became clear that there was no hope of achieving power under
Qasim. As time went on, the projected constitution, with its presumed
legislature, elections, and public legal system, did not appear, and the
political parties gradually disappeared.

The Mahdawi Court and the Rule of Law

The revolution also failed to establish a rule of law. Indeed, official violence practiced by the state increased substantially. Ad hoc trials, random imprisonment, and the use of torture became a regular part of the
state apparatus. Iraq's human rights record, never flawless under the
monarchy, began a steady downward cycle. The most visible mechanism in eroding the rule of law and entrenching Qasim's position was
the notorious Mahdawi Court.

Under the direction of Fadil Abbas al-Mahdawi, a cousin of Qasim's,
the court was established in August 1958 to try old regime leaders. The
first proceedings of the court were conducted in a relatively quiet and
dignified manner. Gradually, however, the tone and proceedings of the
trials altered radically as the court tried new regime opponents. The court
became a platform for attacking the British and Americans and praising
Nasser. Once relations between Iraq and Egypt soured, of course, Nasser
was attacked just as savagely.

The court rapidly became a "show," or, as some said, a circus. Standards of justice deteriorated rapidly. By the end of 1959 the court trials
were discontinued, but by then they had eliminated Qasim's enemies,

thoroughly cowed the opposition, and created sufficient fear in Iraqi political circles to allow Qasim to govern alone.

Qasim, the "Sole Leader"

With the failure of political parties, the collapse of a rule of law, and no constitution on the horizon, Iraq settled down for the first time to a period of genuine military dictatorship from which it would not easily escape. By 1961 all civilian politicians of any note had withdrawn from the cabinet. Thereafter, Qasim appointed either officers obedient to himself or the usual array, prevalent in all military regimes throughout the Middle East, of technocrats and civil servants with no political affiliations.

Qasim had begun his political career with good intentions and democratic leanings, and he succeeded in bringing respected opposition politicians to power. His was the first real attempt at a redistribution of domestic power. But the parties were too fractious and their bases of power too weak to build on. In the end, the institutions of the military and the bureaucracy proved far stronger.

Qasim's own withdrawn and aloof nature became more accentuated after the assassination attempt. He became more withdrawn and isolated, virtually barricading himself in the Ministry of Defense. His grip on affairs slipped markedly. The remainder of Qasim's rule (after 1961) was characterized by his increasing inability to acquire real control over the political situation.

The Social and Economic Revolution

The political struggles of the first two years should not obscure the social and economic revolution that was begun under Qasim as he attempted to move Iraq in the direction of a more modern, egalitarian state and to remove bars to social mobility. The measures he took did more to destroy the edifice of the old regime than to construct the foundations of the new one. Much of the reform effort had an ad hoc quality. Nonetheless, the general thrust was designed to benefit and empower the middle—and sometimes the lower—classes and to use the state apparatus to develop Iraq's resources, especially its oil and industry, as freely as possible from Western control.

Land Reform

The most significant and far-reaching revolutionary program undertaken by the regime was land reform. The 1933 Law of Rights and Duties of Cultivators was replaced, as was the Tribal Disputes Code. Henceforth, all Iraqis would be judged according to common civil and criminal codes, a long overdue step in modernization and national unity. The Agrarian Reform Law, promulgated on 30 September 1958, attempted a large-scale redistribution of landholdings and placed ceilings on ground rents. Holdings were henceforth to be restricted to 1,000 dunams of irrigated land; 2,000 of rain fed. The land was to be distributed among the peasants in lots of 30 to 60 dunams in irrigated areas; 60 to 120 in rain-fed lands.[16] The farmers were expected to pay for the land, with 3 percent interest, over a period of twenty years. Expropriations and distribution, to be completed over a five-year period, would be overseen by a ministerial committee under the prime minister. The law also provided for the establishment of cooperative societies to replace the services the landlords had provided. The fixed rents gave the peasant between 55 and 70 percent of the total crop.[17]

The reform ran into difficulties from the first. Even before the legislation was drafted, peasants in the south took matters into their own hands. In the late summer and fall of 1958, peasants swept through Kut and Amara, looting and sacking landlords' property, burning residences, and destroying accounts and rent registers. The spontaneous movement was quickly joined by the Communists, who urged the peasants on and moved rapidly into the countryside to organize them. The Communists established peasant societies and infiltrated their leadership. The societies were then amalgamated into the National Federation of Peasants, which the Communists then demanded be recognized as the legal authority for land distribution.[18]

These events shocked the landlords, who were frightened by the drift to the left and the specter of incipient anarchy. Many refused to cooperate with the government. They locked up their pumps and machinery and moved to the city, thus putting large areas out of production. In the meantime, disputes over land policy arose in the cabinet between the Communists, who wanted the state to retain as much land as possible and eventually to establish state farms, and the moderates, led by the NDP, who envisioned widespread distribution and the evolution of a class of small landowners. Eventually, the latter won, but not without a slowdown in the application of the law and increased uncertainty about its direction.

Even without political problems, the economic and social difficulties of applying the Agrarian Reform Law were enormous. Most important was the problem of distribution, which required extensive state machinery not yet in existence. As a result, some 4.5 million dunams of land had been expropriated by 1963, but only about 1.5 million had been distributed.[19] Even for those who received some land, inadequate facilities were available for cultivation and marketing. Without supervision, and especially without management of water distribution in the south, the peasant was lost. Moreover, the landlord had frequently been a tribal leader as well, responsible for many social and quasi-governmental functions. These could not be immediately replaced by the government. As a result, throughout much of the countryside the populace lapsed into old ways. The landlord leased his land from the government but continued to function as a patriarch, or his place was often taken by his *sirkal*, or agent. Production declined drastically. By 1961 Iraq had ceased exporting barley and was importing rice and wheat to cover 40 percent of its consumption.[20]

The Personal Status Law

The agrarian sector was not the only area in which Qasim attempted to bring about greater equality. He also helped raise the status of women. In December 1959 he promulgated a significant revision of the personal status code regulating family relations, traditionally governed by Islamic law. One of its provisions (Article 3) severely limited the right of polygamy. Men were forbidden to take a second wife without the authorization of a judge, and then only for legitimate reasons. Articles 8 and 9 stipulated the minimum age for marriage as eighteen, which could be lowered in special cases to sixteen, thus eliminating child marriage. Article 35 protected women against arbitrary divorce by invalidating divorces pronounced by a man under certain circumstances. Most interesting and most revolutionary was a provision (Article 74) that, through an indirect legal mechanism, gave women equal rights with men in matters of inheritance. The new code applied to both Sunnis and Shi'a, thus bringing all Iraqis under one law.[21] Although not as radical as laws promulgated earlier in Turkey or Tunisia, the revised code clearly showed a liberal intent. Unfortunately, it aroused considerable opposition among religious leaders and conservative elements and did not survive without changes after Qasim's regime.

Economic Development

In other fields as well, the revolutionary regime showed a sharp change of direction from its predecessor. Education was greatly expanded. The education budget was raised from nearly ID 13 million ($36 million) in 1958 to ID 24 million ($67 million) in 1960, almost doubling the budget of the old regime.[22] Enrollment increased at every level. Unfortunately, the advance in quantity was often made at the expense of quality.

The new regime also displayed a new attitude toward economic planning and the priorities of investment. It adopted the concept of a planned economy, influenced partly by the Soviet model and partly by a desire for more rapid economic development. The Development Board, with its Western advisers, was dismantled and a ministry of planning created. In December 1959 a provisional revolutionary plan was published with a new set of priorities. Social welfare and investment in housing, health, and education received considerable attention, whereas the share devoted to agriculture and irrigation was greatly reduced. The largest share of investment—30 percent—went to industry.

Qasim's Oil Policy

Perhaps the most far-reaching of Qasim's economic moves was in the field of oil policy. The rationale behind Qasim's policy was to reduce the influence of the foreign oil companies over Iraq's economy and to gain control over the country's major resource. In this the Iraqis were ultimately successful.

In 1961 oil revenue provided 27 percent of total national income and 90 percent of all foreign exchange.[23] Iraq's dependence upon oil was clearly recognized by Iraqi leaders, and in the early months of the revolution, the regime made no move to disturb existing conditions. But the new regime had inherited a number of oil problems, and in the spring of 1959 negotiations were begun with IPC.

There were at least a dozen points of difference with the company. The two most important from the Iraqi point of view were the demand for 20 percent Iraqi ownership of IPC and relinquishment by IPC of the unused portion of the concession area granted to the company for exploration and production. Iraqis insisted that the company relinquish 75 percent of the concession immediately and more later, until it held only 10 percent.

Qasim proved to be an intransigent and somewhat erratic negotiator, but the parent companies in IPC were also clearly insensitive to the Iraqis' real grievances.[24]Although willing to concede minor points, they were not yet ready to compromise on the fundamental changes demanded by the Iraqis, as they would then have to institute these changes in other countries as well—in fact, undoing much of the concessionary system in the area.

On 11 December 1961, Qasim announced Public Law (PL) 80, which dispossessed IPC of 99.5 percent of its concession territory, leaving it to operate only those areas currently in production. He announced the establishment of the Iraq National Oil Company to exploit the new territory. IPC protested and demanded arbitration, which the Iraqis did not accept. Recognition and acceptance of PL 80 by IPC then became a prime Iraqi aim, indeed a sine qua non of future negotiations.

The effects of PL 80 were far-reaching. The law began the battle to remove foreign control over the economy and to isolate the foreign oil interests that had been a key support of the former regime. It put much oil territory into the hands of the government, including the rich Rumaila field in the south, which had previously belonged to the Basra Petroleum Company, a subsidiary of IPC. At the same time, the law did not touch the current flow of oil because IPC continued to produce from the Kirkuk field. The government could now develop its own oil resources in competition with the foreign-owned IPC. This would not happen for some time, however, as the law initiated a long, protracted, and costly struggle with IPC, which resulted in reduced income for Iraq and a slipping production position with respect to other Gulf producers.

Erosion of National Unity

Whatever the benefits of social and economic reforms initiated by Qasim, they could not compensate for the other flaws in his administration: a gradual concentration of power in his own hands, his increasingly erratic and unsophisticated leadership, and lack of a coherent vision for the future. Qasim's regime should have been favorable to ethnic and sectarian integration and the development of an Iraqi identity. Qasim himself came from mixed Sunni-Shi'i and Kurdish parentage and could therefore appeal to all groups. And he focused on domestic reform in Iraq, not on pan-Arabism. The regime was more generous in recognizing Kurdish rights. But in fact the regime failed to prevent serious erosion of Iraq's national unity. The revolution itself had not only weakened government structures but also unleashed forces, including ethnic and religious aspirations, long repressed or dormant. These now reemerged. After the struggles of the first two years and the attempted assassination, the drive for order overtook the impetus for reform. By 1960 Qasim came to think of himself as the embodiment of the nation. As the drive for uniformity and control intensified, Iraq's fragile national unity began to unravel.

The Shi'i Revival

One unintended consequence of the Qasim era, and especially its left-leaning social and economic reforms, was a revival of Shi'i activism, long dormant during the monarchy. The intense secularism of the regime and its support for leftist policies soon provoked a reaction from conservative Shi'i elements and a religious revival among Shi'i youth. The same reforms that garnered support among the poor generated fear and alienation on the part of Shi'i landlords and merchants and, more importantly, opposition from the Shi'i clerics, many of whom had derived income from a religious tax (*khums*) on tribal leaders and wealthy Shi'a. The clergy also disapproved of the Personal Status Law and the appeal of Marxism to Shi'i youth and took steps to counteract both. In 1960 the chief *marji'* (religious source), Muhsin al-Hakim, issued a *fatwa* (religious decree) against communism and was instrumental in the formation of the Islamic Party, reversing a long period of Shi'i political passivity in Iraq.[25] At the same time, the removal of previous regime's constraints and the current regime's loosening political control provided space for the emergence of new groups.

Among the Shi'a two important Islamic groups emerged. Even though both were dedicated to the revival of Islamic ideals, they were different in orientation and support. The Society of Ulama was a group of senior and some junior clerics from Najaf, formed in 1960.[26] Propelled by the rising tide of communism and by the enactment of the Personal Status Law in 1959, the group was committed to reasserting religious values. The society helped spread mosques, schools, and services to other cities and encouraged a wide variety of Shi'i activities and organizations.

Even more important over the long run was the Da'wa (Call), which was rooted in a younger generation of laymen and junior members of the clerical establishment.[27] The Da'wa was interested in reshaping Islam and its teachings to meet the needs of the modern world and in organizing to protect and spread these ideas. A rising young cleric, Muhammad Baqir al-Sadr, was its chief founder and intellectual guide.[28] Although the group was formed in 1957, before the Qasim period, the revolution gave it impetus.[29] Sadr also gave the movement the intellectual vision needed to reshape traditional Shi'i ideas through two seminal studies he published, one on Islamic philosophy (*Falsafatuna* [Our Philosophy], 1959) and the other on Islamic economics (*Iqtisaduna* [Our Economics], 1961). His works had widespread appeal. The Da'wa became a political party—with a cell-based structure like that of the Communist

Party, functioning underground, in secret, for some time. It aimed at the eventual establishment of an Islamic state.

Although these activities did not yet challenge the Iraqi state or its unity, they revitalized Shi'i consciousness and created new organizations and networks able to mobilize large numbers of Shi'a for change within the state. The result was the beginnings of a more modern, but distinct, Shi'i identity, embedded in a framework of opposition to the regime and the state as it was presently structured.

The Reemergence of the Kurdish Question

Even more serious in eroding national unity was the reemergence, in a more invigorated form, of the Kurdish question. Most Kurds had enthusiastically supported the revolution of 1958. One reason was the temporary constitution promulgated by Qasim and Arif, which stipulated that Kurds and Arabs would be partners in the new state, the first time a Kurdish national identity was recognized. Another was the return of Mustafa Barzani and his followers from exile. Barzani was given a triumphal entry into Baghdad, put up in the palace of Nuri's son, and given a cash allowance for himself and his retinue. A Kurdish paper, *Khabat* (The Struggle), was published openly.

However, the honeymoon between Qasim and Barzani did not last long. Qasim, who had brought Barzani back to Baghdad partly as a counterforce to the Arab nationalists, soon began to fear that demands for Kurdish autonomy within the Iraqi state, if truly granted, would lead to Kurdish independence. For his part, the Kurdish leader increasingly came to distrust the Sole Leader's all-embracing concept of himself as leader of a united state. Barzani rightly suspected Qasim of giving only lip service to Kurdish demands for autonomy.

The return of Barzani was critical to the revival of the Kurdish insurgency. Qasim had a formidable opponent in Barzani. At fifty-five Barzani had been fighting the central government and rival tribal groups off and on since 1931 and had demonstrated his military capacity time and again. His strength came from the guerrilla forces he could muster and from the Barzanis, his clan from the village of Barzan, his birthplace and headquarters. It was not long before Barzani began mobilizing tribal support. In this effort he was assisted by Qasim's land reform program, bitterly opposed by Kurdish landlords in the north.

Barzani was not the only factor in the revival of the Kurdish movement. Qasim also had to contend with the Kurdistan Democratic Party—the urban, professional wing of the Kurdish movement. By 1958 the KDP had come under the influence of left-wing intellectuals and adopted a very progressive, anti-imperialist platform.[30] The KDP modeled its party structure on that of the Communist Party. The party was now led by Ibrahim Ahmad, its secretary general, and Jalal Talabani, his younger son-in-law, both leftist, middle-class lawyers. In January 1960, when Qasim licensed parties, the KDP received a license, and in May 1960, at the party's fifth party congress, Barzani was elected its head.

However, relations between the two wings of the Kurdish movement were tense and fractious. Although the splits were papered over, the differences remained profound. Barzani represented the landed establishment and the wealth and power of the *aghas* (tribal leaders); the KDP party leadership consisted of town-bred intellectuals interested in reform as well as Kurdish rights. Both, however, aimed at recognition of Kurdish autonomy.

In 1960 and early 1961 the situation was still fluid. Barzani had gradually become dissatisfied with the lack of progress in meeting Kurdish demands. Qasim began to encourage Barzani's tribal enemies to move against him. Barzani moved from Baghdad to Barzan, where he could mobilize his tribal support and move against his opponents. From these tribal skirmishes Barzani emerged victorious. At the end of August, much strengthened, he sent an ultimatum to Qasim demanding an end to authoritarian rule, recognition of Kurdish autonomy, and restoration of democratic liberties.

The Kurdish War

Earlier in September tribes loyal to Barzani attacked an army column, and Qasim responded by bombarding a Barzan village and other surrounding hamlets. Events moved swiftly, and what had started as a tribal clash now escalated to a full-fledged war for Kurdish autonomy. Before long, it enlisted the support of not only the tribal contingents, always ready to fight, but also the sophisticated urban intellectuals.

Although the KDP had played virtually no role in these tribal events, on 23 September the party was banned in Baghdad and several of the leaders were arrested. In December 1961 the leadership met in the north and agreed to support the revolt. Although far weaker than Barzani, they had about 650 *peshmerga* (party militia) by 1962.

As the fighting began in earnest, Barzani's tribal forces were boosted by Kurdish army officers who deserted the regular army to go over to his side, strengthening the rebels and also providing much-needed arms. At the same time, their defection weakened the regular army. By 1963 many Kurdish tribes had also joined the rebels. Adopting guerrilla tactics, the rebels held their strongholds in the mountains and ambushed army garrisons in the cities, cutting off their supply lines. The rebels never attempted to hold sizable cities (where they often went to buy grain), but gradually the cities became isolated and surrounded, while the more remote outposts were in danger. In these encounters the Kurds came out ahead, consistently growing stronger in morale and in weapons.

Although the war was by no means entirely Qasim's fault, it badly sapped his strength at home and distracted his attention from other problems. Development slowed, and the opposition began to regroup. To garner some needed support, especially among the Arab nationalists and the Ba'thists, Qasim released their members from prison, whereupon they reorganized and began to plot the overthrow of the regime. During the early days of 1963, contact was made between the Ba'thists and the KDP, and a tentative agreement appears to have been reached that if Qasim could be overthrown, Kurdish autonomy would be granted. This unlikely alliance is remarkable mainly in revealing the extent of Qasim's internal isolation.

Foreign Policy Failures

Qasim's domestic isolation was more than matched in foreign affairs. The revolution of 1958 had made a fundamental change in Iraq's foreign policy orientation. Formerly dependent on the West, primarily Great Britain but also the United States, for arms and economic support, Iraq now turned to the Soviet Union as a substitute, swayed mainly by the Qasim regime's anti-imperialist outlook as well as the rising influence of the left. The shift was to prove permanent, putting Iraq in the Soviet orbit for decades and distancing it from the West and its regional allies. On 16 March 1959, Iraq signed an extensive economic agreement with Moscow, the first of several. It provided Iraq with a substantial loan. The funds were to be used for industrial equipment for steel, electrical, glass, and textile industries; railway projects; oil exploration; technical training; and help with the agrarian reform program.[31] Russian technicians increasingly replaced the departing Americans and British. Meanwhile, a series of cultural exchanges took place. By 1959 there were almost eight hundred Iraqi students studying in the USSR, mostly at Soviet expense. Eastern bloc films and books were imported. Tourism to these countries was encouraged, as were exchanges of professional groups.

These cultural and educational exchanges were paralleled by arms deliveries, which would henceforth tie Iraq's military establishment to the Soviet Union rather than to the West. Late in 1958 a squadron of MiG-15 fighters was delivered, followed by later deliveries of MiG-17s and MiG-21s, transport aircraft, and helicopters. In February 1959 the first deliveries of 100 to 150 Soviet tanks took place. More followed. The Iraqi air force was reorganized and modernized under Soviet aegis.[32]

The Rupture with the West

Soviet help, however, did not entirely compensate for Iraq's alienation of the West. Both Britain and the United States were surprised and taken aback by the 1958 revolt, and both considered military action against the regime, urged on by regional allies such as Turkey, Iran, Jordan, and Israel. This was soon rejected as impractical, although both sent forces, temporarily, to the area—the United States to Lebanon, acting under the Eisenhower doctrine of 1957, and the British to Jordan. After the initial shock had dissipated, however, British and American reactions to the regime soon diverged. The British, still smarting from the Suez crisis and the failure of their 1956 tripartite action against Egypt, saw the main regional threat as an expanding Arab nationalism led by Nasser. They soon recognized that Qasim was an Iraqi—not a pan-Arab—nationalist and would not accept Arab unity if it meant subordinating himself to Nasser. In their view, Iraq could be a convenient buffer against expanding Egyptian influence.[33] Even though the United States also feared Nasser's brand of radical Arab nationalism, its fear of communism was greater, and it was slower than the British to recognize Qasim's independent policy. By the time it did, however, the rising tide of communism in Iraq had become Washington's major focus, supplanting Arab nationalism as a threat. Regardless of these Anglo-American differences, neither country was ever able to restore its previous position in Iraq, and in time, Britain, too, became increasingly disillusioned with Qasim. By 1961 acrimonious negotiations over oil and Qasim's abrupt claim to Kuwait had lost him what little British support he had once had.

Tensions with Iran

Iraq's increased alienation from the West was matched by its deteriorating relations with its regional neighbors, especially Turkey and Iran. Turkey was concerned about the rupture of the Baghdad Pact, the increase of Communist and Soviet influence in Baghdad, and, eventually, rising Kurdish insurgency across its border. But relations with Turkey were less threatening than those with Iran, which deteriorated rapidly. The overthrow of the monarchy in Iraq, the leftward shift of Qasim's government, and the increased Soviet influence in Iraq worried the shah. Iraq's withdrawal from the Baghdad Pact all but ended cooperation between these powers on the Kurdish front, and as time went on, the Iranian and Iraqi Kurds began to cooperate across the border.

The first arena of disagreement, however, was over the Shatt al-Arab. Tensions rose, along with accelerated border skirmishes.[34] In November 1959 Iran questioned the validity of the 1937 agreement, which had recognized the border drawn at the low-water mark on the Iranian side and given Iraq control of the shipping channel. In December 1959 Qasim reacted to Iran's reopening of the dispute by nullifying the agreement. Iran then made a counterclaim to a boundary in the center of the channel along the entire Shatt. However, by April of that year the two powers had agreed to settle their differences by negotiation.

Qasim also asserted Arab interests in the Gulf, another shift of policy from the old regime. He began by laying claim to Arabistan (the Arab name for the province of Khuzistan in Iran), which contained a majority of Iranians of Arab descent, an action further alienating Iran.

Meanwhile, Qasim's domestic victory over Arif and the pan-Arabists had profound regional repercussions. Qasim represented a serious obstacle to Nasser's regional influence and even a threat to the recent Syrian-Egyptian union.[35] The open quarrel between Iraq and the UAR became a major feature of the Qasim period. Relations reached a point just as low as they had been under the monarchy. The propaganda war began again, with Iraqis calling Nasser the new "Pharoah of the Nile" and Egyptians calling Qasim the "divider of Iraq," a pun on his name, which means "divider" in Arabic. The crowning blow came in 1961 when Qasim took one final step in foreign affairs that made his isolation virtually complete. This was the notorious Kuwait affair.

The Kuwait Affair

The episode began in June 1961 when Britain and Kuwait agreed to terminate the agreement of 1899, which had made Kuwait a virtual British protectorate, and recognize Kuwait as an independent state.[36] While other countries hastened to send congratulatory cables, Qasim sent the Kuwaiti ruler an ambiguous message, making no mention of independence. In a radio announcement made five days later, on 25 July 1961, Qasim laid claim to Kuwait as an integral part of Iraq, citing as justification the fact that Kuwait had once been a district of the Basra *wilaya* (province) under the Ottomans. Qasim further announced the appointment of the ruler of Kuwait as a *qa'imaqam* (district ruler) of Kuwait, to come under the authority of the *mutasarrif* (governor) of Basra. These claims harked back to the last quarter of the nineteenth century when Kuwait had nominally come under the suzerainty of the Ottoman Empire.

The repercussions were immediate. The Kuwaitis requested British protection, and on 1 July British troops entered Kuwait. Qasim's provocation and the resulting intrusion of the British into Kuwait increased Arab hostility toward Iraq, already inflamed over Qasim's stand on Arab issues. The matter was taken up in the Arab League in July, and the league decided to assemble an Arab force to replace the British. The first contingent arrived in Kuwait in September 1961, and except for the Egyptians, the Arab forces remained until 1962, when the danger appeared to be over.

Events then shifted to the diplomatic front. Kuwait applied to the Arab League for admission and on 20 July was admitted. Iraq thereupon ceased all cooperation with the league. Not content with this, on 26 December 1961, Hashim Jawad, Qasim's foreign minister, announced that Iraq would reconsider diplomatic relations with any country recognizing Kuwait. As the recognitions continued to pour in, Iraq began to recall ambassador after ambassador, though the remaining diplomatic staff was generally left behind. During 1962 the long list came to include, among others, Jordan, Tunisia, Lebanon, and the United States.

The Kuwait affair, although founded on long-standing Iraqi grievances, was grossly mishandled. It isolated Qasim from all his Arab neighbors and solved no problems at home. By the end of 1962, Qasim had no friends left inside Iraq except a weakened Communist Party and a handful of army officers, and none left outside except the Soviet Union, itself increasingly disturbed by the Kurdish war and far more concerned over Egypt than Iraq.

The promise of social revolution begun in 1958 had faltered. Land reform was in deep trouble, industrialization could make no headway, development plans could not be launched, and oil revenues were beginning to fall off. The state structure and the sense of national identity on which it was based had begun to unravel through a festering Kurdish war that could not be brought to conclusion. And political hopes for liberalization had died under the boot of an increasingly erratic dictatorship.

But even though discontent was widespread and ran across a broad spectrum of political and social groups, the question was whether any of these had sufficient motive and means to displace the regime. Democratic-minded elements, such as the NDP, found dictatorship distasteful, but without any grassroots organization or foothold in the military, they were in no position to overthrow the government. Moreover, their views probably came closest to Qasim's. The Kurds were sapping the regime's strength but were unable to replace it on their own. Abroad, the United States and Britain, although alienated from Qasim, on different grounds, were not willing to intervene directly and by 1962 had lost any influence or ability to drive events inside Iraq.

What really undid the Qasim regime was the alienation of the pan-Arab groups, bitter over their failed attempts to gain power and the isolation of the regime in the Arab world. Unlike other opponents of Qasim, however, these had a foothold within the military and in organized, underground movements, like the Ba'th, with potential to mobilize against the regime and to strike it at key vulnerable points. By 1962 these forces, though still weak, were gathering strength and organizing; it would not be long before they would open a second, bloody chapter in the revolution.

The Qasim Regime in the Balance

The Qasim era has been variously estimated by opponents and supporters. Although the regime's record is decidedly mixed, there is little doubt that Qasim made fundamental changes in Iraq and the direction of its policy. The egalitarian thrust of the regime brought much-needed social reform—in the landholding system, in Iraq's ownership of its oil resources, and in the opening up of the education system in a way that would strengthen the middle class. These wrenching changes could not have occurred without some turmoil, but the excesses of the left, especially the Communists, frightened conservatives and nationalists as well as outsiders like the United States, creating a backlash that would help to unseat the regime. The continual instability that resulted also contributed substantially to the establishment of an authoritarian regime.

Qasim also reoriented Iraq in the direction of an Iraq First policy and away from unproductive involvement in Arab unity schemes, a much-needed corrective. He and his supporters also appeared willing, at least initially, to attempt a reorganization of domestic power-sharing arrangements. This should have had a beneficial effect in strengthening the nation-state project, but in fact it did not. Fear of Communist influence helped spark a religious revival among the Shi'a. Far more serious were the return of Barzani and a resuscitation of the Kurdish movement. This gave impetus to the revival of Kurdish separatism and set off an intermittent, but long-running, Kurdish war that would plague the state for decades.

Qasim also changed the direction of Iraq's foreign policy away from the West and toward the Soviet bloc. The aim was greater Iraqi independence, a goal that was achieved in some measure. (Relations with the USSR were never as close as former ties with Britain had been.) But this new direction alienated the United States, fearful of the Communist threat, and eventually Britain, helping to isolate Iraq. Iraq's new orientation also alienated much of the Arab world and its domestic pan-Arab nationalists, who eventually mobilized to overthrow the regime.

In the end, the most important consequence of Qasim's four-and-a-half-year rule was negative: the failure to construct political institutions and processes to govern Iraq. Despite some feeble attempts at opening the political system, no constitution, no representative institutions, and no elections emerged. Instead, Qasim governed, as prime minister, through a cabinet that he controlled, concentrating executive, legislative, and sometimes judicial powers in his hands. The Mahdawi Court made a mockery of justice and permanently damaged the concept and practice of the rule of law.

Above all, the Qasim era opened the door to direct military participation in politics. The military would thenceforth intervene again and again, creating more instability and increasingly authoritarian regimes. The result of this spiraling process was now seen in the next turn of the wheel, as the Ba'thists and Arab nationalists used the military to overthrow the Qasim regime in one of the bloodiest episodes of the revolutionary decade.

6

THE ARAB NATIONALISTS
IN POWER, 1963-1968

The coup that finally put an end to Qasim's regime came from the Arab nationalist quarter.[1] As a result, the era that followed the coup shifted Iraq in the direction of a more pan-Arab policy, with renewed attempts at greater Arab integration. The coup unfolded in a period when regional support for Arab nationalism and socialism was high and when Nasser was seen as a hero. Hence, Arab unity, as the dominant ideology of the time, was an effective tool for mobilizing broader elements to counter Qasim and the left. But the Arab nationalists also had problems of their own. There was no real unity of purpose beyond their common desire to be rid of the "sole leader" and to reorient foreign policy toward some kind of union with other Arab countries. Instead, they were splintered into several groups, the most important of which were the Ba'th and the Nasserites.

The Nasserites did not constitute a political party; rather, they were a collection of individuals who looked to Nasser for leadership and desired some kind of unity with Egypt. While lacking clear leadership, they tended to view Abd al-Salam Arif as their spokesman. Nasserites could also draw on support from conservative elements—landlords and religious leaders—who feared the radical changes introduced by Qasim;

from military leaders, especially those left out of the Qasim regime; and from the Arab Sunni population in the smaller cities and towns of the northwest, especially in Mosul and Ramadi.

The Ba'th Party, with its tightly knit organization, clandestine activities, and militant leadership, was far better organized and better positioned to undertake a coup. The party's chief appeal was a combination of almost mystical belief in Arab unity with a call for the social and economic transformation of society, a view that had appeal across sectarian boundaries.[2] But the party had its own weaknesses. It was composed mainly of young civilians, long on zeal and short on experience, and it had little support in the military, where it would have to rely on older, more conservative elements among the Nasserites. These weaknesses would soon become apparent.

Whatever the motives, the outcome of the coup was a shift for the remainder of the decade from domestic reforms and an Iraq First orientation under Qasim to increased involvement in pan-Arab schemes and a neglect of the home front.

Based on high doses of ideology too little tempered by reality, continual attempts at Arab unity would founder just as badly as had attempts at radical social reform under Qasim. Coups and attempted coups followed, as military politics dominated the state and politicians failed to build civil and political institutions at home. Domestic problems, especially the ongoing Kurdish insurgency, festered. Meanwhile, the foundations of the state and its collective identity would be further eroded. It began with the Ba'th coup of February 1963.

The Iraqi Ba'th in 1963

Although the party was first introduced into Iraq in 1949 by Syrian Ba'th students studying in Baghdad, it gained a real foothold in Iraq in the early 1950s under the leadership of Fu'ad al-Rikabi, a Shi'a from Nasiriyya. Between 1952 and 1958 the Ba'th made inroads in the schools and colleges, from which it drew much of its leadership and support, but its numbers were still small. By the mid-1950s it had only about three hundred full members and possibly five hundred supporters.[3] Many of these young men (a few were women) were Shi'a whose families originated in the south; they were attracted by the party's nonsectarian character and modernizing ideology and, in general, favored the more radical, socialist ideas current at the time. After the revolution of 1958, membership increased and new contacts were made in the officer corps. Not surprisingly, this military cohort was overwhelmingly Sunni and drawn predominantly from the provincial towns north and west of Baghdad. The interests of these officers in the party were pragmatic, even self-serving. They wanted to overthrow Qasim and needed a political base. Ahmad Hasan al-Bakr provides a good example. A practicing Muslim from Tikrit, he had qualms about joining a party led by a Christian (Michel Aflaq).

After the failed attempt on Qasim's life in 1959, the party went through a difficult period. Many members were in prison or in exile, and serious splits developed within the party. A struggle for power between the Ba'th and Nasser led some to support Nasser, while others supported the Ba'th. In 1961 the secession of Syria from the UAR left Syrian politics—and the Ba'th party—in considerable disarray. These internecine struggles indicate that the party was ill prepared to take over and run a government.

Nonetheless, by 1960 a new group of clandestine leaders had emerged in Iraq. They were mostly young and Shi'i. Most important was Ali Salih al-Sa'di, of mixed Kurdish and Arab Sunni stock. Though not a Ba'thist, Abd al-Salam Arif was tough, militant, even ruthless, and he was a good organizer.

The 14 Ramadan Coup

During 1962 plans were laid for the coup. Some of those involved were retired officers; others were in active duty. A Ba'thist civil militia of several thousand was organized and armed. In December, however, Qasim discovered the plot. When Qasim arrested some of the participants, the plotters decided they had to act, and on 8 February 1963—the fourteenth day of Ramadan—the coup took place.[4]

The 14 Ramadan action was no palace coup. Ba'thists and their Arab nationalist allies succeeded in gaining control of the government only after a bitter two-day fight with Qasim's forces that cost hundreds of lives. The coup began early in the morning of 8 February when the Communist air force chief, Jalal al-Auqati, was assassinated and tank units occupied the Abu Ghraib radio station. It was at the Ministry of Defense that the heaviest fighting took place. Qasim had taken refuge in the heavily fortified building with a few of his loyal followers. The battle at the ministry raged all day. Communist demonstrators were mowed down by tanks. Most of the army outside the capital apparently remained neutral. Finally, on 9 February Qasim asked for safe conduct out of the country in return for surrender. His request was refused. Instead, he was dragged before a hastily assembled group of military and party leaders and summarily interrogated about his failures. He and three associates were shot on the spot and their bodies displayed on public TV. The Qasim era had come to an end.[5]

The Ba'th Government

Soon after the coup's initial proclamation, the structure of the new government was announced. The Ba'th members, for the most part young and unknown, wished to have an older, well-established figure at the head of government—preferably one satisfactory to Nasser. For this purpose, Abd al-Salam Arif, now out of prison, was made president and promoted to field marshal. Although his role was supposed to be more symbolic than authoritative, Arif had been friendly toward the Ba'th and was expected to cooperate with it. Military appointments were given to officers who had come out in support of the coup, Ba'thist or otherwise.

A cabinet of twenty-one members put Ba'thists in all key posts and gave the party an absolute majority of seats (twelve). Ahmad Hasan al-Bakr was made prime minister and the party's civilian leader; Ali Salih al-Sa'di, was made deputy prime minister and minister of interior. But the cabinet also included some Arab nationalists (five) and Kurds (two), as well as a few respected professionals.

Behind the cabinet, however, real power was vested in the National Council of the Revolutionary Command (NCRC), established on 8 February. The NCRC was given the legal power to appoint and remove cabinets and to assume the powers of the commander in chief of the armed forces.[6] Membership in the NCRC was kept secret, but it clearly represented the Ba'th Party members who had collaborated in the coup.[7]

This government was meant to establish a Ba'th Party state, but Ba'th control of the government was more apparent than real. Several fault lines soon emerged in these hastily constructed structures. One was the cleavage between the young, civilian wing of the party, represented by Sa'di, and the older, military men, such as Arif and Bakr. There was also an ideological division between conservatives, or pragmatists, aware of the Ba'th's weak power base in the country and the need to compromise with others, and radicals, anxious to push forward rapidly with a Ba'th agenda. Soon a third divide appeared between Ba'th members on the party's Regional Command who held no official positions but were supposed to husband the party's interests and its policy behind the scenes and those now in positions of authority, like Arif and Bakr, who could make and enforce decisions whether or not the party's Regional Command agreed. It was not long before the older, military men in positions of authority began to prevail over the young party militants. The young civilians on the Regional Command were no match for the more seasoned officer-politicians, backed by supporters in the military.[8] In this fluid atmosphere the military began to consolidate its hold on power by forming blocs based not on party affiliation but on tribe and locality. Those from Tikrit gathered around Bakr; those from Dulaim (Ramadi), around the Arif brothers.

Despite these frictions, the Ba'thists soon showed their ruthlessness in rooting out supporters of Qasim and persecuting the Communists. The property of almost a hundred Qasim followers was frozen, and many of his ministers were arrested. Communists were unofficially sought out in their neighborhoods, arrested, and sometimes assassinated. Special investigative committees were set up, torture was practiced, and random executions were authorized by some of those in authority. These actions continued a vendetta begun earlier by the Communists who had persecuted Ba'thists under the Mahdawi Court. In their number, their extrajudicial illegality, and their use of torture, however, these Ba'th actions surpassed those of the Qasim period and boded ill for the conduct of politics in the future.[9]

Ironically, although one of the principles of the Ba'th constitution was socialism, its first actions in government appeared relatively conservative. This was undoubtedly due to the increased influence of more conservative military elements in the regime. Faced with pressure from religious leaders, Sunni and Shi'i, the regime, in one of its first steps, amended the Personal Status Law, modifying the clause granting equality between men and women in inheritance. No socialist measures were passed.

Ba'th foreign policy was equally moderate. Relations with the West, specifically the United States, were strengthened, for example, and Qasim's policy toward the United Arab Republic (which no longer included Syria) was reversed. Even more significant was Iraq's new position toward Kuwait. The Ba'th signed an agreement recognizing Kuwait's sovereignty and independence. Even more remarkable, it agreed on a boundary, although no actual demarcation took place. The apparent quid pro quo for this recognition was a long-term interest-free loan from Kuwait of ID 30 million to cover increasing budget shortages in Iraq.[10]

Ba'th Failures

Despite these moderate beginnings, the Ba'th regime did not last the year. Its leaders' difficulties, mainly of their own making, began soon after the coup. One was the ongoing Kurdish war, which the Ba'th aggravated by its pan-Arab policy.

The Conflict with the Kurds

Initially, the Kurdistan Democratic Party (KDP) had been in touch with the Ba'th and had agreed to support the coup in return for a promise of autonomy. From the first, the issue at stake was just how much self-rule the new government was prepared to offer the Kurds to achieve peace in the north, especially as the Ba'th, unlike its predecessors, was eager to achieve some kind of Arab unity. In March Barzani demanded, among other things, affirmation of the Kurdish right to autonomy, the formation of Kurdish legislative and executive authorities in the north, a Kurdish vice president in Baghdad, a Kurdish legion in the north, and the appointment of Kurds to all posts in Kurdistan. The Kurdish region was to include the provinces of Sulaimaniyya, Arbil, Kirkuk, and the districts in the Mosul and Diyala provinces in which Kurds were a majority. This was well beyond any concessions the Ba'thists were prepared to make.

The real interest of the Ba'th lay in its negotiations with Nasser for some kind of future unity, not in its accommodation of the Kurds. On 17 April an agreement in principle was concluded with Nasser on a future union. The Kurds had already made it clear that if Iraq were to join an Arab federation, they would demand greater autonomy.[11] After the agreement, the Kurds published a memorandum demanding virtually a binational state. From here on, relations with the Kurds rapidly deteriorated. By the end of April, aircraft and troops were deployed northward, and early in June the Kurdish delegation in Baghdad was rounded up and arrested. The war resumed.

The Kurds soon had control of the entire northern region bordering Iran, and Barzani was receiving considerable aid from the Iranian Kurds. Abandoning the defensive strategy followed by Qasim, the government decided to recapture Kurdish territory and crush the Kurdish movement. Iraqi forces bombarded and bulldozed Kurdish villages under their control and began Arabization of strategic areas.[12] The toll taken on the Kurds was greater than previous losses, but the Ba'th policy was no more successful than Qasim's approach had been. By winter the Kurds had regained most of their position. Before long moderates in the army began to turn against the government's policy. So did a number of ministers. The Ba'th inability to either find a solution to the Kurdish problem or win a military victory hastened the regime's downfall.

Arab Unity Failures

The most serious problem resulted from the Ba'th regime's intense embroilment in Arab affairs. The Ba'th coup in Iraq had been followed by a similar event in neighboring Syria; on 8 March the Ba'th came to power in Damascus. The Syrian Ba'thists were interested in a new union with Nasser. To strengthen their position in negotiations with Nasser, they needed the support of their Iraqi colleagues. In Iraq as well, there were reasons for engaging in the unity talks with Cairo. The ideology of the party called for pan-Arabism, and popular expectations for union were high. More important, however, was the need of the new Ba'thist government to propitiate Nasserites and other pan-Arab nationalists at home, who were restless because they had been given only a marginal role in decisionmaking.

An Iraqi delegation and the Syrians joined Nasser in Egypt for unity talks. These soon foundered on mutual mistrust between Nasser and the Ba'th. For a number of reasons, Nasser did not want unity with the Ba'thists in Syria and Iraq. He disliked the idea of sharing leadership in the Arab world with them, he distrusted their doctrinaire ideas, and he was unwilling to become embroiled in Iraq's numerous problems, especially the Kurds.

In May a potential coup by Arab nationalist elements was forestalled in Iraq and a number of civilians and officers were arrested. This event ended any prospects of power sharing with Nasserites.[13] From then on, Nasser encouraged the Ba'th opponents in Iraq to bring about a change of government.[14] With no real prospects for a union with Egypt, the two Ba'th parties in Syria and Iraq then turned to increased cooperation between themselves. In October a military agreement was concluded, followed by an economic pact. This growing rapprochement only increased Egypt's concern.

Party Cleavages

Ultimately, however, the critical factors responsible for bringing down the Ba'th were the deep splits in party leadership over policy as well as tactics, together with its inexperience and ineptitude in handling the task of governing. These differences soon crystalized around two factions, one dubbed "conservative" and the other, radical and more militant. The latter, led by Sa'di, was doctrinaire to the core, interested primarily in upholding party principles and maintaining party control. It adopted such Marxist ideas as socialist planning, collective farms, and workers' control of the means of production. This group was overwhelmingly civilian, young (members were mainly in their early thirties), and thoroughly committed to achieving its revolutionary agenda. These radicals were not interested in gradual evolution or in sharing power, much less democratic institutions, and their inexperience—even naïveté—in the requirements of governing a complex society like Iraq's soon became glaringly apparent. One frankly stated, "We were not prepared for power. We had spent all of our time underground, preparing for conspiracy."[15]

The other, more moderate group was led by Talib Shabib and Hazim Jawad among the civilians but increasingly driven by military Ba'thists, such as Ahmad Hasan al-Bakr. Pragmatism was this group's hallmark. Realizing the weakness of the Ba'th position, it advocated some power sharing with sympathetic non-Ba'thists, especially the Arab nationalists. This group was more interested in keeping the Ba'th in power than in realizing a purist, one-party state. The military contingent, in particular, was uninterested in ideology or rapid social change.

In October 1963 these issues all came to a head at the sixth Ba'th Party conference, held in Damascus.[16] In an election for the party's National Command,[17] Sa'di and his faction succeeded in winning most of the seats allotted to Iraq. He also succeeded in getting his more radical socialist ideas accepted, thereby alienating Michel Aflaq, the party's founder, and other moderates. Victory in Damascus, however, did not mean victory in Baghdad, where Sa'di's opponents were already preparing for his downfall.

Back in Baghdad, contacts among officers, Ba'thist and non-Ba'thist, had been under way for some time, aimed at ousting the radical faction of the party—and its civilian control. In November at a Ba'th Party meeting engineered by the military Ba'thists, the moderates gained control. A new Regional Command then arrested Sa'di and four of his civilian supporters and exiled them to Spain.[18]

The reaction was not long in coming. Sa'di's supporters took to the streets, and the National Guard, the Ba'thist militia controlled by the militants, went on a weeklong rampage. On 12 November, Michel Aflaq arrived in Baghdad with a Ba'th contingent to mediate. The arrival of Syrian Ba'thists to help decide the country's leadership was considered by

Iraqis as blatant foreign interference. On the ground, control was in the hands of more radical Iraqi elements who were demanding the removal of the two "moderate" civilian members of the Regional Command, Shabib and Jawad. A meeting held on 14 November declared the Ba'th election of 11 November null and void, and these two moderates were exiled to Lebanon.

A more unfortunate set of circumstances for the party could not be imagined. The dispute had removed almost the entire leadership of the Ba'th Party that had carried out the coup of 1963, thereby easing the way for Arif and his Arab nationalist supporters in the army to take over. In one brief day of military action, Arif inaugurated a new regime.

On 18 November Arif announced that the armed forces would take control of the country and that a new government would be formed with himself as president of the republic and commander in chief of the armed forces. It was not long before Arif found ways of ridding himself of the key Ba'thists. In January 1964 Bakr's post was abolished and he resigned from the government; other Ba'thists were dismissed. Arif retired over four hundred officers, most of them Ba'thist, and transferred others out of Baghdad, weakening Ba'thist ties to the military, particularly those of Bakr. By early 1964 the Ba'th had been thoroughly removed from power.

In the end, the Ba'th coup of 1963 succeeded only in putting power back in the hands of the military. But this brief, early Ba'th episode in power is important, less for what it accomplished than for the lessons learned by the Ba'th, especially Ahmad Hasan al-Bakr and his young aide and relative, Saddam Husain. Both men appeared to have learned at least three lessons from the disaster of 1963. First, ideological divisions—or any other kind—are to be avoided at all costs. Second, potential military opponents must be moved out of power as soon as possible. Third, it is easier to gain power than to maintain it. In any future government, gaining control over the instruments of state would be paramount. For this purpose, a security apparatus would prove far more effective than a party or the military. These lessons would indelibly shape Iraq's future after the next Ba'th coup in 1968.[19]

The First Arif Regime, 1963–1966

The smooth execution of the November coup and the masterful manipulation of the Ba'th in its aftermath showed that Abd al-Salam Arif had emerged from the turbulent events of the previous four years a somewhat different man from the Arif who had brashly led the coup of 1958. The lessons of his struggle with Qasim, his imprisonment, and his observation of the forces released by the revolution had tempered his impetuosity and given him a greater sense of realism and maturity. Arif was a relatively conservative Muslim and a staunch Sunni, characteristics that would in time raise public accusations of sectarianism. However, his mastery of military politics, his newfound moderation, and his ability to govern in a more open manner were to stand him in good stead in consolidating his power and giving the nation some relaxation from the tensions and clashes of the previous years.

Moderate Arab Socialism

Although the Arif regime went through several stages of development, in general it was dominated by the philosophy and tactics of Nasser's brand of Arab socialism. After removing the Ba'th, Arif relied heavily on the Nasserite elements in Iraq—at least at first—mainly to help consolidate his position internally and to win Nasser's much-needed support for his regime. Much of the political dynamics of the regime can be understood only by examining the push and pull of the two remaining groups in power. On the one hand stood a strong Nasserite element demanding unity and a more state-controlled economy; on the other hand were more pragmatic, "centrist" elements willing to accommodate nominal unity but more concerned with stabilizing Iraq's situation at home and achieving some reasonable balance between Iraq's foreign and domestic demands.

Arif and his supporters clearly fell into the second category. This was apparent in his early actions, which were designed to calm domestic turbulence and normalize Iraq's relations with foreign powers. Although it was clear that the military would be in control, Arif was never as authoritarian as Qasim or as brutal as the Ba'th; greater freedom of speech and action was allowed. The first cabinet stated that it would institute a planned economy that would encourage both private and public sectors, stimulate industry and private investment, and carry out the agrarian reform that had been all but forgotten in the previous few years—all on an equitable basis. Soothed by this start, many Iraqis who had been living abroad returned, and capital flowed into the country once again.

In foreign affairs as well, Arif's government followed a moderate policy, starting with an attempt to mend fences with the West. Between May 1964 and June 1965 Iraq engaged in negotiations with the Iraq Petroleum Company (IPC) and arrived at several agreements that would have resolved outstanding issues had they been implemented. Relations with the Soviet Union were also improved without alienating the West. Arms deliveries were resumed early in 1964; the USSR installed a surface-to-air missile system and delivered MiG-21s and TU-16 medium jet bombers.[20]

It was not long, however, before the Nasserite elements in the regime began to push for more progress on a union with Egypt, and it was this policy that tended to dominate the second phase of the regime, during 1964 and 1965. In January 1964 Arif visited Egypt and talked extensively with Nasser. Neither leader appeared eager to rush headlong into union; both agreed that preliminary steps should first be taken to harmonize their political and economic systems. In Iraq the impetus was seized by the Nasserites. Under their influence, Iraq's internal structure began to be revised along Egyptian lines. On 3 May 1964 a new provisional constitution, modeled on that of Egypt, was announced. It provided that Iraq would be democratic, socialist, Arab, and Islamic; a future national assembly would be elected, but in the interim, legislative power would be exercised by the president and the cabinet. The chief difference with Egypt was that the Iraqi instrument gave more emphasis to Islam and less to socialism. In May 1964 both countries signed an agreement providing for a joint command. By September there were some 5,000 Egyptian troops on Iraqi soil. Presumably there for joint maneuvers, the troops were meant in reality to bolster the regime in the wake of an attempted Ba'th coup.

The Nationalization Laws

These pan-Arab political and military measures were short-lived. Of far more importance for Iraq's internal development were the nationalization laws of 1964. They represented the regime's most substantial step toward a socialist system, one that eventually had far-reaching effects, putting important productive sectors of Iraq's economy in government hands.

The chief architect of nationalization was a young, Cambridge-educated economist, Khair al-Din Hasib, governor of the Central Bank. Hasib and Adib al-Jadir, a cousin who later became minister of industry, were representative of the prounion technocrats who were impressed with Nasser's recent experiments in socialism and wanted to adapt them to Iraq. This group had examined the private sector and found it wanting. They advocated nationalization of banks and key industries, creation of a public sector to act as a catalyst for development, and passage of laws designed to redistribute income.[21]

Published on the anniversary of the July revolution in 1964, the new laws nationalized all banks and insurance companies, all cement and cigarette companies, and some flour and textile industries. A later amendment made the import and distribution of pharmaceuticals, cars, tea, sugar, and other items a government monopoly. Opposed by conservative business elements, the nationalization laws unquestionably discouraged private investment. The suddenness of the decrees and the economic discontinuity they introduced created a climate of uncertainty. Arif felt it necessary to reassure the public that there would be no further nationalization.

Whatever the economic impact of the new laws, politically they marked a major step in converting the economy of the country from a free enterprise system (though an admittedly weak one), modified by concepts of the welfare state, to a system based on a planned economy and on state ownership of the means of production in major industries. The step placed the authority for directing the economy in government hands, where it would remain for the rest of the century. As would soon be apparent, however, Iraq as yet lacked the skilled manpower to run such an establishment.

After the nationalization laws, the next phase of Arif's regime began. By the summer of 1965, Arif began to pull back from the union measures and felt strong enough to initiate a series of astute moves against the Nasserites. In this he was helped by discontent with the socialization decrees and by another failed coup attempt by a Nasserite officer he had appointed as prime minister. Arif was also able to secure his position by appointing his brother and loyal supporters from his own tribal group—the Jumaila from Ramadi—to key military posts.[22] This practice heralded the beginnings of a tribal policy in appointments that was to outlast the regime. With his position secure, Arif now appointed Abd al-Rahman al-Bazzaz as prime minister and gave him the authority to move in a new direction, one designed to civilianize the administration, marginalize the military (and thus circumvent more coups), and launch a modest return to a constitutional system.

Bazzaz: Another Attempt to Liberalize

Abd al-Rahman al-Bazzaz was both a civilian and an Arab nationalist of long standing. As a London-educated lawyer and an experienced man of fifty-two, he would satisfy the moderates and wide segments of the population tired of military rule. More importantly, Bazzaz represented the potential for a return to the rule of law and even an elected assembly.

This new direction was made clear in a number of public statements and speeches by Bazzaz. First, he stressed the rule of law, especially an end to arbitrary arrests and extreme retribution for political opponents. Second, he promised to establish a permanent constitution, to promulgate an election law, and eventually to hold an election for a national assembly. Third, he affirmed that while adhering to agreements with Cairo, the government would now attend to Iraqi territorial unity, a reference understood to mean a renewed attempt to settle the Kurdish issue. Lastly, Bazzaz promised a retreat on the socialist front.

At the same time, the regime was increasingly civilianized. As prime minister, Bazzaz presided over a cabinet that had the fewest military members since 1963. The National Revolutionary Council, which had been an exclusively military group, was dissolved; its functions devolved on the cabinet. Civilian technocrats played an increased role. The relative openness of the regime as compared to its predecessors allowed for planning, discussion, and the normal processes of government to take place.

The Shi'i *Renaissance*

This modest attempt to liberalize, together with a concentration on Iraqi, rather than Arab, unity also brought some positive, if short-lived, results in the Kurdish and Shi'i communities: more social peace in both areas. The Shi'i Islamic movements that had emerged under Qasim to confront the Communist challenge now took advantage of these relatively favorable conditions to expand their organization and influence. Arif, a Sunni, was a practicing Muslim of conservative bent, and he supported public religious observances, including those of the Shi'a. Indeed, under the Arif regime there was something of a Shi'i renaissance. Muhsin al-Hakim, the chief *marji'*, and the Da'wa, still underground, used the new political climate to spread the Shi'i movement widely in schools and college, through charities and in public rituals. So successful were these efforts that some Shi'i scholars have seen this period as a "golden age" for the Islamic movement.[23]

Not all of the results of the Arif regime were positive for the Shi'a, however. The intrusion of the military into politics and its monopoly of positions at upper levels of power had greatly reduced Shi'i participation in decisionmaking and increased the Sunni-Shi'a imbalance in government (see Table A.2). This increased "Sunni-ization" of the political elite had been exacerbated by the removal of the Communists and the radical Ba'thists, both of whom had been predominantly Shi'i in their leadership. This sectarian imbalance was further exacerbated by the nationalization laws, which disproportionately affected the mercantile and financial sectors of the Shi'i middle class. The increasingly Sunni character of the regime brought to the surface the old issue of sectarianism and discrimination against Shi'a. In response, the Shi'i religious and intellectual community began to focus on its own sectarian identity and on the creation of a justification for it. The Da'wa movement directed much of its opposition to reaffirming the Arab character of the Iraqi Shi'i community, emphasizing its majority in Iraq and therefore its right to govern. These sentiments would deepen in succeeding years.[24]

The Attempted Kurdish Accord

Kurdish separatism was a much more serious threat to Iraq's unity and the stability of the regime than were Shi'i feelings of alienation. In February 1964 a cease-fire in the Kurdish conflict was announced. It called for recognition of Kurdish national rights, a general amnesty, and a reinstatement of Kurds in the civil service and the military. It did not mention autonomy and called for the return of the central government administration in the north.[25] This seemed to be a promising beginning, but it did not take into account emerging fissures among the Kurds.

Barzani's acceptance of the cease-fire had angered the hard-line leaders of the KDP because it had been concluded over their heads. In April 1964 when the KDP publicly condemned his position, Barzani elected a new party committee, sent his forces to attack the KDP leaders, and actually forced many of them across the border into Iran.[26] The result was a serious split in the Kurdish movement, which had long been simmering beneath the surface but which now broke into the open.

The rupture had a number of serious and long-lasting effects. It created a continuing source of internal dissension that weakened the Kurdish movement and provided a dissident group that was frequently used by the government against Barzani's forces. Nevertheless, the split had one great virtue, which proved an overwhelming advantage in the short run: It enabled Barzani to put together a tough and seasoned fighting force, capable of confronting the government in the Kurds' mountain strongholds and able to take a coherent stance in negotiations.

By 1965 Barzani had unquestionably emerged as the strongest force within the movement. He had consolidated his hold over a wide stretch of territory in the north and had set up his own de facto Kurdish administration, consisting of a revolutionary council of fifty members (an embryonic parliament) and a smaller executive bureau (an embryonic cabinet). Barzani's control did not extend to the large cities, but it was virtually complete in the countryside.

In April 1965 the government began an offensive by occupying Sulaimaniyya and moving north to Raniyya; for the next year the two sides were engaged once again in hostilities. In April and May of 1966 the tide turned against the central government. In the fierce battle of Handrin, the Kurds scored a significant victory, forcing the Iraqi army to retreat from a strategic mountain pass and thus preserving their de facto autonomy. This event, together with the presence of a new cabinet with a moderate, civilian prime minister, Bazzaz, finally provided the impetus for a pathbreaking accord. The Kurds now had a man in Bazzaz whom they could trust and whose politics—moderate, legal, and Iraqi oriented—matched that of Barzani. In two weeks of negotiation the two sides came to an agreement known as the June 1966 Accord. Announced on 29 June, it provided the Kurds with the most liberal recognition of their rights thus far.[27]

The June 1966 Accord was a twelve-point peace plan that provided for recognition of Kurdish nationality to be specified in a permanent constitution, allowed a high degree of decentralized administration in Kurdish areas, recognized Kurdish as an official language, provided for proportional representation of Kurds in the institutions of state, reintegrated Kurds into the army and civil service, and appropriated funds to rebuild the north.

Unfortunately, this settlement was never implemented due to unexepcted events. In April 1966 Arif had embarked on a speech-making tour of the country in an effort to develop popular support for the regime. On 13 April, shortly after takeoff, his helicopter crashed in Qurna near Basra, apparently because of poor visibility and a sudden sandstorm. All aboard were killed.

The Regime of Arif the Second, 1966–1968

Bazzaz temporarily assumed the office of president, and in accordance with the temporary constitution of 1964, the National Defense Council and the cabinet met to elect a new president. Three candidates were nominated. One was Bazzaz; the other two were military men. The military was unwilling to surrender power, and on 17 April 1966, Arif's brother,

Abd al-Rahman Arif, was elected president. He was a congenial man of relatively weak personality whom the ambitious army officers believed they could manipulate. Although Abd al-Salam Arif's short time at the helm had been marked by political twists and turns, he had a gift for keeping a coalition of forces together and a mastery of military politics, neither of which was shared by his brother.

The Return of Military Politics

Bazzaz continued in office a while longer, but without a strong figure to keep the military in tow, military factionalism soon reasserted itself. Finally, Bazzaz resigned. He was succeeded by Naji Talib, who was a Free Officer, a moderate Arab nationalist, and, more conveniently, a Shi'a. But Talib was unable to solve any basic problems. He reversed Bazzaz's stand on the Kurds, precipitating renewed but desultory fighting on that front. He was unable—or perhaps unwilling—to bring about sufficient unity with Egypt to satisfy the Nasserites, and he ran into economic difficulties over a pipeline dispute with Syria. By now, however, pressures for a change—particularly from military officers anxious for their turn in power—was too great for Talib, and on 10 May 1967 he, too, resigned. Arif himself became prime minister, and a coalition cabinet was formed of various elements. The Arif government had by now become little more than a collection of army officers balancing various interests and ethnic and sectarian groups. Like the new regimes before it, Arif's government had failed to develop political structures or parties to support it or to create a consensus or a framework for action.

This lackluster coalition was unable to survive a series of events that radicalized the political climate in the region and culminated in the 1967 war. One of these was the emergence in Syria of a new Ba'th regime under Salah Jadid that had come to power in February 1966. Virulently anti-imperialist and anti-Israeli, the new Syrian regime turned its attention to the Arab-Israeli situation, initiating a disastrous series of events that eventually led to the outbreak of war in 1967, which polarized the Arab world and dragged other Arab states into an unwanted conflict.

Iraq, saddled with a weak military government and involved in a renewed military engagement with the Kurds, could ill afford to withstand a regional climate increasingly swept by animus against the West and Israel. It is not surprising, therefore, that Iraq's participation in the 1967 war was minimal, although it sent troops to fight on the Jordanian front. Like other Arab regimes, however, the government in Baghdad had to face the responsibility for a humiliating defeat. This unquestionably added to the unpopularity of the military politicians and played a role in eventually toppling a regime already seen as weak and incompetent.

In the aftermath of the 1967 defeat, anti-Western sentiment was at a peak. This feeling was now focused on the remaining vestiges of Western influence inside the country—IPC. The government's oil policy had long been a bone of contention between those oriented toward a pragmatic policy of increasing Iraq's financial benefits, and along with them its ties to the West, and those more concerned with Iraq's controlling its own resources and maintaining a more nationalist and anti-Western foreign policy.

The New Oil Policy

When the first Arif regime came to power, it inherited the unsettled oil problems of the Qasim era. Public Law 80, passed by the Qasim regime, had expropriated almost all of IPC's concession area. However, the law had left open at least the possibility of IPC's future participation in the expropriated territory (in particular the rich southern Rumaila field), alone or in partnership with the government. From then on, IPC attempted to gain control over the Rumaila field, or at least to prevent its competitors from doing so.

In 1963 a new oil minister, Abd al-Aziz al-Wattari, a US-trained engineer and a moderate, took control.[28] In February 1964 Wattari established the Iraq National Oil Company (INOC) and drafted an agreement that provided for a joint venture between IPC and INOC in which IPC would be given a controlling interest. Most important of all, IPC was to have access to all-important producing areas of Iraq, including Rumaila and other areas of proven reserves.

Wattari's agreement produced a bitter reaction, especially from the Nasserite group led by Hasib and Jadir, and nothing was done about the agreement. However, when Tahir Yahya, a Nasserite supporter, returned as prime minister in July 1967, his cabinet passed Public Law 97, giving exclusive rights to INOC to develop the expropriated territory and prohibiting restoration to IPC of the Rumaila field. In April 1968 Adib al-Jadir announced that INOC would reject all outside offers to develop Rumaila and would proceed to develop the field itself.[29] With this statement, Iraq's future oil policy was clear. Those opposed to IPC and "imperialist monopolies" had won. Henceforth, the state would control the expropriated oil resources, although it would have to develop them in cooperation with outside firms. However, a cloud still hung over the development of the field, for IPC did not recognize any of these acts as legal and announced its intention of taking legal action against anyone purchasing oil from the field.

Notwithstanding this liability, INOC began discussions with outside interests on further development of its oil resources. In November 1967 the government signed a service contract with Entreprise de Recherches et d'Activités Pétrolières, the French state-owned oil company group, to develop areas outside Rumaila. In an even sharper departure from precedent, the government signed a letter of intent with the Soviets in December 1967 stipulating that the USSR would provide direct assistance to INOC for development of the Rumaila field. Though the regime was overthrown before much was accomplished, these steps signaled that Iraq was shifting away from a more pro-Western foreign policy and toward the socialist bloc. However, the dispute with the oil companies prevented exploitation of Iraq's rich resources and allowed competitors (Iran, Saudi Arabia, Abu Dhabi) to increase their market share at Iraq's expense.

The Coup of 17 July 1968

The pro-Western forces were not the only ones dissatisfied with the regime. Many believed that Arif, a weak leader, had allowed things to drift. Whereas more conservative forces were dissatisfied with the socialist trend, others wanted more decisive action in remedying the country's economic and social ills. Still others continued to want a more open political system and public elections.

Against this background of rising discontent, a number of groups and individuals were jockeying for position on the political scene toward the end of 1967. On the left were two Communist movements. One was the central committee of the ICP; the other was a splinter group, the central command that had broken away from the party in September 1967 under the leadership of Aziz al-Haj. This group was fighting the regime in a guerrilla action in the south of Iraq.[30] The National Democratic Party was active as well. Kamil al-Chadirchi had publicly asked for free elections and open political parties. On the right were a variety of groups, including the moderate nationalists previously gathered around Bazzaz but now in some disarray. Also arrayed against Abd al-Rahman Arif was a formidable group of military politicians, all determined to regain office. Most important among these were the military Ba'thists such as Bakr, Hardan al-Tikriti, and Salih Mahdi Ammash who had lost power in 1963 and hence had both political and personal reasons for desiring the fall of the regime. The Kurds and the Shi'a, both with active opposition movements, could be relied upon to support the overthrow of a government that was predominantly Arab Sunni. The Kurds in particular were dissatisfied with the government's failure to implement the 1966 agreement. Beneath these broader ideological groups were clusters of military cliques based largely on regional and tribal ties and aimed at protecting their personal interests and, where possible, enhancing their power.

The two different groups that, in an unlikely and uneasy coalition, would finally combine to carry out the coup were the Ba'th Party and a small contingent of disaffected supporters in Arif's inner circle. The latter group was led by Abd al-Razzaq al-Nayif and Ibrahim al-Da'ud. To a considerable extent these two men held the fate of the regime in their hands, Nayif by virtue of his position as deputy director of military intelligence, Da'ud as head of the Republican Guard, responsible for protecting the president and his entourage.

Whatever their motivations, the young officers didn't have the stature, the organization, or the public credibility to maintain a government after a coup. For this a political party or publicly recognized group with some grassroots support was needed. This was the role played by the Ba'th, which, independently of the officers, had been planning the overthrow of the Arif regime for some time.

The Ba'th Party of 1968

The Ba'th Party of 1968, however, was not the same party that had seized power in 1963. In the interim, the party had survived underground struggles, imprisonment of its leaders, and a bitter fight with the Syrian branch. In September 1966 it broke decisively with Syria and elected a new national command. As a result of these struggles, the leadership that emerged in 1968 was a more practical and seasoned group than that of 1963; it was also more ruthless, more conspiratorial, and, above all, more determined to seize power and this time to hold onto it. Using its well-known military figures in the public sphere and its clandestine organization underground, the party was ready by 1968 to make another bid for power. But it was still not strong enough to do so without help from non-Ba'thists in the military.

The Making of the Coup

Early in 1968, if not before, the senior military Ba'thists began probing the military for dissatisfied elements willing to participate in a coup. As Nayif was in a key military position, it is not surprising that he was drawn into such schemes. In April 1968 thirteen retired officers, including former ministers and prime ministers, submitted a memorandum to Arif calling for the removal of Tahir Yahya, the regime's strongman, as prime minister and demanding, among other things, a coalition government of revolutionary elements and establishment of a legislative assembly. However, Arif refused to meet their demands. When Yahya was asked to form a new cabinet in July, it became clear to Nayif and Da'ud that the time had come to act.[31]

On the eve of the coup, Nayif and Da'ud had reactivated contacts with Ahmad Hasan al-Bakr and a few of his chosen colleagues. In return for their participation in the coup, Nayif demanded to be made prime minister and Da'ud, minister of defense. Bakr was to be president. The young officers believed that by controlling these posts, they would control the government and the army.

In the early morning hours of 17 July, the coup began. Nayif and his forces occupied the Ministry of Defense, while Da'ud, with members of the Republican Guard, occupied the broadcasting station. The critical action took place at the Republican Palace, where one of the Ba'th accomplices opened the gates to the Ba'thists. In the middle of the night, Arif was summoned, and after a brief confrontation, he surrendered. He was sent off to England and eventually into exile in Istanbul and later Cairo. (He returned to Iraq in the 1990s.) Almost ten years to the day after the first revolution of 1958, the fourth major change of regime had been effected in Baghdad.

The Revolutionary Decade, Assessed

The revolutionary decade between 1958 and 1968 had a profound impact on Iraq at all levels—well beyond the political sphere. Beginning with Qasim and ending with the second Ba'th coup, the constant political instability ruptured the institutions of state, brought constant and dramatic shifts in policies and orientations, and eroded the country's still fragile national identity. Although some change had been long overdue under the monarchy, the revolutionary era was unable to create viable new policies or to institutionalize change. Parliament and political parties had been removed, considered by most of the new elites not as mechanisms of democracy but as vehicles of an outmoded class structure. In their stead, the military was made the main instrument of politics but in the process became hopelessly factionalized as it became permeated by the contending trends and interests within the larger society.

In the Arab nationalist period, 1963 to 1968, the direction of policy changed but not its methods or rule. Neither the short-lived Ba'th regime nor the more moderate Arif regime could bring stability or coherent policies. The brief attempt to restore a constitutional process and the rule of law under Bazzaz did not survive long enough to materialize. Meanwhile, the Kurdish rebellion deepened and became more intractable. Even the

Kurdish movement, however, ended up split into ideological and social factions. The Shi'a also used the period of upheaval and declining central control to develop a new religious and communal identity at odds with the secular nationalism of the central government and to strengthen Shi'i groups, like the Da'wa and the clergy. Meanwhile, the Ba'th and the Arab nationalists in charge of the government spent an inordinate amount of time and energy in failed attempts to emasculate Iraq's identity and merge with the Arab world.

Perhaps the greatest loss was a sense of civic responsibility, already weak to start with, on the part of governing elites, who fell back on patronage and patrimonialism. Politics became a plaything in the hands sometimes of inexperienced youth, more often of army officers with coercive force at their disposal. Governments came to be toppled almost at a whim. In the brutal struggle for power and political survival, serious contenders for power were driven underground, where they were even less likely to acquire the kind of experience necessary to govern Iraq.

The revolution of 1958 did put power in the hands of the new middle class and spread Iraq's wealth—and access to middle-class status—more widely. It also achieved a long-standing desire for greater independence from the West and a better balance in Iraq's relations with both Cold War blocs. But the period was so disruptive overall that these benefits could not take root or bring substantial advantages.

In this environment of political disruption, loyalty to family, kin, and locality gradually began to fill the political and social gap, especially under the Arifs. These ties did not yet supplant the modern institutions previously built up over four decades—the military, the bureaucracy, the educational establishment—but they became more important. Increasingly, Arab Sunnis came to exercise control over the country's levers of power and wealth. Meanwhile, at the periphery, in the Kurdish north and the Shi'i south, the country faced competing cultural identities, while its "center" pursued will-o'-the-wisp Arab unity schemes. The seeds of the totalitarianism established by the succeeding regime were sown in this watershed decade of revolutionary upheavals.

7

THE ERA OF BA'TH PARTY RULE, 1968-1979

The coup of 17 July 1968 shortly brought the Ba'th Party to full power and inaugurated another, more permanent change in the structure and orientation of government in Iraq. This time the key Ba'th leaders instituted the kind of regime they had failed to achieve in 1963, and they managed to hold on to power, by draconian means, for the remainder of the century.

The early years of the new regime were precarious. The party's base was thin, and Ahmad Hasan al-Bakr and Saddam Husain—the two key figures—had challenges at home and abroad. Their dominance was secured only by instituting a reign of terror—a series of trials, executions, and arrests reminiscent of the Stalin era—that became a hallmark of the regime.

By the mid-1970s, however, the party had stabilized its hold on power at the summit and was on its way to creating the foundations of a totalitarian state—establishing a mass-based, tightly controlled party; a ubiquitous secret police; a reorganized and Ba'thized military; and a burgeoning bureaucracy with virtually total control over society. Woven into this structure at the top were Tikriti family and clan ties. The regime's longevity was helped by a settlement of the Kurdish problem in 1975 that brought a period of stability in the north and by the oil price rise of 1973, which enabled Iraq, like other oil producers, to undertake a major development program. The party not only established a command economy, under the rubric of socialism, but also undertook an industrial program—including extensive weapons development—and provided widespread health, education, and social benefits that went well beyond those of any previous regime. These measures enabled the regime to allay discontent and establish greater control over society. By the late 1970s, Iraq had begun to emerge from its earlier regional and international isolation. Thanks to the economic, social, and political developments just mentioned, Iraq also began to exercise a major influence on the Middle Eastern scene and even in the nonaligned movement, where it expected to play a leading role in the future.

Consolidation of Power, 1968–1973

Within two weeks of the 17 July coup, the Ba'th executed a series of maneuvers that completely removed Abd al-Razzaq al-Nayif, Ibrahim al-Da'ud, and their supporters from power and consolidated its position on the newly formed Revolutionary Command Council (RCC), the new fulcrum of power. On 30 July, President Bakr became prime minister and commander in chief of the armed forces; Hardan al-Tikriti was made minister of defense. Husain was elevated to the second most important post in the RCC, that of Bakr's deputy.

Several features of this new government deserve mention. First, the RCC was completely military. Second, it was dominated by Tikritis; three of the five members of the RCC were Tikritis, and Hammad Shihab and Husain were both related to Bakr. Third, the government was now completely dominated by the Ba'th. The new RCC now included only five members, all Ba'th or Ba'thist supporters.[1] The new leaders had put into operation one key lesson from 1963—not to share power with non-Ba'thists.

Despite these steps, however, the party's position was still precarious. According to the Ba'th's own estimates, it had no more than 5,000 members.[2] Its support in the military was weak thanks in part to constant purges since 1958. The party faced several tasks if it were to retain power and avoid a repetition of its fate in 1963. It had to consolidate its hold over the apparatus of state, it had to avoid disruptive divisions among its leadership, and it had to neutralize—and then remove—the military from decisionmaking positions. Moreover, it had to undertake these tasks at a time when the regime was faced with domestic pressures (from the Kurds) and challenges from abroad (Iran). This difficult and delicate task was accomplished, largely by Husain, between 1968 and 1973.

The consolidation process began in the military. Early on, officers of questionable loyalty were replaced by Ba'thists or Ba'th sympathizers. At the same time, many senior civil servants, including most directors-general, were also replaced by Ba'thists.

The Conspiracy Trials

The most important and dramatic mechanism for achieving Ba'th dominance was a series of trials that not only eliminated real or potential opponents but also cowed the political classes by introducing a reign of terror. The convictions demonstrated the ruthlessness of the regime and made clear that no attempt to overthrow Ba'th rule would be tolerated.

The first to be arrested were members of the previous government. They were charged with corruption and jailed. However, as fellow Arab nationalists and socialists, they were dealt with leniently. No charges were proved, and all were eventually released.

Far more important, pro-Western elements were targeted. On 10 November 1968 Nasir al-Hani, a former foreign minister, was murdered and a number of Iraqi representatives of Western firms were arrested. Then came the arrest of several men accused of spying for Israel and supplying information to Central Treaty Organization countries, especially Iran and the United States.[3] The arrested men included a number of Jews as well as former ministers, including Abd al-Rahman al-Bazzaz. A number of the accused were tried by secret military court, and fourteen were executed. Amid international outcry, they were hanged publicly in Baghdad's main square, where they were viewed at government urging by over half a million people. More trials and executions followed in 1969. Bazzaz did not confess and was given a prison sentence.[4]

No sooner had these trials ended than the regime faced a plot by just the right-wing pro-Western elements it most feared, one apparently supported by Iran and the exiled Nayif. In January 1970 thirty-seven men and women were executed on charges of attempting to overthrow the government and a death sentence was passed in absentia on Nayif. In the same month, Iraq expelled the Iranian ambassador, closed Iranian consulates, and undertook wholesale deportation of Persians and Iraqis of Persian origin, making the point that the regime would tolerate no domestic interference from Iran.

Nor did the Ba'th spare the Communists. When the Iraq Communist Party (ICP) took a position of opposition in the spring of 1970, the regime began arresting its members, and by June 1970 several hundred Communists were in jail.

While the party was moving to eliminate or neutralize threats to its control, it also acted to broaden and institutionalize its power within the state. The first step in this direction was taken on 9 November 1969, when the five-member Revolutionary Command Council was enlarged to fifteen. All those appointed were civilians and Ba'thists. Saddam Husain became vice chairman of the RCC, officially becoming the second most important figure in the regime after Bakr.[5]

The Interim Constitution

The next step came in July 1970 with the formal publication of a new constitution. It defined Iraq as a people's democratic republic aimed at achieving a united Arab state and a socialist system. It claimed that Iraq was formed of two principal nationalities, Arab and Kurd, with recognition of Kurdish national rights. However, a provision aimed at the Kurds declared that no part of Iraq could be given up. Islam was declared to be the state religion, but freedom of religion and of religious practices was guaranteed.

The state was given the authority to plan, direct, and guide the national economy. State ownership of natural resources and the principal instruments of production were stipulated, but private ownership was guaranteed, with some limitations placed on ownership of agricultural land. Free education up to the university level and free medical care were guaranteed. Work was not only guaranteed as a right but was also required.

The constitution also granted dominant power to the RCC, which had the authority to promulgate laws and regulations, to deal with defense and security, to declare war and conclude peace, and to approve the budget. The president, as the executive of the RCC, was made commander in chief of the armed forces and chief executive of the state. He was given the power to appoint, promote, and dismiss judiciary, civil, and military personnel. Article 38 stipulated that newly elected members of the RCC had to be members of the Regional Command, thus enshrining the principle of the one-party state. The constitution put into practice another lesson from 1963—firm party control over the executive and legislative organs of state.

Neutralizing the Military

The next task of the party—preventing leadership divisions—proved more difficult. Both Bakr and Husain were anxious to reduce military influence in politics and to prevent the military Ba'thists from taking over the government once again. The enlargement of the RCC in 1969, which reduced the military component to a little more than a third and added strong civilian party figures, was a first step in this direction.

The next step was the removal of the two key military figures in the regime, Hardan al-Tikriti and Salih Mahdi Ammash, both of whom had ambitions and the constituencies in the party and the military to achieve them. Although there is little doubt that Bakr, who had an obsessive (and justified) fear of coups, desired the removal of both military rivals, it was a task he willingly left to Saddam Husain and his growing security apparatus. In October 1970 Hardan al-Tikriti was relieved of all his posts, and in March 1971 he was assassinated in Kuwait amid rumors that he had been planning a coup. Next Ammash was dropped from the RCC in September 1971 and never again played an important role in Iraqi politics. These moves neutralized the military. Remarkably, by 1974 Bakr was the only former army officer left in a key post.

Equally significant was the gradual removal from the party command and the RCC of a number of Ba'th civilians with long-standing party credentials.[6] Again, this was largely the work of Husain in an attempt to remove any future rivals to himself or to Bakr.

In June 1973 Nazim Kzar, hand-picked head of the party's security system, attempted a coup that very nearly succeeded in ending Bakr's regime. Kzar, a Shi'a who had worked his way up the party ladder, resented the growing monopoly of power by Sunnis and Tikritis. The plot called for the assassination of Bakr at the Baghdad airport on his return from a trip. The plan misfired when Bakr's plane was late. Pursued by loyal Iraqi forces, Kzar fled toward the Iranian border, where he was intercepted and captured.

Ironically, the Kzar episode strengthened the hold of the Tikritis on the security system, as Saddam Husain increasingly turned to his relatives to fill sensitive security posts. The removal of so many top party figures paved the way for the unquestioned domination of two men— Bakr and Husain. Their ability to work together would keep the party in power for decades.

Bakr and Husain

From the first, the relationship between Bakr and Husain was complementary. Bakr, the only senior politician in the regime who had previously held high office, conferred on the party a certain legitimacy. More importantly, he brought support from the army. Bakr provided the regime with a paternal face, projecting himself as a "father figure" who could reassure a public increasingly shocked by brutal purges and public executions. But Bakr also had his weaknesses, including a personal dislike of confrontation. He was thus content to leave the operational details of removing his rivals to someone willing and able to undertake the task.

In Saddam Husain he found the perfect counterpart.[7] Saddam was born into a poor, illiterate peasant family, and his early upbringing was harsh. The environment in his village, Auja, was one in which ties of kin and clan, as well as traditional bedouin values of honor, courage, and even revenge predominated, explaining his later reliance on tribal practices and ideas. His father died before he was born, and his stepfather reputedly abused him. At the age of ten, Husain went to Tikrit to live with his uncle, Khairallah Talfah, previously imprisoned for participation in the Rashid Ali movement, who passed his strong nationalist and anti-British feelings on to Saddam. While attending high school, Saddam plunged into nationalist, anti-regime activities and in 1957 joined the Ba'th Party. He also had an early history of problems with the law, landing in jail with his uncle for six months for a political murder, never proved. These activities contributed to his reputation as a "tough" and as a man to be feared.

After the failed 1959 assassination attempt on Qasim, Husain took refuge in Cairo until 1963, where he finished high school; this is the only lengthy foreign exposure he ever had. On his return to Baghdad in 1963 he married his cousin, Sajida Talfah, and they subsequently had five children—two boys, Udayy and Qusayy, and three girls, Raghad, Rana, and Hala. The marriage to a member of the Talfah family was a step up socially within his clan, and he used the ties and the period to cement ties of loyalty to Bakr, then prime minister. After the collapse of the Ba'th government in 1963, Husain spent several years in prison. He escaped in 1966 and then worked underground to establish the party's apparatus. According to many, he was in charge of the special security forces, which became his forte. It is these underground conspiratorial activities that were most influential in shaping Husain's outlook and mentality. His secretiveness, his suspiciousness, and his distrust of outsiders sprang from years of being hunted—and hunting others—and from his own considerable talents in organizing conspiracy.

In 1968 Husain was a man too young to constitute a challenge to Bakr and with no military links. Although Husain began very early to gather the threads of power into his hands, he was careful not to challenge Bakr's leadership. Indeed, Husain's main avenue of advancement in the party—and the state—was through Bakr and his kinship relationship. Husain's organizational ability, ruthlessness, willingness to take risks, and, above all, instincts for survival were to prove invaluable for Bakr and the party in this early period of challenge. Both men were non-ideological. But Husain was the better organizer and political tactician, able to build mass institutions, to borrow and use the socialist ideology of the left to create a broader constituency for the party, and to tackle tough issues like the Kurds and the nationalization of oil. He appeared as the young, dynamic modernizer.

By 1969 Saddam Husain was clearly a moving force behind the scenes. But in these early years, when Saddam was still in his thirties, he could not do without Bakr's support and patronage. In the last analysis, however, Bakr needed him, and Saddam began gradually to overshadow his patron.

Ba'th Foreign Policy: The Radical Phase, 1969–1973

Not surprisingly, the first years of the Ba'th regime were turbulent externally as well as internally, with foreign and domestic problems constantly intertwined. The radical, new regime, vulnerable at home as it purged its ranks and attempted to stabilize its power, adopted hostile rhetoric against its foreign adversaries—chiefly Iran, Israel, and the United States, which it saw in collusion against it. The rhetoric was designed in part to generate domestic support, or at least to distract attention from some of the severe measures it was taking at home, but it also reflected the regime's perception, not entirely unjustified, that it was isolated internationally and threatened by neighbors anxious to exploit its fragile position at home.

Ba'th accession to power coincided with dramatic changes in the regional environment that worked to its disadvantage. On the Western front, Iraq had to deal with the aftermath of the Arab defeat by Israel in the 1967 war. Iraq's diplomatic relations with the United States, broken during the war, were not restored, cutting it off from the major Western influence in the region. At the same time, Iraq rejected UN Resolution 242, calling for Israeli withdrawal from Arab territory in exchange for peace. Instead, it called for a continuation of "armed struggle."

Iraq was isolated on other fronts as well. Interactions with the rival Syrian regime remained contentious and antagonistic even after the more pragmatic Hafiz al-Asad replaced the radical Salah Jadid regime in 1970. Relations with Egypt also cooled after Nasser accepted the peace plan advanced by the US secretary of state, which called for a negotiated settlement with Israel. By 1970 Egypt and Iraq were engaged in heated press attacks.

Trouble in the Gulf

In the Gulf, Iraq also faced an entirely new situation. Britain's announcement in 1969 of its intended withdrawal from the Gulf (accomplished in 1971) was followed by the emergence of new and relatively weak states there—Bahrain, Qatar, and the federated United Arab Emirates (UAE). In March 1969 the United States announced the "Nixon Doctrine," which offered to furnish support to any regional power able to defend security in the region. Iran stepped forward. Not long after, the flow of US arms to Iran began. Between 1970 and 1977 Iran's defense budget rose by 1,100 percent, while its arms imports increased from $264 million in 1970 to $2.6 billion in 1977.[8] Saudi Arabia was soon added as the second Gulf "pillar" of US policy and also supported with military training and some arms. Gradually, the US military presence expanded in and around the Gulf—in Diego Garcia, Oman, and Bahrain. In time, Iraq came to feel surrounded, although it established diplomatic relations with the new Gulf states.

Iraq's most serious difficulty, however, came from Iran. Confrontation began over the perennial problem of the Shatt al-Arab. In February 1969 Iran announced that Iraq had not fulfilled its obligations under the 1937 treaty and demanded that the boundary between the two countries be drawn along the *thalweg*, the deepwater channel in the middle of the river. Iraq refused. On 19 April the shah publicly abrogated the treaty, and Iran proceeded to pilot its own ships through the Shatt without paying dues to Iraq. The Iraqi reaction was swift. A number of Iranians were expelled from Iraq, a propaganda war ensued, and Iraq began to aid dissidents against the shah's regime. Iran responded with support to Kurdish dissidents.

Iran was not the only Gulf country disturbed by Iraq's radical stance. Saudi Arabia and the conservative Gulf shaikhdoms opposed Iraq's support for South Yemen, its ties to left-wing elements in North Yemen, and its aid to the Popular Front for the Liberation of the Occupied Arabian

Gulf, a Marxist organization dedicated to the overthrow of the conservative regimes in the emirates. The most serious confrontation was with Kuwait; it centered on the two Kuwaiti islands of Warba and Bubiyan, which had assumed increased significance to Iraq with the development of its southern oil fields and its plans to expand the port of Umm Qasr. Iraq demanded that the two islands be transferred or leased to it. When negotiations proved fruitless, Iraq decided to apply force. On 20 March 1973 Iraqi troops attacked Samita, a border post in the northeast corner of Kuwait. Saudi Arabia immediately came to Kuwait's aid and, together with the Arab League, secured Iraq's withdrawal from the post but not from other positions inside Kuwait.[9]

Relations with the USSR

Iraq's isolation, the Iranian threat, and domestic instability, especially a renewal of the Kurdish rebellion in the north, caused the regime to turn to the Soviet bloc as a counterweight to these forces. The USSR provided essential help in developing the Rumaila field, the first significant entry of the Soviet Union into the production of Gulf petroleum.

The high tide of Soviet-Iraqi cooperation came with the conclusion of the Iraqi-Soviet Friendship Treaty of 1972. The accord called for cooperation in the military, political, and economic spheres and required regular consultations on international affairs affecting both parties. On the Soviet side this meant continued supplies of military equipment and training at a high level. On the Iraqi side it meant Soviet access to Iraqi ports and airports, but no base facilities. But the relationship soon cooled. Iraq was irked by the Soviets' sale of oil to Europe at much higher prices than it paid and at the poor quality of the Soviet goods it received in exchange. There was little the Ba'th could do, however, to break its dependence on Soviet arms.

The One-Party State

Saddam Husain had, by now, eliminated key military and civilian competition and was ready to lay out, publicly, the new foundations of party and state. To this end, the party called a regional congress, which met from 8 to 12 January 1974. Organized by Saddam Husain, the congress made clear that its aim was a one-party state with centralized control over all key institutions.

First, the congress elected a new, thirteen-member Regional Command, adding eight new members to the previous five.[10] In November 1974 eight new ministers were appointed, five of whom were new command members. Although ministerial reshuffles occurred with regularity thereafter, the Ba'th share of ministerial posts seldom fell below two-thirds, and key posts were always occupied by Regional Command members. In September 1977 all Regional Command members were appointed members of the Revolutionary Command Council, making these two bodies indistinguishable. Through the overlap of personnel on three essential bodies—the Regional Command of the party, the RCC, and the Council of Ministers—the party could control policy formation, policy legislation, and policy execution.

Party Structure

Buttressing this centralization of power at the top was a grassroots party organization that had taken full shape by 1974.[11] The smallest unit in this organization was the party cell or circle (*khaliyya*), composed of between three and seven members. Cells usually functioned at the neighborhood level, where they met to discuss and carry out party directives. Next on the hierarchical ladder was the party division (*firqa*), made up of several cells and operating in small urban quarters or villages. Professional and occupational units similar to the divisions were also located in offices, factories, schools, and other organizations. Honeycombing the bureaucracy and the military, these units functioned as the party's eyes and ears. Above the division was the section (*shu'ba*), composed of two to five divisions. A section usually had jurisdiction over a territory the size of a large city quarter or county. A branch (*far'*), composed of at least two sections, operated at the provincial level. The Regional Command, elected by the party's congress, operated at the national level. Over and above the Regional Command was the National Command, headed by a secretary-general, Michel Aflaq, and including the party's representatives from other Arab countries as well as Iraqis. While the Regional Command developed the ideological agenda for Iraq, the National Command connected the Iraqi party to its friends and allies in other Arab countries.

Careful attention was paid to the recruitment and indoctrination of party members. Potential recruits were known as party "friends" and "supporters" but technically were not inside party ranks. Such candidates were required to undergo a long probationary period, taking anywhere from five to eight years, during which they would perform party tasks under careful supervision and attend party seminars and courses, before admission to the party. The party grew rapidly in this period, at least at the lower levels. In 1968 party membership may only have been a few hundred. By 1976 there were about 10,000 full members and some 500,000 supporters. By the early 1980s, according to official party sources, full members numbered 25,000; followers, about 1.5 million.[12]

Attached to this structure was a militia or popular army, composed mainly of new party recruits. Initially, its main function was to help defend the party in time of need, to keep order in the neighborhoods, and to give military training to members.

The Security System and the Military

The party was not the only mechanism controlling the state and its citizens, although it was the most visible. Equally important was the security apparatus, which not only grew in the decade after 1968 but also evolved into an elaborate network of institutions watching over one another and intertwined with all state institutions. These were increasingly brought under the control of Saddam Husain, who made security his special province. The history and development of these security organs, some of which predate the 1968 coup, is understandably murky, but by the end of the 1970s they included the Amn al-Amm (Public Security Directorate), the "official" government organization responsible for criminal investigation, traditionally attached to the Ministry of Interior; the Mukhabarat al-Amma (General Intelligence Service), in charge of watching party as well as nonparty political activities at home and abroad; Istikhbarat Askariyya (Military Intelligence), responsible for data on foreign military threats as well as the loyalty of Iraq's officer corps; and the party's Military Bureau, in charge of security in the military. By 1980 still another organization, the Maktab al-Amn al-Qaumi (Bureau of National Security), oversaw the Public Security Directorate, the Mukhabarat, and Military Intelligence officers. Overlapping and compartmentalized, intelligence units not only watched citizens but each other.

The military was also brought under party control. Ba'th cells in the military oversaw recruitment and indoctrination. By the mid-1970s the officer corps was rapidly being Ba'thized, and in July 1978 a decree made any non-Ba'thist political activity in the military punishable by death, essentially transforming the military into an arm of the party.

The party also put special emphasis on education. The public school curriculum, especially in the humanities and social studies, was rewritten, and the party began to restrict admittance to a number of colleges.

The party not only developed and controlled the coercive organs of state but also took over an existing network of popular organizations and used them to generate grassroots support. Some, like the associations for lawyers, engineers, and teachers, were old and well established; others, such as the General Federation of Peasants Associations, the General Federation of Workers Unions, and the Women's Association, had been created after the revolution of 1958. All were encouraged and dominated by the Ba'th.

The Emergence of Personal Rule

While this party institutionalization was under way, an important countertrend was also at work: a shift in the balance of power from Bakr to Husain. By the mid-1970s, Bakr had begun to retire from an active political role. Over time, Husain's office became the central focus of power and decisionmaking in Iraq; Bakr's position became more ceremonial. By 1977 the party bureaus and ministers who, according to the constitution, should have reported to Bakr reported to Husain. Meanwhile, Husain himself became less accessible. The RCC and Regional Command were used less for collective discussions of policy than as instruments to ratify decisions already taken by Husain and a close group of his followers.

As power gravitated to Husain's hands, he exercised it in an increasingly paternalistic fashion. Several hours a week he had an open phone line to receive public complaints, often dealt with summarily on a personal basis. Meanwhile, a cult of personality—even a mythology—grew up around him. The press constantly displayed his picture; his virtues became part of party legend. Newborn babies were named after him, and young party members emulated his walk, his dress, and even his manner of speech.

The Kin and Clan Network

Buttressing Husain's party position and his personal rule was a network of kin and clan relations that was interlaced with and often cut across party lines. At the core of this network was the family relationship between Ahmad Hasan al-Bakr, Saddam Husain, and Adnan Khairallah Talfah. In 1977 Talfah, Saddam's cousin and brother-in-law, was elected to the Regional Command of the party, appointed to the RCC, and made minister of defense to keep an eye on the military. From the mid-1970s on, Husain's half-brothers Barzan, Saba'wi, and Watban Ibrahim assumed increasingly important posts in the security system. From this inner circle, family ties extended outward to include more distant kin in positions of influence. The kinship network, drawn almost wholly from Saddam's tribe, the Albu Nasir of Tikrit, allowed Saddam to bypass the party and the military and keep personal control over these institutions.[13] In this parallel but traditional system of recruitment, loyalty was based on family and clan ties rather than on institutions or ideology.

Relations with the Kurds

When the Ba'th came to power in 1968, it inherited the Kurdish situation left over from the Arif era. The promising settlement concluded by Bazzaz in 1966 had fallen into abeyance. Although a desultory cease-fire

had been maintained, Mustafa Barzani had begun to consolidate his relations with Iran and had established contact with Israel, factors that did
not augur well for a solution, given the intense Arab nationalism of the
Ba'th.[14] By 1968 he had acquired antiaircraft weapons and field artillery.
At the same time, intense factionalism continued within the Kurdish
movement between the followers of Ibrahim Ahmad and Jalal Talabani,
on the one hand, and those of Barzani on the other; the latter now controlled the Kurdistan Democratic Party (KDP).

The new Iraqi regime initially committed itself to implementing the
1966 agreement and offered cabinet seats to representatives of both Kurdish factions. But Barzani was doubtful of Ba'th intentions and refused to
accept any positions in the cabinet. The Ahmad-Talabani faction, however, had no such qualms and, to bolster their position, accepted the offer.
Before long the government was openly supporting this group, and skirmishes between the Kurdish factions took place once again. Barzani now
turned against the government, attacking some of the Iraq Petroleum
Company (IPC) installations in Kirkuk. Four divisions of the Iraqi army
were now sent north, and full-scale war ensued once more. Iran was soon
heavily embroiled in the conflict. By 1969 Barzani was receiving extensive
aid from Iran, and Iranian units were even fighting in Iraqi territory. This
aid helped turn the tide in Barzani's favor. Recognizing the stalemate, the
government reluctantly decided to negotiate with him.

In fact, both sides had good reasons to come to terms. Barzani needed
a respite in the fighting to deal with his opponents, who had gained some
strength in the interim. As a quid pro quo, he insisted that the government abandon the Ahmad-Talabani faction and disarm the Fursan (progovernment Kurdish militia), consisting mainly of his tribal enemies.[15]

The regime had even stronger motives for concluding an agreement.
In 1969 Saddam Husain was still preoccupied with consolidating control over the military wing of the party. He did not want a war that
would strengthen the military faction, as had happened in 1963. Even
more important was government concern over the shah's aid to Barzani
in the midst of Iraq's intense confrontation with Iran over the Shatt. Better, the government reasoned, to grant some concessions to the Kurds on
autonomy than to lose control of the Kurdish situation to Iran.

The March 1970 Agreement

On 11 March 1970 an agreement was concluded with Barzani. It provided for Kurdish autonomy (the first official use of the word),[16] and it guaranteed proportional representation of Kurds within a future legislative body, the appointment of a Kurdish vice president at the national level, the expenditure of an equitable amount of oil revenue in the autonomous region, and the recognition of both Kurdish and Arabic as official languages in Kurdish territory. For his part, Barzani agreed to turn over the heavy weapons of his fighting force, the *peshmerga*, and integrate that force into the Iraqi army.

Both sides doubted the sincerity of the other. The agreement would only come into effect in four years, after a census had determined areas in which Kurds had a majority. Given these mutual misgivings, it is not surprising that the agreement was to prove only temporary. In fact, the main loser, as usual, was the dissident Ahmad-Talabani faction, which had lost support from the government as well as the Barzani Kurds.

Breakdown of the Agreement

Between 1970 and 1974 the situation between the government and the Kurds gradually deteriorated. In July 1970 the KDP nominated its secretary-general, Muhammad Habib Karim, as the Kurdish vice president, but he was rejected by the Ba'th because of his Persian background. Worse, two assassination attempts instigated by Saddam were made on Barzani, in 1971 and 1972.[17] Meanwhile, the government undertook an Arabization program in Mosul and Kirkuk, deporting some 45,000 *faili* (Shi'i) Kurds to Iran and replacing them with Arabs.

Barzani did not keep his part of the bargain, either. He refused to close the border with Iran, continued to import arms, and in 1971 appealed directly to the United States for aid. President Richard Nixon directed the CIA to surreptitiously advance Barzani $16 million in aid. The shah followed with far more massive support.[18] Barzani also resumed his contacts with Israel and received some aid from this source as well. With this infusion of support, he saw no reason to compromise with Baghdad.

By 1974 the split between the Ba'th and Barzani was virtually complete. On 9 March, the Ba'th gave the Kurds two days to accept the government's own autonomy plan. The Kurds rejected the plan and on 11 March, the Ba'th put its plan into effect. By April the war had resumed.

The 1974–1975 War

At first, things went well for the government, and the troops demonstrated better fighting capacity than previously. By May government troops had occupied the great plains area of Kurdistan and consolidated their position in the cities of Kirkuk, Arbil, and Sulaimaniyya. By fall they had taken Rawanduz and reached Qal'at Diza. In response, Iran augmented its military aid, furnishing the Kurds with antitank missiles and artillery and intervening directly in Iraqi territory. Syria, also at odds with Iraq, likewise aided the Kurds. These activities slowed down the Iraqi offensive, and by spring of 1975 a stalemate had been reached. It was during this stalemate, with no further progress by the Iraqi army but with Iran becoming directly and dangerously involved, that talk of an agreement between Iraq and Iran, at the expense of the Kurds, began to surface.

The 1975 Agreement

By 1975 both Iran and Iraq had good reasons for seeking a solution. The Iraqi army had done better than expected on the ground, but Iranian intervention had made it clear that the Iraqi regime could not, on its own, win the military victory it needed to impose its own solution. Moreover, further escalation might well mean full-scale war with Iran, which Iraq could not win. More importantly, Saddam Husain had staked his future on solving the Kurdish problem and could not risk failure.

On the Iranian side, the shah, although he wished to weaken the Baghdad government, did not want the rebellion to spill across his borders, nor was he ready to move to the level of open war with Iraq. Moreover, he was concerned that the Soviets were providing Iraq with sophisticated weaponry, including MiG-23s. In return for a cessation of aid to the Kurds, the shah wanted explicit recognition of Iran's boundary claims on the Shatt al-Arab. On 6 March the two sides finally negotiated an agreement.

The agreement did, in fact, accomplish most of the shah's goals. The official clauses specified that the frontier between Iran and Iraq would be governed by the 1913–1914 Constantinople Protocol but that the demarcation line on the Shatt would be the *thalweg*. In return, both parties agreed to exercise strict control over their frontiers to prevent subversive infiltration, in effect ending Iranian support for the Kurds. The Iraqis also renounced any Arab claims to the Arab-speaking province of Khuzistan, as well as to the islands at the foot of the Gulf.

For the Kurds supporting Barzani, the 1975 settlement was little short of a disaster. Within hours of its signing, the Iranians began to haul away their military equipment. On 7 March the Iraqi army moved into the remaining areas of the north, and on 2 April it reached the border, sealed off the area, and proclaimed the end of the revolt. For his part, Barzani, faced with the cease-fire, decided to give up the fight and fled to Iran, taking most of his *peshmerga* with him. (He died of cancer in Georgetown Hospital in 1979.) Under an amnesty plan, about 70 percent of his *peshmerga* eventually gave themselves up to the Iraqis. Some remained in the hills of Kurdistan to fight again, and about 30,000 went across the border to Iran to join the Kurdish civilian refugees settled there. The result of the agreement was to leave the Kurdish national movement in a state of complete disarray, with its leadership defeated and in exile.

The Aftermath of the Agreement

On 11 March 1974 the Ba'th regime began implementing its own autonomy plan, which stated that Kurdistan was to be autonomous, although forming an integral part of Iraq; that the administrative capital was to be Arbil; and that the region was to be governed by an elected legislative council and an executive council to be elected by a majority vote of the legislative council. The Baghdad government could dismiss the president of the executive council and dissolve the assembly. The autonomous territory excluded Kirkuk and the districts of Sinjar and Khanaqin.

In addition to implementing a degree of Kurdish autonomy, the government took steps on the ground to change fundamentally the political and social dynamics in the north. On the positive side, the Ba'th moved to settle the refugee question. By the end of 1976, all but 30,000 refugees from Iran had been repatriated. The government also moved forcefully to develop the north economically, aided by increased oil revenues. Much of this expenditure went into industrial projects, schools, hospitals, and tourist sites, as well as roads and communications networks, which improved the government's capacity to control the area. Textile, carpet, canning, and tobacco factories were built; student enrollment increased fourfold from 112,000 to 332,000. These actions did bring a measure of prosperity to the north and, in some areas, a new consumer-oriented society; some Kurds became rich, while a new middle class acquired a taste for stability and a higher standard of living.

The government also introduced land reform into the north in a more serious way. About 2.7 million dunams were distributed among Kurds; about four hundred cooperative societies were formed to replace the landlords.[19] While these measures weakened the *agha* class, especially those supporting Barzani, the government also revived the Fursan, the *agha*-led military forces willing to support the government. These grew in size, along with subsidies and favors for those tribal leaders willing to stand with the government.

However, these positive achievements were accompanied by drastic steps taken to assure that no further organized rebellion would take place. These measures focused on large-scale relocation of Kurds as well as continued Arabization of Kurdish areas. By 1976 the Iraqi government had razed all Kurdish villages along an eight-hundred-mile border with Turkey and Iran ranging from five to fifteen miles deep. Some 1,400 villages had been razed by 1978 and some 600,000 villagers displaced.[20] Displaced Kurds were sent to newly constructed collective settlements near major towns, a policy bitterly protested by Kurds. In mixed Kurdish, Arab, and Turkman provinces such as Sinjar, Khanaqin, and Kirkuk, the Kurdish population was reduced and additional Arabs were introduced. In these areas Kurdish was not permitted as the primary language of instruction. The carrot-and-stick approach to the Kurdish area did bring a measure of quiet to the north, especially after 1975, and enabled the government to turn its attention to economic and social development.

The Nationalization of Oil

Despite its socialist aims, the Ba'th did not initially move toward nationalization of oil. Rather, it allowed the Entreprise de Recherche et d'Activités Pétrolières agreement and other arrangements made by the Arif regime to continue in force. The regime undertook measures to exploit the southern fields previously expropriated by Qasim and now under government control. In 1969 new contracts were signed with the Soviet Union to drill in the northern Rumaila field and US and West Germany firms helped construct a new, off-shore terminal, Mina-l-Bakr (now the Al Basra Oil Terminal). Development of the southern fields, however, did not solve the government's continuing problems with IPC, including the company's refusal to recognize Public Law 80. In addition, there was underlying bitterness in Iraq over low levels of production from the Kirkuk fields in the face of increased production everywhere else in the Gulf. Iraq's share of Gulf production fell from 20 percent in 1960 to 10 percent in 1974, while that of Iran, Saudi Arabia, and even Abu Dhabi rose. Much of this imbalance, of course, was due to the lingering dispute with IPC.

Between March and May 1972 IPC dropped production from the Kirkuk field about 44 percent, an action that brought home to Iraq its dependence on the foreign oil company. The Iraqis saw the move as a means of forcing concessions from them on other points of disagreement. When IPC failed to restore production, events then moved to a rapid conclusion. On 1 June 1972 Public Law 69 nationalized IPC. Despite dire predictions of what might befall Iraq after nationalization, in February 1973 a final settlement was reached with IPC clearing the decks of all prior disputes and removing legal actions against purchases of Iraqi oil. In October 1973, all foreign oil companies were put in Iraq's hands.

The Ba'th had finally accomplished a major aim of all revolutionary regimes since 1958. In the short term, nationalization had some negative effects. It disrupted oil production and development programs and

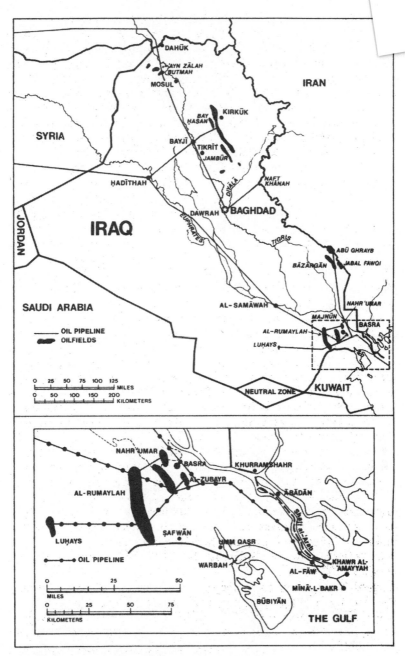

FIGURE 7.1 Oil Fields, Pipelines, and Ports, 1979

helped isolate the regime from the West. However, in the longer term, nationalization had significant benefits. It gave the government complete control over its oil production and sales and paved the way for the regime to profit fully from the oil price rise about to shower bounty on the Gulf producers. Iraq quickly turned to expanding oil production and transport facilities as well as to further exploration. It doubled the pipeline from Kirkuk through Turkey to the Mediterranean and in 1975 completed the so-called strategic pipeline from Haditha south to Rumaila and then to Faw, designed to take Kirkuk oil south to the Gulf and Rumaila oil north to the Mediterranean, thus freeing it from Syrian interference. By 1980 Iraq had doubled production and increased recoverable reserves fourfold.

Iraq's nationalization of oil coincided with the unprecedented oil price rise initiated by the Arab oil embargo of 1973. By 1974 oil prices had quadrupled, and they continually rose throughout the decade, with a second boost in 1979 after the Iranian revolution. This price rise, together with expanded production, provided a flood of wealth in Iraq. Iraq's oil revenues increased from $575 million in 1972 to $26 billion in 1980.[21] This bounty produced an era of unprecedented prosperity, as well as a new economic reality.

Even though nationalization gave Iraq greater economic independence from Western oil companies, Iraq's domestic economy became increasingly dependent on oil revenues and therefore on international oil markets. By 1979 oil production constituted almost 63 percent of Iraq's gross domestic product (GDP) (see Table 7.1).[22] The dramatic increase in income also turned Iraq into a consumer, instead of a producer, society. Oil displaced the productive sectors as the chief source of national income. The government used the new income to spread services, especially health and education, to wide sections of the population, while the population became increasingly accustomed to state-supplied benefits.

Economic Development

Increased revenue provided a brief period of prosperity unmatched in Iraq's previous history. It also enabled the Ba'th regime, which was now

TABLE 7.1 Oil as a Percentage of Iraq's Gross Domestic Product, 1960–1979
(in current ID millions)

	Value in ID millions	% of GDP
1960	209.7	37.1
1965	285.9	33.0
1970	370.5	30.9
1975	2,287.7	57.6
1979	5,686.5	62.7

SOURCE: World Bank, *World Tables,* 3rd ed., vol. 1: *Economic Data* (Baltimore, MD: Johns Hopkins University Press, 1983), pp. 90–91.

fully in control of the government and the country, to make some impressive gains in economic development, encompassed in three interrelated goals set out by the party. The first, adopted under the slogan of a "socialist" economy, was state ownership of national resources and state control over most of the economy. The second was a more broad-based distribution of wealth and services designed to favor the lower and lower middle classes from which most of the leadership was drawn. The aim was greater social justice and a welfare state. The third was rapid industrialization, as a means of diversifying the economy and achieving economic independence. Included in this was a military-industrial program designed to enhance Iraq's power. By 1980 the regime had taken significant steps in all these areas.

The Socialist Economy

Oil revenues gave the government the wherewithal to expand its control over the economy, just as it had done in government. This could be seen even in agriculture, usually difficult for the government to penetrate. The Ba'th began the development of collective farms (along with an extensive land reform program) with the intention of creating large-scale, capital-intensive agriculture. The regime also made substantial investments in barrages, dams, irrigation works, and drainage systems. However, agricultural production, particularly in grain crops, continued to stagnate or decline. In 1981 the regime reversed its policies and abolished the collective farm program.

More significant was the socialization of industry. Much of the oil revenue went into developing large-scale industries, such as iron, steel, and petrochemicals. These were wholly owned and managed by the government, as were most medium-sized plants, which manufactured items such as textiles, food products, and construction materials. Trade likewise came under increased government control, through various mechanisms such as state trading organizations, state retail outlets, import licensing, and direct government purchasing. The share of the socialist, or public, sector rose from 31 percent of domestic production in 1968 to 80 percent in 1977, although it varied according to sector.[23]

Socialization was not without its drawbacks, however. It brought inefficiency, waste, and mismanagement, and there was no indication that the public sector was more productive than the private. Some of these drawbacks were recognized by the regime, but they did not outweigh the regime's commitment to government control.

Redistribution of Wealth and Establishment of the Welfare State

The regime's attempt to redistribute wealth can best be seen in agrarian reform, one of the first areas it tackled. When the regime came to power in 1968, the overwhelming bulk of the expropriated lands remained in government hands, while peasants farmed the remainder under conditions not much improved from the days of the monarchy. In May 1969 Ahmad Hasan al-Bakr announced that peasants would no longer pay for the lands given to them and that landlords henceforth would receive no compensation for expropriated land, a considerable redistribution of income. Finally, in May 1970 a new agrarian reform law was promulgated. It limited landholdings in rain-fed zones to a range of 1,000 to 2,000 dunams; in irrigated zones, from 400 to 600 dunams. Land distributed to peasants was to be limited to 100 to 200 dunams of rain-fed land; 40 to 60 dunams of irrigated land. This was followed by enforcement. By

1973 the percentage of land held by large and very large landholders (over 500 dunams) had dropped to 18 percent from almost 70 percent in 1958; that held by medium landholders (40 to 500 dunams) had risen to almost 60 percent from almost 25 percent in 1958; and that held by smallholders had risen to 23 percent from about 6 percent in 1958 (see Table A.5). After the 1975 settlement of the Kurdish problem, land reform was rapidly pushed forward in the north as well.

The egalitarian thrust of the regime could also be seen in its expansion of education and health services, measures that disproportionately benefited the poorer classes and improved living standards. Education up to the university level and health services, including hospitalization, were free. Between 1968 and 1980 the Ba'th more than doubled student enrollment in schools at every level. By 1980 Iraq had almost 1 million students in secondary schools and almost 100,000 students in higher education (see Table A.4).[24] Nonetheless, illiteracy remained high—53 percent in 1977. In 1978 Iraq mounted a massive literacy campaign. Similar progress was made in health services. The ratio of doctors to the population in 1968 was 1 to 4,200; by 1980 it had been improved to 1 to 1,790.[25] Life expectancy rose from forty-six to fifty-seven years. Per capita income rose tenfold from ID 120 in 1970 to ID 1,181 in 1980.

Some maldistribution of income remained, however, mainly in three areas: between rural and urban communities; between the central region of Iraq, focused on Baghdad, and the northern and southern regions; and within urban areas. In the central region, the average income was a third higher than in the south and a quarter higher than in the north.[26] The traditional agricultural sector contained the bulk of those at the bottom of the income scale.

Industrialization and Diversification

Rapid industrialization was seen as a means not only of development but also of diversification of the economy to achieve economic autonomy. In this area, results were mixed. The Ba'th regime was unsuccessful in lessening the country's dependence on oil, as were other Gulf producers in this period. The mammoth increase in oil revenues in 1973 and

TABLE 7.2 Industrial Establishments and Employees, 1962–1980

| | Large Establishments[a] | | | | Small Establishments | | | | Total | |
	Number	%	Employees	%	Number	%	Employees	%	Number	Employees
1962	1,186	5.5	77,690	64.3	20,191	94.5	43,136	35.7	21,377	120,826
1965	1,243	5.5	88,343	63.3	21,333	94.5	48,344	36.7	22,576	131,677
1971	1,330	4.2	103,909	60.6	29,940	95.8	67,481	39.4	31,270	171,390
1975	1,349	3.3	134,600	56.9	39,275	96.7	101,993	43.1	40,624	236,593
1980	1,494	4.2	180,900	70.4	34,351	95.8	76,247	29.7	36,025	257,147

[a] Includes water and electricity establishments. Large establishments are those employing ten or more workers.
SOURCES: Iraq Ministry of Planning, *Statistical Pocketbook, 1982*, pp. 29, 30, 32; *AAS 1978*, pp. 91, 118; *Statistical Pocketbook, 1976*, p. 40; *AAS 1973*, pp. 168, 169, 172, 173; *AAS 1965*, p. 150; *Statistical Pocketbook, 1960–1970*, pp. 88–89.

the second price rise in 1979 raised the share of oil revenues automatically in the budgets of all oil-producing states. Nevertheless, there was considerable development of industry in Iraq in this period.

In development allocations between 1975 and 1980, 30 percent—almost twice that of any other sector—went to industry. Much of the allocation to industry went into developing the nucleus of a heavy industry in Iraq, with a concentration on iron, steel, and petrochemical facilities. Among the new heavy industries constructed in this period were two sponge iron plants at Zubair, a companion steelworks in the same area, an aluminum company in Nasiriyya, and a massive petrochemical complex in the Basra-Rumaila area.

Meanwhile, lighter industries were added at a somewhat slower pace, among them a vehicle assembly plant and plants to produce electrical equipment, tires, and paper. Infrastructure was also developed, as roads, railroads, ports, and airports were expanded and improved. Along with civilian industry went the construction of a military-industrial complex, expansion of conventional military infrastructure, and the development of a secret program for weapons of mass destruction. In 1974 a three-man strategic development committee, headed by Saddam Husain, was formed with the aim of developing nuclear—as well as chemical and, later, biological—weapons. The same year Iraq concluded an agreement with France for the purchase of a nuclear reactor, allegedly for research. Although the world knew of the reactor purchases, much of the program was secret. The program did not proceed smoothly and in fact received several serious setbacks. In 1979 Israeli agents destroyed reactor cores being shipped to Iraq from France as they were leaving a French port. In 1981 Iraq's main Osiraq reactor was bombed and destroyed by Israel. However, Iraq continued the clandestine program using other methods.

While these expenditures did provide an economic transformation in Iraq, they also produced some negative results. First, a disproportionate amount of resources was siphoned off on military expenditures. One source puts military expenditure as 30 percent of gross national product by 1980.[27]

Second, a relative decline occurred in the productive sectors, especially agriculture. Its contribution to GDP declined from 17 percent in 1970 to 7 percent in 1979. Meanwhile, agricultural imports increased tremendously. By 1977 Iraq was importing 33 percent of its agricultural supply.[28] Although industry grew, it could not keep up with the outsized growth of the service sector and government employment. Manufacturing accounted for 9 percent of GDP in the 1960s but only 7 percent in the 1970s.[29]

Third, the era of prosperity rapidly created a consumer society dependent on government employment. One source estimates that government employment, exclusive of the military, doubled between 1972 and 1978.[30] Another claims that a fifth to a fourth of the population worked directly or indirectly for the government; in cities the figure reached a third.[31]

The Social Transformation

Oil wealth, improved incomes, and the expansion of education also produced a more rapid social transformation and speeded up social mobility. Rural to urban migration, already under way, greatly intensified, permanently changing the demographic distribution of the population. By 1977 Iraq was an urban country, with 64 percent of its people in cities. Of these, four cities—Baghdad, Mosul, Basra, and Kirkuk—had 61 percent of the urban population, 38 percent of the total population.[32] Massive domestic migration, however, may not have brought urbanization as much as ruralization of the cities, as village migrants clustered in poor, substandard satellite towns—like the Thaura township, now renamed Saddam City, in Baghdad—where they reproduced rural customs and practices.

Social change also brought the beginnings of a new class structure. A stratum of nouveaux riches—mainly contractors, entrepreneurs, and other intermediaries—flourished in a new semiprivate sector that fed off government distribution of wealth. A number of these new wealthy were related to leading Ba'th officials or had family ties to senior state officials, reinforcing the traditional patronage system widely used by the Ba'th.[33] The middle class, defined by education and a modern occupation, also grew. Much of the new middle class, especially at upper levels, was professional—doctors, academics, engineers, high-level civil servants—whereas others were white-collar workers in the middle levels of the civil service, teachers, and those in commerce. One study indicates that in 1977 this group constituted 35 percent of the urban population; a lower-middle class probably made up another 20 percent.[34]

An urban working class also grew rapidly. These included semi- and unskilled workers in industrial establishments, as well as new migrants who found employment as police, in construction, and in other menial jobs. The changing social structure was reflected in the shift in Iraq's employment structure, particularly the decline of those employed in agriculture and the increase of those in services. In the 1960s about half of the population was engaged in agriculture; by 1977 only about a third were. Employment in manufacturing rose from 7 to 9 percent, but the percent of the population in services rose from 12 to 15 percent in the 1960s to almost a third of the labor force in the 1970s. Most of these workers were in government employ (see Table 7.3), not in productive sectors. These trends continued into the 1980s. The era of prosperity rapidly created a consumer society dependent on government salaries (see Table A.3).

TABLE 7.3 Civilian Government Employees, 1952–1990

	1952	1968	1972	1977	1987	1990
Workforce (1000s)	n.a.	2,324	2,776	3,010	4,500	4,900
Government employees (1000s)	85	277	386	666	828	826
Percentage of workforce	n.a.	12	14	21	18.4	16.8

SOURCE: Faleh Abdul Jabbar, "The State, Society, Clan, Party, and Army in Iraq," in *From Storm to Thunder*, ed. Faleh Abdul Jabbar, Ahmad Shikara, and Keiki Sakai (Tokyo: Institute of Developing Economies, 1998), p. 12.

Iraq's Foreign Policy:
The Pragmatic Phase, 1975–1980

Iraq's increased oil revenue and its desire for rapid economic development were reflected, after 1975, in an increasingly pragmatic foreign policy, a trend reinforced by the settlement with Iran on the Shatt and peace on the Kurdish front.

The shift was most noticeable in the Gulf, where relations improved with Saudi Arabia and with the conservative Gulf shaikhdoms. In 1975 Iraq established diplomatic relations with Sultan Qabus of Oman. A series of bilateral agreements were concluded with Saudi Arabia, including an agreement on the demarcation of the neutral zone on the countries' joint border. Relations with Kuwait also improved.

Meanwhile, relations with the Soviet Union took a downturn. The economic boom meant that Iraq turned increasingly to the West for purchases of goods and services. During the late 1970s, Iraq's trade with Japan, Germany, France, and even the United States increased, while economic transactions with the Soviet bloc declined to about 5 percent of total trade. The Soviet share of Iraq's arms purchases also dropped from about 95 percent in 1972 to about 63 percent in 1979.[35] France was the main, but not the only, Western beneficiary of this shift. When the USSR invaded Afghanistan in December 1979, Iraq-USSR relations reached a nadir.

Iraq's foreign policy was also affected by regional developments. More than any other factor, the Camp David Accords of September 1978, in which Israel and Egypt agreed on a framework for peace, propelled Iraq into the mainstream of Arab politics. In November 1978 the Iraqi regime took the initiative in organizing a summit of all Arab governments (except Egypt) to counteract the Camp David agreement. Although the summit did not halt Egypt's march toward a peace agreement, it highlighted Iraq's new regional role in isolating Egypt and moving to take its place. In March 1979, after the Egyptian-Israeli peace treaty was signed, the foreign and finance ministers of the Arab League met, again in Baghdad, to expel Egypt from the league.

These steps were accompanied by a mending of fences with Jordan and even with Syria. In June 1979 Saddam Husain paid a visit to Jordan, the first Iraqi head of state to do so since 1958, and a wide variety of agreements—military, economic, and political—were signed. By 1980 work had begun on a number of joint projects with Jordan. Chief among them were the expansion of the Aqaba port, which the Iraqis hoped to use to relieve their own Gulf ports, and the improvement of the road system between Amman and Baghdad.

Even more remarkable was the brief rapprochement with Syria. In an effort to shore up an Arab eastern front to counter the Israeli-Egyptian détente, Asad arrived in Baghdad for a meeting with Bakr and Husain. Although this startling event was clearly an anti-Israeli effort, it temporarily eased mutual Syrian-Iraqi hostility. However, it soon collapsed.

Iraq's initiatives on the Arab front finally culminated in the pronouncement in February 1980 of an Arab charter endorsed by most of the states that had attended the Arab summit. It rejected foreign bases (Soviet and US) on Arab soil, rejected the use of force in Arab (but not non-Arab) disputes, and asked for Arab solidarity against foreign aggression, a clause directed against revolutionary Iran as well as Israel. By the end of the decade, Iraq had moved out of its earlier isolation into a potential leadership role. Husain's ambitions also lay beyond the Gulf and the Arab world to a broader, global stage. In the immediate future, he looked to the nonaligned nations' summit, which Iraq hoped to host in 1982, a position that would give him Third World, as well as Arab world, leadership. The new era of prosperity had brought Iraq—and its leader's expectations—a long way.

Iraq's New Ideological Stand

These changes in Iraq's economic fortunes and its new pragmatic foreign policy were accompanied by a perceptible shift in party ideology. This was most notable on the Arab nationalist front, where the emphasis on Arab unity was replaced by a focus on Iraq as a state and its leadership of the Arab world and beyond. The notion of integral Arab unity reluctantly gave way to acceptance of individual states committed to gradual pan-Arab cooperation. "The glory of the Arabs," stated one report, "stems from the glory of Iraq. . . . That is why we are striving to make Iraq mighty, formidable . . . and developed."[36]

A second ideological feature was an attempt to draw different ethnic and sectarian groups in Iraq together under one ideological "tent." This was sometimes done by assuming that all Iraqis were part of Arab civilization, broadly defined. "The Kurds," Husain stated at one point, "have always been faithful to . . . the battles of the Arab nation to build the Arab civilization. When we talk about the Kurds, we mean the Iraqi Kurds who are a product of civilization six thousand years old."[37]

A third shift occurred in this period—a new emphasis not only on the leading role of a single party but also on a single individual. This individual, Saddam Husain, was now melded with "society" as a whole as representative and leader of its collective aspirations. Husain's speeches and pamphlets became the new ideological guide and the symbol of collective Iraqi consciousness and identity. By the close of the 1970s, the evolution of an ideology glorifying not only the party but also a dominant leader within it was virtually complete.

Opposition to the Regime

Despite the imposing edifice created by the state and the ruthlessness of the party in dealing with dissent, by the end of a decade of rule the Ba'th still faced opposition from a variety of sources. Some came from groups and parties dissatisfied with the regime's political or economic policies. More serious was the traditional opposition from ethnic and religious groups, most specifically, the Kurds and the Shi'a.

Liberal Opposition

The regime still faced difficulties with the liberal end of the political spectrum. This contingent was far less organized and coherent than other groups, but it was rooted in the professional classes and the intelligentsia, on whom the regime relied for its development program. The liberals were singled out for attention by the Ba'th as early as 1974 when the party report of that year stated, "School programs on all levels still fall short of expressing the principles of the Arab Ba'th Socialist Party and the socialist and nationalist revolution. They are still propagating bourgeois and liberal values."[38] To combat these tendencies, the party gradually exercised increased control over faculty and students, requiring courses on Ba'th ideology at the university level and replacing non-Ba'thist faculty with Ba'thists.

Many Iraqi intellectuals expressed their disaffection by leaving Iraq, as evidenced by the sizable number of educated Iraqis working outside Iraq. The intelligentsia also expressed its disaffection through passive resistance to government programs and policies. The poor productivity of the economy was sufficiently worrisome that in the autumn of 1976 the party held a series of seminars on the subject addressed by Saddam Husain himself. Among the complaints were protection of top-level administrators for political reasons and too many layers of decision-making.[39] These difficulties reflected a growing frustration on the part of an educated class, trained to lead, over its members' inability to control their professional lives.

The Communist Party

More significant than the liberal opposition were the Iraq Communist Party and the various left-wing elements that supported it. Friction between the Ba'th and the ICP was exacerbated by the Ba'th's deteriorating relations with the Soviet Union. The Ba'th feared internal subversion from the ICP supported by the USSR, particularly after the Soviet-supported coup in Afghanistan in April 1978. The very next month, to show that the Ba'th would tolerate no repeat of the Afghan situation in

Iraq, it executed twenty-one Communists who had been imprisoned earlier for organizing cells in the army. By April 1979 most of the principal Communist leaders had left the country, and once again the party's leadership was driven underground.

The Kurds in Opposition

The measures taken by the government to end the Kurdish opposition after 1975 failed to do so. Indeed, the government's deportation and resettlement policy probably encouraged continued rebellion. Renewed guerrilla acts in the north began as early as March 1976 as *peshmerga* infiltrated back into the region from Iran. However, without Mustafa Barzani's legendary stature to keep factions in tow, splits in the movement now deepened, especially the perennial divide between Jalal Talabani and the Barzanis. In June 1975 this long-standing fissure was formalized with the establishment of a new party, the Patriotic Union of Kurdistan (PUK), under Talabani's leadership. The program of the PUK was clearly leftist and totally repudiated the leadership of the Barzanis.[40] The PUK was the first to return *peshmerga* to Iraq in 1976.

The old Kurdistan Democratic Party was also revived under Barzani's sons, Idris and Mas'ud. In October 1979 the KDP officially elected Mas'ud the Party's chairman, along with a new congress and political bureau. It called for continued armed struggle against the Ba'th through sustained guerrilla warfare inside Iraq. Unrelated to these factions, an Islamic group took shape in November 1978; eventually it would become the Islamic Movement of Iraqi Kurdistan (IMIK). However, internal conflict weakened Kurdish opposition to Baghdad and enabled the government to play Kurdish parties against each other while relying for support in the north on the pro-government Kurds and the government-supported militias.

Shi'i Opposition

By the late 1970s, the Shi'a had superseded the Kurds as the major concern of the Ba'th. Shi'i disaffection was multifaceted.

The confrontation between the Shi'a and the government began with a series of skirmishes shortly after the Ba'th came to power in 1968. Some of these were due to heightened tensions with Iran during which the regime expelled thousands of Shi'i Iraqis of Iranian origin and confiscated their property.[41] Shi'i opponents of the regime were also caught up in the spy trials of that year, and Mahdi al-Hakim, son of the chief *marji'*, was accused of spying and sentenced to death, although he was smuggled out of the country to safety. Several Shi'i schools were closed. Finally, the regime put restrictions on the annual ritual processions in the holy cities. Hakim protested these actions, to no avail.

In June 1970 Muhsin al-Hakim was succeeded as chief *marji'* by Abu-l-Qasim al-Khu'i, a more traditional cleric who favored a "quietist" approach, avoiding confrontation with the government. As a result, in the early 1970s Shi'i opposition temporarily died down, although the government continued to monitor and sometimes harass the religious establishment.

Despite the surface quiet, however, organized Shi'i forces were still at work. Chief among them was the Da'wa Party, now an international, not just an Iraqi, organization. By the early 1970s, the Da'wa had grown, forging contacts in the universities inside and outside Iraq, especially in Lebanon and the Gulf. Another group also took shape in this period, the Munazimat al-Amal al-Islamiyya (Islamic Action Organization, or IAO). Formed in Karbala by members of the Shirazi family, it was intertwined with the clerical establishment and had strong Persian affiliations. Gradually, the IAO was turned into a political as well as a religious movement. When the Shirazis were persecuted, the IOA turned militant, organizing cells and giving members guerrilla training. By the end of the 1970s, the organization was ready to begin operations against the regime.[42]

Tensions between these Shi'a and the government erupted during ritual ceremonies in November and December 1974; over two dozen Shi'a were sentenced for plots against the government. Five, all Da'wa leaders, were executed. Far more serious and widespread were the Shi'a demonstrations and riots on 5 and 6 February 1977, when the government tried to stop a ritual procession from Najaf to Karbala. A crowd of some 30,000

angry protesters, chanting antigovernment slogans, was confronted by police. The government mobilized helicopter gunships and armored vehicles, and bloodshed ensued. At least sixteen demonstrators were killed and
many more wounded; 2,000 demonstrators were rounded up and some
500 interrogated.

An urban mass demonstration of this size and kind was new for the
regime and was worrisome. A revolutionary court sentenced eight participants to death, but this was considered too lenient by Saddam Husain,
and two of the court's members were dismissed from the party. Nonetheless, Saddam did try to propitiate the Shi'i community. More funds were
sent to the south, and more Shi'a were introduced into the RCC and the
upper levels of the party. But the Ba'th also tightened control on Shi'i political activities, including continued restrictions on rituals.

By the end of 1977, the regime may well have thought that these
draconian measures taken against the activists had brought Shi'i opposition under control. But such an assessment—if made—did not take
into account the earthquake that was about to shake Iran. The onset of
the Islamic revolution in Iran and its riveting example of a successful religious uprising soon changed these calculations. It also galvanized the
Shi'i opposition.

The Impact of the Iranian Revolution

Although the outcome of the Iranian revolution was by no means apparent, early signs of the upheaval had already appeared. As strikes and
unrest escalated inside Iran in 1978, Baghdad became increasingly concerned that the disturbances could spill over into Iraq. Much of the unrest had been instigated by Ayatallah Ruhallah Khumaini, the Iranian
cleric who had fomented the Islamic revolution in Iran and who had
been residing in exile in Najaf for thirteen years. The shah asked for
Khumaini's removal from Iraq in October 1978, and the Ba'th regime
complied. But with Khumaini's departure to Paris and his open leadership of the revolution, Shi'i opposition in Iraq now entered a new phase.
This time the leadership of the movement was taken up by Muhammad
Baqir al-Sadr, who played a key role in the events to transpire.

On 1 February 1979 Khumaini returned triumphant to Tehran at the head of a successful revolution, and the impact of this success changed the political landscape in Iraq—as well as the rest of the Middle East. A wave of enthusiasm swept the Shi'i community in Iraq. In March Sadr signaled clear support for the revolution in a telegram of congratulations to Khumaini, asserting that he looked forward to more Islamic victories. Sadr even went so far as to issue a *fatwa*—not made public at the time—against joining the Ba'th Party, a dangerous act of defiance well beyond any redline the regime might accept.

In May 1979 events reached a crisis over a visit Sadr was reputedly planning to make to Tehran. Whether he was actually going is not clear, but a telegram from Khumaini, publicly broadcast from Tehran on the Arabic service, asked Sadr to remain in Baghdad. This event precipitated a crisis of the first order and elevated Sadr to the rank of a leading challenger to the regime. Starting on 22 May, there were nine days of demonstrations, initiated by the Da'wa, organized around a *bay'a*, or oath of allegiance, to Sadr. Shi'a flocked to Najaf from all over Iraq. The regime allowed the demonstrations to escalate and then on 12 June rounded up and imprisoned hundreds of Da'wa members. Sadr was arrested.

The detention of Sadr then set off a second reaction. Shi'i activists responded with more massive demonstrations. Riots broke out in several cities. In fact, this uprising was the first popular mass movement of its kind in decades. There was also agitation abroad—in the UAE, in Lebanon, in Britain, and in France, where pro-Da'wa and pro-Sadr forces were situated. These protests finally achieved the release of Sadr. The rest of the activists did not fare so well. Although no full accounting exists, several hundred may have been executed or killed under torture. By the summer of 1979, the Da'wa organization had been virtually emasculated.

The 1979 demonstrations widened the fissure in the Ba'th leadership over how to deal with this challenge. One wing of the party, reputedly including Bakr, favored flexibility in dealing with Sadr and caution in handling the new Iranian government. Saddam Husain and his supporters took a hard line. Husain won out. On 1 April a bomb thrown in a public gathering slightly wounded Deputy Prime Minister Tariq Aziz and killed a number of others. A second attempt occurred a few days later. Saddam blamed Sadr and the Shi'a activities and behind them Iran. On 4 April 1980 Sadr was arrested, brutally tortured, and executed.

In retrospect, the Shi'i activists, Sadr included, appeared to have miscalculated. The Da'wa and other militant groups prematurely picked a violent quarrel with the regime before they were ready to withstand the reaction. The result was devastating for the movement itself. But Sadr provided the movement with a martyr and helped create a mighty revival of Shi'i consciousness and revived religious opposition to the regime; both would go underground—and abroad, mainly to Iran—to continue to bedevil the regime.

The Ba'th: The End of Its First Decade

The era of the 1970s ended for the regime on a mixed note. In the capital and the central provinces, from which it drew most of its support, opposition had been thoroughly cowed. The Kurdish insurrection in the north had ended in 1975, and although brutal measures were taken with rural Kurds, the benefits of economic development were already shaping the more urban Kurdish areas, bringing prosperity and some quiet. In the south, it was clear that the Shi'i resurgence, initiated under the Arif regime, presented a worrisome problem. No longer merely domestic, it was now backed by a new and increasingly militant Shi'i regime in Iran. Domestically, however, by the summer of 1979 Shi'i unrest in the south had clearly been brought under control.

Meanwhile, the massive inflow of oil wealth, spent not only in Baghdad but also in the provinces, provided an aura of prosperity used to mitigate tensions and distract attention from the harsh and brutal measures of the regime. Social mobility also blunted discontent. New economic wealth provided the regime with the means to push rapid modernization and development and a new Ba'th vision of Iraq—strong, united, and under the umbrella of a new Salah al-Din. Much of the wealth, of course, was put into building the military sinews of the state and a nascent nuclear program that would allow Saddam to fulfill the vision of

Arab world leadership. Meanwhile, by 1979 the edifice of the monolithic, one-party state, in control not only of the instruments of political and military power but also of society, was complete. Saddam had reason to feel more confident than worried about the future and Iraq's place in it.

8

THE SADDAM HUSAIN
REGIME, 1979–1989

In July 1979, eleven years after helping the Ba'th to power in a coup and after serving as second in command to Ahmad Hasan al-Bakr, Saddam Husain became president of the republic. It was the first peaceful transition of power in over two decades. Despite the seemingly pedestrian nature of this event, in retrospect it heralded a new era in Iraq, one that was to have permanently damaging consequences and change Iraq's possibilities for the future.

The changing of the guard marked a decisive shift, already under way, from a one-party state to a personal, autocratic regime dependent for security—and, increasingly, for decisions—on Saddam Husain and his close family members and cohorts. The party did not disappear, but what little independence it had was broken; it now became an organization subservient to Saddam Husain. At the same time, the party was both absorbed and displaced by another large, mass-based organization, an elected national assembly, which was convened for the first time since 1958.

These changes took place against the backdrop of a virulent and proselytizing Islamic revolution in Iran, with potential threats to both regime and state in Iraq. Iran's extreme rhetoric, as well as its military mobilization and border attacks, played into Saddam's hands. With few domestic checks on his judgment, he took the initiative in attacking Iran, thus beginning a disastrous eight-year war that would shred much of the economic and social capital that Iraq had built up in the previous decade.

The war accomplished none of Iraq's stated purposes in beginning hostilities. The Iranian regime remained in power and was strengthened. Iraqi resources, human and economic, were drained. Above all, Iraq lost a large measure of its economic independence through massive debts both to the West and to the Arab Gulf states. But the Saddam Husain regime, though changed, remained in power and came through the war with a sense of entitlement to benefits from the Arab world as its bulwark or "eastern flank." The population meanwhile expected a "peace dividend." Unfortunately, these assumptions were ill founded and set the stage for the second, and even more disastrous, period to follow.

Saddam as President

It had been widely expected for some time that Saddam Husain would take Bakr's place. It came as no surprise, therefore, when, on 16 July 1979, President Bakr officially resigned and Saddam Husain became president of the republic, secretary-general of the Ba'th Party Regional Command, chairman of the Revolutionary Command Council (RCC), and commander in chief of the armed forces. There is little doubt that Saddam was impatient to assume official title to the power he in fact already held and that he engineered the older man's retirement. In the cabinet reshuffle that ensued, Izzat Ibrahim (al-Duri) was named deputy chairman of the RCC and assistant secretary-general of the party's Regional Command and Taha Ramadan (al-Jazrawi) became first deputy prime minister, indicating that these old party stalwarts had acquiesced in the change.

The Party Massacre

Much was made in public of the smoothness of this transition, but this was a facade. Within days a bizarre episode revealed fissures within the leadership and the potential for instability. An alleged coup attempt was revealed ten days after Saddam's inauguration, on 28 July, when the new president announced the discovery of a plot by a number of Ba'thist leaders to overthrow the government. An outside power (understood to be Syria) was said to be involved. The announcement of the plot had been preceded by the arrest, on 12 July, of Muhyi al-Din Abd al-Husain, a Shi'i member of the RCC and the Regional Command.[1] In an extraordinary session of the party's regional congress televised in a large hall in Baghdad on 22 July, Muhyi al-Din made a public confession of the plot, naming those involved, many of them sitting in the hall.[2]

In a chilling exercise of power, the accused, one by one, were promptly taken into custody. An investigating committee and a court, both composed entirely of RCC members, were immediately set up, and ten days later death sentences were issued for twenty-two of the accused, including five RCC members. They were summarily executed. One of the accused escaped, and thirty-three others were sentenced to prison terms. Thirteen were acquitted.[3]

These events raised questions about the timing of the transition and motivations behind the drastic action taken by their main perpetrator, Saddam Husain. There is little doubt that Husain had been preparing for the transition for some time and that the way seemed propitious because Bakr had been less active over the years as real power shifted to Saddam. But there is no evidence that Bakr was yet ready to step aside or that he took any initiative in the formal transfer of power. This was Saddam's decision.

The troubles in Iran may have played some role in Saddam's decision to replace Bakr. Dealing with domestic Shi'i disturbances had already caused splits in the leadership and appeared to put Bakr, a cautious man, on the side of those more interested in following a "flexible" policy, both toward local Shi'a and toward Iran. Saddam, deeply suspicious of Iran, may have felt the time had come to move. It is also possible that Saddam wanted to put an end to the unity scheme with Syria, then under discussion. Bakr was slated to head the union, with Hafiz al-Asad as second in command. This would have left Saddam Husain third in rank—unacceptable to him.

But the real reason for Saddam's actions appears to have been opposition to his rule from within the party command. Within the closed RCC meeting to arrange the transition, some made it clear they preferred Bakr to remain. And it is this opposition, as well as Saddam's aversion to tolerating any dissent, that explains the allegations of a "coup" and the massacre of party insiders that followed the announcement of Saddam's presidency.

The transition and the party massacre were a watershed in the regime's history. The regime now became a more personal autocracy, focused on one man and his whims. Although weak, Bakr had provided some shelter for those with opposing views—and possible rival ambitions; these were now destroyed in a chilling exercise of Stalinesque terror. Meanwhile, the party was reduced to an appendage of Saddam's personal rule.

The transition and the purge also reduced, temporarily, the power of the RCC and the inner circle. Saddam now undertook a modest restructuring of the political system. To command the heights of the military and the security system, he appointed himself field marshal, enhancing his authority to exercise more direct control over the military. Adnan Khairallah Talfah, a cousin, was made deputy commander in chief. His half-brother Barzan was put in charge of the Mukhabarat al-Amma (General Intelligence Service). At long last, too, the constitutional provisions providing for a national assembly were activated to provide a democratic facade.

The Establishment of the National Assembly

A law promulgated in March 1980 provided for an assembly of 250 members to be elected by secret ballot every four years. All Iraqis over the age of eighteen were eligible to vote, and the country was to be divided into electoral zones of about 250,000 inhabitants each. A key provision stipulated that all candidates had to be reviewed by an election commission before receiving permission to run, thus assuring that only those favorable to Ba'th principles would be elected.

To no one's surprise, the 20 June 1980 elections gave the Ba'th an overwhelming victory, although a number of independents were also elected. Na'im Haddad, an RCC and Regional Command member, was elected speaker, putting a loyal party Shi'a in a visible public position to help allay accusations of "sectarian" politics. The new assembly, while providing a safety valve—even a distraction—for public discontent, did little to obscure the increasingly personal and secretive nature of the autocracy now governing Iraq and the level of brutality that would face any who opposed it.

These developments eliminated any possibility for dissent or correctives to Saddam's judgment as Iraq faced a volatile situation on its border with Iran. Iraq now had a young man, relatively inexperienced in international affairs, willing—indeed eager—to substitute his own judgment for that of others and to use opportunities to advance his own visions of regional leadership. The result would be a serious miscalculation that would be costly for Iraq.

Iraq at War

There is little doubt that the outbreak of the war between Iran and Iraq occurred against a background of long-standing grievances—even a state of permanent tension—between the two countries. Chief among these had been border disputes combined with a larger, even if intangible, Iraqi fear of Persian hegemony. In many Iraqi minds, especially Saddam's, since the 1920s Iran had been gradually encroaching on "Arab" land, including its absorption of the adjacent Arab territory of Khuzistan (formerly Muhammara) in 1925, the incorporation of the waters around Khurramshahr in 1937, and the 1975 agreement that gave Iran half the Shatt al-Arab.

Cultural differences, based partly on language and ethnicity, had always existed but were now brought into sharp focus with the Iranian revolution and Iranian attempts to spread the revolution to Iraq. The "cultural distance" between Iraq and Iran, however, had always been viewed differently by different communities in Iraq. For the Shi'a in southern Iraq, especially those affiliated with the religious establishment, the differences had been muted, but among the power elite in Baghdad, especially those from small-town Arab Sunni backgrounds, traditional suspicion of and prejudice against Iran remained high.

Despite these ongoing tensions, it is unlikely that war would have occurred had the shah remained in power. To the contrary, there is no evidence that Saddam Husain intended to overturn the 1975 agreement while the shah was in power or even in the immediate aftermath of his overthrow. It was the Islamic revolution and the virulent attempt of Ayatallah Khumaini to spread its ideology that shifted the regional balance of power and changed Iraq's calculations.

Provocation from Iran

The impact of the Iranian revolution on Iraq was first felt in the north among the Kurds. In the wake of the revolution, Iran ceased to police its northern borders, and in July 1979 the Barzanis crossed the frontier from Iran to Iraq with Kurdistan Democratic Party (KDP) forces in violation of the 1975 treaty. Kurdish activities escalated in the north, with the Iraqi KDP firmly supporting Khumaini and urging the overthrow of the Baghdad government.[4] In retaliation, the Iraqi government revived its support for dissident Arab groups in Khuzistan that were in open revolt against the Iranian government, making the point that if Iran did not observe the agreement in the north, Iraq would not observe it in the south.[5]

More serious than the Kurdish skirmishes, however, was Iran's open call for the spread of revolution to Iraq, where Shi'i unrest, already apparent, was now deliberately stirred up by the new Iranian government. The hand of Iran was seen in the 1979 demonstrations on behalf of Baqir al-Sadr and in the April 1980 assassination attempt on Tariq Aziz. The regime responded by deporting up to 35,000 Shi'a, allegedly of Persian origin.[6] The campaign also became a personal test of wills between Khumaini and Saddam Husain. Khumaini had no love for the man who had expelled him in 1978. Saddam, for his part, regarded the militant Islamic leader as a threat to his own revolutionary credentials and to his regime as well. Behind the personal struggle was a clash of ideologies, with the Iraqis championing secular Arab nationalism and socialism and Iran preaching the revival of a militant Islam.

The Temptations of a Weakened Iran

Despite Iran's militancy, by the summer of 1979, as revolutionary Iran sank deeper into chaos, as its military fractured and decomposed, and as its international isolation deepened, the potential for Iraq to reverse its previous losses and even make new gains became irresistible. Chief among these aims was Husain's desire to reverse the 1975 decision on the Shatt al-Arab, as well as the possibility of ending the threat of revolutionary Iran once and for all by overthrowing the regime. There were even dreams of "liberating" the Arab population of Khuzistan and creating a new political entity at the head of the Gulf under Iraqi control.

Preemptive Defense

As tensions and skirmishes between the two countries escalated, the idea of the necessity of a "first strike" appears to have grown. In the minds of some, if no preemptive strike were taken at a favorable time to rectify the border issue and, further, to forestall a future intervention from a reorganized but still militant Iran, the Islamic republic would constitute a far greater threat later.[7]

Iraq first tried to help destabilize Iran by using Iranian opposition, such as Shahpur Bakhtiar, the last prime minister under the shah, and General Ghulam Ali Uwaisi, former chief of staff. Iraq funded their efforts to contact both tribal and military opponents inside Iran hoping to overthrow the regime from inside.[8] (These efforts were matched, of course, by Iranian support for Kurdish and Shi'i opponents of the Baghdad regime.) Pro-shah forces tried two military coups in 1980, but both failed. This may have been a key turning point in Baghdad's decision to take the initiative itself.

Iraq was also encouraged by Iran's isolation. The American hostage crisis, initiated by Iranians in November 1979 and culminating in the disastrous US rescue attempt that failed in the Iranian desert in April 1980, ensured that the United States—and the West—would not come to Iran's aid in a war with Iraq. Whatever the mix of motives behind Saddam's decision, in the end opportunity and a growing sense of confidence, rather than defense against a Shi'i rebellion, appeared to dominate.[9]

The Road to War

By late August the situation had escalated, with serious skirmishes on the borders. On 4 September 1980 Iranian armed forces used artillery to shell the Iraqi cities of Khanaqin and Mandali from the disputed border area of Zain al-Qaus, inflicting heavy losses of life and property among civilians. When the shelling was repeated on 7 September, Saddam officially abrogated the 1975 treaty and announced that the Shatt al-Arab was returning to Iraqi sovereignty. Iran rejected this action, and the conflict shifted to the Shatt.[10]

On 19 September the Iranian government began to use heavy artillery and planes to bombard residential areas and vital economic installations on the Iraqi side of the Shatt. The Iranians also attacked foreign merchant ships in the river. This was the trigger Saddam used. Three days later, the Iraqis carried the war to the heart of Iran with a bombing mission that raided ten Iranian air bases and two early-warning stations. The attack was clearly modeled on the Israeli 1967 strike on Egypt.[11] On 23 September the Iraqis began their military advance into Iranian territory.

Iraq's strategic aims in the invasion remained unclear. Was it to regain the Shatt—and possibly all of Khuzistan? Was it to end the domestic threat from Khumaini's regime by ending the regime itself? Whatever the aims, they failed. The war, instead of ensuring Iraq's domestic security or achieving territorial gains, much less ending the Islamic Republic, bogged down in a long, debilitating eight-year conflict that marked the beginning of a continual downturn in Iraq's fortunes that would continue for the remainder of the regime.

The Course of the War

The Failed Iraqi Offensive

Initially, the Iraqis made rapid advances into Iranian territory on several fronts, especially in the center toward Dizful and the south into Khuzistan. Iran responded with air attacks on oil facilities and a naval blockade, slowing Iraq's advance. Declaring his territorial ambitions achieved, on 28 September, Saddam Husain announced a cease-fire, evidently expecting Iranian concessions for the territory won. His terms included acceptance of Iraqi rights on the Shatt al-Arab and "other usurped Iraqi territory" and noninterference in Iraq's domestic affairs. He may also have expected the collapse of the Iranian government. This proved to be a critical error. The Iraqis had failed to take Dizful, a major transport link between the Iranian capital and the south. They likewise failed to capture Abadan and thus did not gain control over the Shatt, one of their professed aims.

One reason for the halt probably lay in Saddam Husain's reluctance to accept the high casualties that would surely have accompanied further advances. Moreover, the bulk of the soldiers were Shi'a, who might have been prone to defect. Military capabilities may also have played a role in the decision. Iraq's capacity to sustain the long lines of communications and to absorb the inevitable losses was questionable. Whatever the reasons for Iraq's military strategy, it is clear that Husain made a catastrophic mistake in underestimating Iran's resources. Despite massive casualties, the Iranians put up an effective defense of their territory, consolidated, and mounted a counteroffensive. By October the Iranians had pushed the Iraqis back across the Karun River and in May 1982 retook Khurramshahr. Rather than weakening the Khumaini regime, the Iraqi offensive provided the opportunity for more militant elements in Iran to gain control of the political system and, in the long run, helped consolidate the regime.

Putting the best face possible on these reversals, Saddam Husain announced in June 1982 an Iraqi withdrawal to the international borders, claiming that Iraq's objective—destroying the Iranian military apparatus—had been achieved. Few inside or outside Iraq were deceived.

The withdrawal announcement failed to contain the Iranian advance as planned. The Iranians now attempted to carry the war to Iraqi territory, with the professed aim of toppling Saddam Husain and his regime and supplanting it with an Islamic republic. Before long, it was apparent that Iran was merely repeating the mistake that Saddam had made earlier. The fateful Iranian decision to continue the war, rather than accepting Iraq's proffered cease-fire terms, initiated the second phase of the war, lasting roughly from 1982 to 1986—a long war of attrition, fought mainly on land but also in the Gulf, that depleted the resources and morale of both sides and, until a sharp and sudden Iranian victory in 1986, was marked mainly by stalemate.

The War of Attrition

During the summer of 1982, Iran went on the offensive, making several major but unsuccessful attempts to take Basra and to cut the main Basra-Baghdad road, a key aim of Iranian war strategy from then on. Holding well-entrenched positions, the Iraqis held back the Iranian attacks and inflicted heavy losses on their enemies. From then on, the ground war bogged down in a stalemate that was to persist almost to the end of the war.

Throughout 1983 and 1984, there were repeated Iranian attacks on a number of fronts using human waves of young irregulars, as well as up to four divisions of the regular army. The Iranians also used dissident Kurdish forces (the KDP) and Iraqi Shi'i exiles. Iraq built huge earthworks and fortifications all along its frontier in the south and set up a static defense. In 1984 Iran captured Majnun, an artificial island created on the site of a recent oil find near Qurna. Majnun gave the Iranians their first substantial bargaining chip on the ground and a possible future source of oil.

It was during the battle for Majnun that reports reached the outside world that the Iraqis were using chemical weapons. In retrospect, mustard gas appears to have been used as early as August 1983.[12] Although controversy over their use came later, there was little, if any, protest from the West at the time.

Iran still had little to show for its efforts, except for Majnun and some pockets of Iraqi territory in the north, but the ground attacks continued. Kurdish guerrillas made inroads. The KDP may have controlled as much as a third of the north. Basra appeared increasingly to be a city under siege, fearing encirclement and losing population as its inhabitants fled north. By 1986, when the battlefield had stabilized, Iran held about three hundred square miles of Iraqi territory but had not been able to take Basra or any other major city.

The Economic and Diplomatic War

Although Iraq was able to fight Iran to a standstill on the ground, it had not been prepared to wage a long war of attrition and now had to compensate for economic losses. Although Iraq had begun the war with a full treasury, the destruction of Iraq's Gulf port facilities in November 1980 and the closure of its pipeline by Syria in April 1982 had drastically reduced Iraq's oil revenue and its financial capacity to wage war. By 1983 the war was costing Iraq ID 312.5 million ($1 billion) a month.

In a major attempt to restore its finances, Iraq turned first to the Arab Gulf countries. By appealing to Arab solidarity and the fear of an Iranian victory, the Iraqis managed to gain financial support from these countries. Iraq then turned to Europe, where it was able to arrange for credits and a rescheduling of its debts. Even the United States extended agricultural credits to Iraq. At home the government introduced an austerity program. By slashing nonessential imports, obtaining new credits and loans, and deferring hard currency payments, Iraq managed to achieve a fragile economic equilibrium, although it had to go into debt to do so.

Iraq also bolstered its position by the acquisition of new armaments. In 1983 Iraq negotiated a loan of five French Super Étendard warplanes, equipped with heat-seeking Exocet missiles and guidance facilities designed mainly for use against ships in the Gulf. More surprisingly, Iraq also repaired its deteriorating relationship with the USSR and was resupplied with Soviet arms.

Iraq also won the diplomatic struggle for world opinion, placing the blame for the continuation of the war on Iran. Even more important, Iraq managed to achieve a US "tilt" toward Iraq in the late summer of 1983 and a trip by US Special Middle East Envoy Donald Rumsfeld to Iraq in December 1983.

The United States, in a subsequent policy known as Operation Staunch, put pressure on its allies and friends to stop supplying Iran with weapons. By 1983 the United States clearly saw a possible Iranian victory and an Iraqi collapse as not in its interests. In November of that year, it took Iraq off its terrorist list and in January 1984 put Iran on. Thereafter, the United States turned a blind eye to arms shipments to Iraq, as it attempted to stem arms flows to Iran. Except for the "Iran-gate" interlude from August 1985 to November 1986, when the United States allowed the secret resupply of some equipment to Iran, the Americans continued Operation Staunch to the end of the war.

Turning Points, 1986–1987

After four years of a grueling war of attrition, two events, one in 1986 and the other in 1987, marked turning points in the stalemate and, in retrospect, led to the end of the war the following year: Iran's capture of Faw in February 1986 and its unsuccessful attack on Basra in early 1987. On 6 February 1986 Iran managed to capture Faw, giving the Islamic Republic a strategic foothold on Iraq's access to the Gulf. From Faw the Iranians were able to threaten Kuwait by launching silkworm missiles on the small Gulf shaikhdom. Buoyed by this success in Faw, Iran mounted what it hoped would be its "final offensive" against Basra. In a fierce campaign during January and February, Iran pushed to within ten miles of the city, but by March it was clear that the offensive had failed and Iran could not take the city. In May and June 1987, Iraq counterattacked, making gains in the north in the Halabja area. In both attacks chemical weapons were used.[13]

The battle for Basra proved to be the turning point of the war. Though casualties were high on both sides, they proved to be insurmountable for Iran. Iran lost not only a large number of soldiers but also many experienced officers. An attempt to recruit for another offensive the following year collapsed in the face of shortfalls. Iran was also unable to replace lost equipment or resupply spare parts as Operation Staunch took its toll. As the 1987 offensive against Basra eventually made clear, Iran was suffering attrition beyond its capacity for replacement or repair.

Internationalization of the War

The ground war, however, was not the only factor moving the war to a close. Equally important was an escalation of the "tanker war" in the Gulf that had begun in 1984. Iraq attacked tankers bound for Iranian ports; Iran then retaliated by striking tankers bound for Kuwait and Saudi Arabia, Iraq's Gulf allies. This sea war intensified in 1985 and 1986 and finally succeeded in "internationalizing" the conflict, bringing the US Navy more deeply into the conflict and finally persuading the United Nations to exert more serious pressure (with US backing) on the combatants.

It had been a major aim of Iraq to involve the superpowers—especially the United States—in putting pressure on Iran to end the conflict. Progress in this direction was slow. Despite the US tilt to Iraq in 1983, the Irangate episode showed just how "neutral" the United States could be. But by 1987 the situation had changed. Public disclosure of the Irangate affair caused a huge public embarrassment in the United States and an outcry among the international community. More importantly, Iraq's defeat in Faw and the subsequent siege of Basra the following year once again raised the specter of an Iranian victory.

US Intervention

Increased US military involvement began with the reflagging of Kuwaiti vessels to provide Kuwaiti tankers with US protection. This US decision was hastened, ironically, by another incident in the Gulf. On 17 May 1987 the US frigate *Stark* was hit by two Iraqi Exocet missiles, killing thirty-seven crew members. Iraq declared the attack an accident, officially apologized, and eventually paid compensation. However, some in the United States considered the attack deliberate, possibly as retaliation for Irangate, which the Iraqis bitterly resented or, as Iranians charged, as a way of dragging the United States into the conflict.[14] Whatever the cause of the *Stark* attack, the result was to hasten the reflagging effort and to increase US involvement in the war.

The United States was drawn increasingly into direct conflict with Iran when on 16 October an Iranian silkworm missile hit one of the US-reflagged ships. The United States retaliated by hitting an Iranian off-shore platform used by the Revolutionary Guards as a communications station.

In April 1988 a US ship hit an Iranian-laid mine. The United States retaliated by striking two Iranian offshore oil platforms. Iranian speed-boats responded by attacking United Arab Emirates (UAE) offshore oil platforms, and in return the United States sank two Iranian frigates, eliminating half of Iran's navy.

On 3 July an Iranian civilian airbus with 290 passengers left Bandar Abbas for Dubayy. The *Vincennes*, a US cruiser, misidentified the airbus as a military aircraft and shot it down, killing all on board. Although many in Iran persisted in seeing this action as intentional rather than ac-cidental, it may have played a role in finally bringing Iran to the point of accepting an end to the war.[15]

By 1987 international diplomacy was working in the same direction. In January UN Secretary General Javier Pérez de Cuéllar called for a commission to determine who was responsible for the war, a concession to one of Iran's major demands. The result was UN Security Council Resolution 598, adopted in July 1987, calling for a cease-fire linked to a withdrawal to internationally recognized frontiers, a prisoner-of-war (POW) exchange, and an investigation into responsibility for the war. If the resolution were not accepted by the combatants, the United Nations would take appropriate action to end the war. It would take another year to get final Iranian acceptance.

The Iraqi Offensive of 1988

By 1988 the tide began to turn in Iraq's favor. Economically, loans and credits had enabled it to import needed military hardware and spare parts for its equipment. The expansion of its pipelines had increased its oil revenues. Iraq was fielding various armed forces of about 1.3 million troops in 130 divisions.[16] Iraq was also ready to go on the offensive, and with new tactics. It did so in February, first with a major bombardment of Iranian cities in a "war of terror" on civilians and then with a ground offensive in a series of actions that finally regained lost territory and decisively defeated Iranian forces.

The renewed war on the cities began 22 February when Baghdad fired some two hundred missiles on a number of Iranian cities, including Isphahan and Qum, but the majority—some 150—rained down on the Iranian capital. Iran replied with a ground attack in the north of Iraq, seizing the town of Halabja. Deciding to counterattack, Iraq used both mustard and nerve gas and killed an estimated 4,000.[17] Partly because of this chemical weapons attack, the Iraqi missile attacks on Iranian cities, in particular Tehran, raised fears of chemical weapons use on civilians. Although chemicals were not used on Iranian cities, the missile attacks created a crisis of morale for Iran. In Tehran about 1.5 million residents eventually fled a city of about 8 million, posing serious problems for the Iranian regime.

The Iraqis now turned to Faw, their major objective. Attacking on the beginning of Ramadan, the Iraqis took the Iranians completely by surprise. Within four days Iraq was in possession once again of the Faw peninsula and followed up with an attack on Salamja, north of Faw. Iran counterattacked, but its losses were high and its forces were finally forced to fall back.

In June Iraq recaptured the Majnun oil fields and in early July advanced into Iranian territory, along with the Mujahidin al-Khalq, the Iranian opposition force. By July Iraq had achieved the upper hand in the war and Iranian forces were in a shambles. These land offensives coincided with increased US naval actions against Iran, reinforcing an Iranian sense of isolation and hopelessness.

By 14 July serious discussions were under way in Tehran over accepting Resolution 598. Iran's official letter of acceptance was delivered to the UN secretary general in New York on 17 July. The same day, Saddam Husain gave a speech offering a five-point peace program: a cease-fire, a return to international borders, an exchange of POWs, a comprehensive peace treaty, and a mutual commitment to noninterference in each other's territory. But Iraq also demanded direct, face-to-face negotiations with Iran in return for the cease-fire, an effort to compel Iranian recognition of its regime.

The Inconclusive Peace

Although the war came to an end, negotiations over the terms of peace, and the application of Resolution 598, were to prove too difficult to resolve. Talks between the foreign ministers of both countries took place in Geneva in 1988 and 1989, under the auspices of Secretary General de Cuéllar, but there was little agreement between the two parties beyond the withdrawal of forces and a reopening of the Shatt al-Arab. By the time of Khumaini's death in June 1989, the peace talks had bogged down. Although the cease-fire held because both sides were too exhausted to resume hostilities, the eight-year conflict ended in a no-war, no-peace situation. Iraq still held Iranian territory, POWs had yet to be exchanged, no commission had been appointed to investigate "blame" for the war, and the boundary along the Shatt remained unresolved. Iraq had little concrete gain to show for eight years of war except defense of its territory. The river itself remained closed, full of ordnance and chemical weapons. Iraq was more landlocked than before and had to rely for export outlets mainly on Umm Qasr and the Khaur Abd Allah channel. This factor compelled Iraq to focus more intensely on Kuwait.

Although international criticism of chemical weapons use had been muted while the war was in progress, once the cease-fire took effect, various international groups in the West focused media attention on this factor. The unfavorable attention soon turned the international community against Iraq. Much of the advantage gained by an opening to the United States in the war was soon lost.

On the positive side, however, the war appeared to confirm the resilience of the Iraqi state. Despite eight years of a bitterly fought war, Iraq's forces and people had managed to defend their country and prevent occupation of their territory by a neighbor three times the country's size. Among most of the population, the war seemed to generate a greater sense of community, even of patriotism. This was truer for the Arab population than for the Kurds. Although most Kurds fought with—not against—Iraqi government forces, the war in the north strengthened and revived the Kurdish opposition. The most remarkable feat—though hardly positive—was that a repressive and autocratic regime, despite some close calls, came through the war with its hold on power strengthened.

The War's Impact on Foreign Policy

The Iran-Iraq war had a major impact on the regime's regional and international position and its foreign policy positions. In 1979 Iraq's position was stable and relatively secure; its economic wealth was growing, and it was able to maintain a high degree of independence in its international relations.[18] Baghdad had begun to play a leading role in the region and even internationally. Eight years later, this position was substantially altered. Much of Iraq's wealth had been dissipated, and it was in debt. Its relative autonomy in the international arena had given way to dependence on regional and global powers.

Iraqi Foreign Policy in the Region

The first casualty of the conflict was Saddam's ambition to assume a leadership role in the region and in the global nonaligned movement. Owing to the war, the location of the nonaligned conference of September 1982 was changed from Baghdad to New Delhi. Instead of Saddam Husain, India's Indira Gandhi assumed the leadership of the nonaligned world for the next four years. The war also ended Saddam's aspirations to play a dominant role in the Gulf. On the contrary, the destruction of Iraq's offshore oil terminals and its reduced income made Iraq heavily dependent financially and politically on the conservative Gulf states that were financing its war effort.

The most important evidence of the shift in the power balance, and the most significant for the future, was the formation of the Gulf

Cooperation Council (GCC) in May 1981, not long after the start of the war. The six-member group included all Arab Gulf states (Kuwait, Saudi Arabia, Qatar, Bahrain, the UAE, and Oman) but pointedly did not include Iraq. Although the idea of the GCC had been entertained earlier, the Arab Gulf states hesitated, partly because of anxiety Iraq would join and then dominate the group. The war conveniently eliminated that possibility. The GCC institutionalized the distance between the Arab Gulf states and Iraq. Even more significant were the deepening military ties between the GCC and the West. Both the formation of the GCC and the US military presence greatly reduced Iraq's room for maneuver in the Gulf and virtually ended its ability to lead any Gulf alliance, even among the Arab states.

The war compelled Iraq to tilt toward the West and its supporters in the Middle East. This was most striking in the case of Egypt. Iraq had earlier taken the lead in ostracizing Egypt for its peace treaty with Israel, but war needs soon reversed Iraq's position. Once the war started, contacts between Egypt and Iraq accelerated. Egyptian munitions, tanks, and volunteers played a role in sustaining the Iraqi war machine. In return, Iraq helped smooth the way for Egypt's reintegration into the Arab world. In November 1987 Egypt was finally readmitted to the Arab League, and almost immediately thereafter Iraq restored diplomatic relations. Egypt's rehabilitation not only restored a more traditional balance of power in the Middle East but also undercut Iraq's earlier tentative steps to supplant Egypt as Arab world leader.

Iraq also became more dependent on Turkey, a pillar of the North Atlantic Treaty Organization, not only because Turkey provided the sole outlet for its oil during much of the war but also because the Turks were policing the Kurds along Iraq's northern frontier while Iraq's troops were engaged with Iran. In 1984 Iraq agreed to let Turkey engage in operations across the border in "hot pursuit" of Turkey's own dissident Kurds. On at least two occasions—August 1986 and March 1987—the Turkish air force undertook raids on Kurdish strongholds in Iraq. Meanwhile, Turkish exports to Iraq increased from $135 million in 1980 to almost $1 billion by 1987; imports, mainly oil, averaged over $1 billion a year.

Relations with Jordan, another pro-Western country, were also greatly strengthened. Jordan provided routes to Aqaba, allowing Iraqi goods to be channeled through this port on the Red Sea. Jordan also helped with the war effort, seconding military officers, supplying tanks, and providing military volunteers. These close links with Jordan were to survive the war.

As relations with pro-Western neighbors improved, Iraqi-Syrian relations deteriorated to the lowest point in years. Syria refused to end its collaboration with Iran, an act viewed in Baghdad as little short of treason to the Arab cause.[19] In October 1980 Baghdad broke diplomatic relations with Damascus and began supporting the Syrian regime's opposition inside Syria and in Lebanon.[20] But Syria cut Iraq's pipeline in April 1982, eliminating half of Iraq's oil exports and costing the country $6 billion. Iraq closed its border with Syria.

One of the most striking changes brought by the war was Iraq's moderation, at least officially, of its stand on the Palestine issue and Israel. In August 1982 in an interview with US Congressman Stephen Solarz, Saddam Husain stated that a condition of security for Israel was necessary for a resolution of the Arab-Israeli conflict. This unprecedented statement was followed by a declaration by Foreign Minister Tariq Aziz that Iraq was "not opposed to a peaceful settlement of the problem, and therefore negotiations with Israel."[21] This shift was designed to propitiate the United States and its regional allies, but even so was remarkable in the wake of the Israeli bombing of Iraq's nuclear reactor in June 1981, which destroyed Iraq's incipient nuclear weapons program.

Iraqi Foreign Policy Toward the Superpowers

The war also affected the way in which Iraq dealt with the superpowers. Iraq was compelled to draw closer to the United States as its difficulties with Iran and its need for superpower support increased. In 1982 Iraq was taken off the US terrorist list, a major step forward for Iraq. The subsequent easing of Iraq's position on Israel made even more progress possible, such as the supplying of US satellite intelligence to the Iraqis during the war, as well as the extension of agricultural credits. But relations with the United States remained fragile. In addition to protests over chemical weapons use, admittedly muted during the war effort, Irangate and the *Stark* episode in 1987 were blows to the relationship, indicating that it was uneasy and based on little more than strategic necessity and the need to contain a common enemy, Iran.[22]

Relations with other Western European countries were likewise strengthened. Iraq relied on France for much of its armaments, including Mirages and the loan of the Super Etendards. By 1983 Iraq was so deeply in debt to France that French financial circles worried about repayment problems, but the French government nevertheless decided to continue its support.

Despite expanding ties to the West, Iraq was only partly able to reduce its dependence on the Soviets for arms. In 1985 Mikhail Gorbachev came to power in the Soviet Union and Saddam Husain visited Moscow in mid-December. The meeting between the Soviet reformer and the troublesome Iraqi client was reportedly cool. Nonetheless, the Soviets agreed to maintain arms support. By 1987 Soviet policy was beginning to shift, as Gorbachev began to change the ground rules of the Cold War. But the real effects of this change came after the cease-fire and did not affect the war's end.

The War's Impact on National Cohesion

One intangible benefit that Iraq appeared to reap—one for which the war was ostensibly fought—was the continued ethnic and sectarian cohesion of the state. The war and its hardships seemed to forge a greater sense of national unity, giving some credence to claims by the Iraqi government and many outside observers that the war had strengthened Iraqi nationhood. But this assessment, although not inaccurate, is incomplete. In fact, the war had a differential impact on Iraq's various communities. Although the regime could generally count on the support of the Arab Sunni population, who most closely identified with the Iraqi nationalist mission, the war put considerable strains on loyalty within the Shi'i and Kurdish communities.

The Shi'a

Shi'i dissidence was the most worrisome for the regime because the Islamic revolution in Iran was the proximate cause of the war and much touted by the Ba'th as its justification. Indeed, the war provided a test case of Shi'i loyalty, not just for the regime but also for the state and the general direction it was pursuing. In fact, the Shi'i community exhibited mixed behavior. There were no massive defections at the front; Iraqi Shi'a fought about as well—or as indifferently—as Iraqi Sunnis. However, the war was not popular in the south, though it was not openly criticized. It is clear that Iraqi Shi'a were not prepared to make common cause with the Shi'a of Iran. Yet they probably fought because of a mixture of motives, among which positive attitudes of loyalty to the state may have been minimal.

In dealing with the Shi'i population, Saddam used his usual carrot-and-stick policy. On the positive side, he moved to integrate more Shi'a into political positions. The party congress held in June 1982 elected a new Regional Command; of the seven new members, a majority were Shi'a.[23] However, these members were not included in the RCC, where most important decisions were made. Greater inclusion was combined with generous public funding in the south for housing projects, hospitals, water and sewage works, electricity, and even improvement and embellishment of mosques. The birthday of Ali, revered by the Shi'a, was made a national holiday.

These moves, however, were accompanied by continued severe persecution of any potential Shi'i opposition. In 1983, after the Islamic Iraqi opposition in Tehran, headed by Muhammad Baqir al-Hakim, decided to constitute itself a government in exile, the Ba'th arrested about eighty members of the family still in Iraq and in May 1983 executed six. In March 1985 a further ten members of the family were executed, and in January 1988 Mahdi al-Hakim, who headed a European-based opposition group, was assassinated in Khartoum.[24]

Major deportations of Iraqis of "Iranian origin," begun in 1980 at the time of Baqir al-Sadr's execution, continued. At the war's end, this group may have totaled 200,000. These moves decapitated Shi'i opposition inside Iraq and moved much of its support base outside the country to Iran. This growing number of alienated, bitter, and frustrated Iraqis provided an ideal resource to be organized by the Iranians and the exiled leadership of the Iraqi Shi'i opposition.

The Formation of SCIRI

The chief mechanism used by Iran to organize these exiled Iraqis after 1980 was the Supreme Council for the Islamic Revolution in Iraq (SCIRI), formed in Tehran on 17 November 1982 at the initiative of Iran.[25] SCIRI was designed as an umbrella group composed of several Shi'i parties—the Da'wa, the Islamic Action Organization, al-Hakim and his supporters, and other groups. In 1986 two tiers were created: an executive committee of fifteen and a general assembly of some eighty members. In 1986 Muhammad Baqir al-Hakim became SCIRI's chairman and its moving force. At this stage SCIRI was committed to the establishment of an Islamic state in Iraq and embraced the key Khumaini concept of the *wilayat al-faqih* (rule of the theological jurist). Both concepts were alien to the majority of Iraqi Shi'a, to say nothing of the Sunnis and secularists.

Whatever the council's ideology, SCIRI's institutional foundation lay in the Iraqi deportees and POWs in Iran and in leadership and support from Iran. From its inception, SCIRI was tied to the Iranian war effort, particularly through its military arm, the Badr Brigade, several thousand strong in 1986. Reportedly, this militia was under Iranian command during the war.[26] In addition to fielding these political and military activities, SCIRI also engaged in destabilizing activities inside Iraq, including sabotage, bombings, and assassination attempts.

Despite its potential for disruption, SCIRI suffered from many shortcomings as a focus for Shi'i loyalty. Its component groups—the Da'wa, the Islamic Action Organization, and SCIRI's core under Hakim—had different constituents, organizations, and leadership. SCIRI's support ultimately came to be focused on Hakim and his followers. The Da'wa was less enthusiastic about ties to Iran or the concept of *wilayat al-faqih*.

SCIRI's strong collaboration with Iran doomed its efforts inside Iraq. Many Shi'a who opposed Saddam and the Ba'th had no desire to be liberated by Tehran or incorporated in a new Islamic empire.

The Kurds

The impact of the war on Kurdish loyalty was more divisive. Kurdish loyalty to the state had always been problematic, but at the start of the war the balance of forces in the north was in favor of the regime. The most serious danger to the state was posed by the continued armed opposition of the KDP, led by the Barzani brothers and by their active military alliance with Iran. The Barzanis, with many of their forces now located in Iran after their disastrous defeat in 1975, had forged close ties with the new Iranian regime and received support in return for their help in curbing the Iranian Kurdish movement (the Kurdistan Democratic Party of Iran).[27] However, in the first few years of the war, the Kurds spent more time fighting among themselves than fighting the government.

In the north, the Fursan was strengthened as Iraqi army forces were withdrawn to the south. However, this situation changed in October 1983 when the KDP joined forces with Iran to attack Banjwin and the Iranians seized Haj Umran, opening a second front in the northern area. In retaliation, the government rounded up some 8,000 male members of the Barzani clan and sent them to an unknown destination; they were never heard from again. This event forced the government to send troops north and to support the Fursan at a time when it was faced with increasing numbers of Kurdish deserters.[28]

Under these new circumstances, a new national defense battalion was formed of Fursan. By the summer of 1986, it may have totaled 150,000, at least three times the number of *peshmerga* under arms. The Fursan contingents, supplied by tribal leaders, were a volunteer force that included villagers and townspeople, farmers and shopkeepers—even some professionals. They helped stabilize the north, especially in and around the cities and communications routes.[29]

But the Fursan groups were not strong enough to hold the north. Mas'ud Barzani and Jalal Talabani began coordinating a broad opposition movement, and in May 1987 an opposition umbrella came into being, including the KDP, the Patriotic Union of Kurdistan (PUK), the Kurdish Socialist Party, the Iraq Communist Party, and the Assyrian Democratic Movement. By 1987 the KDP had control of virtually the entire northern border with Turkey from Syria to Iran, while the PUK controlled the border with Iran from Rawanduz south to Banjwin.

The Anfal Campaign

It was in these circumstances that the government made the decision to take the drastic measures that would dramatically change its relations with the Kurdish population. This began with the appointment on 28 February of Ali Hasan al-Majid as governor of the northern provinces. The problem was seen no longer as one of controlling the borders but of dealing with an insurgency that controlled much of the rural areas. A new scorched-earth policy had as its purpose to clear the region of guerrillas and remove the village environment that protected them. The campaign, generally known as the "Anfal" (Spoils),[30] reached a level of brutality and killing so high and wreaked such devastation on settled life, even for a regime widely known for its brutality, that it finally resulted in international outrage and charges of genocide.

The operation began in April 1987 with attacks on the KDP headquarters in the Dahuk area and on the PUK stronghold in the Balisan valley north of Sulaimaniyya. In this attack, chemical weapons were used for the first time on the civilian population in the north.[31] The pattern to be followed later was established here. Villages were cleared, with chemical weapons if necessary, and villagers were transported to holding areas. The Fursan would follow, occupying the villages and often looting them. If there was resistance, villages were fired on and farms destroyed.[32] Many of those fleeing from detention centers were "disappeared" or were killed.

Between April and June 1987 over five hundred villages were destroyed. In the new camps villagers were held under appalling conditions, and many did not survive. Despite this brutality, however, in this early period of the campaign villagers were apparently given notice to evacuate and offered alternatives. Some went to relatives; others were resettled. It was those who resisted who were murdered or disappeared.[33] The unfolding "Kurdish solution" was so drastic that the policy backfired, creating greater Kurdish defections from the Fursan, who joined the *peshmerga*. But worse was to come.

In January 1988 the threat to Baghdad in the north deepened, with Iran's last attempt to break through the lines in cooperation with the Kurds. The Iraqi government now responded with a series of planned and concerted military attacks designed to destroy and eradicate armed resistance and areas of *peshmerga* control once and for all. First, there were focused assaults on targeted areas that all used chemical weapons and high-explosive air attacks to clear out *peshmerga* strongholds before ground troops entered. Second, once villagers were flushed out, men were separated from women, children, and the elderly; the latter were put in mass holding camps, where considerable numbers died. Many of the men were taken out of sight, where they were apparently indiscriminately shot and buried in mass graves. The villages they had inhabited were cleared and destroyed. It was this series of attacks to which the term *Anfal* has been applied.

One attack in particular, in Halabja, has achieved notoriety. Halabja was important because of its location near the Darbandikhan Dam, which controlled the water supply for the capital. On 15 March the PUK and Iranian forces took the town, driving Iraqi forces out. Halabja then became the scene of one of the worst chemical attacks during the war. On 16 March Iraq bombarded the city with a chemical cocktail; somewhere between 3,500 and 5,000 people were killed.

How many Kurds died in the scorched-earth campaign cannot be known for certain. Human rights investigators claim that at least 50,000 and possibly as many as 100,000 were killed in the Anfal attacks. By the end of the Iran-Iraq war, an estimated 4,000 villages and hamlets had been destroyed and some 1.5 million people forcibly displaced or resettled. But the operations also left a number of refugees across the borders—by August 1988 there were reportedly 60,000 to 150,000 in Turkey and possibly 200,000 in Iran.[34] The Anfal marks one of the most brutal actions in Iraq's modern history and had a profound demographic, economic, and psychological impact on the Kurdish area.

Although the government ended the war in control of its northern areas, the Anfal campaign polarized the Kurdish population. Even a number of the progovernment Kurdish contingents soured on the regime. Much of the north's agricultural production was damaged, making Iraq even more dependent on imports. Meanwhile, the government now had large numbers of hostile Kurds in settlements to watch. However, much of this cleansing campaign was visited on rural areas and the strongholds of the opposition. The urban areas, the stronghold of the government forces, on which considerable economic development had been lavished earlier, remained largely untouched and, in fact, at war's end appeared prosperous.[35] For the time being, the Kurdish insurgency and the Kurdish nationalist parties had been defeated, but at an enormous price. One part of that price was deeper Kurdish alienation. Another was international opprobrium over the use of chemical weapons and the Anfal campaign.

Economic and Social Effects of the War

The war's huge economic bill and the regime's own unwillingness to face the costs marked the beginning of a continual decline for Iraq. By far the most serious blow to the economy was damage to Iraq's oil infrastructure and closure of the Persian Gulf to Iraqi oil exports. As a result, Iraq lost much of its income for the duration of the war—and even beyond. The country's major offshore oil terminals in the south—Mina-l-Bakr (now the Al Basra Oil Terminal) and Khaur al-Amayya—were destroyed, making oil exports through the Gulf impossible. The Basra refinery was severely affected, as were the two fertilizer plants in the area. The petrochemical plant at Zubair, ready for commissioning when the war broke out, was unable to operate for the war's duration. The same was true of the nearby iron and steel plants.

More important than physical destruction was the cutoff of oil exports. When the war began in September 1980, Iraq was producing 3.5 million barrels per day. In the preceding year, it had earned export revenues of $26 billion. By 1982 exports were well under 1 million barrels per day, and by 1983, when Organization of Petroleum Exporting Countries prices began to fall, Iraq's oil revenues were reduced to about $10 billion per annum, roughly a third of prewar levels.[36]

For the first two years, the regime went to some lengths to insulate the population from the war's economic effects, mainly to guard against dissent against an unpopular conflict. As a result, it followed a policy of providing both "guns and butter" by drawing down reserves at $1 billion a month and by borrowing from the Arab Gulf states at an estimated rate of $10 billion a year, putting it well into the red by 1983.

By mid-1982, however, it was apparent that Iraq simply did not have the resources to pay all its bills. The government took several steps. First, an austerity program was begun in November 1982. Most government employee benefits were reduced, imports were pared down by 50 percent, and the development program was cut back. By 1983 only those projects capable of aiding the war effort or expanding Iraq's potential for increased oil production and export were receiving funds.

Second, measures were taken to liberalize the economy. Although the new policy took effect all across the board—in agriculture, industry, trade, and services—it was particularly apparent in agriculture. Public Law 35 of 1983 allowed private individuals and companies to lease from the state large blocks of land—ironically, those large-scale private mechanized farms that had been eliminated in the early years of the land reform. In 1987 new impetus was given to agricultural privatization with the selling of state lands and collective farms to private enterprise, including poultry and dairy enterprises. Privatization was also encouraged in industry and the trade sector. A number of state enterprises were sold to private entrepreneurs, including supermarkets, gas stations, and smaller factories. Even in the service area, the regime came increasingly to rely on private companies and individuals. In health services, critical to the war effort, the government turned to foreign hospital management companies and also encouraged doctors with previous experience in the state sector to establish private hospitals, a clear departure from socialism.

The haste in selling off government enterprises without creating the necessary legal, economic, and financial underpinnings for a private sector led to abuses, creating a new and larger class of private landlords, entrepreneurs, and contractors tied to the regime and therefore inclined to support it. Moreover, despite this development, privatization did not really change the nature of the economic system; the state continued to play the preponderant role in the economy.

Iraq then moved ahead on two fronts to sustain its economy—improving oil exports and borrowing to finance civilian and military imports. In 1982 Iraq expanded its pipeline capacity to 1 million barrels per day through a connection to the Saudi pipeline to the Red Sea. By the war's end, oil exports were up to 2.1 million barrels per day. In addition, trucks carried oil through Jordan and Turkey. To pay for these improvements, as well as the costs of war, substantial loans were negotiated from Western Europe, Japan, and the United States. Meanwhile, financial aid and loans of various kinds continued from Saudi Arabia and Kuwait. Iraq also became indebted to the USSR for arms sales.

Although these measures improved Iraq's economic situation somewhat by 1988, they could not make up for the losses. Iraq's modest improvement in oil exports was offset by a decline in the price of oil, especially in 1986. By 1987 Iraq was earning a mere $11 billion a year in oil revenue, still only a little more than a third of what it had earned the year prior to the war.[37] The war also cost Iraq virtually all its reserves, roughly $35 billion.

Debt

Rather than paying for the war as it dragged on, Iraq had mortgaged its future by borrowing. Iraq came out of the war with an external debt—exclusive of that owed to Arab supporters—of at least $40 billion but more likely $50 billion. Of this, the Soviet bloc was owed about $8 billion, essentially for arms; Western governments and commercial establishments (mainly Germany, Japan, France, and the United States), about $27 billion; and developing countries, such as Brazil, Turkey, and South Korea, about $10 billion. At the start of the war, Iraq's debt had been miniscule—some $2.5 billion. During the war Iraq followed a policy of pressing for a rescheduling, or a rollover, of the debt, along with a further, longer-term advance of credits. The creditors, with little choice if they wished to retrieve their debt, usually obliged. At war's end Iraq's annual payments, principal and interest, on debt to the West were estimated at a huge $7 billion. The overhanging debt and Iraq's new and far weaker credit rating were important impediments to rapid recuperation and development.

The loans and advances from Gulf states, primarily Kuwait and Saudi Arabia, were estimated at another $30 billion to $40 billion. These sums would include oil sold on Iraq's behalf, payments through oil or cash to the USSR for weapons, and nominal loans. Iraq, however, considered these not as loans but as the Gulf contribution to the war effort. With the decline in oil prices in the later 1980s, these "contributions" had caused hardships in Gulf countries now facing their own financial difficulties. These difficulties—as well as the whole question of repayment—would set the stage for the tensions that followed the war.

Closure of the Shatt

At the war's end, Iraq also faced another economic difficulty, the continued closure of the Shatt al-Arab—a real cause for concern because Iraq's control of the Shatt had been a major, if not the major, justification for the war. This situation also curtailed Basra's function as Iraq's major port. Before the war, the Shatt had carried almost two-thirds of Iraq's nonoil cargo. The river remained impassable because it was filled with war-related debris, some of it highly dangerous. The Shatt was also littered with over a hundred ships, some of substantial size and some sunk in the navigable channel. Lastly, the river had not been dredged for eight years, leading to massive accumulations of silt, some of it possibly contaminated with chemical weapons. The cleanup operation was expensive, highly technical, and estimated to take up to five years.

The closure of the Shatt and the difficulty of reopening it shifted Iraq's focus to its alternative port, Umm Qasr, on the Khaur Abd Allah waterway, and to a lesser extent Zubair, to its north. Even though expansion of these alternative ports was possible, Umm Qasr raised the perennial problem of Iraq's long-standing border dispute with Kuwait and, because of Iraq's desire for a secure seaward approach to the port, control over the two Kuwaiti islands, Warba and Bubayan, that lay at the entrance to the waterway. Thus, the closure of the Shatt not only focused Iraq's attention once again on Kuwait but also limited its ability to develop.

Differential Distribution of Destruction

Even more significant for the future was uneven geographic distribution of war damage. Damage to Basra and its environs was extensive. In 1977 Basra had been Iraq's third largest province; by 1987 it was seventh, although it later regained population. The major industrial complex in the south, so recently built up, was shut down by the war. Agriculture, too, was neglected. The same was true in Kurdish areas of the north.

The center of the country was least affected. The concentration of new industry here, as well as population growth, was significant. The capital and its suburbs were the major recipients of most benefits. Tikrit was completely changed, greatly improving the position of its political elite and their supporters.

The Impact on Labor

The war also had significant costs on the labor front and greatly distorted Iraq's employment structure. The military siphoned off much of the skilled and educated workforce, always in short supply, and wasted its potential productivity in eight years of war. According to one report, government offices had their workforces reduced by as much as 45 percent.[38] As the Iraqi army swallowed up available manpower, serious labor shortages occurred.

To ease the shortage, Iraq imported foreign labor on a large scale. Indians, Filipinos, and Koreans flooded the construction industry, while many positions in the bureaucracy—and later in agriculture—were taken by Egyptians. Even menial jobs for unskilled workers fell into foreign hands. Some estimates in the early 1980s put the number of foreign workers at 2 million.[39]

One positive change came in rising employment for women, who also helped fill the gap. This was particularly true for Iraq's increasing numbers of educated women. The percentage of women in the non-agricultural workforce rose from about 17 percent in the 1970s to about 25 percent in the 1980s, a very high figure for the Arab world.

Social Costs

The war also had social costs, although these are more difficult to measure. The most important, of course, was the toll in human casualties. It has been estimated that total military casualties for Iraq were around 380,000, of which about 125,000 were deaths and about 255,000 wounded. Iraqi POWs totaled between 50,000 and 80,000; many of these did not return to Iraq for years after the war. To these casualties must be added the 50,000 to 100,000 of the Anfal campaigns. This would make a military and civilian casualty total over the eight-year period of at least 500,000, or about 2.7 percent of the population.

In addition to the obvious human loss, casualties also represented a substantial loss of manpower and skill. The Iraqis attempted to preserve their skilled population, deferring students until they had finished their studies, but all had to serve at some point, and many were lost. The loss of young lives weakened support for a regime that had gotten the country into an endless war from which it seemed unable to extricate itself. The war ended the sense of buoyancy that had characterized Iraq a decade earlier.

The war also began a change in the social structure. The slowdown in development, cutbacks in imports, and the resulting inflation—28 percent at the end of the war—bit deeply into the newly acquired prosperity of the middle class and impaired the social mobility on which the regime had based so much of its legitimacy. Many Iraqis were forced or pressured into giving up savings for the war effort, thus beginning a process of disinvestment. Many salaried civil servants, who depended on the government for jobs and income, saw their status and standard of living decline as wages failed to keep up with prices of food and housing. Many of these professionals resented the sale of government-owned industry and agricultural property to private interests, who then profited and became rich. The slow but unmistakable decline of Iraq's middle class and its salaried income base began during the war.

Even more striking than the gradual weakening of middle-class standards was the growth of an affluent and wealthy class of merchants, contractors, and businessmen as the government opened up the private sector. Some merchants and landowners became merely affluent, but others became conspicuously rich, with a high concentration of wealth and business in the hands of a few. Although the new commercial and entrepreneurial elite did cut across ethnic and sectarian lines (there were large Kurdish landlords and contractors as well as rich Shi'i merchants and entrepreneurs), many were beholden to the regime for their prosperity, whether through the sale of lands, government-sponsored contracts, or the purchase of factories previously owned by the government.[40]

Eventually, the war even weakened some of the progress made in the status of women. The Ba'th position on women was relatively progressive to start with, encouraging their education, literacy, and professional advancement. Initially, the war encouraged this progress by providing jobs for women and integrating them further into the workforce, particularly professional and educated women. But as the war dragged on, even this Ba'th policy changed. To make up for losses at the front, the regime attempted to raise the birthrate by encouraging large families. Saddam Husain urged every family, including women in their forties, to have five children. Far more important for women, however, was the toll of casualties on marriage and the family. Many women had to put off marriage for a decade for fear of becoming war widows. Even worse was the situation of the many widows or wives of handicapped men left to support families. Postponement of marriage, loss of manpower, and the decade-long delay in starting careers and work for both young women and men took a heavy toll on the family, still the bedrock of Iraqi society.

The War's Political Effects

These economic and social repercussions naturally spilled over into the political arena. Initially the regime had support in the war, but the army's reverses and its retreat to the borders in 1982 unquestionably eroded loyalty to the regime. The first challenge for Husain was to maintain the allegiance of his inner constituency. The second was to maintain political control over an expanding army and prevent military leadership from acting as a countervailing center of power to himself. In the end, the regime survived, but it changed in several ways that strengthened the personal power of Saddam and his centrality to the system.

The Concentration of Power in the Presidency

Within the formal structure of government, the locus of power was gradually shifted from the party, especially the Regional Command, to the office of the president, which Saddam now turned into his personal fief. The presidential office became the most important center for decision-making, reducing the party to an arm of the state. The party itself was transformed from a cadre of ideologically committed individuals to a mass-based organization designed to support the government. But as membership in the party became a touchstone of loyalty, it also became a channel of mobility. Party membership became essential for employment, acceptance to elite schools, and professional advancement.

Elections for the National Assembly were also used to generate a popular base for Saddam's leadership rather than for the party. In fact, it became a competing institution. The election of the first assembly, initiated in June 1980 after Saddam's assumption of the presidency, gave the Ba'th 75 percent of the seats. By the time of the third election, held in 1989, the Ba'th had been reduced to a slim majority. The assembly had no real legislative authority, but it did provide a voice beyond the party for the population at large.[41]

Buttressing this structure was a full-blown personality cult. Already under way well before the war, it reached new heights during the war. Saddam made himself not only head of state but also symbol of the people. His picture, in multiple guises—as peasant, as educated official, as warrior, as religious penitent—became ubiquitous. The celebration of his birthday on 28 April became a national holiday, commemorated with processions from all over Iraq to his hometown of Tikrit. Radio, TV, and press were all saturated with coverage of his pictures, words, and activities. Iraq's revolutionary history was divided into two phases: before Saddam and after him.

Ideological Shifts

As the political structure changed, so, too, did the ideology. Throughout the 1980s, Saddam experimented with different formulations designed to encourage national cohesion and support for the war and his own legitimacy. The metamorphosis from Arab nationalism to Iraqi patriotism was clear. Mesopotamian history and heritage were publicly emphasized, and Saddam was repeatedly referred to as the modern-day Nebuchadnezzar, the ancient Babylonian king who had ruled over the Babylonian Empire at its height.[42] But Iraq's central role in Arab and Islamic history was also emphasized, particularly to counter the penetration of Khumaini's religious propaganda from Iran. Saddam even invented a family lineage that tied him to Muhammad and, in a particular attempt to appeal to the Shi'a, to Ali. The war was known as "Qadisiyyat Saddam," in commemoration of the famous battle in which the Arab Muslims of the seventh century defeated the infidel Persians. All of these ideological myths were designed to generate a greater identity with the state, but even more to justify the legitimacy of the regime personified by Saddam.

Impact on the Military and Security

Meanwhile, the military was kept under control by tight surveillance. The war saw an increase in the security apparatus as well as the army. To the three major security organizations present before the war—the Public Security Directorate (Amn al-Amm) under the Ministry of Interior, Military Intelligence (Istikhbarat Askariyya) under the Ministry of Defense, and the General Intelligence Service (Mukhabarat al-Amma) under the party—was now added the Special Security Organization (Amn al-Khass), essentially under the president. Headed by Husain Kamil in the 1980s, it protected not only the regime but also its weapons of mass destruction program.

Kinship ties were also used to cement control of the military. Adnan Khairallah Talfah, Saddam's cousin and brother-in-law, was maintained as minister of defense during the war. The upper echelons of the expanding military were liberally seeded with Tikritis and related clans. By the war's end, clan-based control at the commanding heights of the military and security systems was well established.

These steps enabled Saddam to surmount crises and even strengthen the regime during the war. But they did not end tensions or opposition. Within Iraq the security apparatus kept the opposition underground, but it was not entirely cowed, as sporadic bombings and assassination attempts indicated. Most opposition groups operated from headquarters in Syria, Iran, or Europe. Among the secular groups, the most important were the Communists, several Kurdish organizations, and a pro-Syrian Ba'th splinter party led by Hasan al-Naqib, a former army colonel.

Even within the party, dissatisfaction with the party's capture by Saddam Husain and his family led to movements in party ranks to reform. Most of these were reflected in pamphlets circulated outside the country. The dissatisfaction of those in the center was more than matched by disaffection from the two traditional poles of regime opposition—the Shi'a and the Kurds. But both of these opposition forces were dealt with brutally. Having surmounted tensions and opposition from within and from without, the regime now faced an entirely new challenge: coping with the outcome—and the costs—of the war.

The Aftermath of the War

These difficulties, however, were not uppermost in the minds of most Iraqis at the time of the cease-fire. To the contrary, Iraqis came out on the streets to celebrate with a sense not only of relief but also of victory. Along with the relief were expectations of a fairly rapid economic revival and renewed possibilities of development. These expectations were encouraged by the government, which took a number of immediate steps to erase war damage and stimulate a sense of economic improvement. First, it initiated a three-month crash program, costing $4 billion, to rebuild Basra. Faw, a much smaller town, was also rebuilt. The port of Umm Qasr was expanded and the industrial complex in the south revived. The encouragement of the private sector, begun earlier, was given ever-greater impetus. The sale of state assets increased, tourism was privatized, and in 1988 alone the private sector was allowed to import billions of dollars of goods, equal to almost half of government imports.

These economic and political steps were accompanied by a major propaganda campaign designed to cement the idea of an Iraqi victory in the popular mind and to encourage expectations that Iraq's prosperity would soon return. Iraqis hailed the cease-fire as "a great victory which Iraq scored in the name of all Arabs and humanity."[43]

These early postwar steps, together with the "victory" propaganda, projected an image of strength and early recuperation. Both were illusions. They could not long disguise the real costs of the war and dissatisfaction among Iraqis with the regime that had brought them. Gradually, these problems began to surface once the euphoria of the cease-fire had dissipated.

These underlying discontents were soon focused on the major political changes that had taken place since the start of the war—the dominance of political life by Saddam Husain and his family and their personal corruption and misbehavior. The misbehavior soon came into view in a stunning episode that occurred in October 1988. Although private in nature, it soon became widely known. During an official reception in Baghdad attended by Suzanne Mubarak, the Egyptian president's wife, Saddam's son Udayy, drunk and unruly, broke into the gathering and provoked a quarrel with Hanna Jajjo, a close aide and confidante of Saddam Husain. In full view of all assembled, Udayy killed Jajjo, reportedly with a blow to his head.[44] The cause of the outburst, soon revealed, was purely personal. Udayy, and his mother, Sajida, blamed Jajjo for having introduced Saddam to Samira Shahbandar, wife of the head of Iraqi Airways, whom the president was rumored to be on the verge of marrying. The murder and the family feud behind it revealed the extent to which personal rule and family concerns had overwhelmed the process of government in Iraq. Saddam responded by briefly imprisoning his son, then exiling him, then pardoning him.

Not long after, family cohesion suffered another blow. On 5 May 1989 Adnan Khairallah Talfah died in a helicopter crash near Hatra on a return from a tour of the Kurdish area. Although his death was attributed to a sudden and violent sandstorm (which actually did occur), his demise was widely attributed to Saddam Husain. Whatever the truth, Khairallah's death intensified popular dismay at the behavior of Saddam and his family. It also removed a key element of family control over the military.

This trouble from inside the regime was accompanied by problems from abroad, especially from the United States, which had been instrumental in providing political and military support for Iraq during the last years of the war. Opposition to the regime from the US Congress and some of the media, most of it stemming from Iraq's use of chemical weapons and other brutal measures against the Kurds in the war's aftermath, began almost as soon as the cease-fire went into effect. On 8 September 1988 the US Department of State announced it had conclusive evidence of Iraq's use of chemical weapons against the Kurds, and Secretary of State George Shultz warned that such use would affect US relations with Iraq. Whatever support Iraq could expect from the United States was evaporating.

Saddam's First Decade

Saddam Husain had managed to survive his first decade since assuming the presidency. However, by concentrating all power in his own hands and silencing even modest dissent, he had made Iraq vulnerable to a seriously flawed decision—to go to war with Iran. Though Iraq was undoubtedly challenged by a new, radical regime in Iran, the new Iraqi president appears to have made his decision for war not based on a desire to ward off an immediate threat but based on calculations of long-term gains and an overestimate of his own capabilities. The result was a long and debilitating conflict that eroded much of the physical and human capital built up in the previous decade.

The war was not a total loss. It had generated a sense of cohesion—even patriotism—among many Iraqis, and the country had been able, despite its losses, to protect some of its human assets and begin rebuilding. But these modest accomplishments could not mask for long the deeper problems. The question was whether Saddam and the regime he now led were ready to recognize the new reality or would believe the myth of victory and strength they were now propagating.

9

THE SADDAM HUSAIN
REGIME, 1990–2003

Although Iraq had emerged from the Iran-Iraq war with its state intact and with some sense of national pride in having outlasted its adversary, the country faced numerous problems. It was operating with a depleted treasury, and there was still no peace with Iran. Iraq also had to deal with changes in the international environment—the end of the Cold War, a deterioration in relations with the United States, and a sudden collapse of the oil market. These accumulating problems produced a gathering storm that became apparent by late spring 1990 and contributed to the disastrous decision to invade Kuwait. The invasion brought decisive international action, leading to a second Gulf war that ended in defeat, harsh and humiliating cease-fire terms for Iraq, and a widespread rebellion in the north and south of the country that tore the fabric of the state.

The regime survived—barely—but the steps it took to do so emphasized its worst features: a narrow power base, reliance on security institutions, and brutality in repressing its population. Saddam's government faced continual opposition in the north from the Kurds, who carved out a self-governing enclave that would make their future reintegration into the Iraqi state more difficult. Shi'i opposition continued in the south, where the population was largely alienated and neglected. And the exile opposition gained a new lease on life in neighboring countries and in the United States. In foreign affairs, the main feature of the decade was the struggle with the West to remove the cease-fire terms—sanctions, weapons inspections, and no-fly zones, with only partial success. The outcome was a continual downward spiral—economically, politically, and socially—from which Iraq could not fully recover before the international invasion of 2003 pushed it over the edge.

The Occupation of Kuwait: Causes and Motivations

The Iraqi decision to invade and occupy Kuwait was so astonishing that it has given rise to much speculation and analysis about why it was made.[1] The most plausible explanation takes account of several factors, domestic and international, that by the late spring of 1990 converged in Iraqi thinking and focused on Kuwait as a solution.

The Kuwaiti Border Issue

One issue was Iraq's long-standing dispute with Kuwait over borders, which became increasingly acrimonious in the aftermath of the Iran-Iraq war. The continued closure of the Shatt al-Arab after the war meant that Iraq needed to expand its access around the port of Umm Qasr. It wanted a border that would give it control of the Khaur Abd Allah channel and the islands of Warba and Bubayan, which dominate access to the waterway. Kuwait had no intention of giving up this territory.

Iraq's Economic Problems

The victory propaganda and the early postwar flurry of rebuilding could not disguise Iraq's growing economic problems. Most important was the shortage of money to pay expenses. A year after the end of hostilities, Iraq was earning only $13 billion from oil revenues but would need an extra $10 billion per annum just to balance its current budget.[2] Meanwhile, the regime found it difficult to expand oil production much beyond 2 million barrels per day without more investment in the industry and repair of its facilities.

The most serious economic problem was Iraq's debt. By 1990 Iraq owed over $50 billion to Western creditors and to Russia. Iraq refused to pay the debt, rolling over interest payments in return for new loans, allowing the debt to mount. As a result, foreign credit began to dry up. To solve this problem, the regime focused its attention not on Western creditors but on creditors in the Gulf and on Kuwait in particular. Iraq wanted this debt forgiven. The loans from Kuwait and Saudi Arabia were portrayed as payment to Iraq for protecting the region.[3] Although Saudi Arabia was willing to write off the debt, Kuwait was not, probably because it wanted to tie any such concession to a settlement of Iraqi claims on the border. In February 1990 Saddam demanded not only a moratorium on wartime loans but also an immediate infusion of funds in the neighborhood of $30 billion, a sort of Arab Marshall Plan to rebuild Iraq and cover its growing financial crisis. The request was accompanied by a threat. The Gulf states should know "that if they do not give this money to me, I will know how to get it."[4] By this time, money had superseded borders as the main issue with Kuwait.

Iraq was also facing an additional financial crisis it had not bargained for—a drop in oil prices that drastically compounded its financial shortfall and drove the situation into a real crisis stage. The cause, in the Iraqi view, was a refusal of some Organization of Petroleum Exporting Countries (OPEC) producers to stick to their assigned oil quotas, thereby flooding the market with petroleum and drastically reducing prices.[5] Kuwait and the United Arab Emirates (UAE) were identified as the culprits. In fact, the claim was not invalid. At the start of 1990, instead of adhering to the its own quota of 22 million barrels per day, OPEC was producing 24 million. Kuwait and the UAE accounted for 75 percent of the excess.

The Changing International Balance of Power

Iraq's worsening economic situation also played out against the dramatic changes in the international balance of power as the Soviet empire collapsed and the newly created states of Eastern Europe took shape. This remarkable development not only weakened the power of the former Soviet Union—Iraq's chief arms supplier and political supporter—but also ended the former bipolar world. The new, truncated Soviet state was too reduced in power to counterbalance the United States and—worse—had joined the West in a new policy of détente.

Meanwhile, Iraq had to face a deterioration in its relations with the United States. The end of the Iran-Iraq war and the Cold War relieved pressures on the United States to support regional clients and allowed domestic anti-Iraqi forces to surface. By the beginning of 1990, criticism of US support for Iraq in Congress and the media was vocal and this time centered on the regime itself. Newspaper articles and then the Voice of America itself, on 15 February, suggested that Saddam Husain should be overthrown.

Iraq's WMD Program

Another indirect cause of the crisis was Iraq's renewed attempts to develop weapons of mass destruction (WMD), both an indigenous nuclear weapons capacity and biological weapons and missiles. According to estimates, by 1990 Iraq had spent up to $10 billion on various means of developing nuclear weapons.[6] At least eight sites were dedicated to nuclear weapons development, and in February 1990 Iraq activated its first uranium enrichment plant at Tarmiyya. Not surprisingly, this renewed interest in WMD gave rise to an active interdiction effort, both by the West (especially the United States and Britain) and by Israel.

As a result, the Israeli issue soon became intertwined with the Kuwait crisis. Iraq's fears of another Israeli strike on its nuclear facilities grew, increasing Baghdad's paranoia. At the same time, Israeli involvement provided Saddam with an issue on which it was always easy to gain Arab support.

On 2 April Saddam disclosed that Iraq had binary chemical weapons and that he would use them to "burn half of Israel" should Israel try to attack Iraq.[7] The statement had a major negative impact in the West and in Israel. But in the Arab world, almost instantly, Saddam was proclaimed a hero for standing up to Israel. And as popular support grew, especially in the Arab "street," it fed Saddam's growing conception of his role as an Arab leader and his pique at the intransigence of a country like Kuwait in thwarting his goals.

The Kuwaiti "Conspiracy"

By May 1990 these various elements had coalesced in Iraqi thinking into an elaborate conspiracy theory that focused on Kuwait. In this theory, Kuwait was responsible for Iraq's financial crisis. Kuwait had refused to cancel Iraq's war debts or to extend the kind of financial help that would contribute to reviving Iraq's economy and covering its budget shortfall.[8] Kuwait was also accused of tapping into the southern tip of the Rumaila oil field, which straddled the border with Kuwait, and of stealing Iraqi oil. Most important of all, it was manipulating oil prices to cause Iraq harm.

These specific charges against Kuwait were now put in the context of the collapse of the USSR, the emergence of increased hostility in the United States, and US/UK efforts, along with those of Israel, to curtail Iraq's WMD program. Kuwait, in this view, was not acting alone but was in collusion with the United States and Israel in this effort to weaken Iraq. Behind these extraordinary charges, one can detect the emerging frustration—and perhaps desperation—of Saddam in the postwar period. In his view, Iraq, as a large, well-endowed military power, should be able to command respect and concessions from Kuwait. These themes were laid out publicly in several meetings but most specifically at the Arab summit meeting in Baghdad on 30 May, where Saddam equated Kuwaiti actions to a "kind of war against Iraq."[9] This meeting marked a key turning point in the march to another war.

Iraq's Invasion of Kuwait

In the secretive world of Baghdad, it is difficult to determine exactly when and how the final decision to invade Kuwait was made, but all the evidence indicates a process kept in the hands of Saddam Husain and a few close cohorts he could trust. There was no prior consultation with the minister of defense, the chief of staff, or most civilian leaders. Although the idea may have been germinating for some time, the planning was clearly haphazard and rushed and may not have crystalized much before mid-July.

By that time, events moved rapidly to a conclusion. On 15 July Iraq went to the Arab League and laid out its case against Kuwait. The very next day, the movement of Republican Guard units to the Kuwaiti border began, and by the last week in July Iraq had in place the military capability for invading and occupying all of Kuwait. The threats and troop movements took most observers, whether inside or outside Iraq, by surprise. Both King Husain of Jordan and Palestinian leader Yasir Arafat attempted to mediate the dispute, but with little effect. Husni Mubarak of Egypt made a sudden visit to Baghdad to talk to Saddam Husain on 24 July; he returned to Cairo mistakenly thinking the crisis had been defused.

More important was the potential response of the United States. On 25 July, the US ambassador to Iraq, April Glaspie, had an interview with Saddam Husain and left Baghdad a few days later, assuming the situation was under control. The interview was controversial. In the Arab world it was widely believed that Saddam's main purpose was to probe potential US reaction in case Iraq decided to invade Kuwait and that Glaspie's failure to strongly warn against this contingency was interpreted by Saddam as a green, or at least amber, light. Others have seen the meeting as a deception, designed to keep US intervention at bay and to provide some time to put the invasion plan in place.[10] If this was the purpose, the meeting succeeded—but at a huge price for Iraq because it played into Saddam's miscalculations.

Iraq also had to take account the reaction from Iran, the front on which many of his forces were still concentrated. On 30 July, Saddam suggested to President Akbar Hashimi Rafsanjani that he would be willing to acquiesce in practice to Iranian demands on the boundary of the Shatt while retaining "sovereignty" over the river; in return he would withdraw Iraqi forces from Iran. Rafsanjani insisted on Saddam's firm adherence to the 1975 accord dividing the river between the two powers.[11] It was not until 14 August, after the invasion, that Saddam finally conceded, essentially relinquishing Iraqi claims to the Shatt al-Arab. This agreement released Iraqi troops in Iran for the Kuwaiti theater and essentially indicated a willingness by Saddam to burn his bridges behind him on the Kuwait venture, substituting future gains in Kuwait for any loss on the Shatt.

Finally, after all these preparatory steps, on 31 July Iraqi and Kuwaiti delegates met in Jidda for negotiations, as agreed. The Iraqis made their demands—territorial concessions, compensation for oil "stolen" from the Rumaila field, forgiveness of debt, and an economic package to compensate Iraq for losses in the war. Unlike Iraq, Kuwait appears to have considered the Jidda meeting the first step in a longer negotiating process during which it could bargain its way to a solution, but shortly before midnight orders were given to Iraqi forces to cross the Kuwaiti frontier. The decision to occupy Kuwait, one of the most fateful in Iraq's modern history, had been taken. Iraq entered Kuwait (much as it had Iran a decade earlier) under one set of expectations but soon encountered a very different reality. Rather than a quick conquest, at relatively minor cost, Iraq found itself facing a major international confrontation and devastating long-term costs and consequences.

The Invasion and Its Impact

The Occupation

Iraqi forces crossed the frontier at 2 am on 2 August 1990 (local time).[12] Republican Guard units moved rapidly toward Kuwait City while special forces secured several key sites, including the two islands of Warba and Bubayan, Kuwaiti air fields, and the palaces of the amir and the crown prince. There was some Kuwaiti resistance around the amir's palace and elsewhere, but this was soon extinguished.

The initial occupation was far more successful than the attempt to establish a temporary government. At 9:30 am on 2 August Baghdad radio announced a "coup" and the establishment of a provisional government in Kuwait, which had allegedly asked for military support from Iraq. It was headed by Ala Husain Ali, a junior officer in the Kuwaiti army who had mixed Kuwaiti-Iraqi parentage and had studied in Baghdad and joined the Ba'th. He was promoted to colonel, made prime minister of the new government, and sent to Baghdad to meet Saddam Husain.[13]

But the amir, the crown prince, and the rest of the ruling family had had just enough advance warning to escape to Saudi Arabia. Here they were able to appeal for international support and within hours were broadcasting to the population, urging it to resist. Not only had the Iraqis failed to capture or annihilate the ruling family, but also a surprisingly vigorous underground resistance to the occupation emerged. Despite efforts by Tariq Aziz and others to find well-known Kuwaitis willing to associate themselves with the "coup," none would cooperate.[14] Finally, a handful of junior Kuwaiti officers were put in a cabinet along with Ala Husain Ali. Iraqi failure to eliminate the Kuwaiti ruling family and to find any credible government replacement as a fig leaf inside Kuwait revealed the operation for what it was—blatant seizure and occupation of a small, rich country by a larger and more powerful neighbor.

International Reaction

The reaction of the international community was immediate and hostile. On 3 August the UN Security Council (UNSC) passed Resolution 660, unequivocally condemning the aggression and calling for Iraq's withdrawal. The United States took immediate steps to deny Iraq access to its own—and to Kuwait's more substantial—overseas assets; other countries followed suit. Under US leadership, Resolution 661, which prohibited all trade (including oil) with Iraq and any transfer of funds except for food, medicine, and necessities of life was passed on 6 August.

The response in the Arab world, however, was more ambivalent, revealing underlying differences on how to react. The Saudis were in the most difficult position. Prior to the invasion, the Saudis had been somewhat sympathetic to some of Iraq's economic demands. But the attempt to remove the Kuwaiti regime and replace it with a provisional "republican" government was a radical challenge—indeed a major threat—to the legitimacy of all Gulf ruling families. Moreover, Iraq's control of Kuwait's oil resources and assets would not only rival Saudi Arabia's financial dominance in the Gulf but also its position as the chief "enforcer"—as swing producer—of OPEC oil prices.

Egypt was also taken aback. Iraq's occupation of Kuwait and its new strategic position in the Gulf would challenge Egypt's own regional role, while Saddam's increasingly radical statements threatened Egypt's moderate posture. Mubarak also felt personally betrayed by Saddam, who, he claimed, had assured him of a negotiated solution. King Husain of Jordan had the most ambivalent Arab response. Jordan's economic ties with Iraq were strong. Even more importantly, Jordan's Palestinian majority was overwhelmingly sympathetic to Iraq and its "Arab" stand on Israel. King Husain wanted the invasion handled without foreign interference. Other Arab states felt similarly.

Despite Arab ambivalence, the United States moved forward on organizing a response. Any action on Iraq would require a military arm, which was not in place. Even a defensive posture to protect Saudi Arabia would require Arab and, of course, Saudi approval. For the Saudis, a decision to host such forces was fraught with dangers. Nonetheless, they took it. King Fahd agreed to a deployment of US forces to protect the kingdom. Not long after, Egypt and Morocco agreed to participate as well.[15] By 7 August the first US deployments had been dispatched.

On 10 August a full Arab League summit was held in Cairo to address the issue. It was stormy and ended by splitting the league. Egypt, Saudi Arabia, the Arab Gulf states, Syria (Iraq's old nemesis), and Morocco were clearly aligned with the West; the Jordanians and Palestinians, as well as Yemen, Sudan, and Algeria, wanted to Arabize the solution. In the end, a vote by a simple majority of twelve (out of twenty) called for Iraqi withdrawal, a return of the ruling family to Kuwait, and support for sending troops to defend Saudi Arabia.[16]

Iraq's Response

Saddam's reaction to these events was continued defiance and steps gradually taken to absorb Kuwait. On 7 August Iraq declared Kuwait a republic, and made the Kuwaiti dinar equal to that of Iraq's. The following day Iraq annexed Kuwait.[17] On 28 August Iraq announced that Kuwait had become the nineteenth province (*wilaya*) of Iraq, ending the provisional government. The top third of Kuwait, along with Warba and Bubayan, was incorporated into Iraq's Basra governorate. Meanwhile, Iraq tightened its grip on Kuwait. Key opponents were arrested and executed. It is estimated that these totaled over 1,000 in the first few days of the occupation alone.

Most important were systematic looting of Kuwait's wealth and a dismantling of much of its infrastructure. The process began with the assets in Kuwait's central bank, apparently a meager $2 billion, less than anticipated. The far larger assets in foreign banks, estimated at over $200 billion, eluded Iraq when the international community froze them.[18] From the first, the security apparatus was under orders to take valuable electronic, communications, and industrial equipment, which it did, but the looting was much more extensive. As a result, the Iraqi market was flooded for months with all sorts of goods, from household staples to luxury items, that helped sustain an economy sinking ever further into a morass under sanctions.

Crisis Stalemate, September 1990–January 1991

Saddam's actions created a dilemma for the international community and Iraq's neighbors, and the crisis settled into a stalemate that persisted right up to the outbreak of war. The coalition insisted on Iraq's unconditional withdrawal from Kuwait and focused on keeping its loose alliance together while using the tools of a harsh economic embargo and the ultimate sanction of military action to achieve Iraqi withdrawal. But Iraq remained intransigent. Indeed, to keep his support at home, Saddam could not now withdraw without something to show for his efforts.

Meanwhile, the costs of occupation were becoming ever more apparent. Both the Saudi-Iraqi pipeline and the pipeline through Turkey were closed. Within a short time, more than 90 percent of Iraq's imports and almost 97 percent of its exports were shut off. The result was soaring prices, and in September Iraq was compelled to introduce rationing.

As time dragged on without movement, Iraq's continued intransigence and the toll taken on Kuwait began to tip US considerations in favor of a military solution. The United States went to the United Nations for international authorization to use force. The result was Resolution 678, authorizing the use of force to compel Iraq to withdraw from Kuwait but giving Iraq a grace period of forty-five days to accomplish the withdrawal. The date of 15 January 1991 was set as the deadline.

Despite last-minute attempts by others to mediate a withdrawal and avoid a war, Saddam refused to budge.[19] The key to his intransigence lay in his own perception that he could not politically survive a withdrawal without some gains, especially after such serious concessions to Iran. He also assumed that the United States would have difficulty bringing troops into a ground war and that if it did, it could not last long under the kinds of casualties he intended his forces to inflict.[20] In the end, overconfidence may also have led him to miscalculate the time he had available for his brinksmanship. When the allied air attack came at 3:00 am (local time) on 17 January, Iraqis seemed genuinely surprised.

The Gulf War, 17 January–28 February 1991

The Gulf War, which began with an air attack on 17 January (local time) and ended on 28 February, was unlike anything Iraqis had experienced before in eight years of war with Iran. Within twenty-four hours the allies had control of the skies. Thereafter, they turned to their strategic targets. These included command and control facilities (including Saddam's palaces, Ba'th Party headquarters, and intelligence and security facilities), power stations, hydroelectric stations, refineries, military-industrial targets, and Iraq's WMD and missile facilities. The country's communications system was essentially incapacitated and its electrical supply reduced by 75 percent. The coalition then turned to the military targets critical to the ground campaign—roads, bridges, and storage facilities. Lastly, it turned to Iraqi troops in the Kuwaiti theater.[21]

On 18 January Iraq launched missiles against Israeli and Saudi targets. The impact in Israel was mainly political; the missiles generated fears of a chemical attack, causing some disruption in Tel Aviv and other cities. Iraq had made the point that Israel was now vulnerable and had been hit at home by an Arab state, and the attack was now added to Saddam's propaganda arsenal. But the main purpose of the attack—to induce retaliation by Israel, thus bringing it into the war on the coalition side and thereby weakening Arab support for the coalition—failed.

Meanwhile in Iraq, the bombing campaign was taking its toll. Although civilians were not targeted, inevitably a number were hit and killed. (The most precise figures given by the Iraqis claim 2,280 killed and almost 6,000 wounded.)[22] The air campaign brought the war home to the population, especially the urban middle-class inhabitants in Baghdad. Daily life became unbearable. There was no electricity or running water in most of Iraq's major cities. Vehicular traffic almost came to a halt for lack of fuel, and medical epidemics were feared.[23]

By the end of January, Saddam faced an increasingly tenuous position. His strategy had been to absorb the air attack but to draw the coalition into a ground war that would inflict heavy casualties and compel negotiations with a favorable end for Iraq. The country had absorbed the bombing, but the morale, equipment, and fighting ability of the Iraqi forces who would have to face the coalition in the "long war of attrition" were eroding to a point of no return. To draw the coalition into a ground war, Saddam ordered an attack on Khafji in eastern Saudi Arabia on 29 January. The result was a destruction of his forces from the air. For the first time, Saddam had to face the meaning of a possible military defeat. On 22 February, shortly before his withdrawal, he set alight the Kuwaiti oil fields, creating an environmental disaster for the region, but this did not stop the coalition attack.

The Ground War

The ground war in Iraq, begun by the coalition forces attack on 24 February 1991, was over in one hundred hours—four days later—on 28 February. The coalition was surprised by the rapidity of its conquest, especially through the main lines of Iraq's defense around Kuwait. As a result, a separate flanking movement across the desert and into Iraq, though it had moved almost 500 kilometers (310 miles) in four days, was not yet in a position to close the gate on the retreating Republican Guard forces in Iraq when President George H. W. Bush declared the cease-fire. Some, though not all, got away with their equipment.

The capture or collapse of the Republican Guard forces would have weakened Saddam and contributed to his overthrow; instead they survived to protect him. Nonetheless, the victory was swift and stunning. On 25 February, Saddam finally ordered a withdrawal, but the coalition did not accept it and dealt with his forces as an army in retreat. Meanwhile, Iraq continued trying to bargain.

The war now became a race between the coalition's determination to destroy as much of Iraq's forces, especially the Republican Guard, as possible and Saddam's need to get a cease-fire to preserve the guard. The Security Council insisted on Iraq's unconditional acceptance of all UN resolutions. With no other recourse for the Iraqis, this finally came on 27 February (Iraqi time).

Iraq's regular army was broken and scattered. The losses in military equipment, especially in the air force, were severe. Iraqi casualties are hard to estimate but were probably in the area of 10,000 to 30,000 dead, many fewer than originally thought.[24] The number of prisoners of war (POWs) who gave themselves up or were captured was 86,000 to 90,000. Morale was shattered. But despite this disarray and the relative disorder of the retreat, much of the Iraqi army and especially the key Republican Guard units in the south of Iraq were able to get away. Some would shortly regroup to help save the regime from its rebellious citizens.

The Cease-Fire and UN Resolution 687

Although the cease-fire ended hostilities, it did not yet result in coalition troop withdrawal. The action now shifted to the United Nations, where a final termination resolution was drawn up and passed on 12 April. Resolution 687's provisions were to place much of Iraq's economy and its military under international control. Although not anticipated in

April 1991, this control would remain—even deepen—over the coming decade.

Under 687 Iraq had several obligations. First, it had to accept the inviolability of the Iraqi-Kuwaiti border, which was to be demarcated by an international commission in which Iraq was expected to participate. Second, Iraq had to accept a UN peacekeeping force on the border. Third, Iraq would have to demolish its weapons of mass destruction and long-range missile capacity and refrain from reviving their production. To accomplish this end, the country was required to submit to the Security Council a full list of all nuclear, chemical, and biological materials and missiles with a range over 150 kilometers (93 miles), together with manufacturing capabilities for these weapons. These would then be destroyed. To verify the validity of the list and to prevent future acquisitions and production, there would be on-site inspection teams. Lastly, Iraq would have to facilitate the return of Kuwaiti property and agree to a level of reparations agreed on by the United Nations. Until these measures were fulfilled, the full trade embargo was to remain in place, except for imports of food, medicine, and other necessities of life. Sanctions would be reviewed every sixty days. In the meantime, no oil could be sold.[25]

Iraq accepted these terms, and on 9 May the last coalition forces were withdrawn. Rather than admitting defeat, however, Saddam propagated another myth. The war had not been a defeat but a victory. Iraq had fought "the mother of battles" by standing against thirty-one armies, including the most technologically advanced forces in the world, and triumphed. The coalition would never have accepted a cease-fire if it had not feared the fist of the Republican Guard. Iraqis were commended for their fortitude and steadfastness in the face of imperialism.[26]

The Costs of the War

But rhetorical claims of victory could not disguise the real outcome of the Gulf War for Iraq and its people. Its economy had sunk to depths that Iraq had not yet had time to appreciate. Sanctions had cut off

Iraq's major source of income—oil—and shut down almost all trade. Inflation had already started its upward trajectory. Coalition bombing had destroyed a good deal of Iraq's industry and infrastructure, making the restoration of a normal peacetime economy a distant dream. Iraq's army was scattered and in retreat (or had deserted and was sitting at home). Nonetheless, the most serious potential threat to the regime came from angry officers and men, outraged at the leadership that had thrust them into such a foolhardy venture, and from its own population, which would soon rise up.

In foreign relations, too, the cost of the war was high. The war, and the long crisis leading up to it, isolated Iraq as never before. The Kuwait occupation and the Gulf War had now made an implacable adversary out of the United States, the world's only superpower. Iraq's relations with Europe were hardly better. All of the coalition members had cut diplomatic ties with Iraq and were participating in the sanctions regime authorized by the United Nations.

These enormous costs came with no new gains for Iraq. To consolidate his efforts in Kuwait, Saddam had publicly given up the one potential gain from the Iran-Iraq war: control over the Shatt. And he was left with no gains in Kuwait; indeed, in return for the occupation, Iraq would now be saddled with economic reparations. Meanwhile, it had to endure sanctions and the imposition of wide-ranging restrictions on its sovereignty in the form of weapons inspections.

By March 1991 it was apparent to all, inside and outside Iraq, despite rhetoric to the contrary, that the occupation of Kuwait had been a miscalculation of breathtaking proportions and that the Gulf War—utterly avoidable if withdrawal instead of intransigence had taken place—had been the most damaging act in Iraq's modern history.

The Intifada of March 1991

One of the most immediate and ultimately fateful costs of the Gulf War would be the *intifada* (uprising) of March 1991. Although not apparent at the time, its effects would be profound in shaping Iraq's future. At the uprising's peak, rebels controlled substantial portions of fourteen of Iraq's eighteen provinces. Although not successful in overthrowing the regime, the *intifada* was a defining moment in Iraq's modern history in revealing attitudes toward the regime and the state.

The Rebellion in the South

According to most accounts, the rebellion broke out in Basra on 1 March, led by retreating soldiers.[27] A soldier, in a fit of anger, turned the gun of his tank in Sa'd Square on an outsized portrait of Saddam. This was the incendiary spark. Armored vehicles then attacked the key points of the regime's authority—the mayor's office, the Ba'th Party headquarters, and security centers. There was looting; people broke into shops, hotels, and even houses. However, by the third day the military began to regroup and reorganize, and by 17 March the *intifada* in Basra was over. Fighting was fierce, and many took refuge across the Shatt in Iran. Thousands were killed or executed, with bodies left in the street.[28]

But the revolt had already spread. By the end of the first week, rebel groups had seized control of most of the provincial towns south of Baghdad.[29] In most areas the rebellion was unruly, unorganized, and sometimes almost as brutal as the regime. But in Najaf and Karbala, the *intifada* took on a different complexion. Accounts here point to some organization beforehand.[30] The slogans were distinctly Shi'i and called for a Shi'i ruler and an Islamic revolution, pointing to clearer signs of influence from the Supreme Council for the Islamic Revolution in Iraq (SCIRI) and Iraqis coming from Iran. The rebellion was not initially encouraged by the chief *marji'*, Abu-l-Qasim al-Khu'i, but when Republican Guards regained control, he was taken to Baghdad and compelled to go on television and support the government.

Despite the rebellion's spread to differing localities, there were striking similarities throughout. Rebels everywhere focused on the symbols of the regime and the seat of its power, especially the party and the hated security forces. Indeed, rebels had considerable success in forcing the collapse of the security system and the party in some areas of the south.

The Collapse of the Intifada *in the South*

The *intifada* in the south failed to take hold and to withstand a concerted government attack when it came. Four factors appear to have been of paramount importance in contributing to its failure.

First, the Badr Brigade and SCIRI played too much of a role in the revolt. Although too few in number to make a significant impact, Iraqi exiles crossed the frontier in the collapse of order after the Gulf War to join—even to lead—the rebellion. The fighters came with banners and slogans from the Islamic revolution, demanding a Shi'i government. The slogans gave rise to fears of sectarianism and of "outside organization" from Iran. They gave the revolt a narrow ideological cast that belied its much broader base and that provided an ideal propaganda ploy for the regime to use in garnering support against the rebellion. It also worried the coalition, especially Saudi Arabia and the United States.[31] In fact, however, the Iranians gave very little support to the revolt.[32]

Second, the chaos and destruction of the *intifada* created images of retribution and disorder that frightened the populace in Baghdad and the country's center and helped convince the more stable elements of the population to stay at home.

Third, the military did not join the *intifada* in the south. Some military men—soldiers and officers—did join the rebellion, but they did so as individuals, not as units. Organized defections from the army to the rebels did not take place.

Fourth, the rebellion in the south received no support from abroad, except in a very minor way from Iran. The United States and the Western forces occupying Iraq were not prepared to provide such support, despite a call from President Bush to overthrow the regime. Saddam's government immediately used helicopter gunships to put the rebellion down, while numerous attempts by rebels to solicit arms and help from the coalition from across the cease-fire lines were turned down. Instead, the coalition indicated in numerous ways that it would not support the rebellion, thus depriving it of hope and material help.[33] The failure of the United States to respond with any help left deep bitterness and frustration.

The Rebellion in the North

In the north the rebellion began on 4 March in Raniyya. The spark for the revolt was provided by a deserter who was chased into the mountains and shot. The next day the townspeople rose. They were joined by the Fursan, which had weapons. News of Raniyya soon spread. On 7 March Sulaimaniyya rose in what was primarily a popular uprising that attacked the Ba'th Party headquarters, the Mukhabarat, and the security headquarters. Here some reports put the number of Ba'th killed at four hundred; the total killed, at seven hundred.[34] Sulaimaniyya was followed in rapid order by Qal'at Diza, Dukan, Darbandikhan, Halabja, Kalar, and Shamshamal. On 13 March, the Kurdish Front announced the establishment of an executive and legislative council for regional self-government. Thus, the Kurdish Front quickly established a civilian administration for the north, promising something more permanent for the future.[35]

The rebels then turned their attention to the prize—Kirkuk. There was no uprising in this mixed Arab-Kurdish-Turkman city, and advancing forces had to put up a fight. After a considerable battle, the Kurdish Front and Fursan were able to take Kirkuk, but it reportedly cost them 3,000 casualties.

In many respects, the *intifada* in the north was similar to that in the south. The population in cities and towns rose spontaneously, the rebellion spread rapidly, and it ended just as suddenly when the regime mobilized its military forces. Despite similarities, however, there were some striking differences as well. In the north, there was a much higher degree of organization and leadership from the traditional Kurdish political parties, the Kurdistan Democratic Party (KDP) and the Patriotic Union of Kurdistan (PUK). There were more planning and coordination with the Kurdish militias supporting the government—the Fursan, which joined the rebellion. Their almost wholesale defection was crucial. Most critical of all, however, was the contact between the Kurdish parties and the West, which ultimately laid a basis for internationalizing the plight of the Kurds and securing a measure of support from the coalition for their aims.

Silence in the Center

In the end, one of the most important outcomes of the *intifada* was where it did not spread. There was no rebellion in the five central provinces of Baghdad, Anbar, Salah al-Din, Ninawa, and Diyala (except for the partly Kurdish towns of Kalar and Kifri in the latter). As news spread of the rebellion, especially in the south, the mainly Sunni urban population thought not of rebellion but of survival. In the regime's reports, the *intifada* was called "sedition" and the rebels "mobs." Iran was blamed for its instigation, and sectarian slogans were exaggerated. The result was that the center greeted the *intifada* not with hope but with fear of a bloodbath and a desire to protect itself and its property. The failure of the *intifada* in the center showed not only the strength of the regime but also the passivity and ambivalence of its population toward a government it did not like but was unwilling to move against.

Repression of the Rebellion

Given the regime's resounding defeat in the war and the collapse and disarray of its military, the swiftness with which it was able to recoup its losses and quell an uprising that had spread to both the north and south of the country surprised many.

The turnaround began 6 March in Basra. The repression was brutal. There was shelling of houses and buildings, and thousands of bodies were left in the streets. The most difficult battles, in Karbala and Najaf, went on for days. Women and children were used as human shields; thousands were rounded up and killed. Tens of thousands fled across the border to Iran. Many also fled across the front lines to coalition forces, eventually ending up in camps in Rafha in Saudi Arabia. There was serious destruction in the shrines and cemeteries in Najaf. The ties of the holy cities to the rebellion and the strong presence of SCIRI in these towns brought strong retribution from the regime.

There is no accurate death toll for the *intifada* in the south. Although those killed by the rebels can probably be numbered in the thousands or even tens of thousands, those killed by the regime may have been well over 100,000. It is likely that the *intifada* as a whole took at least twice as many lives as the war itself.[36]

Among the Shi'i population of the south, alienation from the regime was higher than at any time since the founding of the state. Regardless of whether the population had participated in the uprising or not, its cities and towns and its youth had undergone a devastating experience in brutality. Alienation against the West—and especially the United States—was also high. Even though the *intifada* was domestically driven, the failure of US and coalition forces to provide any aid when asked left an indelible impression on Iraqis. Much bitterness was also directed against Iran as well, mainly for Iran's failure to provide more support. In the end, the Shi'a of the south, who had for the most part led a genuine domestic revolt against a repressive regime, were left brutally repressed and politically and intellectually isolated.

By the last week in March, the government was ready to turn its attention from the south to the north. By 28 March the attack on Kirkuk began. The government then moved on to Sulaimaniyya and Arbil. And within a few days, Zakhu and Dahuk also fell. By the beginning of April, the *intifada* had ended in the north, with the Iraqi forces in control of all major Kurdish cities.

The Unraveling State in the North

Despite the collapse of the Kurdish rebellion, the ultimate outcome of the uprising in the north was very different from that in the south. Owing entirely to unforeseen circumstances, the result was to loosen—not restore—the state's control over the Kurdish population. The government's attack and recapture of the cities of the north led to a mass exodus of Kurds to the borders of Turkey and Iran, spurred by fear of a possible chemical weapons attack. The result was a refugee problem of such scope that it rapidly took on international proportions. Eventually, it involved an estimated 2 million people, roughly half the Kurdish population. The overwhelming majority of fleeing Kurds took refuge in Iran, but Turkey absorbed some 60,000 Iraqi Kurds as well.

Operation Provide Comfort

The Kurds, unlike the Shi'a in the south, owed much to having Western friends they had cultivated for years. These supporters put pressure on the international community, and especially the US administration, to take some action. The outcome was Operation Provide Comfort, an effort to provide the Kurds with humanitarian aid and sufficient protection to induce them to go home. On 5 April the United States ordered Iraq to cease all military activity, including the flying of aircraft, north of the thirty-sixth parallel. This no-fly zone protected aircraft delivering supplies and, later, ground troops operating in northern Iraq. But it also restricted Iraqi sovereignty over its airspace in a wide region, including major cities such as Mosul and Arbil.[37]

Another step taken by the United States and its coalition partners was the creation of a "safe haven" for the Kurds in northern Iraq, under UN control, where refugees would be free from attack. On 16 April Bush agreed to send ground troops into northern Iraq to secure the haven. By June, soothed by the coalition military presence, virtually all the Kurds who needed to be repatriated had returned from the Turkish border, and by the end of the month 600,000 Kurds had returned from Iran, a remarkably successful humanitarian effort. By 15 June all allied forces had withdrawn, except for a small force overseeing humanitarian relief.

Meanwhile, a series of skirmishes ensued in the north between the *peshmerga* and government forces. Kurds attacked Iraqi police posts in Zakhu and Dahuk, displacing Iraqi security forces in both towns. The Kurds soon managed to take and hold Dahuk, Arbil, and Sulaimaniyya. It was the outcome of this ground action and the unpleasant prospect of renewed guerilla war in the north that probably account for the government's next action, its most striking and ultimately most significant in shaping the post-*intifada* period.

Toward the end of October 1991, the Iraqi government decided to withdraw its forces behind a defensible line in the north. It reached a cease-fire with the Kurds and withdrew from the major towns on the plains. It maintained control of Kirkuk, however. The government had

now left much of the Kurdish region in Kurdish hands, retreating behind a new, internal front.

This unprecedented action left Kurds, for the first time, in control
of much of the territory (except for Kirkuk) they desired to control.
They seized the initiative in establishing a new Kurdish government independent of the central authority in Baghdad in all but name. At the
same time, however, the central government imposed an internal economic blockade on the area. Sealing the main roads leading to the
north, it clamped down on trade, attempting to isolate the north and
cripple it economically.

Regime Survival and Reorganization

One of the most remarkable outcomes of the war was the survival of
the regime. Even before the revolt was quelled, the regime began to reorganize and to marshal its support in the four essentially Arab Sunni
provinces of the center and north—Anbar, Salah al-Din, Ninawa, and
Diyala—the "white provinces," so called because they had remained
loyal during the rebellion. (Baghdad was more problematic because it
had a majority Shi'i population that had to be kept under control.)

To propitiate the disaffected, in April 1991 the Revolutionary Command Council (RCC) pardoned Iraqis who had taken part in the rebellion, lifted the ban on international travel, and disbanded the popular
militia. There was even talk of reforming the system. A new cabinet under Sa'dun Hammadi, an educated Shi'a, was formed, and the Ba'th
Party held a new election at all levels. But these efforts soon petered out
and so did talk of reform.

Much more important was the regime's reorganization of its security
mechanism, including major purges and executions within the military,
party, and security services. The regime then concentrated on rebuilding
its multiple and overlapping security and intelligence networks. Key security agencies were put under family control. By 1993 the Special Security Organization (SSO), responsible for thwarting potential coups, was
headed by Saddam's son Qusayy. The Special Republican Guard, the only
heavily armed force permitted inside Baghdad, was headed by a member

of the Majid clan. At the pinnacle of this system was the Himaya (Protection) Force, a small group of thirty to forty men recruited wholly from tribal groups loyal to Saddam. In the bureaucracy and the party, leaders were now overwhelmingly drawn from the Sunni center, in particular the smaller, poorer, and more provincial towns of the northwest.

As a substitute for the collapsing party, Saddam now turned increasingly to tribal groups in the countryside for governance. Those tribes that had supported the regime or remained neutral during the *intifada* were now rearmed—even in some cases with rocket launchers—in return for keeping law and order in their region. Benefits to *shaikhs* and their tribes included redistribution of land previously confiscated, as well as sizable sums of money for personal use.[38]

Finally, a new ideological formulation gave this reorganization focus. After the failure of most of the Arab world to support Iraq in the war, adulation of Arab nationalism was gone. More stress was put on religion. As an indication of the increase in Islamic rhetoric and symbols, in January 1991 "God is Great" was added to the Iraqi flag. Saddam began to see himself as a potential redeemer, claiming Iraq as "a representative of God . . . in the Mother of Battles."[39] This shift—from Arab nationalism and modernity to more traditional forms of organization and belief, such as tribalism and religion—would deepen in the course of the decade, laying the groundwork for a new and different society that was to emerge after 2003 in Iraq.

The Imposition of Foreign Control

Next to survival, the main difficulty the regime faced was dealing with the costly and intrusive cease-fire terms the United States and its coalition allies had fastened on Iraq. The most important elements were contained in UN Resolution 687, which provided for a settlement of Kuwaiti issues and elimination of Iraq's weapons of mass destruction and long-range missiles. Most onerous of all, especially for the population, was the continuance of sanctions until requirements were met.[40]

A second resolution, 688, required Iraq to cease repression of its population. The main purpose of this decree was to protect the Kurds and allow the establishment of the safe haven and the no-fly zone in the north. In August 1992 a second no-fly zone was established south of the thirty-second to protect the Shi'a. (This line was later extended to the thirty-third parallel.) These zones restricted Iraq's control over much of its airspace.

These cease-fire resolutions, especially sanctions, defined the remaining years of the regime, right up to 2003. Both Saddam and the West miscalculated their longevity. Saddam's response was to avoid compliance where possible and acquiesce only where necessary, assuming that he could outlast the international community. The West was unprepared for the degree of intransigence it met and the skill of the regime in resistance.

Recognition of Kuwait and Its Borders

In April 1992 a UN border commission recommended a return to the landline established in a 1963 agreement between Iraq and Kuwait. This stripped Iraq of territory on which it had previously encroached and compelled Iraq to give up several oil wells at the tip of the Rumaila field and a number of naval jetties at the Umm Qasr port.

The border commission then turned to the offshore boundary, an even more contentious issue. Here there was no previous agreement to work from, and as was the case with the Shatt al-Arab, Iraq wanted complete control over its access to the Persian Gulf in the Khaur Abd Allah channel. However, the commission drew the boundary down the middle of the channel. This finding was bitterly protested by Iraq, which claimed it had been made a landlocked country, but the new boundary was formalized in UN Resolution 833 on 27 May 1993.[41] The Iraq National Assembly rejected this boundary, and in October 1994 Iraq sent some 80,000 troops to the Kuwaiti border. This action backfired, bringing military retaliation from the coalition, and on 10 November 1994 the Iraq national Assembly reluctantly accepted the border demarcation.

Resolution 833 also provided for war reparations to be paid by Iraq to individuals and companies for war losses and to Kuwait for loss of oil revenues and destruction of the environment when its wells had been set on fire. The resolution also insisted that Iraq pay all debts incurred by the Iraqi regime; total reparations came to $53 billion, a heavy burden.

The Struggle over WMD

The second and ultimately most contentious issue in the cease-fire agreement was elimination of Iraq's weapons of mass destruction.[42] This struggle was critical for Iraq's domestic situation because removal of sanctions hinged on UNSC agreement that all WMD and long-range missiles had been eliminated in Iraq. The responsibility for the documentation of removal lay with Saddam Husain, but he was clearly not willing to comply. The result was a long-running cat-and-mouse game, punctuated by periodic confrontations, that lasted for most of the decade. Iraq, when compelled, would make only partial disclosure. The United Nations Special Commission (UNSCOM) and the International Atomic Energy Agency (IAEA) would make semiannual reports to the United Nations, but without a final, satisfactory report, the damaging sanctions regime remained in effect.[43]

Notwithstanding these difficulties, UNSCOM and the IAEA went a long way toward unmasking Iraq's WMD program. Between 1991 and 1994 IAEA and UNSCOM uncovered and dismantled a network of about forty nuclear research facilities using three clandestine uranium-enrichment programs. In the chemical field, UNSCOM managed to destroy over 148,000 tons of chemical warfare agents (including mustard gas, sarin, and tabun). In the biological field, Iraq admitted that it had a biological weapons program but said it had destroyed all agents, without offering any proof.

By 1996 UNSCOM, according to its chairman, Rolf Ekeus, had found "all the big things,"[44] but there were numerous elements for which there was still no accounting, including some missiles, some VX nerve agent, and the entire biological weapons program, assumed to be hidden in private homes and other places difficult to enter. UNSCOM focused increasingly on Saddam Husain's concealment mechanisms, while Iraqis accused UNSCOM of spying for the United States and Israel and threatening Iraq's security and survival.

In 1997, this controversy sharpened. Finally, at the end of October 1998 Iraq announced that its cooperation with UNSCOM was at an end, and on 19 December the United States, supported by the United Kingdom, responded with a major bombing campaign, Operation Desert Fox. Operation Desert Fox was the most massive military strike on Iraq since the Gulf War, but its targets were more political than military, aiming at Saddam's concealment and security mechanisms and his palaces. However, the strike finally weakened the coalition. Most of the Arab world opposed the strike. So, too, did Russia, France, and many other European states. Moreover, the strike effectively ended UNSCOM. After 1998 Iraq was left free of any inspection system, seemingly a partial victory for Saddam.

In retrospect, the absence of a satisfactory settlement of the WMD issue and the withdrawal of inspectors would prove to be the Achilles heel of the regime in the post 9/11 environment. In Washington a new, more hard-line administration took power in 2001 and adopted "regime change" in Baghdad as its policy. Seeking a justification for such a shift, the new administration found it in Iraq's breach of UN Resolution 687, on WMD. Had the inspection regime still been in place or had Iraq cooperated more fully on disarmament, the United States would have had more difficulty justifying its subsequent attack on Iraq.

Sanctions

The most serious constraint imposed on Iraq was the sanctions regime, which over a decade profoundly changed Iraq's social and economic structure for the worse. A few figures give some indication of how dire the situation became, especially in the early 1990s. Oil production dropped 85 percent between 1990 and 1991 and began to increase again only after sanctions relief in 1997. Iraq's per capita income, which had stood at just over $2,000 in 1989, fell to $609 by 1992.[45] Skyrocketing inflation made most items unaffordable for average families.[46] In prewar times, 1 dinar had been worth $3.20; by 1996 $1 was worth ID 2,600. Iraq suffered a hemorrhage of its educated and technocratic elite. Famine was avoided only by an effective rationing system. Infant mortality rose steeply. With drugs and essential medical supplies lacking, health services were nearing breakdown.

In August 1991 the United Nations had passed Resolution 706, allowing Iraq to import food, medicine, and essential civilian needs, but Iraq did not accept the legality of sanctions and rejected the resolution outright. In 1995 the United Nations tried again, passing Resolution 986, known as "Oil for Food." It was only in January 1996, when inflation had driven the dinar to its lowest point ever—ID 3,000 for $1—that the Iraq government accepted the resolution.[47] In December oil began to flow for the first time, and in March 1997 the first food shipments reached Iraq. It was only in December 1999 that the United Nations lifted all ceilings on Iraqi oil production and exports, and in May 2002 another UN resolution eased the import of civilian, but not military, goods.

These actions helped stem Iraq's economic downturn but could not reverse the decline. By 2002 GDP per capita had risen to a little over $1,000, but it was still only than half what it had been in 1989 (see Table 9.1). Agriculture was stagnating. The government made some effort to expand production but with little success. Infrastructure was badly neglected. Farmers had shifted from cash cropping to subsistence and in the last years of the 1990s, Iraq suffered serious drought. Once oil revenue rose, Iraq once again turned to agricultural imports. Industrial production also continued to limp. By 2003 there was some increase in local manufactured goods, but only 40 percent of installed electric power was available. Although oil production rose to about 2.4

TABLE 9.1 Growth of GDP, Population, and GDP Per Capita, 1999–2002

	1999	2000	2001	2002*
GDP (billions US$)	23.8	31.8	27.9	26.1
Population*	22.4	22.9	23.6	24.1
GDP Per Capita ($)	1,062	1,385	1,184	1,078

*Based on Estimates.

SOURCES: Economist Intelligence Unit (EIU), *Country Report Iraq, 2002–2003* (London: Economist Intelligence Unit, May 2003); EIU, *Quarterly Economic Report, Iraq,* 1 March 2003.

TABLE 9.2 Crude Oil Production and Export, 1976–2001 (millions of barrels per day)

	Production	Export
1976–1980	2.69	2.5
1981–1986	1.26	.961
1995	.550	.150
1996	.580	.180
1997	1.15	.840
1998	2.11	1.795
1999	2.52	2.203
2000	2.57	2.243
2001	2.36	2.030

SOURCE: Economist Intelligence Unit, *Country Profile Iraq, 2002–2003* (London: Economist Intelligence Unit, 2003).

million barrels per day by 2001, the reservoirs had suffered long-term damage from years of mismanagement (see Table 9.2).

The damage to the education system was also severe. Credible figures show that the literacy rate, which had reached 67 percent in 1980, fell to about 57 percent in 2001.[48] Thus, one of the major gains of the early Ba'th period, like industrial development, was dramatically reversed (see Table A.4). These trends were accompanied by social erosion. Iraq suffered a hemorrhage of its educated and technocratic elite through emigration.

By the early twenty-first century, income and status disparities within Iraq's social structure were much higher than they had been in the 1970s. A new upper and affluent class emerged that included top-level members of the bureaucracy and the party as well as entrepreneurs, who often skimmed profits from the system. Meanwhile, those living only on salaries could not keep up, while unskilled workers simply sank deeper into poverty. Instead of upward social mobility, Iraq now saw downward mobility and the shrinkage of the middle class.

Regional disparities grew as well. By 2003 Baghdad was a megalopolis of over 5 million, while southern provinces had lost population and the northern barely grown (see Table A.1). One of the most important sectors of the population to be affected was Iraq's youth, who lost the benefit of education and a future. The 1997 census shows that over half of the population (56 percent) was below the age of nineteen. An absolute majority of the population had been born and raised after Saddam came to power as president in 1979; his was the only system they knew. There was much evidence among youth of a turn to religion, encouraged by the regime, which allowed more fundamentalist views to take root among Sunni as well as Shi'i youth.

Regime Consolidation and Its Limits

The regime had managed to consolidate its power at the top of the political structure, but it still rested on increasingly shaky pillars. One of these was its continued reliance on a network of kin and clan. By 2003 Saddam's clan occupied central positions in all key security and military institutions. On the Regional Command of the party in 1998, seven out of seventeen members were Albu Nasir or clan allies.[49] This gave the regime a kinship network of considerable depth, but it also brought the political system back to premodern modes of operating.

Even within this structure, however, Saddam faced continual opposition and fissures. Among the first to give Saddam trouble were the Juburis, a key tribal confederation spread over a wide area from Mosul to Hilla, with key positions in the military. Juburis were behind an attempted plot to assassinate Saddam in June 1992. In July 1993 a coup attempt led by well-known Tikriti families revealed how deeply opposition had penetrated the president's own Albu Nasir tribe. In November 1994 members of the Dulaimi tribal confederation revolted, and in the same month Wafiq al-Samarra'i defected as director of military intelligence and joined the opposition in the north.[50]

These difficulties, however, paled in comparison to the split in Saddam's own family that resulted in the flight from Baghdad to Amman of Husain Kamil, Saddam's son-in-law; his brother, Saddam Kamil; and their two wives (Saddam's daughters). The main reason for the defection was hardly opposition to the regime but rather a struggle within the family for power and patronage. Saddam's own sons, Udayy and Qusayy, were emerging as political players in their own right. Udayy, in particular, resented Husain Kamil, who had risen to control Saddam's prized military and WMD industries and was a threat to Udayy's ambitions. Even more bizarre than the defection was the return in 1996 of Husain Kamil and his family. To retrieve his daughters (and restore his family "honor"), Saddam had issued a pardon for the Kamils, but on the return of Husain and Saddam Kamil, they were forced to divorce the daughters. Security forces were then sent to kill them. To make clear that this was family retribution, not action by the state, those involved in the execution were all relatives of Kamil's clan. The action once again shed light on the tribal nature of the regime.[51]

The following year Udayy was attacked as he drove through Baghdad; the perpetrators were a Shi'i opposition group from the southern marsh area. He was not killed, but he was gravely wounded. The attack eliminated Udayy's prospects for succeeding his father. Qusayy moved into that position. Unlike Udayy, Qusayy was quiet but equally ruthless. By the end of the decade, he was virtually the overseer of most key security function.

The tribal nature of the regime was not its only drawback. A second feature of the political structure was its narrow ethnic and sectarian base, unrepresentative of the country as a whole and even of its urban middle class. The RCC and the Regional Command substantially underrepresented both Shi'a and Kurds at top decisionmaking levels (see Table A.2).

Not surprisingly, there was also an imbalance in the geographic area from which the leadership was drawn. In the RCC and the Regional Command of 1998, some 61 percent came from the Arab Sunni area northwest of Baghdad, almost 25 percent came from Tikrit, but only 6 percent came from Baghdad, Iraq's most integrated city. Few came from the northern (mainly Kurdish and Turkman) and the southern (mainly Shi'i) areas.[52] By the end of the decade, the Ba'th leadership failed not only to represent broad regions of the country and certain ethnic and sectarian groups but also to adequately incorporate the most important social force in modern Iraq—the urban, educated middle class, which was modern in its outlook and aspirations.

The second pillar of the regime—its institutional structures—still remained in a weakened state. By 2003 the Ba'th Party may have lost as much as 70 percent of its membership, weakening its capacity as an instrument of control and social engineering.[53] The party had clearly lost any appeal to youth or the population at large and had become mainly an instrument for career advancement. The Regional Command of 1998 shows an aging group, almost all hailing from the generation that had joined the party just before or after 1958.

The military arm of state was also far smaller and weaker than it had been in several decades, although it was still large by regional standards. The chief backbone of the military was no longer the regular army but the better-equipped, better-trained Republican Guard, a seven-division corps of about 60,000 to 70,000. Moreover, it was clear that the military could no longer perform its chief function—defending the country's territorial integrity and its borders. In the north, it had been forced to withdraw from a substantial portion of Iraqi territory, leaving its governance to parties generally hostile to the central government. In this area, the army had no control over Iraq's borders, which were crossed at will by both Turks and Iranians. In the south, the military was able to control the borders, but its control over the population was weak. In the air, Iraqi forces had lost control of two-thirds of Iraq's airspace. By 2003 the role of the military was reduced mainly to protecting the regime and the territory in the center. As repeated coup attempts had shown, the military's loyalty had to be constantly watched.

Changes in Regime Ideology

Decline was also reflected in the chief project of the Ba'th Party—creating a viable nation-state and the vision to go with it. Declining aspirations were seen in the regime's own ideology, directed mainly at the Arab population in the center. By 2003 the early Ba'thist drive to remake Iraq and the Arab world had disappeared. Pan-Arabism and Iraqi leadership of the Arab world were still given lip service, but in the absence of much meaningful help from the Arab world since the 1990 invasion of Kuwait, such leadership appeared increasingly illusory.

Iraq's public rhetoric as well as the regime's actions also tilted heavily in the direction of Islam. The struggle against the United States and the United Kingdom was referred to as a *jihad*, and the population was encouraged to turn to religion. The emphasis on Islam, begun during the Iran-Iraq war as a means of propitiating the Shi'a, grew in the 1990s as the regime's policy and the sanctions regime required ever-greater sacrifices. This may have been designed as an escape mechanism for a weary population or as a response to the growing strength of Islamic movements among the populace. Better to seize control of the movement and help direct it than to have it turn against the regime. By 2003 Islam was firmly embedded in the regime's ideology and symbolism.

But the main thrust of the regime's message to the center—and the rest of the country—was its control over society and the need to defend the country and the regime against foreign enemies. A typical fifth-grade text exhorted students to be loyal to the state, the "revolution," the party, and the "struggler" president, Saddam Husain.[54] The main vehicle for expressing national identity was the military, and students were urged to join paramilitary formations. Overall, patriotism was defined through the values of sacrifice, honor, and courage. This vision of Iraq's future, emphasizing sacrifices and defense against enemies, represented the siege mentality of the regime but was not likely to have widespread appeal to future generations.

The Kurds in the North

Despite the regime's survival in the center, Saddam Husain continued to face opposition from inside and outside Iraq. Chief among these was the gradual, if turbulent, consolidation of control by the Kurds of their territory in the north. The challenge here was less the threat of overthrow than the successful establishment of a separatist regime. Even though the Kurds failed at unity, they did manage to achieve a high degree of independence, thereby defying and weakening Baghdad.

The process began early. In January 1992, when it became apparent that ongoing negotiations with the central government had completely broken down, the Kurds announced that they would hold an election for a new government. On 19 May, voters cast ballots for a parliament of 105 representatives. Fifty-one parliamentary seats were won by the KDP and forty-nine by the PUK; four of the remaining five seats, allocated to minorities, went to the Assyrian Democratic Movement. In a closed-door session lasting several days, the leaders of the two parties essentially revised the results and arranged for an even division of seats in the interests of preserving Kurdish unity. This election "arrangement" between the two parties, the so-called strategic agreement, would remain a fixture of Kurdish political dynamics. Although it preserved the facade of a united Kurdish front, the struggle for power between the two groups would continue, leading to a breakdown of the arrangement and, before long, to a local civil war.

The elections marked a decisive victory for the organized Kurdish political parties against their traditional rivals, the tribal groups and their militias, the Fursan, which had previously dominated the north and cooperated with Saddam. The elections were a turning point in the direction Kurdistan would take, putting power in the north in the hands of the two nationalist Kurdish parties, aiming at greater autonomy, if not eventual independence.

The Kurdish Civil War

On 4 July the new Kurdish Regional Government (KRG) came into being, with the establishment of a council of ministers and then a parliament. But the effect of the election arrangement had been to split not only the parliament but also the executive branch. For every minister of one party, there was a deputy of the other to check him. This arrangement was a formula for deadlock and a renewal of the clash between the two parties that had been the staple of Kurdish politics for decades.

It was clear that this struggle was both political and personal. The two party leaders, Mas'ud Barzani and Jalal Talabani, both aspired to dominate a new Kurdish state-in-the-making. Neither was accustomed to sharing power. The two parties, which had been competing since the mid-1970s, also had different constituencies and operating styles. The KDP, although it attracted a number of urbanites and intellectuals, relied for administration on the Barzani clan and for support on related tribal groups. The PUK considered itself more modern and progressive. Barzani's stronghold was the north, the Bahdinan-speaking area straddling the Turkish border. Mainly rural and tribal, it had few large urban centers. Talabani's strength lay in the south, in the Surani-speaking area, with Sulaimaniyya and its urban intellectuals at its center.

The territory controlled by Barzani contained much rich agricultural land, less affected by the Anfal campaigns. He also controlled the border crossing point with Turkey at Khabur, soon to prove a lucrative source of customs income once transit traffic began to flow again. Talabani's territory, bordering Iran, had received the brunt of the Anfal campaign, and hence its economic base was poorer. Trade with Iran was much less lucrative. Both factors put Talabani at a disadvantage.

These issues came to a head in May 1994 when a minor land dispute in Qal'at Diza slipped out of control and soon engaged local KDP and PUK forces. Fighting soon spread. By August there were 1,000 dead and over 70,000 local Kurds displaced.[55] When fighting broke out between the KDP and PUK, a third party, the Islamic Movement of Iraqi Kurdistan (IMIK), took advantage of the situation to seize the towns of Halabja, Banjwin, and Khurmal. By the time the fighting died down in the autumn, the IMIK was in control of a wide swath of territory around these towns.[56] By March 1995 the PUK controlled about two-thirds of the Kurdish area in the southeast, including Arbil and Sulaimaniyya; the KDP, about one-third in the north and some of the west, including the Turkish border.

The collapse of the KRG and the civil war between the two parties created a political vacuum in which other contending forces could operate. One of these was a relative newcomer to northern Iraq, the Kurdistan Workers Party (Partiya Karkari Kurdistan, PKK), Turkey's radical Kurdish movement.[57] By the mid-1990s, the PKK had become an important and destabilizing force in northern Iraq, occupying the high and inaccessible mountain territory along the northern border with Turkey.

The Iranians also entered the fray. Like the Turks, they had hostile Kurds based in northern Iraq, represented by the Kurdistan Democratic Party of Iran (KPDI), mainly in PUK territory near the Iranian border.

Between 1992 and 1994, fighting between the KDPI and Iran had intensified, making PUK areas vulnerable to attacks by Iran. In July 1995 the Iranians made a major incursion, in collusion with the PUK, into Kurdish territory.

As fighting and tensions continued between the parties, the PKK moved to improve its situation. In August 1996 it attacked the KDP, this time supported by the PUK, Iran, and Syria. Fearing his annihilation, Barzani turned to Baghdad for help, an invitation Saddam could hardly resist. On 31 August Iraqi forces, in conjunction with the KDP, attacked Arbil and succeeded in occupying the city. Under protection of these Iraqi forces, the KDP then routed the PUK. By 11 September the KDP controlled all of Iraqi Kurdistan to the Iranian border.

But this expansion of Saddam's forces met with opposition, not only from the PUK and behind it Iran, but also from the United States. Saddam's breakthrough in the north was a major setback for the United States putting an end to operations by Iraqi opposition forces there and ending the presence of the US Military Coordinating Committee. The United States had to undertake damage control, mediating a settlement with Barzani that kept the Baghdad government out of the north and allowed for a return of the PUK.[58] On 14 October 1996 the PUK recrossed the Iranian border in force, backed by the Iranians, and reached Sulaimaniyya's outskirts. When a cease-fire finally came into effect, the Kurdish area was effectively divided in two again. Although some civil strife continued between the KDP and the PUK during 1997, by March 1998 a new turning point was reached and the situation appeared to improve. From then on, representatives met frequently to establish areas of cooperation and to coordinate education, administration, and other activities, although both parties continued to govern their separate areas. The civil war was effectively over.

"Kurdistan" Taking Root

Despite these difficulties, by 2003 the Kurdish area was doing better economically than much of the central and southern portions of Iraq. The revenues from customs dues on truck traffic from Turkey were increasingly pumped into the KDP region, giving it an air of prosperity.

PUK territory still had less revenue, but it now received income from the Oil for Food program, supplemented by trade with Iran. International aid groups and the United Nations, with direct access to the north, had done a good job in distributing aid. A decade after the *intifada*, many villages had been wholly or partially resettled, health facilities revived, and some trade installed. Three universities operated in Kurdish territory, and statistics showed an infant mortality rate better than that before the Gulf War.

The north was also freer than areas under Baghdad's control. Kurds established their own Kurdish-language newspapers and TV stations, and the Kurdish parties allowed cable TV from outside to be broadcast in their region, giving their population an unprecedented view of the outside world, unavailable elsewhere in Iraq. Both parties also maintained offices and representatives in Turkey, Europe, and the United States. This gave the Kurds a window on the outside world and crucial contacts with the West, which they used to good advantage.

The decade of the 1990s allowed a separate Kurdish identity to take root in the north. The new school curriculum instilled loyalty to a new entity—Kurdistan—and its distinct culture. Students were taught that Kurdistan, their real homeland, included not only the three provinces of Dahuk, Arbil, and Sulaimaniyya but also Kirkuk, with its oil. By 2003 this curriculum was taught in Kurdish in most, though not all, schools, increasingly raising the question of how well the new generation of Kurds would be able to communicate with Iraqi Arabs in a future, more unified state.

The Shi'a in the South

Shi'i opposition to the regime continued in the wake of the *intifada*. Although the regime maintained control of the south, its position there was weak, as evidenced in numerous hit-and-run episodes against Ba'th and military posts and against high-level regime figures traveling in the south. The main area of activity, however, was in the marsh region, which constituted a refuge for dissidents and the chief connecting link across the border to Iran.[59] Once the government had quelled the rebellion, it turned its attention to the local population in the marshes, sending some 40,000 troops south to build new roads and bases in the area and to slash and burn their way through areas with ten-foot-high reeds and palm thickets.[60] It was at this point, in August 1992, that the United States, the United Kingdom, and France, under UN auspices, instituted the southern no-fly zone. Nonetheless, ground actions against the Shi'a continued. By September 1995, the United Nations estimated that 200,000 to 250,000 former inhabitants of the marshes had been driven from the area. Some of these villagers were resettled by the Iraqi government in camps; others were moved to the Kirkuk region in an effort to Arabize Kurdish and Turkman territory.

The government also employed massive—and controversial—drainage schemes to dry up the marshes. By 1994 aerial photos showed near-total destruction of the marshes. As the marshes were drained, the government's ability to move into the area and to control the population increased, but so, too, did opposition from the local population.

Opposition continued to emanate from religious clerics as well, and they met with continued persecution. Especially significant was the killing of Muhammad Sadiq al-Sadr, who had been hand picked by the regime as a *marji'*, because it had reason to believe he would cause no trouble. This proved to be a faulty assumption.

Opposed to the quietist tradition of clerics like Ali al-Sistani, as well as to the exiled clerics like Muhammad Baqir al-Hakim in Iran, Muhammad Sadiq al-Sadr called for a Shi'i leadership that would take an active spiritual and political role in supporting the community. His interpretation had strong strains of mysticism and messianism (preparation for the coming of the Mahdi) and a conservative application of Islamic practices, like dress codes. Most important of all, however, he appealed to poorer elements of society, especially the Shi'a in Saddam City, and rural, tribal areas of the south, focusing on matters affecting their everyday life. Cultivating junior clerics and sending out representatives to these areas, he slowly built the basis of a mass movement, in contrast to the traditional middle-class constituencies of most Shi'i clerics.

Using his mosque in Kufa, Muhammad Sadiq al-Sadr cautiously began to challenge the regime, for example, asking for the release of Shi'i
prisoners and refusing to limit his activities. As he did so, his congrega-
tions increased, and he drew larger and larger crowds, always a danger
for the regime, which tried but failed to curb him. In 1998 Sadr donned
the white shroud that indicated he expected to be a martyr. He was not
wrong. On 19 February 1999 Sadr and two of his sons were attacked
and killed by assailants obviously working for the regime.

In response, the regime faced some serious Shi'i uprisings throughout
the south, turning Sadr into a martyr for the cause. By appealing to the
urban poor, neglected rural and tribal population of the Shi'i south, and
disaffected youth, Muhammad Sadiq had created a nascent mass movement. After his death, it was kept alive by his representatives, midlevel
clerics inside the country, ready to be mobilized by his son, Muqtada, after Saddam's removal in 2003. The movement also revealed fissures in
the Shi'i opposition movement. Traditional Shi'i clerics, like Sistani and
Khu'i, had been willing to keep out of direct interference in politics;
they relied not on mass movements but on the educated middle class.
Sadr was their direct antithesis. His movement also opened up the fissure between Shi'a who remained inside Iraq and had to "suffer" Saddam's brutality under the sanctions regime and those who had left
(especially to Iran) and fought from outside under "foreign" sponsorship. These fissures would become increasingly apparent after 2003.[61]

Opposition from Abroad

The regime also faced continuing opposition from Iraqis outside the
country. Estimates indicate that the number of exiles may have reached
1.5 million prior to the Gulf War. The war, the rebellion, and the ongoing sanctions regime may have pushed this figure to as many as 2 to 3
million by the mid-1990s. The largest group was in Iran, numbering
500,00 to 1 million.[62] Others were in neighboring Arab countries, especially Jordan, Syria, and the Arab Gulf. In Europe the major concentration was in England, which housed hundreds of thousands. Some

were scattered across the United States. Some were poor, but many more were from Iraq's educated and skilled middle class.

By the time of the Gulf War, the main components of this opposition were well known. They included the two Kurdish parties (the KDP and the PUK), the two Shi'i Islamist groups (SCIRI, with its headquarters in Iran, and the Da'wa, now scattered abroad), and the venerable Iraq Communist Party. Also significant for the future was the Iraqi National Accord (INA), led by Ayad Allawi, a Shi'a. The INA had strong ties to former Ba'thists and Iraqi army officers and to Western intelligence organizations in Britain and the United States. Allawi, from a well-known family and a doctor trained in England, had defected from the Ba'th Party in the mid-1970s and worked against the regime in England. In December 1990, under Saudi auspices, he formed the INA.

The weaknesses of this exile opposition soon became clear. Deep ideological divisions within its ranks prevented effective collaboration. Even more significantly, the exile groups often had little or no foothold inside Iraq, especially in the center, where the regime had to be displaced. Only the Kurdish parties had managed to reestablish themselves within the borders of Iraq, but even their ability to operate against the government was limited. Most important of all, the exile parties, including the Kurds, were dependent for support on outside governments, often at odds with one another.

Initially, Iraq's neighbors, especially Iran, Syria, and Saudi Arabia, took the initiative to create a unified opposition group in 1990 and 1991 but failed.[63] However, by 1991 the Gulf War had caused a shift in regional and international dynamics that created challenges—and opportunities—for the opposition. The West was now opposed to Saddam; Iran was less willing to support the opposition within Iraq. The Shi'i Islamist parties now had to adjust, and they did. Although wary of affiliating with the West, the Da'wa shifted gears in 1995, adopting a new political manifesto calling for Iraqi independence and the establishment of political parties. SCIRI, closer to Iran, reluctantly accepted the new US role and was included in subsequent meetings with US officials.[64]

Ahmad Chalabi

But these Islamist groups were soon outflanked by the opposition efforts of a relative newcomer, Ahmad Chalabi, and the contacts he was able to develop in the United States, especially among leading administration and congressional figures, who were now turning against Iraq and its regime. Chalabi, a Western-educated mathematician from a wealthy Shi'i banking family, had left Iraq in 1956. In 1977, as part of his family's operations, he established Petra Bank in Jordan. In the late 1980s the bank collapsed, and he fled Jordan after indictments from the Jordanian government for bank fraud. He now turned his attention full time to opposition activities. Despite his intellectual talents, Chalabi had some obvious drawbacks that would make him extremely controversial. He had not lived in Iraq for years, he was under a cloud for allegations of banking fraud in Jordan, and he was seen to be heavy-handed in dealing with his colleagues. But his organizational abilities, tenacity, and effectiveness in dealing with Western politicians soon made him a leading spokesman for the opposition in the West.

Chalabi now took the lead in trying to organize the disparate opposition groups, independent of the Middle Eastern sponsors. In 1992 a number of these groups met in Vienna and formed a new umbrella group, the Iraq National Congress (INC), which incorporated some, but not all, of the existing parties. A second, more inclusive meeting in northern Iraq later selected an executive committee directed by Chalabi.[65] For a time, the INC made some headway in establishing its presence on Iraqi soil. It acquired a headquarters in Salah al-Din, it operated a radio station that reached into Iraq proper, it had printing facilities that it used to distribute leaflets and a newspaper, and it acted as a magnet to attract defectors, especially from the military. These were housed, fed, and trained as the beginnings of a militia to be added to the Kurdish *peshmerga*. In the course of time, it became apparent that the United States (in fact the CIA) was funding these activities and that it had sent some midlevel operatives into the north to help manage the operation. These operations showed how far Chalabi had succeeded in drawing in US policymakers.

Chalabi had a "periphery strategy" designed to overthrow the regime by revolt or pressure from the Kurds in the north and the Shi'a in the south. A key element in its potential success—in the view of its perpetrators—was air support from the United States. Chalabi and his supporters, especially in the PUK, had by 1995 decided to push forward with an attack on Iraqi forces in two directions—Mosul and Kirkuk. Already in a struggle with the PUK over territory, however, Barzani and the KDP refused to join the operation, seriously weakening it.[66]

Despite these setbacks, the INC and the PUK went forward. On 3 March 1995 the group attacked the regular armed forces in the Kirkuk area and had some success. Some seven hundred Iraqi forces surrendered to *peshmerga*, and the opposition gained a few square miles of territory, but not enough to seriously threaten the regime. Effective US support had failed to materialize, and so, too, had the participation of the KDP, one of the two main pillars of the INC in the north.

The operation also revealed serious splits among policymakers in Washington.[67] The CIA and others in the administration were only willing to give limited support to Chalabi and his strategy. Instead, the CIA put its emphasis on a coup from disaffected officers in the center. In June 1996 the agency supported an attempt by the INA and Allawi, with his former contacts in the Ba'th and the military, to engineer such a coup. This attempt was also unsuccessful. The effort was penetrated by Saddam, and many of the perpetrators in Baghdad were executed, indicating that his overthrow without substantial outside military help would be difficult, if not impossible.

These defeats in the north apparently convinced Chalabi he could not overturn the regime without US military support, and he now turned his attention to this effort. The timing was propitious and accompanied a shift in political dynamics in the United States. The election of a Republican Congress in 1994 and the rise of neoconservative political forces on the American political scene gave Chalabi an opening. The formation in 1997 of a new think tank, the Project for a New American Century, led by many neoconservative politicians (including those who would be influential in the subsequent Bush administration, such as Dick Cheney, Donald Rumsfeld, Paul Wolfowitz, and Zalmay Khalilzad), consistently pressured the administration and Congress to move toward regime change. They not only formed a new base of support for Chalabi but also were clearly influenced by his ideas and their personal contacts with him. Chalabi began to have some success.[68]

In May 1998 Congress appropriated $5 million for the opposition to spend on media and other outreach activities, and in October the Iraq Liberation Act, authorizing $97 million to be drawn down from the defense budget, was signed by the president. These funds were to include military training. Gradually, the US administration shifted to a policy of "regime change" in Iraq, although support for this goal was still modest under the Clinton administration; indeed, very few of the funds appropriated were spent up until 2001. Among those designated to receive funds were the KDP, the PUK, the INC, the INA, and SCIRI. Two others, the IMIK (dropped later when it was taken over by radicals) and a monarchist movement under Sharif Ali, a Hashimite descendent of the former dynasty in Iraq, later fizzled out. SCIRI refused the funding. It is doubtful that any of these efforts would have come to fruition had there not been a change of administration in 2001 or the trauma of 9/11.

A Decade of Stagnation

The aftermath of the Gulf War was one of the worst periods in Iraq's modern history. The regime's repression, the harsh and long-lasting cease-fire terms, and the *intifada* and its outcome weakened state structures and the cohesiveness of the nation. In the north about 10 percent of the country—the self-governing Kurdish area—was left free of central government control. In the south, government control was weak and needed constant reinforcement. Continual dissidence in the center revealed intense unhappiness with the regime. The modest economic and social revival toward the end of the decade was insufficient to undo the damage of a decade of sanctions or to set the country on a path of future growth and normalcy.

The exodus of millions of Iraqis and the depletion of the middle class deprived Iraq of much of its best talent, leaving those who remained isolated and with lower standards of living and little exposure to the outside world. Although the regime survived, it rested on an exceedingly narrow power base, dominated by one community—Sunni Arabs—and only a small portion of that community. The struggle with the West, now narrowing mainly to the United States and the United Kingdom, continued. US policy, however, focused until 2001 on maintaining key cease-fire restrictions on Iraq and little more than encouraging a change of regime. That was to change dramatically after 11 September 2001.

10

THE US ATTEMPT AT NATION-BUILDING IN IRAQ, 2003–2006

Iraq's political, economic, and social structure had already been badly eroded under Saddam Husain, but the inept occupation of 2003 brought unprecedented political and social collapse and by 2006 almost pushed Iraq over the edge into a failed state.

Without substantial international support and lacking in understanding of Iraq or clear planning for Iraq's future, the decision by the United States to occupy Iraq was fraught with dangers. Toppling Saddam proved easy and swift, but replacing the government and the political and social institutions that underpinned the regime was a long, difficult, and costly process—for both the United States and Iraq. The initial attack, followed by unchecked looting and the ill-advised dismantling of the previous political and military structures, created widespread destruction and a political and social vacuum, which foreign personnel proved unable to replace. Iraq soon began to fracture into its ethnic and sectarian components.

At local levels in Kurdish and Shi'i areas, opposition groups moved to fill the vacuum (the Kurdistan Democratic Party [KDP] and the Patriotic Union of Kurdistan [PUK] in the north; the Supreme Council for the Islamic Revolution in Iraq [SCIRI] and the followers of Sadr in the south) while the exile opposition parties elbowed their way into national politics in Baghdad. To shore up the situation, the United States instituted the Coalition Provisional Authority (CPA), under a forceful administrator, Ambassador L. Paul Bremer III, who, together with coalition forces, instituted a period of direct rule, lasting until June 2004, in which the United States attempted—unsuccessfully in most cases—to radically reshape Iraqi society. It was not long, however, before those now excluded from power rebelled, creating an increasing climate of violence that stunted economic growth and generated growing political opposition to the Iraqi venture inside the United States. The main Iraqi opposition came from the Sunnis—the ousted Ba'thists, Sunni religious elements, and al-Qa'ida, which now gained a foothold in Iraq. In addition, a group of poor and disaffected Shi'a, also excluded from power, was mobilized against the occupation by Muqtada al-Sadr, son of the former assassinated cleric Muhammad Sadiq al-Sadr, and the supporters he had left behind.

In the face of growing opposition at home to the nation-building project in Iraq and forthcoming U.S. elections in 2004, the George W. Bush administration abruptly decided in November 2003 to end the CPA and to turn sovereignty over to an "Iraqi" administration by June 2004. A confused period of transition occurred involving a new interim government, an intense struggle for power among Iraqis, and UN mediation. Elections for a constituent assembly were held early in January, a constitution was hastily drafted, and, after a referendum held on it in October, a final election for a new government took place in December—all in 2005. All three elections solidified ethnic and sectarian fragmentation, giving power to Kurds in the north and Shi'i religious parties in the center and south and marginalizing Sunnis.

The emergence of an entirely new constellation of forces in Baghdad and the provinces played out against a background of continued unrest and insurgency, which led in 2006 to a vicious, sectarian war in Baghdad and its environs. Substantial elements of the population were killed or displaced as refugees, further changing Baghdad's social and sectarian demography and entrenching sectarian divisions. The violence also depleted Iraq's educated middle class and left bitterness and deeper divisions over identity and outlook. By the end of 2006, Iraq appeared to be slipping into chaos.

Occupation of Iraq

The forces that finally brought the fall of the Saddam Husain regime were wholly external to Iraq and lay in the terrorist attacks on 11 September 2001. President Bush declared a "war on terrorism" and made preemptive military strikes against regimes that threatened the United States part of the US political arsenal. The United States first turned its attention to Afghanistan and the removal there of the Taliban regime, which had been protecting Usama bin Ladin. Not long after, it focused on Iraq and the potential threat posed by weapons of mass destruction (WMD) in the hands of a hostile dictator like Saddam Husain.

The Decision to Invade

Much ink has been spilled on how, when, and, above all, why the decision to go to war in Iraq was made and need not be detailed here.[1] Regime change had been advocated by a number of politicians on the right for some time and was now justified according to several shifting rationales. One was a link between Usama bin Ladin's network and the Iraqi regime, which would have implicated Iraq in the 11 September attacks.[2] More convincing were arguments centered on Iraq's continued possession of WMD, which could be neither verified nor disproved owing to the absence of on-the-ground inspectors in Iraq.[3] Another argument cited the regime's appalling human rights record and the benefits that would accrue from a more peaceful and democratic leadership in Baghdad. Indeed, some put forth a new and ambitious agenda—creating a democracy in Iraq that would provide a model for the region and shift the very parameters of regional politics. In the year before the invasion, there was some discussion, inside and outside the administration, about the advisability of military action and its ultimate goal. Divisions emerged in the public debate, in Congress, and within the administration itself. In the end, the prevailing assumption of the administration appears to have been that ending the regime would be easy, that the occupation would be widely welcomed by the Iraqi population, and that a modest force of about 150,000 and a short military stay would be all that were necessary.

The Exile Opposition

No aspect of this decision was more difficult than finding a regime replacement. An early US assumption appears to have been that underlying bureaucratic and military structures would be left to govern Iraq while the top political leadership would be replaced—mainly by the exile opposition. The hard core of this group, which had operated outside Baghdad's control in the 1990s and had been designated to receive support under the US Iraq Liberation Act, consisted of the KDP, the PUK, the two secular Shi'i groups (the Iraq National Congress [INC] and the Iraqi National Accord [INA]), and SCIRI. A major ingathering of this opposition in London in mid-December 2002 gave an indication of future problems. The Kurds wanted federalism with a high degree of separatism, opposed by most others; most objected to Ahmad Chalabi's leadership; and secularists had reservations about SCIRI's Islamist agenda. The United States had concerns about SCIRI's ties to Iran. Given these problems, Bush made a decision to forgo any provisional government composed of these opposition leaders before occupation and to put authority in the hands of the United States. The Americans would now invade without any clear plan for a future government.[4]

The Three-Week War

In September 2002, Bush took his case against Iraq and its possible possession of WMD to the UN General Assembly. In November the UN Security Council (UNSC) unanimously passed Resolution 1441, which demanded that Iraq restore WMD inspections on rigorous terms. Meanwhile, the United States, in collaboration with the United Kingdom, began a quiet military buildup in the Gulf. In an attempt to avoid military attack, Iraq accepted Resolution 1441, and in November 2002 a new inspections regime began its work. Iraq cooperated with inspectors but provided no new information. Despite deep divisions in the international community between those wishing to continue with inspections (mainly France, Germany, and Russia) and those impatient to bring the issue to closure while forces were in place to accomplish this (mainly the United States and United Kingdom), the United States decided to act on the authority of UNSC Resolution 1441. On 18 March, President Bush gave Saddam forty-eight hours to leave the country, a clear warning to all that war would follow.

Operation Iraqi Freedom, as the US military campaign was called, was over in virtually three weeks.[5] The main object was the capture of Baghdad, the defeat of Saddam's forces—mainly the Republican Guard protecting the capital—and the fall of the regime. The operation began with an air campaign, meant to "shock and awe" Iraqi forces, on the night of 19 March (the morning of 20 March in Baghdad). It targeted key regime strongholds, command and control facilities, and military installations, not oil installations or electricity grids, because these would be needed to rebuild the country.

The backbone of the campaign was a major ground offensive, designed for speed and surprise, to reach Baghdad as fast as possible, to surround and then capture it, and thus to end the regime. The campaign was specifically not designed to occupy urban areas on the way, where it expected the local population to be friendly, if not openly welcoming. After crossing the border with Kuwait in the south on 20 March (21 March local time), combined US and UK forces first protected the major southern oil fields.[6] British units then peeled off to secure Basra and the key areas in the south, while the main arm of the invasion forces then headed north along the Euphrates to Nasiriyya, Samawa, and Najaf. Not everything went according to plan. Unexpected fighting from Saddam's *fida'iyyin*, a guerrilla force, in Samawa and Nasiriyya slowed the march north. This was a foretaste of future resistance.

The first US attacking units reached the Baghdad airport on 4 April. In probes into Baghdad, US units were again attacked by irregular forces but succeeded on the second day in reaching the Republican Palace, the nerve center of the government, where they set up headquarters. On

9 April, a corporal with a tank came upon a group of Iraqis trying to topple a statue of Saddam Husain in Firdaus Square. He threw a cable around the statue, helping pull it to the ground. With camera crews available, this act, recorded on TV screens around the world, became the iconic symbol of the regime's fall.

In the north of the country, the occupation took an entirely different course. An expected agreement with the Turks to use their territory fell through, largely because of popular opposition in Turkey to the war. Denied passage by the Turkish parliament, the United States was without a northern route for its forces to enter Iraq. With only special forces in the north, together with airpower, the United States was forced to rely on the Kurds and their *peshmerga* for help, although the U.S. government apparently promised the Turks that US forces would prevent Kurdish occupation of Kirkuk and Mosul.

The first area to be attacked was Banjwin on the Iranian border, under the control of Ansar al-Islam, a radical Sunni Islamist group hostile to the PUK.[7] With the help of US air attacks and logistic support, the *peshmerga* retook this area by the end of March.[8] Ansar al-Islam essentially dispersed, mainly across the Iranian border, but some members made their way back into Iraq to help found al-Qa'ida in Iraq (AQI). In the push for Mosul and Kirkuk, however, it proved impossible for the sparse US forces to control the *peshmerga*, who took advantage of the vacuum in forces to expand their control over Kurdish-dominated portions of these provinces, in addition to the three provinces of Dahuk, Arbil, and Sulaimaniyya.

By mid-April it was clear that the regime had been toppled and its forces defeated, Basra was gradually being brought under British control, and US forces were in tenuous control of the Euphrates cites of Nasiriyya, Samawa, Najaf, and Karbala, as well as Kut on the Tigris. But the country had hardly been occupied, and coalition forces were spread extremely thin. They had not yet gotten control of northern towns along the Tigris like Tikrit or in the Sunni center in Anbar, Saddam's former strongholds. And their control of Baghdad would prove tenuous. The entire operation had been based on economy of forces, and the United States was apparently still operating under the assumption of an early withdrawal and a quick handover to an Iraqi administration. By June US forces had been drawn down to about 60 percent of their original size and the British to 40 percent.[9] These assumptions were soon to be proved disastrously wrong.

The Looting and the War's Immediate Aftermath

Although some damage was done by the war—especially the bombing—the real costs of the occupation to the Iraqi people came immediately after the fall of the regime. The failure to bring enough troops to control "occupied" cities and establish some sort of law and order was a critical flaw and did more to affect the outcome than any military action. In the vacuum that ensued with Saddam's fall, widespread looting by the local population went unchecked for days, even weeks, in virtually all major cities and towns, except for the Kurdish area, where it was stopped by the *peshmerga*. Mobs attacked ministries, hospitals, and universities as well as communications facilities, the power grid, and industrial plants. Among the most shocking episodes of looting was that of Baghdad's National Museum, containing priceless treasures. While coalition forces did protect oil installations, they had no orders to fire on unarmed civilians and made few moves to control the situation. The result was spreading chaos as the army, police, and bureaucracy disappeared. The CPA estimated the cost of looting at $12 billion.[10] The looting devastated Iraq's infrastructure, set back its reconstruction effort, and undermined what confidence the population may have had in the new administration. The population had greeted the foreign forces, at least in some parts of Iraq, with clear relief at being free of the previous regime and a sense of hope for the future. Much of this was now punctured, as was the exaggerated sense of optimism under which the occupation had been conducted.

The absence or weakness of occupying US forces allowed the local forces to fill the emerging political vacuum. They established "shadow governments" that often operated beneath the radar of the skeletal structures later established by the coalition.[11] In Basra SCIRI and Badr, two of the outside opposition groups, established local beachheads; in Nasiryya a number of tribes associated with Da'wa took over parts of the city;

and Karbala was penetrated by survivors of the radical Islamic Action Organization.

Most of these groups penetrated from outside Iraq, but the most significant and ultimately disruptive movement—that of Muqtada al-Sadr and his followers—came from inside. Muqtada clearly relied on the legacy, theology, institutions, and representatives left behind after his father's death in 1999.[12] Sadrists were strong among the poorer tribes and marsh dwellers of Amara and Nasiriyya and in semiurbanized areas like Saddam City and the poorer quarters of Basra.

The rise of the movement probably owes as much to Sadr's followers as to Muqtada himself; it was these young clerics who seized control, rapidly, where they could, using "street" supporters as foot soldiers, occupying mosques, hospitals, schools, and social welfare centers.[13] On 11 April, Muqtada gave his first postwar sermon in Kufa, assuming leadership of the movement. Saddam City was renamed Sadr City (after his father). His second sermon a week later stressed the themes he would emphasize over and over—opposition to occupation and criticism of leaders who had gone into exile when the country needed them (SCIRI and Da'wa).

The rapid and sudden emergence of this insider group soon generated an inter-Shi'i struggle for power in the south. Abd al-Majid al-Khu'i, head of the Khu'i Foundation in London and a moderate young Shi'i cleric, had been flown into Najaf from London, under US auspices, to establish a liaison with the leading clerics. Shortly after his arrival, he was brutally attacked and killed by a mob of Sadrist supporters. The extent of Sadr's responsibility for al-Khu'i's death became a major controversy, but there is little doubt that the removal of al-Khu'i, a moderate, relatively pro-Western voice among the Shi'i Islamists, and the resulting boost it gave to Sadrist forces on the ground were major factors in the emerging power struggle that would ensue as the United States tried to establish some sort of local government.

In the north, the two main Kurdish parties and their *peshmerga* forces had already used their cooperation with the United States and the absence of any substantial US forces to move out of their Kurdish Regional Government (KRG) stronghold into disputed areas. Even though they had to relinquish official political control over Mosul City and Kirkuk, their *peshmerga* forces remained in control on the ground in areas the Kurdish leaders eventually wanted to absorb. Indeed, they were already busy in efforts to replace the fleeing Arabs with Kurds from other areas, beginning to change, once again, the demographic balance.

In contrast to these Shi'i Islamist forces and the Kurds, the Western-oriented opposition leaders on whom many in the United States appeared to be counting—mainly Chalabi (INC) and Ayad Allawi (INA)—had no military force or people on the ground. Both Allawi and Chalabi would essentially have to rely on foreign support to gain any power.

Meanwhile, in Sunni areas in Baghdad, Anbar, Salah al-Din, and other strongholds of the former regime, local forces were generally hostile to the occupation. Chief among them was the Association of Muslim Scholars (AMS, or Hayat al-Ulama al-Muslimin) formed among Sunnis and emphasizing a religious/sectarian identity. AMS also had Ba'thist supporters, which gave the movement a nationalist character, soon to crystallize into an insurgency.

Garner's Brief Administration

The US civil administration that faced this local situation was inadequate and unprepared. Its head, Jay Garner, a retired general, had been appointed less than two months before the war and had few guidelines for policy and little time to gather a team. Garner's tenure in Baghdad lasted a brief three weeks, from 21 April to 11 May. Garner was to head the Office of Reconstruction and Humanitarian Assistance (ORHA). He and his team operated on the assumption that there would be an early US troop withdrawal (possibly by September), a short stay for ORHA, and a transition to a provisional government. They expected the Iraqi military, stripped of its top command, to help with security and to engage in reconstruction activities; the bureaucracy, minus its former oppressive leadership, would continue to function. An interim Iraqi government, consisting mainly of the exile opposition leaders plus some additional Iraqis from inside the country, would form a transitional administration, help write a constitution, and then hand off to an elected body. None of these assumptions would prove correct.

On 6 May, Bush replaced Garner with a new civilian administrator, Ambassador L. Paul Bremer III, and announced that the United States would seek a UN resolution giving it status as an occupying power. One reason for this abrupt change was a US desire to reassert some control in Iraq in the face of disorder. Another was the intense suspicion—inside some US government circles and among British allies—of giving authority to exile Iraqi leaders (and especially to Chalabi) without a serious attempt to include those living inside Iraq.

Bremer and the CPA:
Direct Rule and an Attempt at Nation-Building

Bremer's tenure in Iraq, from 11 May 2003 until 28 June 2004, was decisive in shaping Iraq's future political and social direction, for the most part negatively. It was a brief effort by the United States at direct rule and an ambitious attempt at nation-building. Bremer saw, correctly, that real change would require a longer period of transition and direct governance by the United States before control was handed over to any Iraqi government. Nor did Bremer have much faith in the exile opposition leaders. He wanted a broader Iraqi base with specific consideration given to ethnic, sectarian, and gender diversity.

On 16 May, Bremer met with the key opposition leaders to inform them that there would be no "provisional government." Instead, the CPA became the effective government in Iraq, authorized by UN Resolution 1453 to exercise legal power in Iraq as well as to spend Iraqi funds. In addition, considerable authority was given to the military. By mid-July, the remaining allied forces were reorganized into the Combined Joint Task Force-7, headed by Lt. General Ricardo Sanchez. They essentially controlled security in Iraq and, parallel to the CPA, established their own administrative structures in cities, towns, and provinces under their command and dispensed funds under their control for local reconstructions projects.

This rearrangement did bring the security situation sufficiently under control in the remaining months of 2003 to restore some order and allow reconstruction. By October 2003, electricity production had returned to prewar levels; the same was true of water treatment plants. But these short-term positive effects were ultimately undone by Bremer's radical effort to reshape Iraq from the bottom up. That effort—ideologically driven, ill-considered, and woefully understaffed—destroyed more than it built. It dismantled the entire institutional structure of the old regime but had too few resources, staff, or time—and too little understanding of the country—to construct the building blocks of the new Iraq it wished to create.

De-Bathification

The effort began with the first CPA order, issued 16 May—the de-Ba'thification order. The order disestablished the Ba'th Party and aimed to eliminate the party structures to "ensure that representative government in Iraq is not threatened by Ba'thist elements returning to power."[14] It excluded from public-sector employment the top four ranks of the party, immediately affecting about 30,000 individuals.[15] Although some removal of Ba'th elements was essential, the issue was how deep to cut and how to replace the lost expertise. The deep cuts made for an abrupt change from the more gradual process begun by Garner and his ORHA staff.[16] In addition, those removed were, almost by definition, Sunnis, impeding Bremer's intention to achieve sectarian diversity in the leadership.

Nonetheless, de-Ba'thification was popular with most of the population, especially among Shi'a and Kurds. The chief supporter of the process was Chalabi, who wanted the previous ruling class extirpated as a prelude to its replacement by the opposition leadership he hoped to head.

De-Ba'thification rapidly became a key political issue in the new Iraq and a sharp point of disagreement between the new—mainly exile—opposition leaders and a minority who had been affiliated with and benefited from the previous regime. US administrators would soon backtrack on de-Ba'thification, recognizing the need for trained, local personnel and seeking "reconciliation" and a middle ground, but not before the issue had become intensely polarizing.

Dissolution of the Military

Even more disruptive than de-Ba'thification was the total dissolution of Iraq's armed forces and its entire intelligence and security system, which came with the second CPA order, on 23 May.[17] Whereas the de-Ba'thification order had been popular, the sudden end of the Iraqi army came as a shock to much of the population. Moreover, this dissolution order involved as many as 400,000 Iraqis (and their families), who had now lost not only their jobs but also their pensions. (This latter mistake was soon rectified when Bremer agreed to pay the pensions of about 250,000 "retired" military men.)

Unlike the de-Ba'thification order, this sweeping decision appears to have been made mainly by Bremer and represented a distinct change of thinking about the army among most of the military officers who had been in charge of the forces on the ground.[18] The main argument advanced for this decision was that there was no longer an Iraqi army in existence but some elements of the previous structure could have been reassembled. Once again, the order was driven by the ambition to restructure Iraq from the ground up. The refusal to reconstitute and use Iraq's regular army contributed more than anything else to the rapidly deteriorating security situation in the country. The United States not only lost control of Iraq's borders but also of most of its local population centers, while alienating the largest and most lethal portion of the population likely to be opposed to US policies.

Meanwhile, recruitment for the new army, minus its old officer corps, began in August. So, too, did an attempt to rebuild the police, both pillars of local security. By the end of the CPA's tenure, the armed forces had increased to about 180,000, but—as the coming insurgency would demonstrate—rapid recruitment and an inexperienced force of new recruits and officers, with competing loyalties to political groups, could not produce a professional military.[19] Much the same result occurred with the police.

At local levels and in Baghdad, policing fell to US combat forces untrained and unprepared for such action.[20] Increasingly they used harsh tactics, often treating the public in humiliating ways offensive to the local culture, thereby raising, rather than reducing, tensions. The absence of security allowed—indeed encouraged—the emergence of militias. These often intimidated the local population but also provided the only security mechanism. Meanwhile, unprotected borders allowed fighters and insurgents of all kinds to enter, smugglers to engage in illegal but highly lucrative trade (especially in oil), and all kinds of criminal activities to flourish.

In May 2003, the CPA had forbidden militias but made an exception for the *peshmerga* in the north, probably necessary given realities on the ground, but this action raised hackles elsewhere in Iraq because it appeared to give legal underpinning to Kurdish separatism. Although the Badr Brigade had officially renounced its arms (in theory but not yet in practice), it gradually became absorbed into the national police and other security forces, essentially becoming an arm of the newly emerging state. Elsewhere militias flourished.

Economic Change

On the economic front, the CPA made an equally bold attempt to restructure Iraq along the lines of a free-market economy. The new governors of Iraq hoped to dismantle the Ba'thist command economy and substitute a capitalist system, which, they assumed, would flourish if Iraqis were able to exercise individual initiative. The CPA began by attempting to privatize state-owned industries, liberate trade from government control, encourage foreign investment, and end protection for local industry. The one area in which the CPA did not interfere—wisely—was oil and natural resources, recognizing that this was a sensitive issue best left for a future Iraqi government.[21]

Here, too, the effort soon floundered. Difficult trade-offs had to be made between essential short-term goals—the need to jump-start a broken economy, rapidly repair infrastructure, and, above all, employ the Iraqi labor force—and long-term restructuring goals.[22] Many of the moves toward a market economy were difficult to implement and often had to be reversed.

The best example was the attempt to privatize state enterprises. It soon became apparent that virtually none were economically viable and no buyers could be found. Rather than being resuscitated, the factories were purposely neglected, contributing to rising unemployment. A more mixed example was the CPA effort to liberalize trade and open the door to foreign investment. A CPA order permitted 100 percent foreign investment and ownership in Iraqi businesses, except for natural resources (oil), banks, and insurance companies. Iraq attracted virtually no foreign investment because of rising insecurity. More significant and enduring was the opening to foreign trade. Tariffs on foreign trade were abolished, and a simple 5 percent flat tax imposed on most imports and exports. The Iraqi market was soon flooded with consumer goods—air conditioners, refrigerators, cell phones, cars—that a starved public craved, and as a result a new merchant class of local retailers and wholesalers flourished. This effort unquestionably raised living standards but hurt efforts to get indigenous industries started.

The most successful long-term measure taken by the CPA was the stabilization of Iraq's currency. It made the Central Bank of Iraq an independent institution, responsible for monetary policy.[23] It then created a new Iraqi dinar, eliminating the two different currencies that had been circulating—at wildly different rates—in the Kurdish north and the rest of Iraq. The measure helped unify the economy, reduce inflation, and improve prospects for trade.[24]

These measures, together with renewed government employment of civil servants at better-than-average wages and salaries, unquestionably improved standards of living for the middle class—especially in Baghdad—but it also increased demand, which could not yet be satisfied. Improvements in infrastructure (especially electricity, power, and water facilities) could not keep up with rising demand, and in the absence of sufficient expansion of local industry and services, unemployment remained high. Indeed, short-term goals soon overtook the ambitious restructuring project, which, like its political counterpart, ended by destroying more than it could create.

The Establishment of the Interim Governing Council

Meanwhile, the CPA had to address the critical issue of who would replace the Ba'th. The core group of exile opposition leaders—all outsiders—had expanded its group, now called the Iraq Liberation Council (ILC), to include the Da'wa (led by Ibrahim al-Ja'fari) and the secular NDP. This did not satisfy Bremer, who wanted more insiders.[25] However, it was one thing to ask for a broader base of leadership to replace the old regime and another to develop it at such short notice. The CPA would have to contend not only with the ILC but also with the newly emerging political forces released in the wake of occupation.

Bremer's attempt to form the Interim Governing Council (IGC) soon ran into difficulties. The two Kurdish parties were not interested in joining the IGC, which would have little power in Baghdad; rather, they wanted to focus on consolidating power in their own autonomous region in the north. On 12 June, they finally unified and formed one Kurdish administration, intensifying Kurdish aspirations for self-government.

Even more significant was the rising strength of Shi'i forces and political consciousness. The politics of Shi'i identity, emphasizing former discrimination against Shi'a in government and the need for a unified Shi'i majority to reverse this phenomenon, became increasingly explicit. There were several elements in this current. One was SCIRI, whose leader, Muhammad Baqir al-Hakim, had returned to Iraq, where he assumed a position as a leading Shi'i spokesman. He envisioned a religio-political role for himself—something akin to a "political *marji'*"—and saw his party as the vanguard organization in creating a Shi'i-dominated Islamic republic.[26] Another was the Da'wa. Added to these known exile Shi'i parties was the eruption of the insider Sadrist movement and its offshoot, the Fadila (Virtue) Party, a quieter version of Sadr's movement. All of these efforts provided powerful support for a growing—if diverse—political dynamic of Shi'i communal identity.

Identity politics was also encouraged by trends in the Sunni community. Under the Ba'th, Sunnis had avoided open identification with sectarian politics—despite their obvious dominance. This now changed in the face of rising Kurdish and Shi'i identity and Sunni marginalization. However, Sunnis were divided. Some, including many exiles in opposition who were generally secular and Western oriented, soon accepted reality and were willing to join the political process, including the Iraqi Islamic Party (IIP). But the bulk of the Sunni community, especially those abruptly displaced by the Bremer administration, refused to join and before long would be engaged in active insurgency.

Finally, in an attempt to enlist some of the local population, in May and June 2003, Bremer's team fanned out across all eighteen provinces in Iraq searching for Iraqis who could represent their communities on the IGC.[27] The process was ad hoc at best. At least a dozen local figures were found and added to nominees suggested by the ILC, which, in fact, became the backbone of a new governing body. On 13 July, the Interim Governing Council was announced. Its main task was to advise the CPA, draw up a draft constitution, and function as a nominal Iraqi government.

The resulting IGC had twenty-five members but was dominated by the exile ILC opposition parties. Most local figures selected by the CPA were unknown. In keeping with the CPA demand for ethnic and sectarian representation, thirteen—just over half—were Shi'a, five were Sunni Arabs, and five were Kurds. One Turkman and one Christian were included. Three were women.

But the CPA also tried to include a wide spectrum of political parties, with an edge given to those that could be characterized as secular and more liberal in tendency. Of the twelve identifiable parties on the IGC, half met the secular characterization—eight if the KDP and PUK are added. Only four were identifiably religious and sectarian (SCIRI, Da'wa, IIP, and the Kurdish Islamic Union [KIU]).[28] No one connected with the emerging Sadrist movement—or Fadila—was included.

However inclusive the IGC was on political grounds, it was still dominated by Shi'i exiles and the Kurds. Even among these, traditional divisions soon emerged. Early on, the IGC failed to agree on a president who could lead its efforts and in August ended by creating a "presidency" that rotated among the top twelve IGC members each month.[29] This first attempt by the IGC to develop a cohesive executive authority and delegate responsibility among its members revealed a pattern that would persist through all subsequent Iraqi governments—intense mistrust, a fall back on traditional consensus politics, and, as a result, a slow and often ineffective decisionmaking process. The IGC was asked to nominate a cabinet of twenty-five. Rather than broadening its base, the council appointed ministers of the same parties, thus strengthening its hold over the levers of power in Baghdad.

Local administration also began to take shape in these early CPA months in an ad hoc manner. In April, the US Agency for International Development set up a structured provincial government in Baghdad, creating some eighty-eight neighborhood advisory councils, nine district councils, a city council, and, eventually, a provincial council. The CPA began to replicate that model throughout the fifteen non-Kurdish districts. These new administrative layers had to take account of the actual distribution of power on the ground and the Iraq political forces that had already established local bases. SCIRI and its now-transformed militia, Badr, for example, were well on their way to entrenching themselves in parts of Baghdad, Basra, Najaf, Kut, Diyala, and Amara.

In addition to establishing a new governing order, the CPA continued its effort to extirpate the Ba'th regime, seizing and capturing key Saddam-era figures still at large. There were several dramatic successes. One was the discovery on 22 July of Udayy and Qusayy Husain in a safehouse in Mosul. Both died in a shootout with coalition forces. Even more dramatic was the final capture of Saddam himself on 13 December in an underground hideout in the backyard of a farmhouse near Tikrit. Dirty and disheveled, he was displayed on TV prior to being taken to an American-run prison to be held for trial.

Opposition to the Occupation

By the end of the year, Bremer and the military had brought some order out of chaos, revived commerce, rehired bureaucrats, and even put together a temporary Iraqi government. But the failure of the United States to understand the politics and culture of the society in which it was operating and the abrupt and inept destruction of what little was left of Iraq's previous institutional structure would soon prove the undoing of much of the progress made and undermine the entire enterprise.

Virulent opposition to Bremer and an entrenched occupation began to appear on three fronts: the Sunnis, the Sadrists, and, most importantly, at home in the United States. This opposition would soon bring a new "transition" in Iraq.

The Sunni Insurgency

A widespread Sunni Arab insurgency soon became a major feature of the post-Saddam era, based on a mixture of motives. One was obvious—shock and rejection of foreign occupation and rule, accompanied by outrage at de-Ba'thification and the displacement of Sunni Arab leaders by exiles and opposition elements. Sunnis were also dismayed at the increasing ethnic and sectarian basis of rule, which seemed to be undermining state unity.

The insurgency also grew out of mishandled military clashes between occupation forces and the local population. On 28 April, US forces shot at demonstrators in Falluja protesting the American takeover of a local school for their barracks, killing seventeen and wounding seventy others. This episode galvanized the population, and opposition grew among Sunni Arab cities and towns.

The opposition came from several directions. First were the mosques. The AMS under Harith al-Dari developed a support network of Sunni Arab imams and clerics in mosques and schools throughout Sunni Arab areas.[30] Their message was a combination of religion and nationalism; they openly urged Sunnis to resist and to shun any participation in the government while occupation lasted. While publicly abjuring violence against Iraqi citizens, they had murky ties with emerging underground militias.[31] Some of the religious opposition came from groups with a more Salafist, or Sunni fundamentalist, orientation. One of the best known of these was the Army of Muhammad, an underground militia reportedly headed by a former Republican Guard commander who had adopted a militant religious terminology. In the heartland of Anbar—Falluja, Ramadi, and the smaller cities and towns of the upper Euphrates—where mosques had been centers of this campaign, these groups were affected by more conservative, "Wahhabi" ideas coming out of Saudi Arabia.[32] They considered militant opposition to the new order a religious duty.[33]

A second source of the insurgency drew on a more locally rooted nationalism, often intermixed with tribally based codes of honor. This opposition was swollen by former army officers and other newly discharged veterans of the Ba'th intelligence and military apparatus. They not only had the military expertise to organize and coordinate armed, underground opposition, but they also had access to weapons, finances, and a deep network of tribal and family ties essential to any underground network. The absence of employment opportunities and services was also a major factor in the insurgency, making it easier to employ local youths with no jobs.

A third source of opposition came from foreign elements, most notably those loosely associated with al-Qa'ida. These were always small in number, but they were able to exploit local opposition to increase their support. The al-Qa'ida group apparently had its origins in Ansar al-Islam fighters who had fled from Kurdistan, but they were soon joined by other foreign Islamists coming across the border, mostly through Syria. They soon came under the leadership of Abu Mus'ab al-Zarqawi, a Jordanian who had already engaged in terrorist activities in Jordan, fought in Afghanistan, and had links with al-Qa'ida. This group espoused a very puritan version of Islam distinctly foreign to Iraq and was willing to use harsh tactics to enforce its rule among Iraqi civilians. The aim was not merely to end occupation or overthrow the new regime but also to establish an Islamic amirate in Iraq.

This group's work was soon seen in three spectacular, grim events in August. A car bombing of the Jordanian Embassy on 7 August killed eighteen. On 19 August another car bomb struck the headquarters of the UN mission, killing twenty-two, including Sergio de Mello, the mission's head. Third was an even more devastating attack that killed Ayatallah Muhammad Baqir al-Hakim and almost one hundred others as he was leaving the Imam Ali mosque in Najaf after Friday prayers on 29 August. The murder of Hakim was a huge setback for Shi'i Islamists in general and SCIRI in particular. In fact, SCIRI was never quite able to recover from the loss of Hakim's leadership. And the killing was a harbinger of the kind of sectarian conflict that al-Qa'ida (along with its Sunni Arab allies) was willing to foment in Iraq to achieve its goals.[34]

By the summer of 2003, a number of shadowy underground militias had emerged representing various strands of this opposition. They numbered in the dozens and may have brought together over 30,000 men, but they were fractured and episodic in their formation; in time, however, some became more effective in coordination and in tactics and strategy. Events were not helped by the publication in October of pictures of US military police forces scandalously maltreating Iraqi detainees at the Abu Ghraib prison, an event widely publicized in the Arab world and the West.

By November, insurgent acts had increased and included sabotage of power, water, and, above all, oil installations; assassinations of leading political figures; criminal activities like kidnapping; disruption of convoys and killing of foreign forces by lethal roadside improvised explosive devices; and spectacular, random killings of civilians for media attention. The insurgency even reached the Kurds. On 1 February 2004 suicide bombers attacked KDP and PUK centers in Arbil, killing scores of high officials, including KDP member Sami Abd al-Rahman. The bombing hastened and intensified Kurdish moves toward separation from the rest of Iraq and a central government that could no longer provide security.

By April 2004, the spread of the insurgency to Arab Sunni areas reached a point of no return. On 31 March four American security guards driving through Falluja took a wrong turn and were ambushed. Their bodies were mutilated and burned, and two were hung from the main bridge, a grizzly spectacle shown widely on TV. Even though there were divisions in the CPA and the military over what to do, both Bremer and the White House wanted insurgents cleared out of the city.

Initiating the first siege of Falluja (Falluja I) on 5 April, US Marine forces attacked the city, but insurgents put up stiff resistance and the battle dragged on amid mounting civilian casualties and much destruction. The siege created enormous friction in the cabinet, with two Sunni Arabs resigning. Worse, the newly crafted Iraqi Security Forces (ISF) cooperating in the effort did not hold together; one unit deserted, and a civil defense corps joined the insurgents. Falluja became a rallying cry for Sunni Arab opponents. Finally, a local Falluja brigade was formed to keep the peace and a hasty cease-fire was negotiated, but it proved to be a short-lived solution to a problem that would only grow worse. The Sunni Arab insurgency had put down roots.

The Sadrists

The Sunnis were not the only disaffected group to mount an insurgency. A second major force emerged in this period—the Sadrists—to challenge the coalition and the IGC, as well as the traditional *hawza* and the more moderate Shi'i leaders now gaining power, thus splitting the Shi'i Islamist movement. And it was not long before the Sadrists became armed and militant.

They had some obvious similarities with the disaffected Sunni ex-Ba'thists. They were adamantly opposed to the US occupation. They were insiders who had endured Iraq under Saddam and who resented the "exile" opposition. And they had not been included in the emerging government structure. But the Sadrists were a separate and distinct movement with a very different theological orientation from the Salafists who were gaining ascendancy among the Sunnis. The Sadrists also had a very different constituency—the young and the poor in Sadr City and other towns of the south.

In the summer of 2003, Sadr announced the establishment of the Mahdi Army, the military arm of the movement. By fall, Sadrist forces were ambushing US forces. On 11 October, Sadr proclaimed his own government. Sadrists also clashed with their rivals, SCIRI, over control in Karbala, and more Americans were killed as they moved to restore order.

By early 2004, there were increasing reports of Sadrists taking over mosques and universities in Baghdad, setting up *shari'a* courts, and enforcing Islamic law, even on Christians and minorities. The group's military training and bomb-making capacity also increased. Finally, the CPA issued an arrest warrant for Sadr (in connection with Khu'i's death). Sadr then called for an open revolt against US forces from his mosque in Kufa. Thousands of Sadr supporters flooded south from Baghdad to take key buildings in Najaf, Kufa, Nasiriyya, and Amara, and they occupied the CPA headquarters in Kut and Nasiriyya.

Worried that Sadr was spoiling their chances to take power through elections, the key Shi'i Islamist parties quietly gave the green light to the CPA to deal with Sadr—but not to the point of extinction. Sadr's radicalism also turned much of the local Shi'i population against him as violence increasingly disturbed normalcy. Sadrist forces themselves were too thinly spread and disorganized to hold on to many of the positions they had taken, and they abandoned them. Sadr, with his future at stake (and with the arrest warrant now issued), took refuge in the Najaf shrine.

On 5 May the US forces began an assault on the Mahdi Army in Najaf. The Mahdi Army was no match for US tanks and air strikes and was badly decimated. Realizing he could not withstand the attack, Sadr turned to mediation with the clerics, primarily Ali al-Sistani. They arranged for Sadr to withdraw from Najaf and Karbala, but he was not required to disarm. The Mahdi Army would survive to fight another day.

Both the Sunni and Shi'i insurgencies were strong challenges to the occupation and the process of government formation in which coalition forces were engaged. Both risings put real strains on a foreign military that had too few resources to deal with them. Although they were thwarted, neither movement—the Sunni insurgents nor the Sadrists—was yet ready to give up the fight. But neither did they want to lose. A truce bought time for all sides.

By the fall of 2003, it was already apparent to many in Washington that the situation in Iraq was becoming untenable. Violence was rising, particularly from al-Qa'ida attacks; so was militancy from the Sadrists. On 29 October, US combat deaths reached 117, more than had died before combat was declared over. More importantly, domestic opposition to the Iraq venture inside and outside Congress was rising, just as the critical 2004 election season approached. No weapons of mass destruction had been found. In January 2004 David Kay, head of the Iraq Survey Group charged with finding WMDs, concluded that Saddam had destroyed them early in the 1990s. "Everyone was wrong," he said.[35] Nor were any allies coming to shore up the US position on the ground. A change of policy was needed—and soon.

The 15 November Agreement: Changes in US Plans

UN Resolution 1511 had mandated that by December 2003 the United States present a plan for a transition to an Iraqi government. On 8 September, Bremer presented a plan for such a transfer, which involved a constitution (written by an unelected group), a referendum on that constitution, an election, and only then a turnover of authority to Iraqis.[36] This plan implied a long process—too long for those in the administration who wanted to accelerate a transfer of authority to an Iraqi government by June 2004—before the US elections in November. The question was to whom and how such a transfer would be made. And could a reasonably democratic regime, relatively friendly to US interests, be found? Although a solution was eventually hammered out, the search for a plan ushered in a period of relative confusion in which local forces once again came to the fore.

Essentially, the United States proposed a national assembly to be chosen through a complex series of local caucuses, a process allowing considerable US influence. This assembly would then pick a new Iraqi government, which would assume sovereignty by June 2004. This government would be responsible for conducting a new election by March 2005 for a constituent assembly, whose sole purpose would be to draft a constitution and hold a referendum on it. If the referendum were successful, a second election would be held, by December 2005, for a new national assembly, which would then form Iraq's first constitutional government. The plan, although allowing for an elected constituent assembly, would postpone the drafting of a constitution for about fifteen months and the election of an Iraqi government for about two years. To govern Iraq in the interim, the plan called for the CPA and the IGC to draw up a transitional administrative law (TAL), basically a provisional constitution.

Whereas some members of the IGC were wary of the caucuses and the interim government it would produce—which might exclude them—most were delighted at an early turnover of sovereignty, and they accepted the US plan. The resulting agreement was announced on 15 November.

Ayatallah Sistani and His Political Role

Even before the announcement of the 15 November Agreement, however, it had run into trouble from a number of sources. The most important was Ayatallah Ali al-Sistani, long recognized as a leading *marji'* for Shi'a inside and outside Iraq, who was rapidly becoming the decisive voice among Shi'i politicians. Sistani was known as a "quietist" who did not want direct rule by the clergy. But in the new post-2003 situation, he had moved out of the shadows to play a more open and increasingly decisive role. He wanted to ensure that the "new Iraq" emerged as an Islamic state.[37]

To advance that end, Sistani had opposed the earlier Bremer plan because it had not provided for an elected constituent assembly. He now opposed the 15 November Agreement because of its complicated caucuses and unelected interim government. Sistani wanted an early election, which was essential in bringing the Shi'i majority—especially the Islamists—to power in the face of more Westernized, secular groups vying for power (the Kurds, the CPA, exile politicians). His views and his hold over the majority Shi'i community were decisive in forcing a change in the process.

Bremer was taken aback by Sistani's insistence on an early election.[38] He understood that an early election was likely to put power in the hands of the Islamists and thwart the more secular, liberal order he desired. Moreover, mechanisms were not in place to hold an election before the turnover of authority in 2004. Recognizing the informal power of Sistani, who would not talk directly to the United States as the occupying power, the United States turned to the United Nations to mediate the dispute. The result was the appointment of Lakhdar Brahimi, an Algerian and a veteran UN diplomat, to head a mediation mission. Meanwhile, the CPA turned its attention to the TAL, hoping to cement the provisions of the 15 November Agreement and provide a model for the future constitution.

The TAL

The TAL was negotiated by several different groups behind closed doors between 8 February and 8 March 2004. It clearly set the framework for the future permanent constitution. Even more significantly, the struggles over the TAL among groups clearly foreshadowed the key issues that would dominate Iraq's future political process.

One group was liberal. In coordination with the CPA, it began drafting a constitution that emphasized civil rights, a central government with an independent judiciary, and a separation of powers in government. Little was said about Islam or Islamic law. A second group consisted of the Kurds, worried that an unexpectedly rapid turnover of authority to Iraqis and a simultaneous reduction in US influence would endanger their autonomy. Some Kurds saw an opportunity to lay the groundwork for possible future independence. They proposed a draft focused heavily on federalism and a confederation. This proposal soon ran into difficulty, and Bremer had to make several trips to the north, essentially setting up a separate negotiating track for the Kurds. After extensive negotiations between the two drafting groups, the TAL was announced on 8 March by the CPA and the IGC.

The TAL laid out the structure of the new "interim" government, which was to consist of a presidency council, a national assembly, and a council of ministers. The prime minister and his cabinet were vested with the real governing power. The president had to be elected by two-thirds of the National Assembly; the prime minister and cabinet, by a simple a majority. Although not specified as such, this provision was clearly designed to make sure that all ethnic and sectarian communities had a voice and could act as a check on one another. No recent member of the Ba'th Party could be a member of the National Assembly. The system was highly decentralized and gave the Kurds a victory by recognizing KRG control in the north and allowing it to continue government functions in these regions, to retain control over police and security, and to tax in KRG areas.[39]

The Brahimi Mission and the UN Role

Lakhdar Brahimi, appointed UN special envoy to Iraq, had several tasks. One was to secure Sistani's agreement to the 15 November Agreement, especially the postponement of Iraq's first open election—that is, the election for a constituent assembly. The second was his agreement on an appointed interim government, which would presumably hold power until the end of 2005. Brahimi made several trips to Iraq and did secure Sistani's agreement on postponing Iraq's first election, but the CPA was compelled to compromise on the longevity of the "appointed" interim government. Its responsibility would now end early in 2005 with the election of the constituent assembly, which would also function as a new national assembly with the right to appoint a "transitional" government. This pushed the election of an Iraqi government to an earlier date by almost a year, a decision that would turn out to be decisive in shifting power in Iraq's political structure.

Brahimi also had to mediate the creation of the interim government. Brahimi wanted to cut the exile politicians free from power and force them to run for election to maintain their positions. But both the United States and the IGC members themselves wanted more control over the process. In the end, the process of appointing the new interim government involved bargaining behind closed door by those with the biggest stake—Bremer, the White House, the CPA, Brahimi, and the IGC members.

In this process Ahmed Chalabi was finally sidelined. Chalabi's public attacks on Brahimi and his mission angered the United States, which began to marginalize him.[40] Much more significantly, though the allegations could not be publicly verified, Chalabi was accused of warning Iran that the United States had cracked its code, a warning that broke US laws and endangered US security. Even though Chalabi would remain active in Iraqi politics, whatever support he had had in Washington circles had been irrevocably severed.

The schedule for the turn over was provided in the TAL. A new Iraqi government would be appointed by 30 June and would assume sovereignty. National elections for a transitional national assembly would be held by January 2005. That assembly would form a government, write a constitution, and submit it for referendum by October 2005. Assuming its acceptance, a second election would be held by the end of 2005 to form Iraq's first permanent constitutional government.

On 2 June the new Iraqi Interim Government (IIG) was appointed and the UNSC recognized Iraq's full sovereignty, effective 30 June. On June 28, two days before the scheduled turnover, Bremer handed over authority to the IIG, marking the end of an ambitious attempt to remake Iraq. Bremer's place was taken by a new US ambassador, John Negroponte, a traditional diplomat little interested in nation-building or backseat bargaining in Baghdad. One milestone had been reached, but the struggle for the future of Iraq among its political participants had just begun.

The IIG of Ayad Allawi, June 2004–May 2005

The IIG, led by Ayad Allawi as prime minister, was the last appointed government in Iraq and, in retrospect, the last opportunity for the more secular, nonsectarian Iraqis to take control of the political process. There was a continued emphasis on "ethnic and sectarian balance." The president, Ghazi Ajil al-Yawar, was an Arab Sunni; by design, he had two vice presidents, Ibrahim al-Ja'fari (Da'wa), a Shi'a, and Raush Shawais (KDP), a Kurd, to ensure a check on single-community dominance. Allawi (INA), a secular Shi'a had a Kurdish deputy, Barham Salih (PUK). The key ministries went to the old ILC parties: foreign affairs to Hushyar Zibari (KDP), finance to Adil Abd al-Mahdi (SCIRI), defense to Hazim al-Sha'lan (INC), interior to Falih Hasan al-Naqib, a supporter of Allawi, and oil to Thamir Ghadban, a technocrat.

The IIG unquestionably marginalized the Shi'i Islamists in favor of the more secular nationalist contingent. Shi'i Islamists held only two top posts (vice president and minister of finance). In fact, this was a cabinet dominated by Allawi's INA.

Political Orientation of the IIG

The composition of the new government was reflected in its political orientation—secular, Western, and anti-Iranian. The seeming resurgence of secularists and former Ba'thists worried the Shi'i Islamists, but there was little they could do about it. In fact, they regarded the cabinet as short-lived and were focused on winning the upcoming elections.

Ties with the United States, especially its intelligence community, were strong. The coalition forces, now renamed the MNF-I (Multi-national Forces–Iraq), under a new commander, General George W. Casey, still had the responsibility for security, the most important function of governance. In November 2004, thanks mainly to US efforts, the Paris Club agreed to write off 80 percent of Iraq's debt—a total of US $30 billion. Although the follow-through on this agreement was weak, the cooperation of European creditors in alleviating Iraq's debt was a major step forward.

Meanwhile, there was a distinct shift in Allawi's regional policy toward the Arab states and away from Iran. Iran favored a rapid departure of the US forces and wanted a Shi'i-dominated government in Baghdad friendly to its interests—best secured by the Islamists. Iran considered the secular Allawi government, with its close ties to the United States and its anti-Iranian, nonreligious orientation, to be a potential obstacle to its aims and one that could split the Shi'i community in the coming election.

The Allawi government also engaged in outreach to insurgents, especially Sunnis, playing on the prime minister's former Ba'thist ties. The government's aim was to separate the nationalists, unhappy with occupation, from the foreign and mainly Salafist radicals, especially those linked to al-Qa'ida. The quid pro quo was to offer more jobs in the administration and a stake in the political process through the coming election. However, these efforts failed.

The Second Sadr Conflict

The IIG's tenure witnessed a renewed confrontation between the MNF and Sadr. The previous military conflict had weakened both Sadr and the Mahdi Army but had not ended their influence. Iran had begun aiding the Mahdi Army by arming them, training Mahdi forces in camps just across the border, and supplying officers. The MNF, for its part, was anxious to eliminate the Mahdi Army as part of a renewed attempt to end militias.

A new collision came at the beginning of August when an MNF patrol was attacked in Najaf near Sadr's house. Major fighting broke out in which the Mahdi Army took on the MNF, supported by the Iraqi police and National Guard. Sadr barricaded himself in the Najaf shrine. Fighting was severe, much of it around the shrine, and hundreds were killed. As the fighting went on and the capture of Sadr himself became a real possibility, anxieties grew in the Shi'i community as Islamists feared that they were going to be pushed out of power by a new "security government" and as the secularists worried about a Shi'i "minority" allied with Iran.

Once again, Sistani emerged as the solution. Sadr, recognizing the futility of his position, agreed to leave the shrine and turn over the keys—but only to Sistani. On 26 August, Sistani agreed to take control of the shrine, but only under certain conditions: (1) Sadr and his Mahdi Army would stand down; (2) Najaf would return to control of the *hawza*; (3) in return, the Mahdi Army would be allowed to keep its arms; and (4) it would remain intact. This agreement ended the second major military confrontation with Sadr and his Mahdi Army.

Though Sadr remained a force to be reckoned with, he was greatly weakened. The main winner was Sistani, now undisputed leader of the *hawza* and the Shi'i community. The outcome left Sistani in a powerful position to influence the coming election—in favor of Shi'i Islamists rather than secularists. The hostility of Allawi and his chief advisers to Iran, and their willingness to take on Sadr and even to eliminate him, gave the Shi'i Islamists pause. Their old fear of a strong, secular state, which would repress Shi'i identity and use military force to achieve its aims, sharpened.[41] This new breach would work to Allawi's detriment.

Falluja II

A second major event facing the IIG was a renewal of the Falluja conflict. The so-called truce in Falluja was rapidly becoming unglued and required decisive and serious action. By summer, the Sunni insurgency had heated up again. Allawi's policy of reaching out to nationalist Sunni insurgents had failed.[42] Rather, Sunni insurgents were spreading their influence elsewhere, attempting to encircle Baghdad and taking control of a belt of territory southeast and west of the city and cleansing it of Shi'a. In Samarra', a city with a major Shi'i shrine but a Sunni majority, they began to infiltrate and take control. Meanwhile, the insurgency spread elsewhere in the "Sunni triangle"—to Ramadi, Haditha, and Mosul, where some fighting broke out. But the insurgency's center was still Falluja, now something of a mini-Islamic state unto itself. Local Iraqi Salafists, reinforced by Jordanian, Saudi, and Yemeni fighters, imposed draconian religious measures on Falluja—dress codes and prohibitions against alcohol, beauty parlors, and music.[43] By the fall of 2004 there was no doubt that the MNF—and the new IIG—would have to go back in and clean the city of its insurgents. Allawi reluctantly agreed.

On 7 November MNF forces attacked. The fall of the city took several weeks, and fighting was hard. Some 92 US soldiers were killed, and some 1,200 insurgents died. There were claims of a loss of close to 6,000 civilians dead and up to 200,000 who had fled the city.[44] Destruction of the city was substantial. Over 60 of the city's 200 mosques (which had been used to store weapons) were destroyed and nearly 20 percent of its buildings.

The immediate fallout of the battle was political. Sunnis were incensed and increased their hostility to the occupation—and to the election for which campaigning was well under way. The IIP resigned from the cabinet, removing its major Sunni component.[45] Sunni groups called for a postponement and then, when the United States would not agree, a boycott of the election. Sunnis also hardened attitudes to Shi'a, who had generally sided with the attack and even cheered the outcome.

The most significant political outcome of these events was to weaken Allawi and the forces gathered behind a more secular, nonsectarian state. Whether these forces could have overcome other difficulties—personal failings, lack of organization, too little support on the ground—is not clear, but the two insurgencies widened the sectarian gap and diminished Allawi's political fortunes. Sistani, not Allawi, emerged as the key

Shi'i leader. These two battles, and the deepening sectarian divide, set the stage for the coming elections.

The Elections of 2005:
The Emergence of the "New" Iraq

During 2005 several events occurred that would define Iraq's political system: three elections (two for a national assembly and one a referendum on the constitution), the drafting of the constitution itself, and the process of forming indigenous national and provincial governments based on election results. These were the first genuinely free elections in Iraq's modern history, but they also solidified trends already under way—fragmentation of the state along ethnic and sectarian lines, a weak central government, and a deeply divided political elite.

The January 2005 Elections

The first of these elections, as specified in the TAL, was to be held on 30 January for a 275-seat national assembly, as well as provincial assemblies in each of the eighteen provinces and a Kurdish regional assembly of 111 seats.[46] The election would be run by the newly appointed Independent Electoral Commission of Iraq (IECI).

The election law, promulgated on 15 June 2004, provided for a single district, nationwide, proportional representation system. It was also a "closed list" system, meaning voters would choose a party, a coalition, or an individual from a list of candidates whose order on the list (and therefore likelihood of being chosen) would have already been decided by the parties before the election. In the absence of district representation, the election became almost purely a national identity referendum. It also left some areas, like those inhabited by boycotting Sunnis, with little representation.[47]

The major political groups were clear—SCIRI, Da'wa, and the now fading INC of Chalabi among the Shi'a; Allawi's INA and assorted liberals, such as Adnan Pachachi, representing secularists; the two strong

Kurdish parties; and the IIP representing Sunnis. In short, the old ILC plus the IIP. If Shi'a voted on the basis of sectarian identity, they would automatically dominate, but the Shi'a—like other communities—were divided on political views.

On 8 December, the United Iraqi Alliance (UIA) was formed. Led by SCIRI, now headed by Abd al-Aziz al-Hakim, brother of the deceased Muhummad Baqir, it included all the major Shi'i religious groups. Ayad Allawi, a nominal Shi'a, was invited to join, but he refused. He did not want to accept Sistani's leadership and was uncomfortable in a religiously oriented bloc tied more closely to Iran than he liked. The UIA's primary, though unstated, goal was keeping Shi'a together so as to win power and the ability to shape the direction of the new regime.

Allawi and his more secular, Iraqi nationalist followers also put together a ticket, led by himself and his INA party, the Iraqi National List, or Iraqiyya. To do well, Allawi would have had to secure a large chunk of the Shi'i vote, much of the Sunni vote, and possibly the northern Christian and Turkmen as well.

The Kurdish parties ran a unified ticket, the Kurdistan Alliance, dominated by the KDP and the PUK but incorporating the smaller Kurdish parties as well. Their aim was to win a solid bloc in the new assembly that could maintain—and if possible enlarge—what they had succeeded in getting under the TAL. They purposely declined to join any other blocs prior to the election.

The missing component in the election list was any meaningful ticket comprising Sunnis. The IIP, which had resigned from the cabinet on the Falluja issue, quietly put a ticket together but late in December, bowing to overwhelming Sunni pressure to boycott the elections, withdrew. The absence of any substantial Sunni presence on the ballot was a serious blow to the whole election outcome and clearly affected the results. It was a lesson the Sunnis learned quickly, but not before Iraq's first election set a pattern for those that followed.

The elections were accomplished relatively smoothly. By law, one out of every three candidates was female, and Iraqis abroad were eligible to vote. About 275,000, most of them in Iran, did so. The IECI—together with almost a quarter million Iraqis—oversaw the elections with a few foreign observers and help from MNF security forces. Despite a number of irregularities and charges of fraud, the results were ultimately accepted.

Three blocs emerged to dominate the coming 275-member assembly. The UIA was first with 140 seats (51 percent), the Kurdistan Alliance came second with 75 (27 percent), and a relatively distant third was occupied by Iraqiyya with 40 (14 percent). A few smaller coalitions also got seats (see Table A.6).[48]

The results indicated that the new government would continue to be led by the exile opposition parties and their leaders, with a significant shift from the more secular, liberal, "nationalist" elements to the more religiously oriented Shi'i parties and the Kurds. Even more significantly, the election showed—indeed solidified—national fragmentation along ethnic and sectarian lines. Allawi's bloc, the main secular ticket, and the only major one that won votes across sectarian lines, came in a weak third. The biggest losers were the Sunni Arabs. Sunni groups won only six parliamentary seats (2 percent) although a few Arab Sunnis ran on other party labels. This left Sunnis with little voice in the constitutional process.[49]

Provincial Elections

The January election cycle also included the election of provincial councils for all eighteen governorates and for the regional KRG assembly. The same political parties that dominated at the national level swept the local elections: SCIRI won the largest number of votes in seven provinces, and the Kurdish alliance won control in six provinces. In Anbar, where only about 2 percent of the population turned out to vote, the IIP got the most seats. The KRG also elected its own parliament. In that assembly almost 90 percent of the seats went to the joint KDP-PUK alliance, allowing it to run the KRG as it wished.[50]

But it was one thing to achieve electoral dominance and another to enforce it in the provinces where nongovernmental actors, such as tribal and religious leaders, militias, and local forces interested in controlling resources, competed for influence. Splits within coalitions made governance difficult. In Basra, for example, there was a constant struggle over control of the police and resources among SCIRI/Badr, the Sadrists, and Fadila, all of which had won some seats. According to one source, Fadila managed the oil industry, SCIRI controlled the security apparatus, and the Sadrists controlled the streets and the port. The province was soon out of control and wracked by violence.[51]

Governance was even more difficult in provinces in mixed ethnic areas where councils were unbalanced. A prime example was Ninawa, with a Sunni Arab majority but a Kurdish minority. A lopsided vote in favor of the Kurdish parties gave them control over the provincial council and key administrative and security positions, which they used to press their ethnic agenda on the rest of the population.[52] The result was ethnic tension, widespread Sunni Arab opposition, and increased violence, which gave al-Qa'ida its opportunity to penetrate the area.

Overall, the provincial elections led to complex power struggles in many areas, including Baghdad, where the power vacuums soon allowed sectarian—and even ethnic—conflict to spiral out of control.

The Ja'fari Government, May 2005–May 2006

The new government appointed after the election was, again, a temporary caretaker charged with drawing up and shepherding the constitution through the National Assembly and getting it ratified. Nonetheless, the two winning coalitions, the UIA and Kurdistan Alliance, now expected to reap the rewards of victory by gaining a proportionate share of power and resources. But the giant coalitions had a problem: They were themselves divided among parties and factions representing different constituencies, interests, and leaders who would have to be satisfied. Hence, the real distribution of power and influence in the cabinet would take place not through the election but through bargaining in Baghdad—a process that proved long and laborious.

The formation of the new Ja'fari government took ninety-three days and was not sworn in until 20 May, leaving Iraq with no legitimate government for four months. The main battle took place within the winning coalition, the UIA, for the prime minister. SCIRI had expected to dominate and govern in alliance with its allies, the Kurds. But the Sadrists were not favorably disposed toward either group and managed to force a compromise in the top post, which was given to the Da'wa. When finally completed, the cabinet was huge and unwieldy—consisting of thirty-two ministers with portfolios and six ministers of state without—a total of thirty-eight. In terms of ethnic and sectarian "quotas," the cabinet was dominated by Shi'a, who took at least eighteen seats; Kurds took at least eight, and Sunni Arabs, six. But the key positions were taken by Shi'i Islamists—prime minister (Ibrahim al-Ja'fari/Da'wa), vice president (Adil Abd al-Mahdi/SCIRI), deputy prime minister (Ahmad Chalabi/INC), and, above all, minister of interior (Bayan Jabr/SCIRI). The Kurdish alliance got the presidency (Jalal Talabani/PUK). Sunnis got one vice president and the Defense Ministry. Most of the leading representatives of the old ILC—except for Allawi—were represented. Exiles managed to maintain their dominance, securing all but two of the top thirteen positions. A few "insiders" made their way into the cabinet, but only in marginal positions. Chief among them were the Sadrists, who had difficulty producing qualified, experienced candidates to run their ministries.

Compared to previous governments, this was a leadership group that tilted heavily toward the Shi'i Islamists and, secondarily, the Kurds. De-Ba'thification, which had been put on hold by Allawi, was reactivated by Chalabi.[53] This action, taken as sectarian conflict increased in and around Baghdad, illustrates the intense mutual suspicion that the political parties had for one another.

The huge cabinet, with built-in checks and balances, appointed mainly to award representation to various groups and parties, however, proved to be dysfunctional. Each minister considered his ministry a fief over which he had complete control, and ministries followed their own dictates. The prime minister found himself having to constantly bargain to get anything done. The traditional mode of decisionmaking by consensus consumed enormous amounts of time, making day-to-day government including delivery of services and timely decisions impossible. Each party, interested in maintaining its hold on power, used its ministries to reward its supporters and relatives, often through corruption, nepotism, and patronage.

Drafting the Constitution

The main function of the new government and its elected parliament was to draft a constitution. Negotiations for the constitution, like the elections, were rushed, propelled mainly by the United States and the TAL deadline for a referendum on 15 October. The complexity of issues to be resolved and the depth of disagreement on them were formidable. These included questions of identity and the role of religion in the new state, the nature of government and the degree of decentralization desired, and how power—as well as resources—was to be shared among communities and regions.

The absence of Sunni Arabs in the National Assembly represented another stumbling block. In June, a new US ambassador, Zalmay Khalilzad, arrived in Baghdad. He was a Sunni Afghan by origin, with strong connections to Bush, and he pushed to bring Sunni Arabs into the political process. Meanwhile, a group of Sunni Arabs, the Iraq National Dialogue Front, emerged to participate. On 15 July, under US pressure, fifteen of them were added to the constitutional committee as full voting members.[54]

The drafting process also proved controversial. The National Assembly's constitutional committee worked on a draft constitution but found the issues too contentious and the divisions too great to agree. Finally on 8 August, the American ambassador convened a closed-door meeting that assembled a sort of "kitchen cabinet" to thrash out the issues. A series of second-track meetings was held that did not include any Sunni Arabs.[55] Two drafts emerged—a Shi'i-driven assembly draft and the new "kitchen cabinet" draft, now shown to the Sunni Arabs to either take or leave. They chose the latter.[56] The two drafts had to be merged, helping account for the ambiguities and the murky, often contradictory, language in the final product.

The time pressure, the secretive procedure, and the absence of real Sunni participation increased Sunni Arab hostility to the resulting constitution. They also left unresolved many key issues that would have to be faced in the future.[57]

Constitutional Issues

"Federalism" was undoubtedly the most contentious issue in the deliberations—along with the establishment of "regions" and how much power and authority should be given to the central government. On this issue, the Kurds won virtually all their arguments. They insisted on a distribution of power between the central government and regions, which gave the latter priority. The Kurds worked to weaken the authority of the central government on issues such as taxation, health, and education. In essence, the Kurds wanted a virtually independent state in the north in a voluntary union with Iraq—a confederation—with a right to secede. Even though they did not get this, they did manage to get a weak central government and a highly decentralized polity.

Secular Arabs and Sunnis opposed strong regions and a regionalization of Iraq. Favoring a unified Iraq with a professional army and bureaucracy, closer to the state that had previously existed, these groups feared that regionalization would mean the breakup of the state. The Shi'i contingent, however, was divided on the issue. The Sadrists and to a large extent the Da'wa did not favor the creation of new regions, but SCIRI did, thus siding with the Kurds. In August, SCIRI had proposed the establishment of a region of the center and the south, which would include all nine governorates south of Baghdad, mainly because these provinces were largely under SCIRI's control. SCIRI felt it could dominate a new "Shi'astan," including Basra, with its oil.

Another issue, related to federalism, was ownership and management of national resources (oil and gas) and distribution of their revenues. This, too, was largely driven by the Kurds, who wanted control over the fields in the north, including those in Kirkuk. On this issue there was a deep divide between most of the Shi'i negotiators and the Kurds, but again the Kurds largely prevailed, getting provisions requiring a referendum on Kirkuk by December 2007 and language giving them considerable control over their oil fields.[58]

Still another set of issues concerned Islam and the degree to which *shari'a* and Islamic practice should be incorporated into the constitution.

This controversy also affected the status of women. Shi'i Islamists, especially SCIRI, pushed for greater Islamization, but they were only marginally successful. A proposal to make *shari'a* "the" basis of Iraqi law failed; in the end it was made only "a" basis of law, one of several. But Islamists had success in defining the basis of the state and society as the "family," rather than the "citizen," as secularists wanted. There was even more controversy over whether to include *shari'a* provisions governing personal status (marriage, divorce, inheritance) in the constitution; such inclusion could limit some of the rights previously given to women. Shi'i Islamists fought—and won—the battle for inclusion.

Iraq's identity also became an issue. Sunni Arabs wanted Iraq defined as an "Arab" state. Kurds refused. Instead, Iraq was defined as a member of the Arab League. The issue of de-Ba'thification was raised again, and here the Shi'i contingent was adamant, insisting on prohibiting "Saddamist" Ba'thism in Iraq, revealing again the depth of distrust and suspicion between the new Shi'i leaders and the ousted Sunnis and secularists, many of whom had worked under the Ba'th.

On one key issue there was little disagreement or division—the democratic basis of the new government, already largely laid out in the TAL. The new constitution provided for an election process to be regulated by law; a parliamentary form of government, with the prime minister as the key executive; a formal and largely symbolic president to keep the country unified; and a separation of powers, including an independent court system. It was also fairly strong in outlining human rights. On these critical issues there was virtually no debate, indicating relative unanimity on the principle under which the "new" Iraq would be run. This was no small achievement.

Provisions of the Constitution

The constitution put up for referendum defined Iraq as republican, representative, democratic, and federal, with a guarantee of its "unity" (Article 1).[59] Iraq was to be made up of a "decentralized capital," regions, and governorates. All powers, except those stipulated as "exclusive authorities of the federal government," were vested in regions. In case of a conflict between regional and national legislation, the region would prevail (Article 111).

The federal government was given few exclusive authorities. These included formulating foreign policy and national security policy, exercising control over Iraq's armed forces, securing the country's borders, defending Iraq, formulating fiscal policy, drawing up a national budget, and planning policies on water sources external to Iraq (Article 108). Although taxation was not explicitly included, it might well be interpreted as part of fiscal authority.

Provisions on oil and gas were often ambiguous and sometimes contradictory. Oil and gas were owned by all the people of Iraq "in regions and governorates" (Article 109), but management of these resources from "current fields" was to be undertaken "with" producing regions and governorates, making this a shared responsibility; so, too, was the distribution of proceeds, in proportion to the population (Article 110).

Legislative power was vested in an elected council of representatives (CoR)—with a four-year term. Executive power was vested in a president and a council of ministers (Article 64). The president was to be elected by a two-thirds vote of the CoR and for the first term was to have two vice presidents—a concession to ethnic and sectarian diversity. Most importantly, the president was to nominate as prime minister the "candidate of the parliamentary majority" (Article 74). The prime minister was the "direct executive authority, responsible for general policy" and commander in chief of the armed forces (Article 76). An elaborate federal judiciary was created, including a higher juridical council with oversight of judicial affairs and a new federal supreme court with the authority to interpret provisions of the constitution.

On identity, the constitution declared Islam the official religion of the state and specified that no law could contradict established provisions of Islam—or principles of democracy (Article 2). It specified that the High Commission for De-Ba'thification would continue to function (Article 145). It also laid out a fairly extensive list of civil and political rights, including many unrealizable economic and social rights, such as the right to work and to achieve a decent standard of living. Interestingly, the constitution also promised to strengthen civil society, including Iraqi "clans and tribes," but prohibited tribal traditions in conflict with human rights, presumably honor crimes (Article 43).

Whatever its shortcomings, the constitution did lay out a relatively clear structure for the future—a democratic, parliamentary system of government, with elections, and a strong set of decentralizing guarantees to allow for ethnic, regional, and local interests. It would now be up to the Iraqis to make this structure work and to develop the institutions to give it specificity.

The 15 October Referendum

Even though the draft constitution had passed the National Assembly, it now had to face the electorate, where its passage was more questionable. The Sunni negotiators rejected the draft but had learned their lesson from their previous boycott. They began registering to vote in large numbers. The TAL had specified that if two-thirds of any three provinces voted "no," the referendum would fail. There was a fear in US circles that the draft constitution might be rejected. Turnout on 15 October was relatively high—63 percent over the entire country. The two entirely Sunni Arab provinces of Anbar and Salah al-Din voted overwhelmingly against the constitution, and Ninawa rejected it by a close 55 percent. Elsewhere the "yes" vote was over 94 percent. The constitution passed. The referendum left the Sunni Arabs, who wanted a stronger, more centralized state, dissatisfied but determined to participate in the coming political process.

The December 2005 Election

The next step in the process laid out in the TAL was election of a new, permanent Iraqi government to replace all of the previous temporary iterations. This government would be in power for four years and be far more determinative of Iraq's future. Campaigning for the critical December election had already begun well before the referendum. As campaign rhetoric increased, a wave of assassinations and armed attacks took place in Baghdad and other cities, a number of them on Sunni politicians. On 19 October, the trial of Saddam Husain began, adding to tensions. He was charged with crimes against humanity. To meet this rising crisis and to maintain security during the election, US troops were increased to a record high of 160,000; they engaged in a pre-election military campaign to clear insurgents from Sunni cities along the Euphrates.

In an effort to correct the imbalance of the January election that had virtually excluded Sunni provinces, the December vote was conducted under a revised election law that employed a two-tier system. Political parties and coalitions had to run in each province rather than in the country as a whole. Almost 80 percent (230 out of the 275) seats in the election were allocated to governorates; the rest were filled on a national basis, depending on how well parties or groups did nationwide.

Two new coalitions ran slates of candidates representing Sunni voters. Tawafuq (Iraqi Accord Front) represented a loose amalgam of groups hastily brought together mainly by the IIP for the purpose of contesting the election.[60] It was weak on organization, funding, and reputation among voters, and it was fragmented between those with a nationalist, secular agenda and those with a more religious orientation. The second Sunni newcomer was the Iraqi Front for National Dialogue, headed by Salih al-Mutlak, a former Ba'thist. Both of these new Sunni-dominated coalitions opposed the constitution as written, favored a unified country with an Arab identity, and wanted a cessation of de-Ba'thification. Their nationalism was often strident, and their opponents soon tarred them with accusations of ties to the outlawed Ba'th and to insurgents who were continually wreaking havoc on the new regime and innocent civilians.

The other major coalitions were essentially the same as those that had run in January. The main secularist group, with Ayad Allawi and his INA in the lead was Iraqiyya (Iraqi National List). Its platform did not differ from its previous one. The Shi'a also assembled a coalition, essentially with the same components—the UIA, which was often just referred to as I'tilaf (Coalition). However, on this ticket the Sadrists increased their participation and influence. The UIA once again had been able to bring all Shi'i forces under one umbrella and could look forward to getting most of the Shi'i vote. However, although Sistani did not endorse any party officially, SCIRI and the UIA as a whole suffered nonetheless from charges of sectarianism and strong ties to Iran.

Finally, the Kurds ran a similarly allied ticket, although this time the Kurdistan Islamic Union ran separately and did manage to get some seats. The Kurdistan Alliance made clear that its willingness to be part of Iraq was conditional on implementation of the loose federal structure in which Kurdistan's autonomy would be recognized.

Once again, the winner of the election was the UIA with 128 seats (46.5 percent), followed by the Kurdistan Alliance with 53 seats (19.2 percent), Tawafuq with 44 seats (16 percent), Iraqiyya with 25 seats (9 percent), and Mutlak's Dialogue Front with 11 seats (4 percent). The KIU managed to get 5 seats on its own. In the end, the 2005 elections reinforced Iraq's growing ethnic and sectarian divide. It also established the three or four main parties and blocs that would dominate Iraq for the next four years.

The Formation of the Maliki Government

The December election also reinforced the previous difficulties in forming a government, despite the overwhelming victory of the UIA and its Kurdish partners. The existence of a new Sunni bloc that would insist on inclusion in the government added to the difficulty. The United States and especially its forceful ambassador, Khalilzad, pushed for a "unity" government that would include all ethnic and sectarian communities. The main problem arose again because of a struggle in the Shi'i coalition. Ja'fari won as candidate for prime minister by one vote. But Ja'fari had his opponents, including the Kurds and the United States, which saw him as inconclusive. As a compromise, Nuri al-Maliki, another Da'wa member and a real "dark horse," was nominated. On 22 April, the CoR approved Talabani (PUK) as president and Mahmud al-Mishhadani, an Arab Sunni and a member of Tawafuq, as chairman of the CoR. Talabani nominated Maliki as prime minister. It took nearly a month for Maliki to assemble a cabinet of thirty-seven people, all of whom had to satisfy the many components of various blocs, and 20 May the cabinet was approved in parliament, some four months after the first announcement of the election results.

The new Maliki government included all of the top vote-getters in the election—SCIRI, Da'wa, KDP, PUK, and IIP/Tawafuq. Allawi was totally missing, as was Chalabi. In fact, these two key secular members of the exile opposition were the main losers. The Maliki government continued the dramatic decline in power of the secular, nonsectarian parties. Sunni Arabs (mainly Islamists) finally got a slice of the pie. The Kurds lost some of their clout, however, as a result of Sunni gains (see Table A.6). Sadrists were included in the cabinet, but their position was uneasy, as was that of the new Sunni coalition, which was still seen as suspect by the dominant Shi'i-Kurdish axis.

Presiding over this delicate balance was a relatively inexperienced man, Nuri al-Maliki, a Da'wa stalwart, but one of a different temperament than Ja'fari. Like other Da'wa leaders, Maliki had fled Iraq in 1979 and finally settled in Syria, where he became the party's leader. Initially secretive and reportedly overreliant on a small, inner circle of advisers, Maliki would soon prove that he could master the art of political maneuver and make decisions in the new political environment. Although he was surprised to find himself in the top political position, he would outlast many who had underestimated him.

The Sectarian Civil War in Baghdad, 2006–2007

The long delay in forming a cabinet and indecision on the distribution of power came at a price. The most serious was a rise in sectarian tensions that finally reached a breaking point on 22 February 2006 with the bombing of the Askari Mosque in Samarra', one of the holiest shrines in Shi'i Islam. A weeklong spasm of gruesome sectarian violence ensued as Shi'i militias in Baghdad finally turned on Sunnis, despite calls for restraint by clerics.

The Samarra' mosque bombing has been widely identified—not without justification—as the catalyst that unleashed almost two years of brutal sectarian conflict. But the reality was more complex. Tensions between the communities had been building up since the outbursts of extremist activity in 2004—the fight with the Sunni insurgency in Falluja and the battle with Sadrists forces in Najaf. Meanwhile, the elections of 2005 and the marginalization of the Sunni community in the constitutional process increasingly galvanized the Sunni community. Sunnis began to think in sectarian, rather than national, terms. As the results of the 2005 elections became apparent, Sunnis became fearful of a decisive and permanent shift to a Shi'i sectarian government and the subsequent exclusion of Sunnis from the political process. The fear was reinforced by the capture of much of the security apparatus, especially in the Ministry of Interior, by Shi'a, especially members of the Badr Brigade. Calls by Hakim and members of SCIRI for a separate Shi'i region in the center and south also poisoned the atmosphere, encouraging fear of Iraq's collapsing into ethnic and sectarian components. In short, the gradual but decisive shift in power to the Shi'i religious parties, aligned with their Kurdish allies, and their potential ability to consolidate that power once and for all using elections and control of the government became increasingly clear and was seen as threatening by Sunnis Arabs.

The Shi'a, for their part, also had their fears. They had just gained power through elections for the first time in Iraq's modern history, giving them a sense of legitimacy Sunnis could not match, and they were intent on preserving it. And their anxiety over Sunni extremists, such as AQI, was only too justified. So, too, was their concern that many Sunni insurgents were anxious not simply to end occupation but also to prevent Shi'i rule. Indeed, the Shi'i parties had resisted Ambassador Khalilzad's efforts at outreach to the Sunni community and instead made an accommodation with Sadr during the election cycle. Shi'i religious parties had managed to neutralize opposition from his Mahdi Army—at least the elements he was able to control. As a result, the only forces still fighting the new government were increasingly Arab Sunni (a number under AQI control), using increasingly sectarian rhetoric and actions.

Well before Samarra', Baghdad had already shown signs of civil war. During the Falluja campaigns, Sunnis fled from the city to the western outer suburbs of Baghdad, such as Ghazaliyya and Abu Ghraib, and to the solidly Sunni quarters of the city, such as Adamiyya. During 2005,

Shi'i families were increasingly driven out of Sunni-dominated neighborhoods by threats and assassinations. In these areas, Sunni religious extremists began to kill barbers (who shaved beards), real-estate agents (who sold houses), and ice venders (on the grounds that there was no ice in Muhammad's time). Shi'i militias responded in kind with their own killings and assassinations.[61] In January 2006, a month before Samarra', there were seven hundred murders, the highest number up to that date.[62]

Notwithstanding this escalation of sectarian distrust and hostility during 2005, there is little doubt that one party in particular played a leading role in fomenting it. From the first, AQI had been determined to stir up a sectarian war in Iraq as a necessary prelude to government collapse and a future takeover. Unlike other insurgents, AQI attacked not only the foreign forces and the new government but also specific Shi'i targets, such as the Imam Ali Mosque in Najaf in 2003. The Zarqawi letter to bin Ladin released by the *New York Times* in February 2004 and widely believed authentic had spelled out AQI's anti-Shi'a campaign and its purposes. The AQI bombing in Samarra' now opened the floodgates, and the Shi'i militias, already operating in Baghdad inside and outside the government, came out of the woodwork. By mid-2006, the tide turned against the Sunnis as Shi'a turned on them in fury—and with increasing effectiveness. Baghdad, Iraq's center of political gravity, now tipped decisively into a full-scale, unbelievably brutal, sectarian war.

Just as Sunni extremists had earlier consolidated their position in the towns in the western and south belt around Baghdad, Shi'i militias—primarily elements of the Mahdi Army and Badr paramilitary formations—now moved into mixed areas of Baghdad, gradually cleansing them of Sunnis and consolidating their hold over a wide swath of the city. Shi'i militias attacked mosques and people, dumping bodies in the streets. Sunni insurgents responded in kind, using spectacular bomb attacks on markets and mosques. Ordinary civilians living in this atmosphere essentially made the choice either to affiliate with a sectarian militia for protection or to leave and join their respective sectarian community elsewhere in Iraq. Many left the country. A substantial outflow of refugees and internally displaced persons, ultimately measured in millions, resulted. Meanwhile, sectarian propaganda increased and sectarian banners marked off distinct Shi'i and Sunni areas. By 2007, these battles had turned their neighborhoods into wastelands. An end-of-the-year estimate by the United Nations put Iraq's death toll for 2006 at 34,400.[63] In this atmosphere, trust between ordinary citizens who had lived and worked together for years was totally shattered.

In this battle, the Sunnis, long the dominant political and social force, were now the losers. By the end of 2006, the tide was turning decisively against them, as Shi'a emerged victorious on the ground. AQI suffered several political blows. On 7 June 2006, Abu Mus'ab al-Zarqawi was cornered in a house in Ba'quba and killed, in part by cooperation between the MNF and the ISF. By this time, the Sunni insurgency was already showing serious signs of fracturing between its international "salafi" wing (mainly AQI) and the local Iraqi nationalist groups, mainly interested in ending occupation, not in waging a sectarian war.[64] Under increasing attack on all fronts—from the United States, the Iraqi government forces, and now Shi'i militias—the nationalist groups were showing increasing signs of cutting their losses and turning to the United States for support.

At the end of 2006, Sunni insurgents, especially the Ba'thists, suffered another blow to any thoughts of a "comeback"—the execution of Saddam. Saddam was sentenced to death on 5 November 2006 for crimes against humanity. On 30 December, Maliki signed the execution order, determined to end Saddam's life and his role in Iraq. The hanging itself was witnessed by some members of the government in circumstances later widely criticized. Photos, taken surreptitiously and then leaked to the press, showed people taunting the dictator just before his execution. Maliki and his close associates were accused by Sunnis of sectarian motives and the exercise of "revenge" rather than justice. Saddam's exit, more dignified than expected, renewed Sunni feelings of loss and retribution. But his death left the Ba'th wing of the insurgency a spent force.

By the end of 2006, Iraq was collapsing. An occupation and an ambitious nation-building project, begun with more optimism than realism, had begun to unravel. Iraqi society was fragmenting along ethnic and sectarian lines, while a newly elected government, composed mainly of outsiders, had just taken over a new, and as yet untried, political structure. The United States had ended one threat—an aggressive regional regime—but created another: a potentially failing state.

11

THE STABILIZATION OF IRAQ, 2007-2011

In 2007, three factors finally turned the deteriorating situation around: a surge of forces from the United States, a change of heart on the part of the Sunni opposition, and further marginalization of the Sadrists. These steps allowed the new Maliki government to gain its footing. In the following years (2008–2011), Nuri al-Maliki strengthened his position and that of the central government, at least in Arab areas. Increased stability allowed for a measure of economic development, including new oil concessions, and an agreement with the United States to withdraw its forces by the end of 2011. Gradually, Iraq settled down into a pattern representing normalcy.

The process was difficult, episodic, and filled with many challenges. One was the challenge to state cohesion from the Kurds, who were busy consolidating their position in the north. However, as events would show, the Kurds also faced problems. Another was continuing Shi'i-Sunni tensions aroused by the civil war, although these were reduced. A third was the challenge of developing a functioning government that could deliver services and development. Maliki soon became the focal point in a tug of war among competing forces, as he gradually gathered more power into his hands.

These conflicting currents of Iraqi politics finally came to a head with three elections: the first, in 2009, for fourteen provincial assemblies in Iraq; the second, also in 2009, for a new Kurdish Regional Government (KRG) parliament in the north; and the third, and most significant, in 2010 for Iraq's National Assembly and a new government. The outcomes of these elections showed a high degree of continuity, with Maliki (barely) continuing as prime minister, heading a still weak, highly decentralized state, but one that had succeeded in bringing contending forces into a constitutional political process with a measure of stability and prospects for further economic, social, and political development.

The Subsiding of the Civil War

Although fighting and displacement continued well into 2007, a mixture of events and shifts in the political dynamics in both Baghdad and Washington finally calmed the situation. A number of intertwined factors were involved.

The Surge and Counterinsurgency

One was a change of policy in Washington. By the fall of 2006, the situation in Iraq had led to consternation within the administration that Iraq was slipping into irrevocable chaos and could become a failed state. The National Security Council conducted a quiet policy review and concluded that the sectarian situation was dire and needed to be reversed. On 10 January 2007, President George W. Bush announced a "surge" of 50,000 US troops, to be placed primarily in Baghdad. At the same time, he pushed for more Provincial Reconstruction Teams, along with economic aid, to further development at local and provincial levels. Even more important than a commitment of more troops and resources, however, was a full embrace of a new counterinsurgency (COIN) strategy. The previous aim of the US military mission—eliminating the enemy (al-Qa'ida in Iraq [AQI]) and its supporters—would be superseded by the goal of providing protection for local Iraqis, which would allow them to turn against those perpetrating violence. If calm could be restored, it was hoped, a degree of confidence would return that would allow political actors to make political compromises.

Gradually in the course of 2007, more American troops arrived in Iraq. They were now commanded by General David Petraeus, the leading exponent of the COIN strategy. Although the toll in lives was higher at first, as the year wore on the troops helped turn the tide in the capital. Also significant was the appointment in March of a new American ambassador, Ryan Crocker, an experienced diplomat who spoke fluent Arabic and had had years of experience in the Arab world, including Iraq. The new US team members were determined to work together, and their excellent knowledge of Iraq and its political personalities enabled them to exercise both pressure and persuasion on Iraqis to step back from the brink and to make some necessary accommodations.

The Sunni Turn Against the Insurgency

A second reason for the turnaround was a split in the Sunni insurgency and the emergence of a movement, known as the Sahwa (Awakening), among the Sunni tribes of Anbar, who turned decisively against al-Qa'ida and the violence of the insurgency. This shift had begun well before the surge was announced. A key breakthrough came in Ramadi in September 2006 when Abd al-Sattar Abu Risha, chief of the Albu Risha clan, began to enlist his tribesmen to combat al-Qa'ida and encourage them to join the local police.[1] They formed the Anbar Salvation Council, and by the spring of 2007 over forty-one clans and tribal groups had joined; together they began pushing al-Qa'ida out of Anbar. The Sahwa movement provided a local force with which the United States could work to fight al-Qa'ida and other violent insurgents in their Sunni stronghold.

There were many reasons for this Sunni Arab shift in willingness to work with the United States. Most important was local outrage at AQI's brutal tactics and alien practices. AQI's attacks on Iraqi civilians—not only Shi'i but also, increasingly, Sunni opponents—as well as gruesome practices, such as beheading and physical torture, alienated the population. Nor were the Islamic strictures imposed by AQI part of Iraqi culture—full-face veils, beards, banning of music, and the like. There were economic reasons as well. Many local tribal leaders were involved in cross-border trade and smuggling with Syria and Jordan; AQI's activities disrupted this, badly affecting the local economic situation. It may have been significant, too, that the older generation of tribal leaders, many of whom had been deeply involved with Saddam Husain and more committed to his regime, had already left for Amman or Damascus; a younger generation was anxious to secure its position and future in Iraq, including the patronage that Americans and even the new Shi'i government could provide.[2] At base, however, was the fact that most Sunnis in Anbar and elsewhere—especially those in the insurgency—were nationalists fighting for local, Iraqi aims. They did not share the transnational aims or the Salafist ideology espoused by AQI. This divide became even clearer after AQI established the Islamic State of Iraq (ISI) in October 2006 and announced as its goal the establishment of an Islamic caliphate in Iraq, not the independent Iraqi state desired by most Sunni insurgents.

By May 2007, the Sahwa movement had spread to Baghdad itself. One interesting example of how this occurred took place in the Amiriyya quarter. Amiriyya had been a haven for Sunni insurgents, but most of the inhabitants were modern, Westernized professionals—former army officers, officials, and others who had lost their jobs. They had made a bargain with AQI in the insurgency, but most were not prepared for AQI's harsh, Taliban-style measures. At the end of May, Iraqi inhabitants decided to attack AQI. They asked for US help and got it, turning the battle to their advantage.[3] (By this time, the Multinational Forces [MNF] and Iraqi forces were engaged in securing a number of key quarters in the city.) In Amiriyya, a salvation brigade of about one thousand locals was formed, cooperating with both American and Iraqi government forces to secure the quarter. The results were telling. Civilian deaths plummeted from twenty-six a month in May to less than one by the end of the year; after August, the US battalion in Amiriyya was never attacked again.[4]

By the end of 2007, such local councils had spread not only in Baghdad but also to local areas outside. By July Falluja was able to identify four tribal clans to cooperate with the MNF, and Falluja was turned over to these leaders in September. In Diyala as well, a Diyala salvation council was formed and met with some success. Many of these local councils, variously called the Sons of Iraq (SOI) or Concerned Local Citizens, were put on the US payroll, obviously helping with the economic situation and sopping up the unemployment that had helped in insurgency recruitment.

It was one thing to cooperate with the United States, but it was not yet clear whether these Sunnis—Sons of Iraq and others—would be fully accepted by the newly elected Shi'i-dominated government into the military and police as equal partners as they desired. Indeed, to the Shi'i government, these new groups looked like Sunni Arab militias, independent of state control and filled with former insurgents who might turn against the regime in the future. Distrust between both sides remained deep.

Fissures within the Shi'i Front

A third factor in calming the situation was a slower but equally significant curbing of the Shi'i extremists, especially the Sadrists but also Badr. Ultimately, the Shi'i political front was no more homogeneous than the Sunni, and it began to fracture and to realign in the course of 2007. Muqtada al-Sadr had always had trouble controlling his militia, which suffered continual fracturing, with some militia groups going their own way under their own leaders, who were only loosely tied to Sadr. Some of these, referred to as "Special Groups," were under Iranian supervision; others operated on their own and often financed their activities by kidnapping, ransom, and other criminal activities. The government did little to control them because Sadr and his forces were still largely under the protection of Maliki, who had won election as prime minister by Sadrist votes and needed Sadrist support in the Council of Representatives (CoR). However, in early 2007 the Sadrists withdrew from the cabinet over a dispute with Maliki on extending the timeline for U.S. withdrawal of troops. This deprived Sadr of a source of patronage and resources. It also ruptured his alliance with Maliki, with its potential protection. Maliki now turned to the Supreme Council for the Islamic Revolution in Iraq (SCIRI) as a partner, which welcomed the move. SCIRI itself was in the process of reorganization, turning itself into a more organized political party with an Iraqi orientation. In May 2007, it changed its name to the Islamic Supreme Council of Iraq (ISCI, as it is referred to hereafter), dropping "revolution" from its title.

However, the real turning point in Sadr's fortunes came on 27 August during a Shi'i religious holiday when Sadrists in Karbala provoked a fight with ISCI while the city was filled with pilgrims. The incident set off a two-day battle that killed fifty pilgrims and injured many more. Maliki was infuriated, and he personally went to Karbala, where he gave the police chief carte blanche to go after the Mahdi Army.[5] The episode badly tarnished Sadr's image. On 29 August, he announced a cease-fire as well as a prohibition on firing on MNF forces. Several days later, he signed a pact with ISCI agreeing to reduce tensions. He had left earlier in the year for Iran and now announced his intention of remaining there to study under clerics in Qum for status as a *mujtahid*, thereby removing himself from Iraq. Sadr had apparently decided to follow a different route to political power than the street.[6] By the end of 2007, only Special Groups among the Shi'a, backed by Iran, and now led by Akram al-Ka'bi, were fomenting violence in Baghdad.[7]

Other factors also helped calm the situation on the Shi'i side. Political pressure on the new Iraqi government to put "neutral" ministers in Defense and Interior began to pay dividends. Under the more technocratic administration of Jawad al-Bulani, the minister of the interior, the Iraqi National Police, which assisted in counterinsurgency operations, was purged of units engaging in sectarian violence. Gradually, too, the Iraq Security Forces (ISF) increased by 140,000 and were better controlled and officered. These additional forces were now operating with some 50,000 new US troops from the surge and about 103,000 Sons of Iraq to keep order.[8] Their efforts at policing helped reduce violence, which by the end of the year had declined by 90 percent. There were still violent episodes of various kinds, but the sectarian war was essentially over.

The Effects of Sectarian Strife

Nonetheless, the long-term effects of the sectarian war and its legacy remained. The number of refugees has been estimated as high as 2 million and the internally displaced persons at 1.6 million, although many careful observers claim that these figures are too high.[9] Much of this population included Iraq's educated, professional class, which now fled to other countries, mainly Jordan, Syria, and the Arab Gulf, where they constituted a disaffected community on Iraq's borders.[10]

Many refugees were Sunni, although there are no hard figures on the sectarian breakdown, further shifting the demographic balance in the capital in favor of the Shi'a. Indeed, this outcome was probably a main factor in moving Sunnis away from violence and into the political process. They ultimately decided to cut their losses before these became irreparable and to try gaining some leverage with foreign forces before they left.

A second legacy of the conflict was the Balkanization of Baghdad. Much of the decline in violence was obtained by building walls and military barriers around quarters and neighborhoods. Within these enclaves, militias, including the Sons of Iraq as well as Shi'i groups, protected the population and sealed citizens off from outsiders. Baghdad, historically a cosmopolitan, relatively tolerant city in which different sects, religions, and ethnic groups, including foreigners, had lived and worked together, now became much more compartmentalized, with various sections literally walled off from one another.

A third legacy was more intangible. Among ordinary citizens, tired of random and obscure violence, a deep distrust of others and a much greater sectarian identification than had been the case before took root in a way that was new to Iraq. Indeed, exhaustion and a desire for a return to normalcy among those involved may ultimately have been the reason for the return to relative calm. The war had just played itself out.

Kurdish Development

While this devastation and destruction was affecting Arab areas, the Kurds were strengthening their position in the north. Between 2006 and 2010, using their better-developed *peshmerga* and security apparatus, they sealed off their area and maintained a zone of relative peace that included most of the "disputed territories" they had absorbed since

2003. In this new "Iraqi Kurdistan," leaders expanded the economy and undertook development of their political, social, and cultural institutions, consciously setting Kurdistan apart from the rest of Iraq in as many ways as they could. In this endeavor, they were now fortified by the legal provisions of the Transitional Administrative Law (TAL) and the new Iraqi constitution, which recognized the KRG as a region with greatly enhanced legal authority. They were also aided by the weakness of the new central government in Baghdad and the chaos enveloping lower Iraq.

Economic Progress

Most important was the KRG development of "new" oil resources, that is, oil and gas in the three provinces recognized in the federal constitution as constituting the KRG.[11] In this area, the KRG moved ahead rapidly. As early as July 2004, it had concluded a contract with DNO of Norway,[12] later to become controversial, and it continued to award concessions to foreign firms. By September 2008, the KRG had sealed over twenty foreign oil and gas contracts. Almost all of these companies were small, without the resources to do much development, but they could start exploring and drilling. A few, such as Hunt Oil and DNO, were medium sized and could develop a productive capacity. DNO not only developed the Tawke field near the Turkish border but also built a short pipeline (four miles) to connect it with the Iraq-Turkish pipeline to Ceyhan, thus allowing export.

Oil was not the only economic front on which the Kurds moved. They soon made vigorous efforts to attract foreign investment in a number of areas, with considerable success. Turkey, Iran, and the United Arab Emirates, among others, responded. In addition, the Kurds were now assured of 17 percent of the national Iraqi budget agreed to by the central government. In an era of higher oil revenues, income from the 17 percent rose from $2.5 billion in 2005 to $6 billion in 2009.[13] The Kurds also got foreign aid, especially from the United States, channeled mainly into the provinces.

Kurdish development expenditure went into infrastructure, such as water treatment plants, power transmissions, roads, and microwave links. Two modern airports were opened with direct international flights to Istanbul, Frankfurt, Vienna, and Amman, opening the KRG to the outside world. Private-sector development consisted mainly of houses, office buildings, shopping centers, and hotels.

The KRG also invested in education, health, and services, attempting to create social and cultural capital. By the year 2009, the KRG had 1.1 million students in primary schools and 208,600 in secondary.[14] In an effort to overcome decades of isolation and stagnation, there was some investment in high-quality higher education. The three major universities in Dahuk, Arbil, and Sulaimaniyya were expanded; a private US university—American University in Iraq-Sulaimani—opened with KRG funding; and other private institutions opened as well.

Although the economy grew from 8 to 25 percent a year between 2004 and 2009,[15] rapid economic growth had some downsides as well, bringing inflation, rapidly rising housing prices, and increased inequalities in income and living standards. Much of this money flowed into the hands of political leaders through the traditional system of *wasta*, use of a "go-between," especially to the Barzanis and Talabanis, creating more corruption and social cleavages. Without a vigorous productive sector or indigenous industries, the government was still the main employer—by 2008 the KRG was still providing monthly employment stipends to an estimated 1.5 million, or about 75 percent of the population.[16] High prices and the boom also created a new class of working poor engaged in two or three jobs to make ends meet. The main impact fell on youths, seeking jobs and new opportunities that did not yet exist. This was soon to create new political tensions as well.

Meanwhile, the Kurds also continued their efforts to establish an independent identity for their region and underpin it with cultural and historical foundations—not only in the KRG itself but also in Kurdish areas of Kirkuk. The KRG altered the school curriculum, substituting Kurdish history and culture for those of Arabic.[17] Although some Arabic was taught in all schools and some Arabic schools existed for Arab speakers, a younger generation of Kurds essentially unable to operate in Arabic was being produced.

Political Consolidation and Its Challenges

At the same time, the Kurds continued to consolidate their control over the KRG and disputed territories. Their efforts were focused on three fronts. One was unification of their region and resolution of the long-standing conflict between the two parties and their leaders over power-sharing. A second was their evolving relationship with the central government under the constitution, where the Kurds attempted to gain as much independence as possible. A third was the legal absorption of Kirkuk and the disputed territories. Although the Kurds had considerable success in this endeavor, on all three fronts they continued to face challenges.

Unification

The unification process began right after the January 2005 elections, but soon ran into problems. While a parliament and government had existed in Arbil since the 1990s, so, too, did separate Kurdistan Democratic Party (KDP) and Patriotic Union of Kurdistan (PUK) regional governments. The issue now was how to merge these two regions to form a single, new, federal KRG under a more open and transparent constitution. Disagreements on how power would be divided in the KRG extended as well to the yet-to-be-incorporated Kirkuk.[18] At base was the old dispute between Ma'sud Barzani and Jalal Talabani over Kurdish leadership. This was partly settled in April 2005 when Talabani was elected Iraqi president by the new Iraqi parliament. In June, the newly elected Kurdish National Assembly (KNA) convened in Arbil and elected Barzani KRG president.[19] However, it took until May 2006 to get sufficient agreement between the two leaders to be able to form a joint KRG cabinet. On 21 January 2006 Talabani and Barzani published a "unification agreement," agreeing in principle to rotate the key KRG posts (prime minister and parliament speaker) between the two parties periodically and to share other posts and the budget. However, it was not until June 2006 that the first KRG cabinet was announced. At the top of the structure, virtually all key posts went to the two parties.

As this process indicated, the two parties, not the official structures of the KRG, dominated the political process, which, like Baghdad, functioned largely on a personal and neopatrimonial basis. Real power remained vested in the party politbureaus (both dating from the Soviet era) and on personal and family ties. This was clearest in the case of the Barzanis but increasingly true of the Talabani family in Sulaimaniyya. Under both parties, patronage and *wasta* were the rule in securing political positions, jobs, and other benefits. In addition, budgetary control was maintained by the parties and much budgetary information remained secret.[20]

Oil and Kurdish Autonomy

Another challenge faced by the Kurds was their dispute with the central government over the degree of autonomy the KRG was allowed under the constitution. Nowhere was this dispute more contentious than over the issue of who had control of oil resources and whether the KRG had the right, under the constitution, to conclude independent oil contracts in its own territory.

This dispute was exacerbated by the absence of a national hydrocarbon law, which would have spelled out the terms under which contracts could be concluded, oil and gas produced and exported, and revenues shared. Without such a law, there would be no legal protections for foreign firms in cases of dispute. The sticking point was not just Kurdish desires to develop an independent oil sector in KRG territory, but also differing attitudes toward foreign investment. The Kurds were much more "market friendly" than the central government and more willing to entice international companies with better terms—such as production-sharing agreements. The central government, with its long history of distrust of Western oil companies, was less market friendly.

After numerous attempts to reconcile these differences, the KRG finally published its own hydrocarbon law on 6 August 2007 and proceeded to act on it. This law included provisions for "new" fields, as well as "old" fields in Kirkuk and elsewhere that the Kurds expected to have in their territory eventually. The Kurds were willing to distribute the proceeds of this oil to the rest of Iraq provided they got their 17 percent share after the companies had recovered their costs.

It was not long, however, before the central government put a damper on the KRG's oil production and development. Husain al-Shahristani, minister of oil in Baghdad, refused to recognize as legal the contracts concluded by the KRG. Furthermore, he announced that the central government would bar any international company with a contract in the north from bidding for the much more lucrative fields in the south. This prohibition frightened away the major international oil companies (IOCs), thereby reducing the KRG's prospects for development. The dispute became particularly acute after DNO started producing from the Tawke field in 2009. To export, the KRG was compelled to use the Turkish pipeline controlled by the central government; the central government also controlled the distribution of revenues. Although it was willing to give the KRG its 17 percent share of the proceeds, it refused to pay the company's costs, which the DNO expected to recover through production and sale. The KRG also refused to pay the DNO, and the well was shut down pending a solution.[21]

By 2009, income and money had become a dominant issue for the KRG in relations with the central government. In addition to oil contracts, there were increasingly contentions disputes over the KRG's 17 percent of the federal budget. Although accounts vary, one authority puts this subsidy at 95 percent of the KRG's income, making the KRG's economic dependency on the central government clear.[22] Achieving economic—not just political and military—independence was becoming a chief goal of the KRG.

Kirkuk and the Disputed Territories

No dispute with the central government was as difficult or as important as Kirkuk and the disputed territories. Kirkuk was not only symbolic—since at least 1970 the Kurds had been claiming Kirkuk as a Kurdish city and their "capital"—but also economically essential.[23] If the Kurdish parties succeeded in absorbing Kirkuk and its oil, they would have the wherewithal to become independent and command recognition from surrounding countries and the United States, a crucial fact recognized by both the Kurds and the new leaders of the Iraqi state.

The Kurds staked their claim to Kirkuk mainly—though not wholly—on demography. They claimed a traditional Kurdish majority in the province, which had been forcefully Arabized by the central government, especially in the Saddam era.[24] They wanted normalization, which meant a "methodical reversal of Arabization."[25] This was to be accomplished through a return of displaced persons (Kurds) and a resettlement of the persons brought in by the former regime (mainly Arabs). The Kurds began a Kurdification process soon after gaining political and military control of the areas in 2003. With the events of 2003, some Arabs fled and Kurds were encouraged to take their place; in a number of cases, the process was forceful—Arabs were intimidated and pushed out and Kurds with no previous claims in Kirkuk were encouraged to settle in their place. Kurdish sources claim that by early January 2004 almost 4,000 Kurdish families (about 20,000 people) had returned; at the same time, 2,300 Arab families (about 21,000 people) had moved out. Some 200,000 registered displaced Kurds were set to move in (some put the figure as high as 300,000).[26] These figures, although sketchy, give some sense of the scope of these movements, but without a census, they cannot be confirmed.[27]

However, Kurdish claims to Kirkuk and other areas were based not only on demographic facts but also on geography and history; the Kurds were careful to define their territory as Kurdistani—not simply Kurdish—thereby making room for minorities. Much of the territory claimed, said the Kurds, was historically part of the Ottoman province of Shahrazur, which had existed until the administrative reorganization of 1869.

Both Turkmen and Arabs disputed this narrative. To the Turkmen, the *wilaya* of Mosul, formed in 1869, was essentially Turkman, and they considered towns such as Kirkuk, Kifri, Tuz Khurmatu, Altun Kipri, and Tal Afar as originally Turkman. They recognized themselves as a group that came in during Seljuk times, formed the Turkman dynasties that dominated the area in the thirteenth and fourteenth centuries, and served as soldiers and administrators during the Ottoman period.[28] The Arabs in the region came mainly from the neighboring Jubur, Ubaid, and Hadid tribes south and west of the area. Although they did not claim to

FIGURE 11.1 Disputed Territories Claimed by the KRG

This map has been produced by the International Crisis Group. It is a modified version of a similar map appearing in Crisis Group Middle East Report N°80, *Oil for Soil: Toward a Grand Bargain on Iraq and the Kurds* (28 October 2008). Only the northern boundary of the disputed territories has been adjusted to add more detail.

be original inhabitants, they regarded the area as mixed; they wanted it to remain under the central government, not the KRG. Kurdish claims were also challenged by the central government in Baghdad and a broad sector of the Arab population in Iraq.

The TAL and the Iraqi constitution had specified that a referendum on Kirkuk, which the Kurds expected to win, should be held by the end of 2007. In 2006, the Kurds supported Maliki as prime minister on the supposition that he would move ahead rapidly on normalization, but he failed to do so. By 2007, as Maliki began to assert more authority, the tide began to turn against an early referendum.

The United States also shifted its policy. Prior to this time, the United States had supported the Kurds—up to a point—in part because of the US need for Kurdish support on the security front. But this began to change in 2007. The near collapse of the new government in Baghdad, the disastrous sectarian war, and, above all, the new counterinsurgency strategy all influenced US support for the Sunni Awakening in its fight against AQI and US need to incorporate Sunnis into the emerging government in Baghdad. These factors changed the US attitude toward the old exile opposition allies, including the Kurds. The Kurdish parties would now be forced to "reconcile" with and accommodate Sunni Arabs, just like their Shi'i allies in Baghdad had to.

On 10 August 2007, the United Nations passed Resolution 1770, unquestionably supported by the United States, which gave the United Nations a role as mediator to resolve the disputed territories issue. This indicated for the first time that a procedure other than reliance on a referendum could be applied. The Kirkuk issue was now likely to be settled by negotiations of some sort before a referendum, a disposition much less favorable to the Kurds.

Further setbacks to Kurdish hopes for more autonomy occurred in October 2007 when the Partiya Karkari Kurdistan (PKK), always anathema to the Turks, ambushed and killed fifteen Turkish soldiers in northern Iraq. The Turkish parliament voted to allow the Turkish army to conduct cross-border raids into Iraq. To smooth the way, Prime Minister Recep Tayyip Erdoğan visited Washington in November, and Washington agreed to the raid. The incursion came on 16 December, along with a bombing campaign to destroy PKK hideouts in the mountains of Iraq. The Kurds saw this move as US support for Turkey, as a setting of limits on Kurdish autonomy, and as a reaffirmation of US support for Iraq's territorial integrity. Despite these challenges and setbacks, however, the staying power and progress of the KRG as an increasingly autonomous polity indicated that it would continue to be a challenge to the central government in Baghdad and possibly the cohesion of the state.

Maliki's Consolidation of Power, 2007–2009

Meanwhile, in Baghdad the central government under Maliki began, with US support, to strengthen its position. Nuri al-Maliki had started his tenure as a weak, relatively unknown political figure embedded in a Shi'i coalition in which his party, the Da'wa, was the weaker member. But early on, Maliki began to demonstrate political toughness and persistence as well as a penchant for concentrating power in his own hands. Beginning in 2007, he began to increase his control over the army and the security services by appointing people loyal to him personally and bypassing institutional structures. He used the Baghdad Operations Center, created at the beginning of the surge to centralize command and control of military and police forces in selected cities and provinces, as a tool to control the security services, appointing his own generals at these centers. He created the Office of the Commander in Chief and put a civilian loyalist (Basima-l-Jadri) in charge, using the office to increase his direct control over the army. The United States (mainly Petraeus and Crocker) intervened behind the scenes to prevent what it saw as politicization of the military and a weakening of institutions and to encourage incorporation of the new Sahwa forces into government structures, but this was an uphill battle. Maliki was especially reluctant to accommodate the new Sunni Sahwa groups, which he feared would slip back into insurgency and which were, in any case, political adversaries. He wanted a security force loyal to him personally.

Not surprisingly, his opponents, including some in the United States, accused him of being sectarian and working to consolidate the Shi'i hold over the security forces. The Sunnis were unhappy over lack of reconciliation, and the Kurds wanted more support on the Kirkuk referendum. Others claimed he relied on a small circle of advisers, current or former Da'wa members, and was unwilling to widen this circle or cooperate with others in the cabinet. They demanded his removal and replacement through a no-confidence vote in parliament—a crisis he faced twice during 2007. The situation illustrated Iraq's conundrum: a new political system with untested rules of operation, a dysfunctional government that was too inclusive to make decisions, and continued fear among politicians of concentrating power in anyone's hands.

The first crisis reached a head during the summer of 2007. By this time, Maliki's cabinet had already begun to fracture. The Sadrist members had left in April, but Maliki still relied on their support in the CoR. On 26 June Tawafuq left the cabinet as well, and on 7 August five secular ministers from Iraqiyya also left, demanding reform and a new prime minister. This made seventeen absentee ministers, almost half the cabinet. Finally, after a good bit of US pressure, five top Iraqi leaders (of KDP, PUK, ISCI, Da'wa, and Tawafuq) reached an agreement on 26 August to develop a core group under the presidency to meet and work out problems and to shore up discipline in the CoR. Nonetheless, at the end of the year Maliki faced another threat of removal when opponents claimed he was not implementing the 26 August agreement. US Secretary of Defense Robert Gates and National Security Adviser Condoleeza Rice visited Baghdad in December and again applied pressure on the cabinet for compromise. In the end, Maliki was saved once again. In the US view, Maliki, despite his obvious shortcomings, was more of a nationalist than a sectarian and could be nudged over time in a different direction.[29] More important, however, was their recognition of the fractious and intransigent political environment Maliki faced, the weakness of his support base, and, above all, the time it would take to find a substitute—time that could, once again, lead to renewed violence and state collapse.

Using this support, Maliki now moved ahead to establish stronger control over the government. Gradually, he staked out a position for himself as a "nationalist" and a "centrist" rather than a sectarian leader, and he managed to do so without relinquishing his ties and roots to his own Shi'i constituency. From an initially weak figure, he took a number of steps to make himself the main political contender in a fragmented political landscape and to gain control over the central government.

Parliamentary Action

He began with parliament. Helped by behind-the-scenes US efforts, Maliki shepherded two important pieces of legislation through the fractious CoR. The first was the Accountability and Justice Law, which dealt with de-Ba'thification. Passed on 12 January 2008, the law was designed to propitiate demands from Sunnis and ex-Ba'thists for reinstatement in their former government positions. It allowed Ba'thists who had been at the lowest levels of the party's leadership to be reemployed, and it restored the pensions of all who had been dismissed up to and including the next ranking level. However, in some ways the law expanded de-Ba'thification by mandating dismissal of all former members of the Ba'th-era security and intelligence agencies whether or not they had been Ba'thist.

The second law was the Provincial Powers Act, passed on 12 February 2008, which provided for the governance of all provinces outside of regions. It stipulated that Provincial Councils would be elected by secret ballot and that each council would elect a council chairman and a provincial governor. The law shifted some power, but not all, to the provinces. The council could legislate administrative and financial laws but did not control such issues as health, education, transportation, or environment, which were under appropriate ministries in the federal government. Provincial funds were to be received from the central government, but Provincial Councils did have the right to raise revenues from taxes, government services, and investments. The Provincial Powers Act also stipulated that an election law would be drawn up within ninety days.

Originally, provincial elections were expected to be held by October. The potential for an upcoming election—together with prospects for a shift in the balance of local control—focused the central government on politics for the rest of the year. All parties and political factions now had to consider a potentially changed landscape, particularly as a forerunner to the national election mandated in 2010. Maliki, in a bid for power, now began to exert a degree of independence, both from the United States and his Shi'i coalition partners, as he gradually neutralized opposition. His second step in pulling ahead of the pack was soon taken in Basra, where, once again, he challenged Sadr.

The Basra Incursion

A government incursion into Basra, which began on 25 March, was publicly billed as an attempt to bring errant militias to heel and to wrest Iraq's port city from their control, but it was almost wholly directed against

Sadr's Mahdi Army. Nonetheless, even though the move—and its timing—may have had political motives, Basra clearly posed a major problem for the central government that had to be tackled. Basra was Iraq's second largest city, its only access to the Gulf, and its major oil-exporting center, but the city had fallen prey to Shi'i militias and criminal gangs (often indistinguishable). The various local factions engaged in a conflict over port facilities and oil exports that often spilled over into violence. Many used smuggling activities, including oil, to finance their activities. One oil smuggler was so brazen he was willing to be interviewed on CNN demonstrating how he stole oil from a pipeline and shipped it to Iran.[30] ISCI, both Da'wa factions, Sadrists, Fadila, and smaller Shi'i groups vied for control, with their militias having thoroughly penetrated police and security forces. Iranian penetration and arms smuggling were rife, and feuding frequently turned violent. In addition, the local population was harassed about Islamic restrictions and often terrorized by militias.[31]

Apparently, Maliki expected to disband local militias "peaceably," replacing them with government forces sent to the south. Although some planning for the operation had been under way earlier, Maliki made the decision to go into Basra in March on his own, apparently informing the United States only the day before and insisting that it would be an Iraqi operation. On 25 March the ISF entered the neighborhood of al-Ta'miyya, a Sadrist stronghold, where government forces soon faced resistance. Fighting rapidly spread to other neighborhoods as the Mahdi Army fought back. Maliki issued a seventy-two-hour ultimatum for the resisters to surrender their arms; when this did not occur, he asked for coalition aid. Americans and British provided air and artillery support, which helped turn the tide.

One reason the operation ran into difficulty soon became apparent: desertions and even defections to the other side by a number of Iraqi forces. These were mainly in the police, a weak link, but some of the army were also involved, especially a brigade only recently trained in combat operations. Many, if not most, of these deserting forces were from the Basra area, indicating the problems involved in the use of local forces. After the battle, the Iraqi government dismissed 1,300 soldiers and police for disloyalty.[32]

But it is also clear that the Sadrists were under stress as well. Muqtada al-Sadr sought support from Ayatallah Ali al-Sistani, but the chief *marji'* would not come to Sadr's aid this time, claiming that all arms should be in government hands. On 30 March, Sadr ordered a cease-fire, and the parties turned to Iran to mediate. Maliki sent a negotiating team to Iran; Qasim Sulaimani, commander of Iran's Quds Force, was also involved. Eventually, a cease-fire was arranged. Once the bulk of the Madhi Army had stood down, the government's forces were able to move in and take control of the rest of the city. On 24 April, they announced that Basra was now under government control. Law and order had returned to the city.

Pursuit of the Mahdi Army did not end there. In fact, some fighting spread to centers throughout the south, and a second operation was undertaken in Sadr City. In these operations, coalition forces were more heavily involved; indeed, they walled off the southernmost section of Sadr City and cleaned it out. Fighting continued here until 11 May, when another cease-fire, arranged in Iran, was finally signed. Thereafter, Iraqi forces were able to deploy and control most of Sadr City. They also conducted operations in Amara, a Sadr stronghold, where Iranian arms smuggling had been rife.

Whatever the initial difficulties, the Basra operation was a success in restoring government control. Moreover, it was immensely popular in Basra, where citizens welcomed a return to normalcy. And much of the political gain went to Maliki. Whatever his motives, he had extended government control over a key province, once again weakened Sadr, and emerged as someone who looked more like an Iraqi leader than a sectarian partisan—a role he would increasingly play.

Dealing with the Sunnis

Maliki did not limit himself to his Shi'i rivals; he also directed his maneuvers at Sunnis. In general, Sunnis, who had always favored a stronger government, were pleased by the Basra action, but Maliki had no intention of alienating his own Shi'i base for former adversaries. Despite local concessions to the Sahwa in Anbar, he continued to resist integration of the Sons of Iraq elsewhere, doing so only reluctantly and under US pressure. He regarded the SOI, like the Sadrists, as a militia outside government control, and he did not want former fighters hostile to the Shi'i coalition inside his security forces. Apparently, he also regarded the SOI as a spent force that did not necessarily have to be propitiated.

Indeed, Maliki now turned against some of Sunnis, particularly those formerly active in the insurgency. In some cases he was supported by Tawafuq, now challenged by many of these same Sahwa leaders in the upcoming provincial election. The most notorious case was that of Abu Abid (Saif Sa'ad Ahmad al-Ubaidi), the SOI leader in Amiriyya, who was already trying to become a local power and was organizing Sons of Iraq in Baghdad and elsewhere in northern Iraq to challenge Tawafuq politically. Abu Abid was charged with murder while he was out of the country, and his property was confiscated. He did not return. Later in the year, Maliki also arrested several key Sahwa leaders in Diyala. And he froze the activities of the committee set up—under US arm-twisting—to work on integrating the US-backed Sunni fighters into the security system. In Maliki's view, the Sahwa and payment of its salaries were a US problem, not his.

Maliki not only rejected Sunni Sahwa leaders but also cultivated his own tribal contingents in the south, making sure they came under his influence, not that of the Americans. He incorporated a number of tribes in the Basra area into the ISF during the Basra incursion. Elsewhere in the south he set up his own tribal councils loyal to the government, that is, to himself. Indeed, he increasingly used government patronage for these efforts. Iraq's oil revenues for 2008 were estimated to be over $79 billion, providing Maliki with the wherewithal to proffer benefits, jobs, and local projects to these areas and tribal groups just as a provincial election was warming up.[33] The effort was noticed—and attacked—by almost all his opponents, both Shi'i and Sunni.

On 19 July, Tawafuq finally came back into Maliki's cabinet after virtually a year's absence. Tawafuq had benefited from Maliki's "help" in curbing Sahwa competition. In addition, Tawafuq needed seats in the

cabinet to help provide patronage in the forthcoming elections. Whatever the motives, Tawafuq's return strengthened Maliki's position and allowed him to take some credit in his own Shi'i community.

Dealing with the Kurds

Maliki soon took another step in solidifying his position, this time pushing back on the Kurds. Kurdish separatism had never been popular within
the Da'wa or with Maliki himself, and a move to regain control over some
of the disputed territory now in Kurdish hands was not surprising. In August, Maliki launched a military campaign in Diyala, presumably to fight
al-Qa'ida, but government forces took the opportunity to engage some
Kurdish *peshmerga* troops in disputed areas under Kurdish control—in
Jalaula, Sa'diyya, and Qara Tepe, subdistricts in the Khanaqin district. He
succeeded in pushing Kurdish troops out of these areas and restoring
government sovereignty.[34] Kurds were furious, but after negotiations they
agreed to remove 4,000 *peshmerga* from Khanaqin and Qara Tepe and
headquarter them in Kurdistan.

    Maliki then went further. The army began deploying its twelfth divi-
sion in the Kirkuk governorate, establishing its headquarters in Kirkuk
in October 2008, which was put under the command of an army brigade.[35] And in preparations for the elections, Maliki shifted the command of units in charge of areas in Salah al-Din to Arabs. Again, the
Kurds were angered but could not resist, lest their moves be interpreted
as insubordination.

    These steps clearly mark the progress Maliki was making in out-
flanking not only real opponents, such as the Sahwa and former Sunni
insurgents, but also members of his own government coalition, such as
Sadr, the Kurds, and even ISCI. On 8 November 2008, he finally took
aim at the latter in a campaign speech that clearly outlined his emerging position. In it he clearly supported a strong central government,
defining what he meant by federalism. "We must build a strong federal
state," he said, "whose government will assume responsibility for sovereignty, security, external policy and other matters. The powers must in
the first place belong to the federal government. . . . If some powers are

not specified [in the constitution], they will be given to the trunk and not to the branches."[36]

Relations with the United States:
The Status of Forces Agreement

Maliki's march to prominence was based not only on outmaneuvering his domestic opponents but also on negotiating a new agreement with his major international overseer—the United States—that would give Iraq a surprising degree of independence. A case can be made that Maliki's most important achievement in 2008 was the Status of Forces Agreement (SOFA) with the United States, a pact that promised withdrawal of US forces by 2011 and a shift to a more civilian-dominated relationship defined in a long-term strategic framework agreement. Maliki got the agreement—and continued military dependence on US forces for another three years—approved by the CoR, no small achievement. Nor was the tough bargain he struck with the Bush administration on a relatively rapid withdrawal a small accomplishment.

Although Iraq had a long history of opposition to foreign treaties and a foreign military presence on the nation's soil, there were clear reasons for majority support for the SOFA from most political actors. The Kurds, a major pillar of the coalition in power, were the most supportive. They had gained most from the occupation and American support and strongly favored its continuance. The Shi'i coalition—mainly the Da'wa and ISCI—were less favorably disposed, and both, especially ISCI, faced strong pressure from Iran for withdrawal. But they recognized only too well their fragile domestic position. They owed the dramatic power shift in Iraq in their favor mainly to the US occupation, and their ability to remain in power would depend on the development of well-trained security forces loyal to themselves—far from an accomplished fact in the face of hostile militias, al-Qa'ida terrorism, and Sunni adversaries. But the Shi'a in power were not Western oriented. They were anxious to regain control over domestic forces and reduce dependence on the United States. Maliki, in particular, had maneuvered to gain control over the military and appeared anxious to achieve independence. As early as July

2007, he had told Senator Barack Obama, during a visit to Iraq, that he wanted the withdrawal of US combat troops from Iraq by the end of 2010—a promise Obama went on to fulfill as president.[37] By the following year, in August 2008 after military actions in Basra and Diyala, Maliki apparently felt confident enough of his forces to tell the Americans he wanted the withdrawal of all troops by 2011.

Even Sunnis, who had been the most vociferous opponents of the US presence, had largely come around to support for some continuing forces—indeed, many now saw themselves as the potential victims if withdrawal were too rapid or accomplished before their inclusion in the political system. The Sahwa wanted US protection, even though it might be politically unpopular. And no one wanted the continuing US military tie, especially its equipment and training, more than the military itself, so long as it came with the proper terms. The issue with all of these parties was the timing of withdrawal—that is, the need for a date by which Iraq's complete control would be established. To regain full sovereignty, Iraq also wanted and needed the removal of UN Resolution 661 and its onerous restrictions and had to secure US support to get it.

The only real opponents of the SOFA were extreme elements. The Sadrists, who were essentially out of power and saw little hope of getting in, virulently opposed the agreement and wanted "immediate" withdrawal. Behind them was the main regional opponent of a US presence—Iran—which exercised as much pressure as it could to hasten withdrawal. Among the Sunnis, only the most extreme—al-Qa'ida and militant Sunnis—whose numbers had now dwindled, were really opposed, and they had been reduced to the margins by 2008.

Significantly, withdrawal sentiments in Baghdad were now matched in the United States. At first blush, the conclusion of such an agreement might have appeared to be a startling reversal from the initial, ambitious intentions of the Bush administration in 2003 and 2004, with its goal of "remaking" Iraq and establishing a long-term partnership with it. But the shift had been quietly under way for several years as chaos in Iraq and disillusion in the United States had followed the early years and opposition from the electorate had resulted in a loss of Congress to the Democrats in the 2006 election. And the United States itself faced a critical presidential election in 2008. The administration needed something that looked like a victory after the surge, and a gradual drawdown of troops and a clear date for a withdrawal were the best outcomes. Washington, too, saw the withdrawal as a necessity.

At stake now were the terms and the timing. The terms that emerged favored steady drawdown and a date for a complete troop withdrawal—Maliki's preferred position. The results were agreed on by the cabinet and put before the CoR in November 2008. The Sadrists were the most vocal opponents on the street, as expected, but the Sunnis and other opponents tried to drive a harder bargain in the National Assembly, mainly to extract concessions from Maliki on the constitution and other political reforms. Possibly to propitiate them, on 11 November the Iraqi army began paying Sahwa council members stipends, fulfilling one of the key Sunni demands.[38]

After extensive debate, on 27 November the CoR passed the needed legislation, which included three separate acts. The first and most important was the SOFA, the second was the long-term Strategic Framework Agreement with the United States, and the third was a "decision" on reforms.

The SOFA provided for US troop withdrawal and the terms that would regulate US troops while they were still in Iraq. The United States agreed to withdraw all its forces from cities, villages, and localities by 30 June 2009 and from all Iraqi territory no later than 31 December 2011. In the interim the Iraqi government requested the "temporary assistance" of the United States in maintaining security; in conducting operations against al-Qa'ida, other terrorists, outlaws, and "remnants of the former regime"; and in training, equipping, supporting, and supplying the Iraqi forces. All such operations had to be coordinated with Iraqi authorities and would be placed under the authority of a joint military operations coordination committee. Iraq gained the right to exercise legal jurisdiction over all US forces and private contractors while outside the jurisdiction of their bases and when not conducting operations. In return, the United States promised to use its best efforts to terminate the Chapter VII mandate of UN Resolution 661 (the legal basis for placing international sanctions on Iraq, passed after Iraq's invasion of Kuwait in

1990) and to secure forgiveness of Iraq's debt. The SOFA also promised that Iraqi land, sea, or air was not to be used as a launching pad for attacks against other countries—an obvious reference to Iran.

The second act, the Strategic Framework Agreement, made certain that the United States and Iraq would not sever relations with the withdrawal of US forces in 2011. It provided for a number of cooperative efforts on a broad front—cultural, economic, and social. On the cultural side the agreement emphasized promotion of higher education and scientific research, leadership exchanges, and help in preserving (and repairing) Iraq's cultural heritage. On the economic front it promised energy development, investment promotion, bilateral trade, regional integration, improvement of communications, and help developing agriculture and industry. On the social side the United States promised to improve the health infrastructure, train medical and scientific cadres, and improve the environment. The agreement clearly shifted the relationship from the military front to the civilian.

The third piece of legislation was the price exacted by the opposition in the CoR, mainly Sunnis, for its agreement to the SOFA and the strategic partnership. It came in the form of a "decision" to undertake reform by implementing the release of all detainees, amending the constitution, returning displaced persons, and absorbing the Sahwas into the armed forces or the institutions of state. Unlike the other two agreements, this statement was not binding, but it did keep the opposition issues on the agenda.[39]

As a whole, the SOFA and the long-term security agreement were regarded as a victory for Maliki's agenda. Although the SOFA did extend the US presence for another three years, the withdrawal dates were specific and the terms put control in Iraqi hands. The strategic partnership was of benefit to all. The "reform" agenda was hardly new—or binding—and would only be tested in application. The SOFA could also be seen as an accomplishment for the new political system, achieving an orderly withdrawal of forces and a security pact with the United States without major disruption. Much of the credit, too, could be attributed to the experienced US team and the hard lessons learned over the last few years. In a situation of relative calm the following year, Petraeus and Crocker were replaced by a new military commander and a new ambassador functioning under an entirely new administration in Washington. The SOFA thus marked the end of one era and a transition to a new one, which would reduce US influence and put more control in Iraqi hands. However inept and dysfunctional the Bush era had been at the start in Iraq, it ended in a more rational and orderly fashion. The struggles and problems created by the occupation would continue in Baghdad, but they would play out henceforth mainly in the political, rather than the military, arena.

The Provincial Elections of 2009

The provincial elections of 2009 were regarded by all as a bellwether and a preparation for the more important parliamentary elections of 2010, which would determine who would govern Iraq for the next four years. The 2009 elections would also be taken as a referendum on Maliki, a factor on which he now played. The passage of the provincial election law had taken place earlier in September 2008, but it was not signed into law until 7 October; hence the elections had to be postponed until 31 January 2009. Failure to solve the Kirkuk conundrum meant that that province would be left out of the elections along with the KRG. Hence, provincial elections were held in only fourteen of Iraq's eighteen provinces, but these included virtually all of Arab Iraq and most of its mixed provinces, such as Baghdad, Ninawa, and Diyala, providing a good indicator of changing attitudes in Iraq since 2005. Although the new provincial law still tended to favor organized parties and coalition lists, it did open the door to more individual initiative and was expected to allow for new faces to appear—especially from "inside" Iraq. Whatever else occurred, it was certain to afford better representation to Sunni Arabs, almost wholly absent from the 2005 process.[40]

Campaigning began in earnest in September 2008 when candidates and parties registered. Over 14,400 candidates ran for a total of some 440 seats. Coalitions varied from province to province; nonetheless, the major contenders were clear—and familiar. Among the Shi'a, the main coalitions included the ISCI-Badr faction at one end of the spectrum and the more amorphous Sadrists at the other, with Maliki's Da'wa in

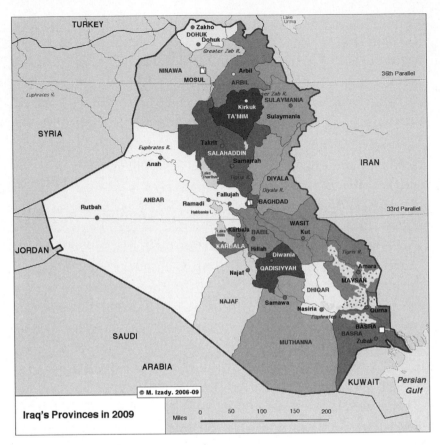

FIGURE 11.2 Iraq's Provinces in 2009

SOURCE: Authored by Dr. M. R. Izady and posted by the Gulf2000 project at Columbia University, New York, http://gulf2000.columbia.edu/maps.shtml.

between. ISCI, with its strong provincial dominance in most of the south, went into the election with control of six of the nine southern provinces, including Baghdad, with consequent control of the security apparatus. Its strength lay in its organization, finances, network of mosques and preachers, and patronage. But its failure to deliver services during its years in power was a major negative factor.

The Sadrists were an unorganized force, still representing the poorer, underprivileged forces that had yet to gain a foothold in power.

Despite numerous military, social, and political defeats over the previous three years, and the absence of their leader, Muqtada, in Iran, they still represented an ever-present, even formidable, opposition force of unpredictable strength.

Rather than running on a Da'wa ticket, or in a Shi'i coalition with ISCI, Maliki put together an entirely new list called "Daulat al-Qanun" (State of Law). Although his ticket included Da'wa and Da'wa Tandim members, nowhere was the name "Da'wa" mentioned. The new name and the party makeover were obviously designed to appeal to a more nationalist strand among the Shi'a, as well as Sunnis and secularists, and to all those tired of anarchy, chaos, sectarianism, and division. Maliki's November speech on federalism left little doubt about his intention to build a strong central government, based on his own leadership, but his new party split the Shi'i front.

Other, smaller splinters in the Shi'i coalition also ran in the south. One was the party formed by Ibrahim al-Ja'fari, the National Reform Trend (Islah), established in 2006 once Maliki assumed the leadership of the Da'wa Party. The other was Fadila, which proved to have little strength outside of the Basra area.

The provincial elections were also a new opportunity for various elements among the Sunni Arab population, which had been essentially marginalized politically since 2005. The Sunnis' main flag bearer was still Tawafuq, but Tawafuq as a coalition had begun to fracture once the Sunni Sahwa emerged. The Sahwa was certainly anxious to replace Tawafuq but was itself fractured, a perennial difficulty with tribally based groups. The leader of the Awakening Council, Ahmad Abu Risha (brother of its founder, Abd al-Sattar, who had been assassinated in September 2007) ran on an Awakening ticket, but so, too, did another tribal leader, Hamid al-Hayis. This fragmentation boded ill for a distinctly Sunni front.

The Kurdish political front (the KDP-PUK alliance) did not expect to play more than a marginal role in these elections because no provincial elections were being held in the KRG or Kirkuk. But it did run a united ticket in several key provinces, Ninawa and Diyala, which included disputed territories and substantial Kurdish minorities.

The secular non-sectarian Iraqi nationalist ticket, Iraqiyya, headed by Ayad Allawi, also ran in a substantial number of provinces, including staunchly Sunni provinces such as Anbar and Salah al-Din, the Shi'i provinces of the south, and mixed provinces, especially Baghdad and Diyala. Other secular but mainly Sunni parties entered the race, including Salih al-Mutlak's Iraqi Front for National Dialogue and an entirely new party that ran in Ninawa, al-Hadba' (Bent), the name of Mosul's most famous mosque, which has a bent minaret. Led by Athil al-Najaifi, brother of CoR member Usama al-Najaifi, it was Arab nationalist and Sunni and appealed strongly to those opposed to Kurdish expansionist aims in the province. These three "secular" parties also noticeably represented, in their ranks and even in their leadership, former bureaucrats and politicians of the Ba'thist era, indicating a comeback by that stratum.

If any theme resonated in the campaign, it was dissatisfaction with the local incumbents, particularly for their failure to deliver services (electricity, clean water, jobs, better schools) and, in some cases, security. Throughout the Shi'i south, disillusion with "exile" politicians and sectarianism had set in. "People now understand that religion has been used," said one politician.[41] "Parties used to display posters of al-Sadr, al-Sistani, and other religious figures," said another, "but this is not going to work any more."[42] Elsewhere, especially in the more northern Sunni and mixed provinces, like Anbar and Baghdad, that had suffered through insurgency and a vicious sectarian war, the desire for an end to fighting and divisions was palpable. "We are the sons of the Tigris and Euphrates," said a politician from Salah al-Din. "We think the same way whether we are from the north or the south."[43] Even though some realism had set in, there was also plenty of old-fashioned patronage, promises to deliver favors in return for a vote, and appeals to local lineage, prestigious relations, and family ties, as well as ties to networks in the federal government that could bring home benefits.

Voting took place on 31 January. Despite speculation that security problems would hamper voting and fears that the Iraqi forces would not meet the challenges, the election was both relatively calm and successful. Turnout was lower than the 2005 election but was, on average, a respectable 51 percent. On the whole, Iraq had passed an early test of both its ability to maintain at least acceptable security under a challenging situation and its willingness to use the ballot box, rather than violence, to resolve political struggles.

The results, announced in February, did indeed bring many new faces and groups into power in the provinces, where the key message of the voters was, as expected, punishment of incumbents for failure to deliver services. Throughout the south in particular, the shift away from sectarian politics to a more practical, centrist orientation was clear, if not decisive. Not surprisingly, ISCI, as the main incumbent, fared badly, though it was by no means wiped out. It lost control in Baghdad, where it got only 12.5 percent of seats, and did not get a plurality in any province. The Kurdish alliance also lost. In Ninawa it was reduced to 32.4 percent of the seats, and it lost the controlling voice in Diyala.

If there was any "winner," it was Maliki's State of Law. Out of 440 provincial seats up for election, his party won the most—126, or 28.6 percent. In Basra, he won a clear majority (57.1 percent), enabling his party to take control of the province, and in the diverse province of Baghdad, he just missed a majority with 49 percent of the seats. He either won or shared a plurality of seats with another party (usually ISCI) in eight other southern provinces. On a national level, his nearest competitor was ISCI, with less than half as many seats (55, or 12.5 percent). Third came the Sadrists, with 43 seats (or almost 10 percent); followed by Tawafuq/IIP, with 32 seats (7.2 percent); Iraqiyya, with 26 seats (5.2 percent); Ja'fari's Reform Party, with 23 seats (5.2 percent); the Kurdistan Alliance, with 20 seats (4.5 percent); and Mutlak's Dialogue Party and Hadba', tied with 19 seats (4.3 percent). It seemed clear that Maliki's shift to a more nationalist posture and his support for a strong central government and some law and order had resonated.

Despite the good showing for Maliki, however, the most important result of the election was still fragmentation. Only in two provinces (Basra/Maliki and Ninawa/Hadba') was any party or group able to get a majority. In every other province, seats were split among parties and individuals, indicating that all groups, including Maliki's, could govern only by forming coalitions.

The KRG Election of 2009

A second, separate election was held in the KRG in July 2009 for a new parliament and president. It, too, was a bellwether of change. Despite the separate status of the Kurdish region, trends showed similar tendencies with the rest of Iraq—a shift away from ethnocentrism to pragmatism and fissures among the leadership. By 2009, political, social, and economic tensions in the KRG, almost entirely the result of domestic KRG developments, had begun to fragment the solid political front so carefully constructed by the two parties. One tension resulted from the recent economic boom and the unequal distribution of its benefits, all too evident in the conspicuous consumption and lavish lifestyles of high-ranking party members and others with connections to them. Closely related to these social inequalities was a lack of political openness and transparency by both parties. Dissatisfaction was most acute among the younger generation, which had aspirations for a more democratic structure and resented the political stranglehold exercised by party apparatchiks and Soviet-era parties. As in the rest of Iraq, the main interest of young voters was in jobs, economic opportunity, and a more open, transparent political system that made room for them. Although they certainly wanted a separate—if not independent—Kurdistan, by this time most took their autonomy for granted and were moving on to other concerns.[44]

These tensions coincided with leadership problems in the PUK, in which a number of politbureau members, notably Naushirwan Mustafa Amin and Muhammad Taufiq, both founding members, had challenged Talabani's leadership, demanding reforms in the party. In 2007, after resigning from the party, Naushirwan founded an independent newspaper, a Web site, and an international satellite TV channel, and in February 2009 he founded a new movement—Goran (Change)—which in the July election ran on a separate ticket. Goran demanded a change in leadership and modus operandi in the PUK and in the KRG as a whole.

Goran was not the only opposition party. The well-established Kurdish Islamic Union (KIU) and the Islamic Group of Kurdistan (a splinter from the older Islamic Movement of Iraqi Kurdistan Party) allied with two small socialist parties, calling their ticket, notably, Reform and Services. The election, held on 25 July, brought some startling results—real opposition to the two established parties for the first time. In the election for president of the KRG, Barzani, as expected, received almost 70 percent of the vote. However, even though the two-party alliance managed to retain a majority of seats in the parliament—59 out of 111 (53 percent)—its majority was considerably reduced. Goran took 25 seats (23 percent), and opposition parties as a whole took 41 seats (37 percent). For the first time, the KDP-PUK grip on power could be openly criticized, if not seriously challenged.

There were several consequences of this outcome. One was a serious weakening of the PUK, which suffered the brunt of Goran's successful run. Goran devastated the PUK in its home base of Sulaimaniyya, where it barely won a majority for the first time. The election also raised the issue of whether the "strategic agreement" for power-sharing between the PUK and the KDP would apply in the future. Results clearly shifted the balance of power in the KRG in favor of the KDP, which would now play the dominant role. Despite the rapid rise of Goran, however, it still had great weaknesses: no formal political structure of elected leadership, access only to private finances, and a new and fragile organization based mainly on a swell of youth support.

Despite the PUK's setback, when the new Kurdish government was formed in Arbil, the strategic agreement was honored as Barham Salih, one of the Kurds'—and the PUK's—most accomplished statesmen, was named KRG prime minister. A new KRG cabinet continued to put key posts in the hands of party stalwarts. However, most of the power in the new government had gravitated to the president, whose personal (and family) control had, if anything, increased, leaving Barham Salih and the PUK much weaker.[45] Despite these continuities, the election revealed changing attitudes in the Kurdish north as the population, especially its youth, turned away from ideology to a concern for a better future.

Maliki and the National Scene in Baghdad

In Baghdad, Maliki savored the results of his apparent victory while he and many others prepared for the more important election in January

2010. But Maliki now faced a new challenge: opposition from all of his other mainstream competitors. His success and his actions in manipulating appointments and moving to dominate the political process during the previous two years had alienated all of his rivals. The Sadrists, originally his key supporters, had born the brunt of his military attacks and were unwilling to support him again. The Sahwa forces were alienated by his foot-dragging on hiring them and his weak efforts at "reconciliation." The Kurdish parties were openly opposed to his efforts to push them out of disputed territory in the north. They had taken to calling him "a new Saddam." ISCI and its chief foreign supporters in Iran also had reason to turn against him because they had been weakened by his refusal to join them in a common Shi'i front.

Despite these factors, Maliki continued to hold his own, and Iraq made slow, uneven, but unmistakable progress in 2009. Al-Qa'ida—mainly AQI and whatever Sunni support it could muster—had now been undercut by the Sahwa movement and Sunni participation in the political process. It was reduced, mainly, to spectacular killings of Iraqi civilians and army and police recruits, clearly aimed at discrediting the government and making Iraq seem ungovernable. Even though there were numerous—almost daily—terrorist attacks (they became almost a fixture of life), they no longer disrupted normal life, which gradually began to revive, especially in Baghdad. The Iraqi death toll declined dramatically. However, there were three spectacular attacks in 2009 that did have an impact on the government and on Maliki's claim to have brought "law and order" to Iraq.

On 19 August coordinated explosions hit the Ministry of Foreign Affairs and the Ministry of Finance, killing over 100 civilians and wounding over 560. Based on the confessions of one of the captured attackers, Maliki accused several Iraqi Ba'thists located in Syria and demanded their extradition. Syria denied being implicated and refused. Relations with Syria had been warming over the previous few years, but this trend was now abruptly curtailed. The Iraqi ambassador was recalled from Syria, and the Syrians recalled their ambassador to Iraq, returning relations to their previous state of noncooperation.[46]

The August bombings were followed on 25 October by attacks striking the Ministry of Justice, the Baghdad Provincial Council building, and the Ministry of Municipalities and Public Works. This time 155 people were killed and at least 720 wounded. Again, AQI was the likely perpetrator. The third main attack took place on 8 December in at least four places in Baghdad, killing at least 127 and injuring 448. ISI claimed responsibility. All of these actions indicated that, although Iraq had made progress in reducing violence and had probably ended its sectarian war, a relapse to worse conditions remained possible.

A second continuing challenge for Maliki, as for all previous governments, was corruption, which ate away at economic development, prospects for increased foreign investment, and confidence in the government and its legitimacy. Corruption, however defined, clearly permeated government and was proving difficult to root out, despite the establishment of a high-level Integrity Commission designed to do just that. (Corruption also involved US officials and contractors, who were numerous and who were subject to investigations in the United States.) Corruption came in many guises, including payoffs and kickbacks on government contracts from the highest to the lowest levels, widespread nepotism, outright theft of government property and resources (especially oil), criminal protection rackets (aided by the almost universal need of government workers and politicians for security protection), and a variety of other largely illegal activities. According to one agency, Transparency International, which ranked 178 countries, only Somalia and Myanmar, tied with Afghanistan, were more corrupt than Iraq.[47]

In May 2009, Maliki faced a corruption case of dramatic and spectacular proportions, which illustrates both the nature and the difficulties of the challenge. The case involved Abd al-Falah al-Sudani, who had been minister of trade, responsible for handling foreign contracts for food and grain imports and managing the remnants of the Oil for Food program, which managed food subsidies and imports of huge amounts of wheat, sugar, rice, and other foodstuffs. Two of Sudani's brothers had been hired to work in the ministry. On 3 May, the Integrity Commission issued an arrest warrant on corruption charges for eight officials, including these two brothers. When an official arrived at the ministry to take them into custody, there was a fifteen-minute gun battle between Iraqi troops and ministry bodyguards, but the brothers managed to escape. As a result of the fracas, Sudani resigned and then attempted to fly to Dubai, but his plane was forced to turn around and return on orders from the government—presumably Maliki. Sudani was held in a Baghdad jail for investigation—a victory for the CoR and the Integrity Commission—but the charges against him were dismissed in April 2010 because of lack of evidence, indicating either the political nature of the charges or the difficulty in making corruption accusations stick or both. The issue did not redound to Maliki's benefit.

But in two other areas, Maliki scored some advances in 2009. One advance was in the perception of increased sovereignty for Iraq. The SOFA had promised a withdrawal of US troops from cities by mid-2009, and this took place on schedule. This greatly reduced the US profile, as US troops disappeared from the streets of Iraqi cities, leaving the Iraqi security forces very visibly in charge. This removed a huge irritant in Iraqi-US relations and also reinforced the idea that security was now the responsibility of the Iraqi government rather than of the United States. Maliki was not shy about taking political credit. On 30 June, Iraqis were given a national holiday to celebrate the country's "sovereignty," and this they did, with parades, fireworks, and parties.

A second advance was in opening the door to foreign investment in the oil industry, especially in the rich fields of the south, essential to any further economic development. In the course of 2009, Maliki made substantial progress in negotiating and signing contracts with major IOCs. Although improvement in oil infrastructure and production would take time, Iraq's ability to secure these commitments gave a boost to expectations for a better future. It also enhanced Maliki's prospects in the coming election.

The Election of 2010 and Its Results

The election of 2010 and its outcome would determine Iraq's government for the next four years and indicate its progress in creating a functioning state. Before a national election could be held, however, a new election law had to be passed. The old law used in 2005 had required parliamentary representation based on population size—one seat for every 100,000 citizens—but this required a recalculation of population to take account of growth since then. In the absence of any census, this was controversial, especially in Kirkuk, where Arabs and Turkmen feared the influx of Kurds. Discussions on elections soon bogged down over Kirkuk, and elections were delayed once again. The United States together with the United Nations Assistance Mission for Iraq had to intervene intensively to get the process back on track. Elections were rescheduled for 7 March, five weeks later than constitutionally mandated.[48] The length of time it took to iron out difficulties indicated how deep political divisions were and how much outside "pressure" was necessary to get a resolution of problems—a harbinger of what was to come in the election.

Parties and Contenders

Electioneering, well under way by September of 2009, involved the usual pre-election attempts by the major parties to put together coalitions designed to get as many votes as possible from core constituencies without having to compromise on their main issues or on the candidate they would run for prime minister or president. And just as before, these coalitions (often involving unlikely or even incompatible partners) would wait until after the electoral outcome to bargain with other coalitions in forming a parliamentary majority. The main contending coalitions—all relatively familiar—were now down to four: Shi'i Islamists, Malaki's State of Law, the Kurds, and a combination of secularists and Sunnis.

Shi'i Islamists

First were the Shi'i Islamists, the former United Iraqi Alliance, now reformed as the Iraqi National Alliance (INA), attempting once again to assemble all Shi'i parties under one umbrella. In this, they were undoubtedly encouraged by Iran. Maliki would not join, but the INA did succeed in including virtually all other Shi'i parties. The backbone, as in

2005, was ISCI partnering with the Sadrists, an unlikely and uncomfortable combination but one designed to bury the hatchet in an attempt to gather in the Shi'i vote. Added to these were the Badr Organization, the Da'wa Tandim Party, Ibrahim al-Ja'fari's National Reform Trend, Fadila, and Ahmad Chalabi's Iraq National Congress (INC), as well as some secular Shi'i independents, such as Qasim Da'ud.

ISCI's strengths included an established organization, well-known political figures, good financial backing (presumably from both religious and Iranian sources), and a solid, middle-class constituency. But the provincial elections had also revealed its weaknesses: an electorate tired of sectarianism, religion, lack of services, and Iranian "meddling" and desiring a more pragmatic, nationalist regime in Baghdad. ISCI attempted to move in that direction in its campaign, emphasizing its Iraqi nationalist identity (the title of its alliance) and its commitment to a pragmatic, consensus-building solution to Iraq's problems.

The Sadrists, the other main component of the INA ticket, was an unpredictable ally, undoubtedly persuaded to align with ISCI by Iran, the main foreign sponsor of this alliance. Sadr had been curbing the violence of his movement, seeking to play a role in the political process, but the movement still lacked organization and coherence. Moreover, the Sadrists were, aside from the extreme Sunni fringe, the major opponents of cooperating with the United States—a main Iranian aim but a liability for any Iraqi party going forward. But the Sadrists had one big advantage—a strong constituency inside Iraq. They still drew on support from the Shi'i underclass—the poor and the lower middle classes, both urban and rural, and a substantial portion of Shi'i youths enticed by Sadr's more radical and anti-Western rhetoric and oppositionist stance. Indeed, the Sadrists, though weakened militarily and politically by Maliki and the United States, would be an important vote-getting component of any coalition. Even if they could not aspire to a top position themselves, the Sadrists might hope to emerge as "kingmakers" in any new election. The primary strategy of the INA was to try to straddle a difficult ideological fence, drawing on latent Shi'i identity to preserve the shift of power to Shi'i hands, but reaching out to a broader constituency. However, the INA had one other important political aim: a desire to make sure that Malaki would not be the next prime minister.

Maliki's State of Law

The second major Shi'i coalition was that run by Maliki's State of Law. He intended to reprise his victory in the provincial elections by drawing on the Shi'i vote and extending his constituency to secularists and, if possible, Sunni Arabs as well, based on his pragmatic, nationalist, "law and order" platform. Maliki had a choice in this election—to join the INA but forgo the prime minister's seat or take the risk and run on his own for the top spot. He chose the latter. He attempted some outreach to Sunni and secular constituencies, and he did manage to get some respected individual Sunnis, but as one Sunni leader claimed, "Maliki can bring in Sunni politicians, whom he will give positions to in government, but he cannot bring in Sunni constituencies."[49]

Maliki's other weaknesses were also clear. He had little political organization, aside from the Da'wa Party, a seemingly narrow group of Shi'i elite on whom he relied for advice. Unlike ISCI, the Da'wa had eschewed the route of mosques and ritualistic outpourings that had characterized much Shi'i activity since 2003, and hence it could not draw on their financial and political support. Rather, Maliki had turned in time-honored fashion to government resources for patronage and tribal outreach through his government sponsored *isnads* (tribal support councils). He made no bones about his platform: the development of a strong, central government, albeit within the constitution.[50] Naturally, he expected to be the prime minister, the main issue at stake among the Shi'a.

The Kurds

The Kurdistan Alliance, the third major coalition, ran a ticket composed, as usual, of the KDP and the PUK and a number of smaller groups. There was no question in this alliance of any collaboration with other Iraqis before the election; the Kurdish strategy was to gather as much strength as possible in the election among Kurds for the alliance's national agenda and then bargain with whomever won in Baghdad for participation in government, hoping to retain the earlier position as kingmakers. If possible, the Kurds wanted to maintain their hold on the presidency—Talabani wanted to run again, despite ill health. The main items on their agenda were well known—the Kirkuk referendum, control over disputed territory, settling of oil contract disputes, and a greater share of the national budget. There was also a new element, "integration" of Kurdish *peshmerga* into the newly emerging national army—that is, giving them training equal to that given by the United States to Iraqi armed forces. The Kurds could see a shifting balance of power here and wanted to maintain military parity.

But all was not rosy for the Kurds either. One problem was the apparent collapse of the PUK; another was the fact that the Kurdistan coalition now faced a new Kurdish party, Goran, which would be running on a separate ticket, weakening the coalition's hitherto solid front. The two religious parties, the KIU and the Islamic Group of Kurdistan, representing the more Islamic constituency of the KRG, also ran on separate tickets. Although these smaller parties had agreed to a pact, authored by Barzani, to stick to a single agenda on Kurdish national issues in Baghdad, the political situation was now more fluid.

The Secularists and Sunnis

The fourth main coalition—a secular, cross-sectarian ticket with strong Sunni support—represented a change in the political landscape. The Iraqi Nationalist Movement, headed by Allawi, was led by the now-familiar Iraqiyya group, normally non-sectarian. But this time the coalition also included several substantial Sunni blocs that had run independently in 2009, notably the Iraqi Front for National Dialogue (led by Mutlak), Hadba' (led by Athil al-Najaifi), and even a new group, the Renewal List (led by Tariq al-Hashimi, who had deserted the IIP and Tawafuq).

In some senses, this coalition appealed to some of the same voters—more pragmatic Iraqi nationalists—as Maliki did, but unlike Maliki, whose ticket was almost wholly Shi'i and relatively cohesive, this one, even more than the INA, was cobbled together from disparate groups. Allawi was well known for his secularism, opposition to Iran, former Ba'th membership, and tough "strongman" image. But new to this coalition was the strong Sunni Arab participation, indicating that these groups had learned from previous experience that fragmentation would not work in getting a seat at the table. Because Allawi's nationalist positions were little different from their own, they decided to coalesce behind him on one ticket. Both Mutlak and Hadba' were strongly Arab nationalist, and both had former Ba'thist bureaucrats or army officers in their ranks. Indeed, the emergence of this ex-Ba'th contingent, especially among Sunni Arabs, would soon be attacked by Shi'i rivals.

It was not clear how this new coalition would do, given its status as a newcomer. However, Allawi did have considerable success gaining support from some Arab states, especially Saudi Arabia, for whom a Shi'i regime in Baghdad was anathema, and Syria, which also preferred a secular government in Baghdad. There was support from Turkey as well, probably with an eye to Hadba's stance against Kurdish expansion in the north.

The last coalition to run was Tawafuq as the Iraqi Accord Front (IAF). Under new leadership since the defection of Hashimi, the IAF included the IIP (led by Ayad al-Samarra'i), the Ahl al-Iraq, and the Turkman Justice Party. The IAF's platform presumed to represent the Sunni population, but the front's weaknesses were apparent: A number of its high-profile figures had cast their lot with Iraqiyya, it had been crippled by the emergence of Awakening groups in Sunni areas, and its failure to gain many benefits from the Maliki government weakened its prospects.

The Election Campaign

The election process and the willingness of the electorate to accept the results were seen as a test for Iraq's new government and its ability to manage a fair and open contest. Although the campaign exhibited all the external trappings of campaigns elsewhere—posters, radio and TV ads, Internet punditry, political attacks, and other less salutary features such as vote buying—the competition for the next government of Iraq was taken seriously; indeed, the struggle for power was fiercely contested. The most important controversy occurred in mid-January when the Supreme National

Commission for Accountability and Justice (the High Commission for De-Ba'thification reconstituted in 2006 and still heavily influenced by Chalabi), charged with vetting candidates associated with the Ba'th Party, disqualified over five hundred candidates, almost a sixth of the total.[51] The charge reopened the wounds of sectarianism and raised countercharges by Sunnis that the move was targeting them.

Despite these difficulties, the election occurred on 7 March. Some violence ensued before, during, and after the election—between 12 February and 7 March some 228 people were killed—but that did not stop people from all areas and provinces from going to the polls. Turnout was a respectable 62 percent. Despite some foreboding among outside analysts, the election process itself, under Iraqi management, was a success.

Election Results

Four major blocs emerged as dominant, but the winner was unexpected. The top vote-getter, by a razor-thin, 2-seat margin was Allawi's Iraqiyya coalition with 91 seats (28 percent). Maliki's State of Law took 89 seats (27.4 percent). The INA came in third with 70 seats (21.5 percent). The Kurdistan Alliance, in fourth place, garnered 43 seats (13.2 percent). However, Kurdish groups as a whole—counting Goran and others—got 57 seats (17.5 percent). Tawafuq, the biggest loser, got only 6 seats (1.8 percent) (see Table A.6).

The main change, even from the previous year's provincial election, was the improved showing of Allawi's secular, cross-sectarian coalition. In 2005 he had won only 25 seats (9 percent), and even in the provincial election the coalition had not been able to get more than about 6 percent of provincial seats. The difference in 2010 was support from new Sunni parties, mainly Mutlak's Dialogue and Najaifi's Hadba', which decided they would do better to concentrate their vote behind someone whose platform resembled their own, rather than scattering their votes. The vote for Allawi indicated a resurgence of more secular and pragmatic trends, especially in Iraq's central provinces.

The reverse occurred with the Shi'i Islamist parties. With the Shi'i vote split, the INA dropped from 128 seats (46.5 percent) in the outgoing

CoR to only 70 (21.5 percent) in the new one. More interesting was the distribution of seats within the INA coalition itself. ISCI, together with its partner Badr received only 17 (24 percent) of the INA seats; the Sadrists had 39 seats (56 percent), giving them a dominant voice in the coalition. This put the recalcitrant and difficult Sadrists in a position, once again, to influence the choice of prime minister. It is hard to avoid the conclusion that ISCI had lost ground since 2005, along with the Shi'i Islamist position.

The Kurdistan Alliance also lost ground. It dropped from 53 seats (19 percent) in the outgoing CoR to 43 (13 percent), or if all Kurdish parties stuck together, 57 seats (17.5 percent), in the new CoR. Most significant was the vote in Kirkuk province, where the Kurds had expected the results to confirm their dominance after a shift of population. They just broke even, taking half the seats—6—with Iraqiyya taking the same amount, an indication of the numbers of those in the province who saw their future in Iraq rather than in the KRG.

Overall, the most striking result of the election was fragmentation. There was no clear winner, despite Allawi's 2-seat margin, revealing deep divisions over the direction Iraq should take, ranging from religious and sectarian identity at one end of the spectrum to a more pragmatic, Iraqi nationalism in the center and ethnic separatist identity among the Kurds at the other end. There was virtually no cross-ethnic or cross-sectarian voting. The Shi'i majority provinces of the south voted overwhelmingly for one of the two Shi'i parties. The Sunni Arab majority provinces voted overwhelmingly for Iraqiyya. The Kurdish provinces voted for Kurdish parties. The mixed provinces did divide their votes, but in the end Iraqiyya was the only group that could garner cross-ethnic and cross-sectarian votes. The underlying lesson of the election, then, was that voters were still voting on ethnic and sectarian grounds to get power, but that within these parameters they wanted more pragmatic, interest-based policies.

The Postelection Stalemate

Voting was one thing; assembling a government was another. A postelection stalemate went on for months.[52] First came challenges to the election from those claiming fraud or unhappy with the results. These included Allawi and Iraqiyya, Chalabi's faction of the INA, and most importantly, Maliki, who demanded a recount of Baghdad's vote by hand. The recount was laborious, finally ending on 17 May, and showed no signs of fraud.

Second came negotiations for a government and the inevitable breakdown of the coalitions that had combined for elections. The two Shi'i coalitions (INA and State of Law) appeared determined to prevent a return of Allawi's Iraqiyya, with its secular agenda and its predominantly Sunni (and ex-Ba'thist) components. On 5 May, both the INA and State of Law realigned as a bloc, even though INA did not want to see Maliki as prime minister. The new "bloc" would now have 159 seats in the CoR, just 4 short of the necessary 163 for a majority. The constitution specified that the parliamentary majority should be charged with forming a cabinet. Allawi claimed that his bloc was the majority because it won the most votes; the new Shi'i coalition under Maliki claimed that it should form the cabinet because it was now the largest bloc in the CoR. The Iraqi Supreme Court upheld Maliki's interpretation.

But that did not end the problem. Despite the formation of the new Shi'i bloc, it had to agree on a prime minister. Neither ISCI nor the Sadrists nor Ja'fari—who had aspirations for the job himself—would agree to nominate Maliki. However, Maliki showed no signs that he intended to relinquish the prime ministership. The bargaining went on for a record eight months after the election and was only settled in mid-November. During the interlude, the extent of foreign interference in Iraq's weak government became apparent. Iran summoned the Shi'i parties and the Kurds (Talabani) to Iran for negotiations in an effort to get them together. Allawi and Sadr were brought to Damascus to negotiate with each other and with the Turkish foreign minister. Vice President Joe Biden, responsible for the Iraq file in the United States, came to Baghdad to speed up the process and reportedly pushed a coalition government, one that would include Allawi and the Kurds but marginalize Sadr.

The key issues, however, were Maliki's refusal to step down as prime minister and the difficulty of others, especially ISCI, in accepting him. Finally, early in October, the Sadrists, presumably under Iranian urging, broke ranks and agreed to support him, essentially leaving the rest of the Shi'i coalition with little choice. On 10 November, an agreement was reached to allow Maliki to remain as prime minister. It was also agreed to allow Talabani to continue as president. Iraqiyya was given the chairmanship of the CoR, for which Usama al-Najaifi was nominated. Thus, the three main positions in government were given to the three main ethnic and sectarian groups, just as had occurred in 2006. The two most important seats were held by the same two people, Maliki and Talabani. The following day the CoR met and approved the agreement, and Maliki began the formation of a new government.

The New Maliki Government

After tortuous negotiations with all parties, Maliki formed his new government, which was approved by the CoR on 21 December. At the top of the structure, the president, Talabani, was given two vice presidents, one a Sunni Arab (Tariq al-Hashimi) and the other a Shi'a (Adil Abd al-Mahdi), to retain communal balance. The same was true for the chairman of the CoR, a Sunni Arab, who had two deputies, a Shi'a, Qusayy al-Suhail, and a Kurd, Arif Taifur. In addition to the prime minister and his three deputies, the cabinet had twenty-seven full ministers and twelve ministers of state, a total of forty-three, a large, unwieldy group unlikely to function as a cohesive unit.

The distribution of seats in the government assured that the *muhassasa* system would remain. The prime minister, a Shi'a, had three deputies, one Kurd, one Shi'a, and one Arab Sunni. The three remaining top positions (foreign affairs, finance, and oil) were given to a Kurd, an Arab Sunni, and a Shi'a, respectively. In the cabinet as a whole, among the thirty-five positions filled, there were twenty-one Shi'a (60 percent), eight Arab Sunnis (23 percent), and four Kurds (11 percent). In addition, there was one Turkman, one Christian, and one woman. The dominance of the Shi'a was clear, but the new dispensation also reflected increasing Arab Sunni participation in government, both at the top of the structure and as a whole. The Kurds still occupied key positions, but their overall influence had been reduced as they shifted their emphasis to the north.

Equally significant was the balance of parties. A breakdown shows the degree of political fragmentation. Maliki's State of Law had three top positions (prime minister, deputy prime minister, and minister of oil); in the cabinet as a whole, a total of eight. Iraqiyya had two positions at the top (deputy prime minister and finance) and a total of nine, but Allawi was not among them. In fact, Iraqiyya's positions were split up among a number of smaller groups in which Mutlak's Iraqi Front for National Dialogue came out with the most—three. Maliki's main Shi'i competitor in the election, the Iraqi National Alliance, received nine posts, none at the top, but most of these were won by Sadrists (six) or Fadila (two). The INA had been irretrievably broken up. The biggest loser was ISCI, with only one post. Among the Kurdistan Alliance, the KDP took two seats (both at the top), the PUK took one, and the KIU received one.

The main victor was Maliki, who after a long struggle and much persistence had kept the top position. But he had done so only through alliance with and support from the Sadrists, as in 2006. They were a volatile group he would have to manage. However, fragmentation offered Maliki the opportunity to play parties and groups against one another to achieve a degree of dominance.

Facing these circumstances, Maliki began, in 2011, to maneuver once again to acquire as much control over the system as possible, indicating a continuation of his previous tactics. The cabinet was incomplete. A number of seats, including the critical security ministries—Interior, Defense, and National Security—were left unfilled; Maliki temporarily assumed the security ministries and made clear he intended to put his supporters in these positions. The United States pushed for the formation of a national security council to include these key ministries and to be headed by Allawi, in part to exercise a check on Maliki, but he again outwaited and outmaneuvered his opponents, and the arrangement eventually fell through. As a result, Allawi did not assume any position in the government, eliminating a key secular rival.

In March, Maliki continued to strengthen his position in the government. The Supreme Court, apparently under Maliki's influence, issued a decree putting three independent commissions—the Independent High Electoral Commission, charged with running elections; the Integrity

Commission, charged with investigating corruption; and the Central Bank, a key player in the economy—under his office, although the court asserted, after considerable outcry, that it would remain "independent." The same month, after demonstrations in Baghdad and elsewhere protested lack of services and transparency, Maliki closed down the offices of two secular opposition parties, the Iraq Communist Party and Mithal al-Alusi's Democratic Party of the Iraqi Nation. The demonstrations, part of uprisings throughout the Middle East that were themselves part of a widespread democracy movement called "the Arab spring," were faced with a determined crackdown, resulting in deaths and injuries. But there were few calls for the overthrow of the regime, indicating that Iraq had achieved a modicum of stability and acceptance of its government, however fragile.

Implications of the Election: Continuity and Change

Even a cursory glance at the 2010 election and the newly formed government reveals that there had been a high degree of continuity in Iraq's leadership and parties competing to run the new Iraq seven years after 2003. Despite insurgency, civil war, and population displacement, exiles and former opposition leaders still prevailed. The original "outsider" opposition groups that had dominated the opposition movement before the fall of Saddam and had managed to gain a grip on power in the first months of government formation in postoccupation Iraq were still largely in place. So, too, were many of the same leaders. The two main Shi'i Islamist parties, ISCI and the Da'wa, still dominated the government. ISCI's top leadership had changed, but the party was still in the hands of the Hakim family, and most of ISCI's exile leaders were still in important positions, notably Adil Abd al-Mahdi, vice president. The Da'wa was the main player, albeit under a new leader and a new name, but many of Maliki's advisers were old Da'wa hands. Their key partners in government were still the two Kurdish parties, whose leaders, Barzani and Talabani, by political skill and hard-earned experience, had prospered well beyond their earlier expectations and were coming close to achieving Kurdish national aspirations denied for over a century.

Despite the persistence of these outsiders, however, political dynamics had changed in subtle ways in Iraq. The opposition exiles who had succeeded in the domestic power struggles—Maliki was the prime example—had now gained considerable experience inside Iraq, learning how to navigate in the new political landscape. The weaker elements among them, especially those who could not generate local support, such as Chalabi and, more recently, Allawi, had been marginalized. Moreover, many well-known exile figures who had played a role in opposition politics for years failed to win seats in the new CoR.[53]

After seven years, the "insider-outsider" distinction had begun to fade as other issues came to the fore. The best example was Sadr's movement, which had earlier made much of its "insider" status but had not yet managed to get a significant foothold in power. The irony is that Sadr's challenge to both the occupation forces and the Shi'i exile leadership in place had resulted in his exile, impeding his access to power and his credentials as an "insider," which grew ever weaker with his residence in Qum and his obvious vulnerability to Iranian manipulation. Nevertheless, his movement was learning how to maneuver in the new political system, as his strong position in the new CoR indicated.

Some new faces had emerged. One was Qusayy al-Suhail, a well-regarded young Sadrist in a key position as deputy chairman of the CoR. Others included Sunni Arabs, chief among them the Najaifi brothers—one (Athil) the provincial governor of Mosul (Hadba' Party) and the other (Usama) chairman of the CoR. Another was Rafi'-l-Issawi from Anbar, the new minister of finance. Both Usama and Issawi ran on the Iraqiyya ticket.

These new elements were important, but the real indication of change was the election itself and the process of government formation. Both revealed that the old Ba'thist structure of government had been permanently broken, with a unified state and a highly centralized government unlikely in the foreseeable future. Although Arab areas—whether Shi'i or Sunni—had demonstrated growing cohesion, the sectarian divide and appeal to communal identity were clearly still fundamental to any election strategy and continued to affect government formation. But the divide itself was less about religion than about a shift of power to the Shi'a and a barring of the return of anything resembling the old Ba'th regime, a formulation that adversely affected the Sunni Arabs and even secular Iraqis.

The ethnic divide between Kurdish and Arab areas, based mainly on language and now a growing institutional separation in the north, would be much more difficult to bridge and could become increasingly permanent. Instead, a new structure—the *muhassasa* system, introduced by the United States and the first occupation government and supported by the opposition parties that had come to power—had taken root, although the strong showing by Allawi's cross-sectarian coalition indicated that it was not irreversible. But *muhassasa* was not based merely on ethnic and communal identity. These communities themselves were fragmented into different constituencies, roughly represented by parties, following different tendencies, ideologies, and even interests and appealing to different groups—all wanting a seat at the political table. Governing would now consist of bargaining and negotiating among these factions before decisions could be made, a process that would provide more freedom for groups but a slower process of development.

Fracturing of communities had also allowed for the emergence of a nascent class system. The weakening of the old, more educated Ba'thist class had allowed new leaders of different origins to come to power. Through a government patronage system and considerable corruption, a new upper and affluent class was now developing, dependent on access to power, similar to the last decade of the old regime. Meanwhile, a new lower class, which had seen very few of the benefits from a shift in power, had gravitated to a more radical movement, the Sadrists. Generational changes were also beginning to affect the older parties, as could be seen in the new Goran movement in Kurdistan but also at provincial levels in the rest of Iraq, where a new, more practical orientation was emerging among the youth.

Most of the new 2010 leaders, whether outsiders or insiders, had been educated in and had strong ties to the Middle East, rather than the West. The leading Shi'i figures, such as Maliki, ISCI's leaders, and Sadr, had been educated in Iraq and exiled in Iran or Syria. The Western-educated elite, such as Allawi and Chalabi, was fading from the scene and being replaced by younger successors with far less exposure to the West. This, in part, helped explain the emergence of more traditional values and practices, including the shift toward more communal and kinship identities.

These factors indicate that Iraq will probably have a relatively weak, incoherent government for some time to come in which getting decisions made will be difficult. Controlling the patrimonial basis of power, the patronage system on which it is based, and therefore continued corruption at some level will also be difficult. A stronger, more effective government, such as Maliki desired, will also have a narrower base and likely be more authoritarian. Although such a government may accomplish more in terms of economic development and effective policy, it will also be less democratic and generate more opposition, including militancy, from those excluded, unless Iraq develops the necessary trust among groups. Development of a stronger parliament with a real opposition party or coalition of parties, although not impossible, appears distant.

12

ECONOMIC, SOCIAL, AND CULTURAL CHANGE IN IRAQ, 2007–2011

The restoration of law and order in 2007 allowed a return to some normalcy and economic development in Baghdad and the south. The scourge of the sectarian conflict and the demographic changes that accompanied it would make both social and economic repair more difficult, but as in the political sphere, the ensuing years saw progress in both areas, despite some setbacks. There were also indications of cultural changes that would shape the new Iraq, especially in the media and in education, as the country struggled to find a new identity and ways of coping with its new freedoms.

Development of Oil Contracts

On the economic front, one of the chief areas of accomplishment was in development of Iraq's oil resources. Securing foreign investment in Iraq's lagging oil industry was a virtual sine qua non for any economic progress.

Numerous problems bedeviled Iraq's oil industry and prevented its early recuperation. Despite having the world's fourth largest proved reserves, Iraq was only its twelfth largest producer in 2009.[1] For most of the post-Saddam period, production hovered between 2 and 2.4 million barrels per day (mbd), not exceeding levels in Saddam's last years. Various international institutions estimated that it would take an additional $1 billion annually just to sustain production at current levels; actual reconstruction could take as much as $100 billion, even before exploration for additional sources, which undoubtedly existed.[2] Not just money but also acquisition of the necessary skills, technology, and spare parts was essential. Iraq's infrastructure constraints were also daunting—the need for water or gas injection for wells, greater supplies of electrical power, and major upgrades to refining and export facilities, such as pipelines. For this, direct foreign investment and cooperation with foreign oil firms would be necessary.

Such cooperation raised old problems in Iraq. First, Iraq had had a long and contentious history with the international oil companies (IOCs) before nationalization of oil in 1972, and a number of politicians, as well as the public, did not want to do business with them again. As the discussions of oil contracts and drafting of a hydrocarbon law progressed in the cabinet and the Council of Representatives (CoR), these criticisms surfaced. The CoR demanded transparency on contracts and "tough" terms. In April 2007, for example, Vice President Tariq al-Hashimi announced that he wanted to deal only with state-owned companies.

In general, Nuri al-Maliki and his oil minister, Husain al-Shahristani, favored "service contracts": that is, OICs would spend most or all of their investment in improving the wells and would receive only a per-barrel fee after production had reached a certain point. In contrast, the Kurds wanted more rapid development of the oil sector. They worried less about privatization and favored greater participation of foreign companies, with their expertise and technology. The Kurds argued for "production-sharing agreements" in which IOCs would "own" a share of production, which they could take in profits. Indeed, this is what the Kurds offered in the Kurdish Regional Government (KRG) as they began to conclude their own contracts. Such deals were politically difficult, if not impossible, in Baghdad.

Second, oil development required the drafting and passage of a hydrocarbon law for the entire country, which would include the terms of future contracts, who could conclude them (the KRG and/or the central government), and the distribution of the revenues.[3] Included within this issue were the now deep-seated divisions over the disposition of Kirkuk. Without such a law, foreign companies were reluctant to begin investments in Iraq on the scale necessary, whether in the north or the south, because any disputes involving the government or other companies would have no adjudication process for resolution.

In June 2007, the central government and the Kurds agreed on a revenue-sharing deal. The central government would establish a fund for oil revenues, automatically transferring 17 percent to the KRG. A hydrocarbon law also appeared close, but it failed, and by November the KRG had already gone ahead with concluding its own foreign oil contracts. By 2008, the central government also started to negotiate some smaller contracts, first with the Chinese National Petroleum Company (CNPC) to develop the Ahdab field in Wasit and then with Shell to develop natural gas in the south.

These were not major deals, but they were still criticized in the CoR for their lack of transparency and for their leniency of terms. However, the price of oil, of much more immediate importance to Iraq's well-being, was then at a high $147 a barrel (July 2008), up from $60 in 2006, giving the Iraqi budget a windfall and making the contract issue less urgent. By December, however, the price had fallen precipitously to $32 a barrel. With budgetary shortfalls looming and with a national election on the horizon in 2010, the oil issue began to be more salient.

Third, attracting foreign investment in Iraq's uncertain political environment was difficult. In February 2009 shortly after the provincial elections, Maliki's government held a meeting with major foreign oil companies in Istanbul to clarify the terms of participation in Iraq's oil industry. Iraq intended to hold two bidding auctions for Iraq's producing wells, one at the end of June and the other in December. But there was still no hydrocarbon law, and fights were ensuing behind the scenes between the Kurds and the central government over both the terms of contracts and the development of Kurdish fields. Finally, al-Shahristani made clear that the Kurdish contracts in the north were not considered legal by the central government. Companies that had bid in the north would be barred from bidding in the south. The central government went ahead with its bids, without an oil law.

In June 2009, Iraq held an open auction for a number of the southern fields. The results were poor. Despite the richness of the fields, only one major bid was publicly accepted, for the Rumaila field. It was given to BP, in partnership with the CNPC. The field was a prize, with an estimated 17 billion barrels in reserves; BP promised to boost production from 2.4 mbd to 4.[4] Eventually Exxon-Mobil and Occidental were also given contracts under this round. Although the fields were known to produce—and hence did not come with risks of exploration—there were serious downsides to investment for the OICs, including a still-uncertain security situation, no hydrocarbon law, a complete absence of labor and management skills locally, and the huge amounts of investment needed to get the wells functioning properly. But in December these and other fields were again put up for auction, on terms only slightly adjusted, and this time more companies did bid—undoubtedly because they were afraid to be left out of one of the major known global sources of oil anywhere. This time the results were much more favorable to Iraq.

The December 2009 auction was notable for its transparency; it was held on public television, although the final contracts were ironed out piecemeal afterward. This time major IOCs participated.[5] These bids let out most, though not all, of the supergiant and giant fields of the south. Despite IOC participation, most of the bids went to state-owned companies, such as those of China, Russia, Malaysia, Angola, and others, raising questions whether the fields—reportedly able to reach somewhere near 10 mbd when fully developed—would get the technology, investment, and human training of Iraqis required to move ahead on Iraq's oil development rapidly. Although the awards gave a boost to Iraqi expectations of a better future, all anticipated a long and difficult path ahead in repairing Iraq's battered oil sector, training its population on a multitude of lost skills, and raising its production and export capacity to levels competitive with its Gulf neighbors. But the first, important step had been taken in this process, and by the end of 2010 the oil companies were already at work building the structures and networks necessary to boost production.

Economic Development

Oil contracts represented a vote of confidence in Iraq's future, but much work remained to be done to improve the economy. On the positive side, the central bank had reduced inflation and higher oil prices, which peaked in July 2008, had brought in about $59 billion in 2008.[6] By 2008 the government had succeeded in eliminating fuel subsidies, which had constituted 13 percent of gross domestic product (GDP).[7] In May 2007, the Maliki government had concluded an agreement with the United Nations known as the International Compact with Iraq (ICI), designed to partner with the international community and bring Iraq into the regional and global economy. The ICI focused on public resource management, government institutions, economic reform, and investment in energy and agriculture.[8] Early in 2009, the World Bank provided an interim strategy outlining development needs and targets for Iraq for the period 2009–2011.[9] Despite ups and downs, Iraq had made some modest economic improvements by 2010.

Oil production rose from 2.09 mbd in 2007 to about 2.4 mbd in 2009 (see Table 12.1). GDP rose from $62.4 billion in 2007 to an estimated $74.7 in 2009. In the same years GDP per capita also rose from about $3,700 to $3,800 in the same years (see Table 12.2). Although much of this improvement reflected rising oil prices, the most important factor in Iraq's economy, some was due to higher oil production and other benefits of improved security.

Although macroeconomic figures do not indicate how much improvement is filtering down to the average person, there were other, tangible signs of progress as well. Real estate was booming in Baghdad, Basra, and many provincial towns by the turn of the decade. Retail and wholesale trade also picked up. Sales of secondhand cars, home appliances, TVs, and

TABLE 12.1 Crude Oil Production and Export, 2001–2009
            (millions of barrels per day)

	Production	*Export*
2001	2.45	n.a.
2002	2.03	n.a.
2003	2.2	1.7
2004	2.25	1.49
2005	2.09	1.42
2006	2.13	1.5
2007	2.09	1.67
2008	2.39	1.83
2009	2.4	1.91

Based on estimates

SOURCE: CIA, *The World Factbook,* 2003–2009.

TABLE 12.2. Growth of GDP, Population, and GDP Per Capita, 2005–2009

	1999–2002 average[a]	*2005*[b]	*2006*[b]	*2007*[b]	*2008*[b]	*2009*[b]
GDP (billions US$)	25.2	34.0	42.2	62.4	84.7	74.7
GDP Per Capita ($ at PPP)	1,000	1,800	1,900	3,700	3,200	3,800
GDP Growth Rate	–2.35	3.3%	6.2%	1.5%	7.8%	4.5%

[a]Based on author's calculations from Political Risk Services, *Iraq Country Forecast: Iraq Data Bank,* (New York, November 2009).
[b]London Economist, Economist Intelligence Unit (EIU), *Country Report Iraq* (London, December 2006, November 2007, June 2010).

SOURCES: Economist Intelligence Unit, *Country Report Iraq* (London: Economist Intelligence Unit, December 2006, November 2007, June 2010); CIA, *The World Factbook: Iraq,* 2003–2009.

electronic equipment rose. Freewheeling trade in all types of commodities took place, although it often straddled the line between legitimate and illegitimate business as merchants took advantage of low import taxes and the virtual absence of import controls.[10]

Tourism also flourished in Najaf and Karbala with an influx of pilgrims, mainly from Iran, but increasingly from Arab countries as well.

This increased local spending on hotels, housing, shopping centers, and services. Although much of the investment in this area came from Iran, Gulf Arab states, especially the United Arab Emirates (UAE), increasingly stepped in. The downside of this development, however, was that Iraq turned into an "import nation," producing few of its own goods and services. By 2009, Iraq exports totaled $40.8 billion (of which crude oil was over 90 percent), while imports (food, medicine, manufactured items, and even refined oil products) totaled $35.7 billion.[11]

Another positive achievement, with US assistance, was considerable reduction of Iraq's international debt and consequently an improved credit rating. Debt with the Paris Club creditors, resulting from the Gulf War, was rescheduled between 2004 and 2008.[12] However, problems still remained with a number of Gulf neighbors, especially Kuwait, unwilling as yet to forgive its debts or reparations. (The UAE was an exception.) By 2009, Iraq's total external debt was down to $50 billion, from an estimated $142 billion in 2004 before debt rescheduling.[13]

Another area of improvement, not only economic but also social, was a massive jump in the telecommunications sector, opening Iraq to the outside world. In 2000, there were only 2.7 telephone subscribers per 100 of the population, and these were entirely based on landlines. By 2005, this number had climbed to 9.4 and by 2008, 61.8. These latter numbers were due almost entirely to cell phones. One source put the number of cell phones in use in 2009 at 20 million.[14] Internet use also came to Iraq, but much more modestly. In 2000, Internet users were virtually nonexistent. By 2008, the number of users had risen to 1 per 100, a substantial increase, though still low by Western standards.[15]

Foreign Investment

With a return of security, there was a marked increase in foreign direct investment (FDI), especially from neighbors. By 2009, FDI reached $156 billion, a 241 percent increase over 2008.[16] Iran exported goods and services to Iraq and invested in tourist enterprises (especially those related to pilgrims in Najaf and Karbala) and in housing and hotels in Basra and elsewhere. By 2009, Iran was Iraq's largest trading partner, with bilateral trade worth $4 billion a year.[17] Iran also invested in infrastructure, especially electricity and power lines, and opened bank branches in a number of cities. But Iranian efforts also encountered a negative reaction among many Iraqis, who complained that Iranian business was smothering Iraqi industry and agriculture by flooding the market with cheap goods. The Iranian government subsidized its exports and levied import taxes on inbound goods, making it difficult for Iraqis to compete.[18]

The Turks were another neighbor with strong and increasing ties to Iraq. They invested heavily in northern Iraq—in construction, industry, and infrastructure—a development welcomed by the Kurds. Between 2003 and 2009, Turkey averaged about $5 billion in trade with Iraq, half of which went to the KRG. By 2010, Turkish companies were heavily invested in oil and energy projects in the KRG, and they operated an airline service to the KRG. But Turkish investment was not limited to the north; the Turks also expanded elsewhere in Iraq and concluded an agreement with the central government to expand the Ceyhan oil pipeline, which did not run through the KRG.

Substantial flows of money came from the wealthy Gulf states as well, especially the UAE. In 2009, the UAE became the largest outside investor in Iraq, surpassing even the United States. Between 2003 and 2009, the UAE invested $31 billion,[19] much of it in oil, gas, and real-estate projects. Other investing neighbors included Qatar, Kuwait, Lebanon, Jordan, and Syria.

Infrastructure

However, despite these promising developments, Iraq's economy still faced enormous hurdles in development and its long-term needs were daunting. Iraq's unemployment remained extremely high, electricity demand continued to exceed supply, and access to clean water and sanitation was the lowest in the region.[20] Infrastructure—especially the electricity grid—was in very bad condition owing to the long era of sanctions, wars, and destruction by insurgents. But figures show that the grid's capacity did improve over time. One source claimed that prewar electricity was able to provide Iraq with 3,958 megawatts—4 to 8 hours a day. By December 2008, it could provide 4,740 megawatts, about 14.1 hours a day, but this still left inhabitants with woeful shortages.[21] Although some of the shortage was owing to mismanagement, the main reason was growth in the economy, increased imports of household appliances, and misuse of resources.

Other infrastructure was hardly in better shape, especially water supply and oil infrastructure. World Bank figures indicated that potable water was available to only about 70 percent of Baghdad inhabitants and in some rural areas it was as low as 48 percent.[22] Just how bad the oil pipeline infrastructure was surfaced in reports circulated in October 2010, one commissioned by the US government. They indicated that Al Basra Oil Terminal's offshore lines, stretching 32 miles into the Gulf, were fifteen years past their shelf life and so corroded that they risked failing at any time. A massive oil spill would not only reduce Iraq's income and global oil supply but also have a major impact on Gulf neighbors, including clogging desalination plants in Kuwait, Saudi Arabia, and other Gulf countries that relied on them for water supply.[23]

Road, rail, and air transport improved, but not enough. Poor control over Iraq's borders was listed as one of the top concerns for those doing business in Iraq. Uncertain border conditions were the leading reason for high levels of smuggling, theft, and even piracy (especially on the Shatt al-Arab). By 2010, six commercial airports had opened in Iraq: in Baghdad, Basra, Najaf, Sulaimaniyya, Arbil, and Mosul. However, international flights were still limited and procedures were cumbersome.

Education and Health

The greatest need in Iraq's economy was for development of the country's human resources. Unfortunately, replenishing Iraq's skills would take decades at best, and initiatives yielded slow progress. The budget for education increased from 3 percent in 2006 to 5 percent in 2008. The construction of new schools also increased, but the effort was more "brick and mortar" than quality. Between 2005 and 2007, the number of children enrolled in primary schools rose 5.7 percent, from 3.5 million to 3.7 million students. Enrollment of children at the middle and high school levels climbed 27 percent during the same period, from 1.1 million to 1.4 million.[24]

Concern for quality education was reflected in a program introduced in higher education for 10,000 government scholarships to study abroad each year for five years, many in US, European, and Australian universities and institutes. But it would take time for this program to produce qualified faculty. Meanwhile, schools and universities continued to expand. Medical schools, for example, increased from seven in 2003 to twenty by the end of 2007 in the midst of a brain drain of doctors, raising questions about teaching staff. Some of these schools did not even have a medical library or proper laboratory.[25]

In 2009, the literacy rate for those over fifteen was 74 percent. These figures were low by comparison with Iraq's comparable neighbors. In 2003, Jordan had a literacy rate of almost 90 percent; Syria, 79.6 percent.[26]

Health facilities, too, had declined badly. Like all other institutions, hospitals and clinics had been badly hit by war, insurgency, and violence; the supply of doctors had declined drastically, especially from emigration. Health improvements took place, but they were painfully slow. Life expectancy had been 64 in 1990; in 2010 it was better but still only 70.5. Infant mortality was still high at 41.6 per 1,000.[27]

Industry and Agriculture

Not much progress had been made, either, in Iraq's productive sectors: industry and agriculture. Some development took place in industries such as construction materials, food processing, and production of everyday goods, but there was little talk of growth in local industries, much less revival of the larger ones, such as steel, aluminum, petrochemicals, and high-tech industry. One reason was their lack of competitiveness, as the flood of imports in manufactured goods indicated. Another was the shortage of power generation. Nor had much foreign investment gone into this sector. A few examples stood out, mainly as exceptions—a small steel mill to produce 500,000 tons a year in Sulaimaniyya and date and cement factories in Najaf. Virtually all of these were aimed at the local market. One authority concluded that the "new Iraq" had failed to produce a private sector and that its economy was still functioning as it always had—with the government existing on oil revenues and putting its citizens on the payroll.[28]

The agriculture sector was targeted for investment, but its production had been hard hit by several years of draught, as well as neglect. By 2010, agriculture was producing only 8.4 percent of Iraq's GDP and employing about 21 percent of its workforce. In 2008, Iraq imported 74 percent of its wheat from abroad.[29]

In addition to neglect, the agriculture sector faced a serious, long-term problem, not of Iraq's making, that had greatly reduced water supply. Iraq depends on irrigation from the Tigris and Euphrates, but as the downstream user of these rivers, it is the last to receive the supply. In recent decades, dams on the headwaters of both rivers in Turkey, as well as the Euphrates in Syria, had drastically reduced the flow. Iraq estimated its water needs would grow by 50 percent by 2015 but supply would continue to drop as more dams were built.[30] Drought and lack of irrigation had turned fields around Amara in the south into dry beds. Lack of water also affected the supply of hydroelectric power.

In addition, Iraq now faced a new problem—salination in the Shatt al-Arab. This was the result mainly of the diversion of rivers in Iran—mainly the Karun, which flows into the Shatt al-Arab. According to the minister of water resources, the Karun had completely dried up where it flowed into the Shatt.[31] The result was a backflow of seawater into the Shatt, resulting in a shortage of drinking water in Basra as well as salinization of the soil. According to local reports, the Faw district had seawater and farmers had stopped irrigating crops or breeding cattle.[32]

Iraq, according to the same minister, had almost 75,000 miles of canals, which would take years to clear and restore. In addition, more modern methods of irrigation needed to be introduced to save and manage water resources. Iraq was also trying to restore the southern marshlands and the wetlands habitat (intentionally dried up by Saddam to curtail dissent in the area) and with it the fishing industry. Increased aridity in southern Iraq also created creeping desertification of once arable land and an increase of sandstorms.

Labor Force

The main problem in the economy, however, was less infrastructure than human resources. Insufficient income flows went into improvements in living standards and the economic well-being of the populace. As a result, by 2011 Iraq still had a large impoverished population, lack of basic services, and few employment opportunities for a growing youth cohort. Unemployment was very high. Officially, it was reported at 15 percent, but unofficially it was at least at 30 percent.[33] Some estimates of underemployment put it as high as 60 percent. Most jobs were in the military, security-related services, and government.

An estimate of the labor-force distribution in 2010 showed about 21 percent in agriculture, 18 percent in industry, and almost 60 percent in services.[34] In 2006, 31 percent of the labor force was working for the public sector, according to the Iraqi Ministry of Planning, and this was expected to climb to 35 percent by 2008, only about 5 percent short of Saddam's era.[35] Corruption and government inefficiency, as well as traditional ideologies wedded to a command economy, made it difficult to open up the economy to the private sector and domestic and global enterprise. A World Bank Report on "Doing Business in 2011" ranked Iraq 166 out of 183 countries as a place to do business.[36]

These indications showed that by 2010, although the Iraqi economy had begun to revive, its difficulties were still severe. They included corruption—ranked as a high risk—a government primarily absorbed with politics rather than improvement of standards of living, high unemployment, and very low technological and management skills. Although repair of physical damage (infrastructure) was necessary, the real damage to Iraq of the events since 2003 had been to its human resources.

Demographic Change

By 2007, war, occupation, and violence from insurgencies had inflicted considerable population losses on Iraq. Figures on these losses are controversial and somewhat uncertain. A rough estimate of civilian deaths through 2010 would total at least 100,000 and possibly twice as much, with wounded probably double those killed.[37] In October 2009, Iraq's Ministry of Human rights said 86,690 people were killed in the four-year period 2004–2008, with 147,190 wounded. A London-based group, Iraq Body Count, put casualties at 93,500 by October 2009, although most think deaths were higher because thousands were still missing or buried in the chaos of war.[38]

Even more significant was the unprecedented population shift resulting from the sectarian cleansing of 2006 and 2007, including both exodus of refugees from the country (refugees) and internally displaced persons (IDPs). At the end of 2008, the United Nations High Commissioner for Refugees (UNHCR) put the number of Iraqi refugees in neighboring countries (mainly Syria and Jordan) at 1.7 to 2.3 million. According to the International Organization for Migration, the number of people displaced internally from February 2006 until mid-2008 totaled 1.6 million (5.5 percent of the population).[39] By 2010, however, these figures had been reduced. Some of the displaced had returned, and international organizations and specialists also revised earlier estimates downward.[40] Whatever the actual total remaining, the numbers were huge.

Impact of the Demographic Upheaval

The social impact of this demographic upheaval was already visible, especially in the capital. Baghdad, Iraq's largest and most cosmopolitan city, had been hollowed out and rearranged. In both Baghdad and neighboring Diyala, mixed population areas, although not totally eliminated, had been greatly reduced. Baghdad had once been a city in which mixed marriages and residential patterns, combined with habits of working with a variety of ethnic, religious, and social groups, had been most prevalent. These habits were now greatly weakened. The population shift also affected the ethnic and sectarian balance in the country and created serious segmentation in living patterns. Even though the Kurdish areas, especially in Kirkuk and the disputed territories, had gone through ethnic displacement since 2003, it was the Sunni Arab population that bore the brunt of the sectarian war. The majority of refugees, especially in Syria and Jordan, were Sunni. According to UNHCR, some 58 percent of those in Syria and 59 percent of those in Jordan were Sunni; Shi'a, about 20 and 27 percent.[41] (Christians made up most of the remainder.) The extent to which this exodus affected the overall Sunni-Shi'i balance in the country would not be clear for some time, but it left Baghdad a much more Shi'i city than it had been.

Moreover, internal displacement also segmented the rest of Iraq, both in ethnic and sectarian terms. Some 98 percent of Shi'a who fled Baghdad went to Shi'i areas of the south, while Sunnis often went to Anbar or Salah al-Din or, in some cases, Kurdistan. Even within Baghdad, greater segmentation took place. After 2007, the situation slowly improved, as refugees and IDPs trickled back to their quarters and commerce revived. Nonetheless, the new reality of Baghdad, even after some of the walls built by the "surge" were dismantled, was a far more divided city, in which separate neighborhoods of like religious background dominated life and business. By 2011, interaction between segmented quarters was still limited. One professional claimed that if he were to start a business in Baghdad, he would think not of the city as a whole, but of his neighborhood, seeking engineers, partners, and labor only from his quarter. Another businessman admitted that, even though people from Kadamain and Adamiyya could visit each other, they could not successfully operate a business in the other quarter.[42]

Minorities, especially Christians, were also disproportionately affected by the violence. Christians were a high percentage of those emigrating. Some 14–15 percent of those in Syria and 12–13 percent of those in Jordan were Christian. Christians, who had once totaled 800,000–1.2 million (about 3 percent) of the population, may have been reduced to about 500,000–700,000. They generally fled from mixed areas in the center of Iraq to religious enclaves in the north—mainly Mosul and the Ninawa plain. In the wake of several spectacular attacks on churches and clergy, many feared the ultimate disappearance of the community, much like that of the Jews earlier.[43] The result contributed to an increased Islamization of society and reduced diversity. The dispersion also led to demands by some Christians for a distinct region on the Ninawa plain where Christians and other non-Arab or Kurdish minorities would predominate to protect the identity and presence of the Christians. Yazidis and Sabians were also affected and migrated, mainly to Syria and Turkey. All of these developments contributed to ethnic and sectarian segmentation and sharpened communal identity.

The population shift also had a marked impact on social structure. In general, it was Iraq's upper and middle classes that departed Baghdad and Iraq, leaving the poorer and relatively unskilled behind. Some analysis indicated that the "sectarian strife" might have been a "class struggle" as well. In the Baghdad quarter of Baya', for example, east Baya' was a mixed area of Sunni and Shi'i inhabitants, but, more importantly, it was middle class and professional. The "other side of the town" was inhabited mainly by Shi'a who were uneducated laborers poorly integrated into society and often prone to fights, drinking, and unruly behavior. The struggle here was less about religion than class and lifestyle. The epitome of this "class" difference was Sadr City, filled with earlier migrants from the Shi'i south only partially integrated into urban life and still following a more rural and traditional lifestyle. The newer, upscale areas of Baghdad across the river, like the university quarter and Mansur, with its well-to-do college graduates (whether Shi'a or Sunni) living in well-appointed villas, had always feared an onslaught from this area in times of crisis. In effect, this is what happened during the "sectarian" violence.

Baghdad, the center of Iraq's political and cultural life, was now more heavily weighted toward the poor and lower middle class than toward an educated middle class. This shift in the class structure helps explain the ease of recruiting into militias, like the Mahdi Army, as well as the resurgence of more traditional mores, religious rituals, and social conservatism, which became a feature of social life. These changes may also have shifted the population further in the direction of youth as well, rather than the experienced older generation. Both of these trends affected political and intellectual life. Rapid and disruptive social change threw Iraqi society back on traditional social mechanisms and institutions for survival—family and religion.

The Brain Drain

Among the most serious impacts of the demographic shift was the massive brain drain it caused. Although Iraq had been undergoing a successive bleeding of its educated middle class for years, the huge outpouring of doctors, professors, lawyers, engineers, scientists, writers, artists, and bureaucrats, especially after 2006, may have crippled the educated class.[44] Indeed, members of this class were personally targeted by extremists. In August 2009, the *Brussels Tribunal,* which tracks these matters, listed 431 assassinated Iraqi academics, the vast majority of them Ph.Ds. Some 247 Iraqi media professionals had been murdered by mid-2007. The Iraqi Lawyers Association claimed that 210 lawyers and judges had been killed. The Iraqi Red Crescent believed that about 50 percent of Iraq's doctors and 70 percent of medical specialists left in the exodus.[45]

A brain drain on this scale affected every aspect of Iraqi society. Government institutions, bereft of an educated and experienced civil service below the very top levels (and even at top levels), were crippled in their ability to operate and deliver much-needed services. Economic development, including in the oil industry, advanced only slowly in the absence of needed technical skills. Writers, artists, journalists, scholars, and others responsible for shaping Iraq's intellectual and cultural future, and for which Iraq had been famous, also fled. Education at every level, from kindergarten to the university, suffered from the scarcity of qualified teachers. Two years after the end of Saddam Husain's regime, a report by the United Nations on Iraq's higher education institutions claimed that teaching staff was underqualified—33 percent held only bachelor's degrees, 30 percent had master's degrees, and only 28 percent had received doctorates.[46] The dean of an engineering school in one of the universities claimed that thermodynamics, an essential subject, was no longer taught because of lack of professors. Nor was surveying, necessary for civil engineering, undertaken because sending students on field trips was too risky.[47] This situation had improved only marginally by 2011. The impact of the brain drain could still be seen in every sector of Iraq's life—health, education, economic development, the bureaucracy, and the efforts to achieve a more democratic political structure.

Youth

In some respects, the disruption was hardest on the younger generation. Many came to maturity under the restrictive and limited regime of the sanctions, which undercut their education and job opportunities. The violence of the post-Saddam period and the enormous demographic displacement of the sectarian war disrupted their education. UNICEF estimated, for example, that in 2007 as many as 250,000 displaced children of primary school age had had their education interrupted.[48] A measure of normalcy returned to education after 2008, but the effects on young people would likely be more lasting.

Health and poverty also affected children at a higher rate. Most important was the impact of trauma. An Iraq mental health survey in 2007 estimated that almost one in five Iraqis had some mental illness. Young adults were no exception. A survey of school children in Mosul found that almost four of every ten children under sixteen had a mental disorder.[49]

Members of the younger generation also had to overcome a background of limited exposure to the outside world for most of their lives. Nevertheless, young people in Iraq, as elsewhere, appeared to be resilient, especially those with access to higher education. They appeared to be emerging with a more practical agenda than their elders, interested in bettering their lives, getting good jobs, and willing to work anywhere, including outside Iraq, to do so. However, there was also considerable frustration.[50] One of the possible effects of this tension may be a new brain drain if Iraq fails to provide enough opportunities at home. For those with less education and opportunity, such frustration could mean unrest and instability.

Intellectual and Cultural Change

In the post-2007 period, intellectual and cultural trends already underway came into focus more clearly. These were unquestionably informed by political events and the outcome of recent struggles and upheavals. Despite the multiplicity of voices that came with greater freedom of expression, several trends stood out.

Identity

One trend was a search for a common Iraqi identity, intensified by the profound shift in power since 2003, and especially 2007, among Iraq's ethnic and sectarian communities. This search was likely to continue for some time, and its outcome would determine Iraq's national cohesion—even its continued existence as a state. The chief divide was now between the Kurds, emphasizing ethnicity and the development of a separate and distinct "national" identity, and the Arab Iraqis (and some Turkmen and Christians), wanting to keep Iraq together but also driven by their own differences, especially sectarian ones. The Kurds increasingly engaged in their own, quite separate discourse—in their press and media, in their literature, and in their education system (in Kurdish)—although they also sustained another discourse with Arab Iraq.

Among the Arab population, the Shi'i-Sunni divide was less pronounced and was often folded into the public discourse as a difference between Sunni "ex-Ba'thists," who were often more secular in orientation and wanted a stronger state in which they played a larger role, and more Islamist Shi'a, who wanted to infuse Iraq with a more Shi'i-oriented Islamic orientation and who still feared a strong state, especially one that could slip from their grasp. But since 2007 the idea of an Iraqi identity that would reduce—if not eliminate—sectarian and other identities and unite Iraq clearly gained ground in Arab areas of Iraq, sharpening the differences with the Kurds.

Revival of Religion

Another trend was a revival of religion as many attempted to redefine Iraq as an Islamic, rather than a secular, nationalist, state. This tendency was more prevalent in Arab, and Shi'i, parts of Iraq than in the north, but religiosity increased in Kurdish areas as well. The trend could be seen in the revival of Shi'i rituals such as the celebration of Ashura (the ritual to commemorate Imam Husain's death), *ziyaras* (visits) to the shrines of the Shi'i imams, and pilgrimages to the holy cities. It could also be seen in the social sphere; here traditional Islamic practices increased, particularly pressures to enforce dress codes and other forms of modest behavior between the sexes. Noticeable, too, were disagreements between secularists and Islamists over the degree to which music, art, dance, theater, and other performing and visual arts should be encouraged and supported. This was evident even at the popular level. When Sadrist control in Sadr City was curbed, for example, it had a marked effect on revival of dancing and music among the populace on occasions such as weddings, indicating a strong undercurrent of interest in these activities.

The impact of this social conservatism on the status of women was particularly evident. The constitution had mandated a 25 percent quota for women in parliament to open doors to their participation, but in reality many women who were intruded onto political tickets were supporters of conservative Islamic positions on women's roles. By 2011, few women had reached a cabinet position, even though cabinets had increased in size. Social conservatism also worked against women's equal participation in social life, even in education. According to the Ministry of Education, the ratio of girls to boys attending schools in the south dropped from two to three before 2003 to one in four after.[51] Most striking, however, was the return to tribal customs, embedded in "honor killings" for immoral behavior, as older social norms surfaced. The United Nations Assistance Mission for Iraq expressed concerns over the rise in incidence of honor crimes in Kurdish areas and noted that 255 women had been killed in these circumstances in the first six months of 2007 alone.[52] The same was true in the south.

Freedom of Expression

But these more traditional forces ran up against countertrends, reflecting the influence of more secular, liberal ideals often expressed in a desire for democracy and more freedom of expression, inevitably leading to more diversity. This could be seen most clearly in the new freedoms given to the press and media and to public expression of differing views, as well as to the inevitable spread of information via the Internet tying Iraq to the outside world. By 2011, the number of newspapers, journals, and other publications had mushroomed; the same was true for TV, radio, and, of course, Internet blogs. By the end of 2010, Iraq may have been producing around 200 print publications of various kinds, including government publications, independent commercial publications, and those owned by parties, Islamic organizations, and others. TV channels also proliferated; Iraq may have had over 100 satellite channels, though most transmitted from outside Iraq. Foreign channels such as the BBC and the UAE's MBC operated there as well, but al-Jazeera's office was closed down in August 2004 because of negative reporting and activities supportive of al-Qa'ida in Iraq.

These freedoms brought mixed results. Many publications were staunchly partisan and probably contributed to ongoing violence. But Iraq's freedom and diversity of expression—as well as unvarnished criticism of government actions—were new and virtually unprecedented in the Arab world. Commentators and TV personalities found imaginative ways to shed light on their societies and to achieve their aims. One example was a TV show called *Patron of the Oppressed*, appearing on a channel owned by the Sunni Iraqi Islamic Party. Its host, a woman, fielded telephone calls from Iraqis whose relatives had vanished either as victims of sectarian killings or as prisoners in Iraq's often brutal and inefficient justice system. Each broadcast offered an implicit critique of the Shi'i-led government.[53] Shi'i publications were equally vocal in their disapproval of some Sunni politicians. In the KRG, the publications of the new opposition party, Goran, openly accused the KRG government— both Mas'ud Barzani and Jalal Talabani—of outright corruption, misuse of public funds, and other illegal actions.

However, media freedom came with a price. Life for journalists, TV personalities, and newspaper editors was hazardous, and they faced increasing repression from government through various means, including intimidation and violence. Nevertheless, despite this discrepancy between word and deed, public advocacy of democracy and human rights remained a strong theme in public discourse in the media and in schools. Iraq now had a ministry of human rights, which issued reports on abuses, and thousands of human rights organizations and nongovernmental organizations, including branches of well-known groups such as Amnesty International and Human Rights Watch. The constitution and the numerous rights enumerated in it were often cited as a distinguishing feature of the "new Iraq."

Education

These intellectual trends and shifts in the new Iraq could best be seen in the education system. In 2010, new social studies and history textbooks were published, replacing those of the Saddam era in public schools from elementary through high school in Iraq, south of Kurdish-controlled areas. These books reflected what Iraq's new leaders wanted the next generation of Iraqis to learn and the direction in which they wanted Iraq to go.[54] Several features stood out in these texts. One was the dominance of Islamic subjects and Islamic history, practices, and ideas as the foundation for building character and laying the basis for the new state. Islam or Islamic history was taught in all three years of intermediate schools and in two years of high school. The intermediate-level texts drew on *hadiths* (sayings of the Prophet), which were explained and related to everyday practices and emphasized values such as unity among Muslims, responsibilities (such as caring for the poor), the value that Islam placed on work, and an obligation to pay taxes. Stories and details about the Prophet's life, his message, and the establishment of the early Islamic state and society were also emphasized. Higher-level texts featured Islamic history.

In addition, students were given courses on "civics," with an emphasis on freedom, democracy, and various human rights. The new Iraqi constitution was explained clearly and simply, highlighting Iraq's pluralism with respect to nationalities, religions, and sects. A good statement on the rights of citizens included coverage of equality of opportunity and equal rights for men and women, as well as freedoms guaranteed by the constitution. The federal system was discussed, with considerable emphasis placed on local government in provinces and localities.

Equally noteworthy was what was missing from the texts. There was little discussion of the Kurds or the KRG government, although the unity of Iraq was urged. In fact, the new texts were a tacit recognition of separate Kurdish social studies and history texts in the KRG. Introduced in the 1990s, these texts had long emphasized Kurdish language, history, and culture. By 2011, these texts had been introduced into Kirkuk and other disputed territories for the Kurdish-speaking population. Another missing element was any attempt to integrate the essentially secular, democratic elements of the new constitutional order with the Islamic material taught alongside it. Most striking was the omission of any discussion of current Iraqi society, its deep and manifest problems, or its prospects for the future.

Likewise, the history books designed for the middle and upper grades taught very little about the modern Iraqi state from its founding in 1920 through 1958 and absolutely nothing about the Ba'th period from 1968 to 2003, the occupation, or the establishment of a new regime in Iraq since then. These subjects were simply too controversial and the difficulty of reconciling disparate points of view too great. When Iraqi history was dealt with, it was woven into a story of the Arab world as a whole, in which the main theme was the Arab struggle against European imperialism, which brought divisions and oppressive governments to the Arab world. For example, students were given a sequence at the intermediate level on Arab Islamic history from the rise of Islam to the fall of the Abbasid Empire to the Mongols in the thirteenth century, followed by modern Arab history from the Mongol period to the contemporary Arab world. The main focus of the second volume was the post–World War I period: the division of the Arab world into its current countries, Zionism and the Palestine problem, and various Arab efforts to gain independence. A final chapter was devoted to the founding of the Iraqi state by the British and successive attempts to throw off foreign rule, culminating with the Free Officers revolt in 1958, which brought independence and a new republic. This is where the story ended.

Students were taught modern European history, including the French and American revolutions, the industrial revolution, and the new imperialist system rising from European economic competition. Woodrow Wilson's Fourteen Points, the League of Nations, and international concern for human rights were also developed. Another high school text detailed the history of the Arab world in modern times, focusing on the history of each Arab country as part of an "Arab nation," the reawakening of Arab thought, and the struggle against European imperialism. Once again,

Iraq was fit into this pattern—briefly—with mention of various revolts against foreign domination, specifically 1920, 1941, 1948, 1952, 1956, and finally, successfully, 1958. The book ended with the 1967 war.

Iraq's education system clearly had improved on Saddam era texts and brought new ideas of democracy and human rights. But they also reflected the country's difficulties in coming to terms with its new identity or its current situation as well as its fear of opening wounds that had only recently begun to heal.

The Future of Iraq

Eight years after the occupation, the creation of the new Iraq is still a work in progress. The country's future direction remains uncertain, but Iraq has reached a modicum of stability and an uneasy equilibrium among its domestic forces, while its political shape is emerging more clearly. New, more democratic forms of governance have been introduced, along with more openness to the outside world, both of which promise a better future. But these forces of change continue to contend with traditional patterns and habits of governance—authoritarianism, patrimonialism, and patronage-based relations—that are more difficult to change. Even more important are the effects of the upheaval and conflict brought by the occupation, which need to be overcome to make progress sustainable.

In this transition, Iraq's new leaders face four interrelated challenges. The first is the consolidation of Iraq's national cohesion based on a greater degree of consensus among its various communities than has prevailed in the past. The sectarian strife that erupted in Baghdad and its environs in 2006–2007 and resulted in displacement and shifts in population left deep divisions between Shi'a and Sunnis. Gradually, these sectarian rifts are being reduced as oppositionist Sunnis and Sadrists join the political process, but they are still sharp. Relations between the Kurdish population, now ensconced in a recognized region in the north, and the rest of Iraq—mainly Arab—remain divisive, making the solution of economic and political problems more difficult. How Iraqis handle this issue will determine whether the nation-state will survive and move forward or whether a more decentralized polity—even a collapse of the state—will ensue.

A second challenge is the development of Iraq's economic resources and the repair of its torn social fabric. Iraq's favorable resource base, including oil and human resources, is well known, but economic development requires more attention than recent turbulent events have allowed. The erosion of these resources by wars, sanctions under Saddam, and then occupation, looting, and civil strife has been devastating. However, by 2007 the tide had begun to turn. Foreign investment and oil contracts as well as trade and local business began to revive, indicating a turn in the economic situation, which could provide a path to long-term improvement. Nevertheless, full-scale oil development was still hampered by disputes between the central government and the KRG.

Repairing the social fabric caused by the violence and social disruption since 2003 will be harder. Chief among these tasks will be the education of a new generation of Iraqis and the replacement of the expertise that has left Iraq since the occupation. The departure of the educated middle class has not only set back Iraq's expertise but also redefined its social structure and cultural orientation. Poorer, less-well-educated elements of the population, mainly concentrated among the youth, now form a much larger percentage of the population, while more traditional and conservative customs have revived, including Islamic norms and kinship relations, some of which may slow the modernization process.

Third, and most critical, is the challenge of governance. Here the record of the new regime has been mixed. It has made major improvements over Saddam's era of oppression, providing Iraq with a new, more democratic framework. It has a new constitution (albeit flawed) and a political leadership that includes all segments of the population, and it has conducted two free and fair elections for a national parliament, all with "unpredictable outcomes." Iraq also has more freedom of expression and access to the outside world. But these new advances have brought their own problems—a dysfunctional government in which it is difficult to make decisions, a weak and fractious political landscape, and an obsession by politicians with getting and keeping power at the expense of broader economic and social development. In the ensuing struggle for power, more traditional patterns of government have emerged—reliance on kin and clan, restoration of the patronage system and *wasta*, with their inevitable corruption. Genuine political parties based on an alignment of interest are still in an initial stage.

The last challenge for Iraq is dealing with foreign influence and control and Iraq's traditional desire for independence. One such problem—the occupation—is well on its way to closure. By the end of 2011, the withdrawal of all US forces will be completed, although some military "presence," however small, may continue under agreement with Iraq, and the US mission to equip and train Iraqi forces is likely to remain. Civilian influence is also likely to remain through support for various endeavors in education, health, and civil society. This reduced position, however, will now be matched by increased influence from regional competitors, especially Iran, but also Turkey and Arab neighbors, such as Syria and Saudi Arabia. Some of this regional influence may be negative. States like Saudi Arabia and Syria have withheld cooperation or, worse, stirred local instability. Saudis, in particular, fear Iraq's ties with Iran. Iraq, now a weak state, will have to develop more domestic cohesion to be able to speak with one voice and to exercise a more significant regional role.

The most important ingredients for making progress in overcoming these challenges will be time and a more benign external environment that allows the country and its leadership to sort through Iraq's multiple problems and challenges. Otherwise, Iraq could slip back into more of the disruption and discontinuity that have been the chief feature of the post-Saddam era and, indeed, much of Iraq's modern history.

APPENDIX

TABLE A.1 Distribution of Iraq's Population by Region, 1977–2002 (percentages)

	1977	1987	2002
Central Governorates			
Total	47.5	48.8	50.8
Baghdad	26.5	23.5	32
Ninawa, Salah al-Din, Anbar, Diyala	21	24.4	18.8
Southern Governorates			
Total	35.8	36	31.8
Basra	8.4	5.3	8.1
Babil, Wasit, Karbala, Najaf, Qadisiyya, Maysan, Muthanna	27.4	30.7	23.7
Northern Governorates			
Total	16.5	16	17.4
Ta'mim	4.1	3.7	3.9
Dahuk, Arbil, Sulaimaniyya	12.4	12.3	13.5

SOURCES: Iraq, Ministry of Planning, *AAS 1978*, p. 26; *AAS 1992*, p. 43; Economic Intelligence Unit, *Iraq, 2002–2003*, Country Profile (London: Economist Intelligence Unit, 2003), p. 18.

TABLE A.2 Ethnic and Sectarian Background of Political Leaders, 1948–2006

	Arab Sunnis	*Arab Shi'a*	*Kurd/ Turkmen*	*Other*[a] *Unknown*	*Total*
Old Regime **1948–1958**					
Upper level[b]	24 (61%)	8 (21%)	6 (15%)	1 (3%)	39
Lower level[c]	17 (31%)	23 (43%)	12 (22%)	2 (4%)	54
Both levels	41 (44%)	31 (33%)	18 (19%)	3 (3%)	93
Military Regimes **1958–1968**					
Upper level[d]	30 (79%)	6 (16%)	2 (5%)	—	38
Lower level[c]	57 (46%)	43 (35%)	16 (13%)	8 (6%)	124
Both levels	87 (54%)	49 (30%)	18 (11%)	8 (5%)	162
The Ba'th Regime **1977–1978**					
Upper level[e]	10 (48%)	6 (29%)	—	5 (24%)	21
Lower level[f]	13 (52%)	4 (16%)	6 (24%)	2 (8%)	25
Both levels	23 (57%)	10 (22%)	6 (13%)	7 (15%)	46
1986–1987					
Upper level	9 (53%)	6 (35%)	1 (6%)	1 (6%)	17
Lower level	8 (38%)	4 (19%)	6 (29%)	3 (14%)	21
Both levels	17 (45%)	10 (26%)	7 (18%)	4 (11%)	38
1998					
Upper level	11 (61%)	5 (28%)	1 (6%)	1 (6%)	18
Lower level	7 (26%)	8 (30%)	3 (11%)	9 (33%)	27
Both levels	18 (40%)	13 (29%)	4 (9%)	10 (22%)	45
2006					
Upper level[g]	4 (33%)	5 (42%)	3 (25%)	—	12
Lower level[h]	6 (19%)	16 (51%)	5 (16%)	4 (13%)	31
Both levels	10 (23%)	21 (49%)	8 (19%)	4 (9%)	43

[a] Includes Christians.

[b] Includes the regent, prime ministers, deputy prime ministers, and the ministers of interior, defense, finance, and foreign affairs.

[c] Includes all other ministers.

[d] Includes the president in place of the regent.

[e] Includes the RCC and the Regional Command of the Party (RL).

[f] All ministers not on the RCC and the RL.

[g] Includes president; vice presidents; prime minister; deputy prime ministers; ministers of interior, defense, finance, foreign affairs, and oil; and chairman of the CoR.

[h] Includes all other ministers.

SOURCES: Phebe Marr, "Iraq's Leadership Dilemma," *Middle East Journal* 24 (1970): 288; Amatzia Baram, "The Ruling Political Elite in Ba'thi Iraq, 1968-1986," *IJMES* 21 (1989): appendix 1; unpublished data collected by the author.

TABLE A.3 Employment of the Population by Economic Sector, 1967–1987 (in thousands)

	1967		1977		1987	
	No.	*%*	*No.*	*%*	*No.*	*%*
Agriculture	11,774	53.5	9,438	30.1	4,930	13.0
Mining	145	0.7	368	1.2	451	1.2
Manufacturing	1,400	6.4	2,843	9.1	2,669	7.0
Electricity, water, gas	126	0.6	231	0.7	362	0.96
Construction	591	2.5	3,216	10.3	3,412	9.0
Trade*	1,350	6.1	2,241	7.2	2,156	5.7
Transportation/ Communication	1,370	6.2	1,778	5.7	2,242	5.9
Services**	2,850	13.0	9,890	31.6	19,881	53.0
Other	2,400	11.0	1,329	4.2	1,678	4.4
Total	22,006		32,157		37,720	

*Includes restaurants and hotels.
**Includes finance, banking, and insurance.

SOURCES: Iraq, Ministry of Planning, *AAS 1973,* p. 358; *AAS 1978,* pp. 38–39; Europa Publications, *The Middle East and North Africa,* 1996 (London), p. 516.

TABLE A.4 Growth of Education, 1958–1994

	Number of Schools	Students	Teachers
Primary Schools			
1958	n.a.	416,000	n.a.
1973	4,594	1,297,756	54,979
1980	11,280	2,612,332	93,917
1985	8,127	2,812,516	118,492
1990	8,917	3,328,212	134,081
1994	n.a.	3,251,000	n.a.
Secondary Schools			
1958	n.a.	51,500	n.a.
1973	904	601,895	14,338
1980	1,891	950,142	28,453
1985	2,238	1,031,560	35,051
1990	2,719	1,023,710	44,772
1994	n.a.	1,103,000	n.a.
Universities and Scientific Institutes			
1958	3	5,679	n.a.
1973	7	49,194	1,721
1980	n.a.	96,301	6,515
1985	n.a.	136,688	7,616
1990	11	175,000	10,592
1994	n.a.	203,000	n.a.

SOURCES: Iraq, Ministry of Planning, *Statistical Abstract on Education, 1958* (Baghdad: Government Press, 1959), pp. 6, 9, 14–16, 20, 21, 26; Iraq, Ministry of Planning, *AAS 1973*, pp. 508–510, 519–521, 528, 531, 545; *AAS 1983*, pp. 210, 214, 228, 231; *AAS 1986*, pp. 208, 212, 226, 229; *AAS 1992*, pp. 290, 294, 310; Iraqi Economists Association, *Human Development Report 1995* (Baghdad, 1995), p. 40.

TABLE A.5 Comparative Distribution of Landholdings, 1958 and 1973

Size of Holdings (in dunams)	Percentage of Total Holdings	Percentage of Total Area
1958		
Landless	n.a.	n.a.
Small holders (under 1 to 50)	73	6.3
Medium holders (50–500)	24.2	24.4
Large holders (500–2,000)	1.9	14.2
Very large holders (2,000 and over)	1	55.14
1973		
Landless	8.8	0
Small holders (under 1 to 40)	62.1	23
Medium holders (40–500)	28.6	59
Large holders (500–2,000)	.37	8.1
Very large holders (2,000 and over)	.08	10

SOURCES: Adapted from Hanna Batatu, *The Old Social Classes and Revolutionary Movements of Iraq* (Princeton, NJ: Princeton University Press, 1978), p. 54; Republic of Iraq, Ministry of Planning, *AAS 1973* (Baghdad: Central Statistical Organization, n.d.), p. 71.

TABLE A.6 Elections 2005–2010: Seats Won in the Council of Representatives

List / Party	January 2005 Seats	%	December 2005 Seats	%	March 2010 Seats	%
Shi'i Islamist Groups	*145*	*52.73*	*130*	*47.27*	*159*	*48.92*
United Iraqi Alliance/ Iraqi National Alliance	140	50.91	128	46.55	70	21.54
State of Law	—		—		89	27.38
Independent Cadres (Sadrist)	3	1.009	—		—	
Upholders of the Message (Sadrist)	—		2	0.73	—	
Islamic Action, General Command	2	0.73	—		—	
Kurdish Groups	*77*	*28.00*	*58*	*21.09*	*57*	*17.54*
Kurdistan Alliance (KA)	75	27.27	53	19.27	43	13.23
Kurdish Islamic Union	*(with KA)*		5	1.82	4	1.23
Islamic Group of Kurdistan	2	0.73	*(with KA)*		2	0.62
Movement for Change (Goran)	—		—		8	2.46
Nonsectarian Groups	*43*	*15.64*	*25*	*9.09*	*91*	*28.00*
Iraqi National List (Iraqiyya)	40	14.55	25	9.09	91	28.00
People's Unity (Communist)	2	0.73	*(with Iraqiyya)*		*(with Iraqiyya)*	
National Democratic Alliance (Chadirchi)	1	0.36	—		—	
Sunni Groups	*6*	*2.18*	*59*	*21.45*	*10*	*3.08*
Iraqi Accord Front (Tawafuq)	—		44	16.00	6	1.85
The Iraqis (Ghazi al-Yawar)	5	1.82	*(with Iraqiyya)*		*(with Iraqiyya)*	
Iraqi Front for National Dialogue (Mutlak)	—		11	4.00	*(with Iraqiyya)*	
Unity of Iraq Alliance (Bulani, Abu Risha)	—		—		4	1.23
Reconciliation and Liberation Bloc (Juburi)	1	0.36	3	1.09		
Mithal al-Alusi List	—		1	0.36	—	
Minority Interest Groups	*4*	*1.45*	*3*	*1.09*	*8*	*2.46*
Iraqi Turkman Front	3	1.09	1	0.36	*(with Iraqiyya)*	
Mesopotamia List (Christian)	1	0.36	1	0.36	—	
Yazidi Movement for Reform & Progress	—		1	0.36	—	
Assorted Minorities					8	2.46
Total Seats	275	100.00	275	100.00	326	100.00

SOURCE: Independent Election Commission of Iraq (IECI), 2005; Independent High Electoral Commission (IHEC), 2010.

NOTES

Chapter 1: The Land and People of Modern Iraq

1. Georges Roux, *Ancient Iraq* (London: Allen and Unwin, 1964), pp. 302–305.

2. Abd al-'Aziz al-Duri, "Baghdad," in *Encyclopedia of Islam* (Leiden, The Netherlands: E. J. Brill, 1960), p. 925.

3. Yitzhak Nakash, *The Shi'is of Iraq* (Princeton, NJ: Princeton University Press, 1966), pp. 15–16; Pierre-Jean Luizard, *La Formation de l'Irak Contemporain* (The Formation of Contemporary Iraq) (Paris: Édition de Centre National de la Recherche Scientifique, 1991), pp. 136–138, 145, 183–185, 189.

4. M. S. Hasan, "Growth and Structure of Iraq's Population, 1867–1947," in *The Economic History of the Middle East, 1800–1914*, ed. Charles Issawi (Chicago: University of Chicago Press, 1966), pp. 155–157.

5. For convenience, the term *Iraq* will be used throughout the book to designate the territory constituting the modern state, even in periods prior to the twentieth century, when the state did not exist as such. Before 1920 parts of the country were known by various names. The most common was Mesopotamia, which in ancient times included the two river valleys. The early Muslim Arabs called the southern delta lands al-Iraq and the northern portion the Jazira (island). By the twentieth century, Europeans were again using the term *Mesopotamia* in its ancient sense as the lands between the two rivers. The country was named Iraq only when it became a state within its present borders in the twentieth century. On the controversy over what to call Iraq, see Alastair Northredge, "al-Iraq al-Arabi," and Reidar Visser, "Introduction," in *An Iraq of Its Regions*, ed. Reidar Visser and Gareth Stansfield (New York: Columbia University Press, 2008).

6. Encyclopaedia Britannica, "Iraq," *2011 Book of the Year* (Chicago: Encyclopaedia Britannica, 2011), p. 413.

7. Because of the dispute between Iran and the Arab countries over the name of the Persian/Arabian Gulf, it will be referred to throughout this work as the Gulf.

8. U.S. Energy Information Administration, "Country Analysis Briefs Header: Iraq," September 2010, www.eia.doe.gov/cabs/iraq/full.html.

9. For a discussion of the historical dimension of this identity issue, see Phebe Marr, "One Iraq or Many? What Has Happened to Iraqi Identity?" in *Iraq Between Occupations: Perspectives from 1920 to the Present*, ed. Amatzia Baram et al. (New York: Palgrave Macmillan, 2010).

10. The population figures on the Kurds vary widely depending on the source. These figures are taken from the Encyclopaedia Britannica, *2011 Book of the Year*, pp. 603, 604, 709, 718. A good list of figures is found in Gareth Stansfield, *Iraqi Kurdistan: Political Development and Emergent Democracy* (London: Routledge Curzon, 2003), p. 33.

11. CIA *Factbook*, Iraq, December 2010.

12. Although there is a rich oral tradition in the Kurdish language, no written literature from early times has survived. Some early written poetry in Kurdish dialects survives from the eleventh century onward (Mehrdad R. Izady, *The Kurds* [Washington, DC: Crane Russak, 1992], p. 176). A Kurdish literature, written in Persian, Arabic, and Turkish, especially from the thirteenth century on, also exists. For example, Sharif Khan, of Bitlis, wrote the *Sharafnama*, an authoritative medieval account of Kurdish history, in Persian (Joyce Blau, "Kurdish Written Literature," in *Kurdish Culture and Identity*, ed. Philip Kreyenbroek and Christine Allison [London: Zed Books, 1996], p. 21).

13. Richard Nyrop, ed., *Iraq: A Country Study* (Washington, DC: Government Printing Office, 1979), p. 67. Some put the figure as high as 6 percent. Encyclopaedia Britannica, "Iraq," *2010 Book of the Year* (Chicago: Encyclopaedia Britannica, 2010), p. 604.

14. Nyrop, *Iraq*, p. 63. The figures on the Persian-speaking population vary. Hanna Batatu estimated them at 1.2 percent of the population in 1947 (Hanna Batatu, *The Old Social Classes and the Revolutionary Movements of Iraq: A Study of Iraq's Old Landed and Commercial Classes and of Its Communists, Ba'thists, and Free Officers* [Princeton, NJ: Princeton University Press, 1978], p. 40). Expulsions after 1980 of Persian-speaking and native Iraqi Shi'a with Persian citizenship probably reduced this group to well under 1 percent of the population, but their numbers have increased considerably since 2003, when many of those expelled returned from Iran.

15. The Lurs speak a dialect of Persian that some consider a separate language (Bruce Ingham, "Languages of the Persian Gulf," in *The Persian Gulf States*, ed.

Alvin J. Cottrell [Baltimore, MD: Johns Hopkins University Press, 1980], p. 329). Others consider the Lur dialect a variant of Kurdish and the *faili* Kurds merely Shi'i Kurds. In the early 1970s tens of thousands of *faili* Kurds were expelled by the government, reducing their numbers in Iraq.

16. Lawless estimated the non-Muslim population at about 5 percent in 1972: R. I. Lawless, "Iraq: Changing Population Patterns," in *Populations of the Middle East and North Africa*, ed. J. I. Clarke and W. F. Fisher (London: University of London Press, 1972), pp. 101, 107. Nyrop gave a similar figure for 1977: Nyrop, *Iraq*, p. 67. Owing to considerable Christian migration in the last three decades, this figure may be lower. Encyclopaedia Britannica put it at about 4 percent: Encyclopaedia Britannica, "Iraq," *2010 Book of the Year,* p. 440.

17. Foreign Area Studies (American University), *Area Handbook for Iraq* (Washington, DC: Government Printing Office, 1969), p. 64.

18. Virtually all Yazidis speak the Kurmanji dialect of Kurdish.

19. Stephen Longrigg, *Iraq, 1900 to 1950* (London: Oxford University Press, 1953), p. 22.

20. Memorandum by King Faisal, cited in Abd al-Razzaq al-Hasani, *Ta'rikh al-Wizarat al-Iraqiyya* (The History of Iraqi Cabinets) (Sidon, Lebanon: Matba'at al-Irfan, 1953–1967), 3:287.

21. Great Britain, Naval Intelligence Division, *Iraq and the Persian Gulf* (London, 1944), pp. 353–354.

Chapter 2: The British Mandate, 1920–1932

1. The occupation was not without setbacks. An initial attempt to take Kut, in 1916, met with defeat and a retreat. The city of Mosul was occupied only after the armistice was declared and was challenged—for years—by Turkey.

2. Peter Sluglett, *Britain in Iraq, 1914–1932* (New York: Columbia University Press, 2007), chap. 6.

3. For the 1920 revolt, see Pierre-Jean Luizard, *La Formation de l'Irak Contemporain* (The Formation of Contemporary Iraq) (Paris: Éditions du Centre National de la Recherche Scientifique, 1991), pp. 403–413; Yitzhak Nakash, *The Shi'is of Iraq* (Princeton, NJ: Princeton University Press, 1994), pp. 66–72; Ghassan Atiyyah, *Iraq, 1908–1921: A Political Study* (Beirut: Arab Institute for Research and Publishing, 1973), pp. 326–338; Abdul Hadi Hairi, *Shiism and Constitutionalism in Iran* (Leiden, The Netherlands: E. J. Brill, 1977), pp. 125–126; and Muhammad Mahdi al-Basir, *Ta'rikh al-Qadiyya-l-Iraqiyya,* 2nd ed. (London: LAAM, 1990).

4. Stephen Longrigg, *Iraq, 1900 to 1950* (London: Oxford University Press, 1953), p. 112; 'Abd al-Razzaq al-Hasani, *al-Thaura-l-Iraqiyya-l-Kubra* (The Great Iraqi Revolt) (Sidon, Lebanon: Matba'at al-Irfan, 1952), pp. 124–170.

5. For diverse interpretations of the revolt, see Luizard, *La Formation de l'Irak*, pp. 414–422; for an excellent summary of works on the revolt, see pp. 383–384. For the role of various groups in the revolt, see Atiyyah, *Iraq*, pp. 270–354.

6. Philip Ireland, *Iraq: A Study in Political Development* (New York: Macmillan, 1938), p. 273; Longrigg, *Iraq, 1900–1950*, p. 123.

7. For an excellent study of the structures and method of rule under the mandate, see Toby Dodge, *Inventing Iraq: The Failure of Nation-Building and a History Denied* (New York: Columbia University Press) 2003.

8. For Husri's role on the curriculum and especially his clash with the Shi'a and Kurds, see Sati'-l-Husri, *Mudhakkirati fi-l-Iraq* (My Memoirs in Iraq) (Beirut: Dar al-Tali'a, 1967), 1: 79–80, 215–216, 271–277, 377–378, 401–402, 457–464, 585, 588–602; and William Cleveland, *The Making of an Arab Nationalist* (Princeton, NJ: Princeton University Press), 1971, pp. 62–70. For criticism of that role, see Abd al-Karim al-Uzri, *Mushkilat al-Hukm fi-l-Iraq* (The Problem of Governance in Iraq) (London: n.p., 1991), chap. 5; and Muhammad Mahdi al-Jawahiri, *Dhikrayati* (My Memoirs) (Damascus: Dar al-Rafidain, 1988–1991), 1:chap. 3.

9. For the treaty, see Abd al-Razzaq al-Hasani, *Ta'rikh al-Wizarat al-Iraqiyya* (The History of Iraqi Cabinets) (Sidon, Lebanon: Matba'at al-Irfan, 1953–1967), 1:94–98; for the agreements, see 1:223–258.

10. For an account of the tortuous British diplomacy on this issue, see David McDowall, *A Modern History of the Kurds* (London: I. B. Tauris, 1997), pp. 163–171.

11. Hilton Young, *Report on Economic Conditions and Policy and Loan Policy* (Baghdad: Government Press, 1930), p. 12.

12. Iraq, Ministry of Planning, *Report on Education in Iraq* (Baghdad: Government Press, 1959), pp. 20–21.

13. For this episode and its implications, see Nakash, *The Shi'is of Iraq*, pp. 75–88; Luizard, *La Formation de l'Irak*, pp. 440–493; and Hairi, *Shi'ism and Constitutionalism*, pp. 131–134.

14. For a succinct biography of Nuri al-Sa'id, see Louay Bahry and Phebe Marr, "Nuri Said," in *Political Leaders of the Contemporary Middle East and North Africa*, ed. Bernard Reich (New York: Greenwood Press, 1990), pp. 467–475.

15. Great Britain, Colonial Office, *Special Report on the Progress of Iraq, 1920–1931* (London: H. M. Stationery Office, 1932), pp. 289–292.

Chapter 3: The Erosion of the British Legacy, 1932–1945

1. Khaldun S. Husry, "The Assyrian Affair of 1933, I," *International Journal of Middle East Studies* 5:2 (1974) (hereafter, *IJMES*).

2. This account has been drawn from Stephen Longrigg, *Iraq, 1900 to 1950* (London: Oxford University Press, 1953), pp. 229–237; and R. S. Stafford, *The Tragedy of the Assyrians* (London: Allen and Unwin, 1935). For a critical view of this perspective, see Husry, "The Assyrian Affair of 1933, I"; and Khaldun S. Husry, "The Assyrian Affair of 1933, II," *IJMES* 5:3 (1974).

3. Khaldun al-Husri, interview with author, Beirut, 12 December 1967.

4. On this problem, see Hanna Batatu, *The Old Social Classes and the Revolutionary Movements of Iraq: A Study of Iraq's Old Landed and Commercial Classes and of Its Communists, Ba'thists, and Free Officers* (Princeton, NJ: Princeton University Press, 1978), chaps. 5, 6; Samira Haj, *The Making of Iraq, 1900–1963* (Albany: State University of New York Press, 1997), chaps. 1, 2; and Ernest Dowson, *An Inquiry into Land Tenure and Related Questions* (Letchworth, UK: Garden City Press, 1932), pp. 16–39.

5. Iraq, Ministry of Justice, *Compilation of Laws and Regulations, 1932* (Baghdad: Government Press, 1933), pp. 42–43.

6. Yitzhak Nakash, *The Shi'is of Iraq* (Princeton, NJ: Princeton University Press, 1966), pp. 109–111, 117–120; Ali al-Wardi, *Dirasa fi Tabi 'at al-Mujtama'-l-Iraqi* (A Study of the Nature of Iraqi Society) (Qum: Matba'at Amir, n.d.), pp. 344–345.

7. Nakash, *The Shi'is of Iraq*, p. 113. For an exposition of Shi'i views on this subject, see Hasan al-Alawi, *al-Shi'a wa-l-Daula-l-Qaumiyya* (The Shi'a and the Nationalist State) (France: CEDI, 1989), pp. 240–247, 252–253, 258; and Abd al-Karim al-Uzri, *Mushkilat al-Hukm fi-l-Iraq* (The Problem of Governance in Iraq) (London: n.p., 1991), pp. 231, 260. For an exposition of the way this prejudice was taught at the popular level, see Sa'id al-Samarra'i, *Ta'ifiyya fil-Iraq* (Sectarianism in Iraq) (London: al-Fajr, 1993), p. 84.

8. Abd al-Razzaq al-Hasani, *Ta'rikh al-Wizarat al-Iraqiyya* (The History of Iraqi Cabinets) (Sidon, Lebanon: Matba'at al-Irfan, 1953–1967), 3:220–221; Nakash, *The Shi'is of Iraq*, p. 114; Uzri, *The Problem of Governance*, pp. 215–239.

9. For the Mithaq, see Hasani, *The History of Iraqi Cabinets*, 4:48–49.

10. On these revolts, see Hasani, *The History of Iraqi Cabinets*, 4:106–132, 139–144, 150–180; and Nakash, *The Shi'is of Iraq*, pp. 120–125.

11. Longrigg, *Iraq, 1900–1950*, p. 246.

12. *Jaridat al-Bilad* (Baghdad), 25 June 1936.

13. Examples of this thinking were to be found in several newspapers but especially *al-Bilad*. See *al-Bilad*, 28 May 1936; and Sati'-l-Husri, *Ara wa Aha-dith fi-l-Ta'rikh wa-l-Ijtima'* (Ideas and Discussion on History and Society) (Cairo: n.p., 1957). For German influence and the *futuwwa* movement, see Reeva Simon, *Iraq Between the Two World Wars* (New York: Columbia University Press, 2004), pp. 31–35, 101–105.

14. Abd al-Fattah Ibrahim, *Mutal'at fi-l-Sha'biyya* (Studies in Populism), Ahali series, no. 3 (Baghdad: Ahali Press, 1935), cited in Majid Khadduri, *Independent Iraq, 1932–1958* (London: Oxford University Press, 1960), pp. 70–73; Kamil al-Chadirchi, *Mudhakkirat* (My Memoirs) (Beirut: Dar al-Tali'a, 1970), pp. 49–50. For the formation and ideas of the Ahali, see Orit Bashkin, *The Other Iraq: Pluralism and Culture in Hashemite Iraq* (Stanford, CA: Stanford University Press, 2009), pp. 61–69.

15. Hasani, *The History of Iraqi Cabinets*, 4:192–194; Khadduri, *Independent Iraq*, pp. 78–82; Bashkin, *The Other Iraq*, pp. 70–71.

16. For the events of the coup, see Hasani, *The History of Iraqi Cabinets*, 4:192–202; Khadduri, *Independent Iraq*, pp. 80–92; and Longrigg, *Iraq, 1900–1950*, pp. 245–250.

17. For a good analysis of the Bakr Sidqi coup and its subsequent government, see Mohammad A. Tarbush, *The Role of the Military in Politics: A Case Study of Iraq to 1941* (London: Kegan Paul, 1982), chap. 6.

18. "The Conflict with Iran," *Arab World File 177* (1977): I i9; Majid Khadduri, *The Gulf War: The Origins and Implications of the Iraq-Iran Conflict* (New York: Oxford University Press, 1988), pp. 37–40. On the government's pro-Turkish orientation, see Tarbush, *The Role of the Military*, pp. 139–141.

19. For this program, see al-Hasani, *The History of Iraqi Cabinets*, 4:265–267.

20. Among the officers were Muhammad Fahmi Sa'id and Mahmud Salman, both of whom later figured in the 1941 coup (Hasani, *The History of Iraqi Cabinets*, 4:314, n1).

21. The personal vendetta sprang, in part, from the killing of his brother-in-law, Ja'far al-Askari, a leading Iraqi politician and minister of defense during the Bakr Sidqi coup. Sidqi was undoubtedly responsible for his death.

22. For this version, see Salah al-Din al-Sabbagh, *Mudhakkirati* (My Memoirs) (Damascus: n.p., 1956), pp. 80–97; and Talib Mushtaq, *Awraq Ayyami* (Papers from My Days) (Beirut: Dar al-Tali'a, 1968), pp. 314–325.

23. On the selection of Abd al-Ilah, see Taha al-Hashimi, *Mudhakkirati, 1919–1943* (My Memoirs, 1919–1943) (Beirut: Dar al-Tali'a, 1967), p. 305; Sabbagh, *My Memoirs*, p. 79; and Hasani, *The History of Iraqi Cabinets*, 5:75–

76. Information on Abd al-Ilah is taken from interviews with men who knew him well. An excellent assessment of his character is also found in Falih Hanzal, *Asrar Maqtal al-A'ila-l-Malika fi-l-Iraq, 14 Tammuz 1958* (Secrets of the Murder of the Royal Family in Iraq, 14 July 1958) (n.pl.: n.p., 1971), pp. 31–47.

24. Mahmud al-Durra, *al-Harb al-Iraqiyya-l-Baritaniyya, 1941* (The Iraqi-British War of 1941) (Beirut: Dar al-Tali'a, 1969), pp. 90–97.

25. For the background and views of these key officers, see Sabbagh, *My Memoirs*; for Yunis al-Sab'awi, see Khairi-l-Umari, *Yunis al-Sab'awi: Sira Siyasi Isami* (Yunis al-Sab'awi: Biography of a Self-Made Politician) (Baghdad: Ministry of Culture and Information, 1980).

26. On the Rashid Ali movement, see Isma'il Ahmad Yaghi, *Harakat Rashid Ali al-Kailani* (The Rashid Ali Movement) (Beirut: Dar al-Tali'a, 1974); Hashimi, *My Memoirs, 1919–1943*, pp. 314–430; Durra, *The Iraqi-British War*, pp. 120–237; Sabbagh, *My Memoirs*, pp. 135–223; Taufiq al-Suwaidi, *Mudhakkirat* (Memoirs) (n.pl.: Dar al-Kitab al-Arabi, 1969), pp. 343–374; Uthman Haddad, *Harakat Rashid Ali al-Kailani* (The Rashid Ali al-Kailani Movement) (Sidon, Lebanon: al-Maktabat-l-Asriyya, n.d.); Hasani, *The History of Iraqi Cabinets*, 5:121–231; Abd al-Razzaq al-Hasani, *al-Asrar al-Khafiyya* (The Hidden Secrets) (Sidon, Lebanon: Matba'at al-Irfan, 1958); Khairi-l-Umari, *Yunis al-Sab'awi*; and Khadduri, *Independent Iraq*, pp. 157–243.

27. For an excellent analysis of the historical impact of the Rashid Ali coup, see the introduction by Khaldun al-Husry in Hashimi, *My Memoirs, 1919–1943*, pp. 21–40.

28. Durra, an ardent nationalist, claims there were over 1,000: Durra, *The Iraqi-British War*, p. 417. Talib Mushtaq, an internee, claims about 750: Talib, *Papers from My Days*, p. 455. Progovernment sources put it at not more than 500, most of whom were released as early as 1942. Most were out by 1943 (Ali Mumtaz, interview with author, Beirut, 5 December 1967).

29. For a good analysis of the texts and the role of education in creating a climate of nationalism, see Simon, *Iraq Between the Two World Wars*, chap. 4.

30. In the seven cabinets formed between March 1941 (after the Rashid Ali affair) and May 1946, Arab Sunnis constituted half or less of the members, not the usual majority. In at least three of these cabinets—the one led by Nuri al-Sa'id (December 1943–June 1944), that led by Hamdi al-Pachachi (August 1944–January 1046), and that led by Taufiq al-Suwaidi (February–May 1946)—Arab Sunnis were a minority, outnumbered, collectively, by Shi'a, Kurds, Turkmen, and a Christian.

31. Iraq, *Statistical Abstract 1947*, p. 235.

32. Iraq, *Statistical Abstract 1947*, p. 211.

33. Hasani, *The History of Iraqi Cabinets*, 6:72. Batatu estimated that the wages of unskilled laborers rose 400 percent between 1939 and 1948, while the price of food rose 800 percent, the salaries of lower-level civil servants rose less than 150 percent, and the wholesale price index rose to 690: Batatu, *The Old Social Classes*, pp. 472–473.

34. Iraq, *Statistical Abstract 1958*, p. 123.

Chapter 4: The End of the Monarchy, 1946–1958

1. For the establishment of the Istiqlal and its program, see Muhammad Mahdi Kubba, *Mudhakkirati* (My Memoirs) (Beirut: Dar al-Tali'a, 1965), pp. 108–208; Abd al-Amir Hadi al-Akam, *Ta'rikh Hizb al-Istiqlal al-Iraqi, 1946–1958* (History of the Iraqi Independence Party, 1946–1958) (Baghdad: Ministry of Culture and Information, 1980), pp. 11–70; and Orit Bashkin, *The Other Iraq* (Stanford, CA: Stanford University Press, 2009), pp. 94–96.

2. For the establishment of the National Democratic Party and its program, see Kamil al-Chadirchi, *Mudhakkirat* (Memoirs) (Beirut: Dar al-Tali'a, 1970), pp. 53–103, 179–225; Kamil al-Chadirchi, *Min Awraq Kamil al-Chadirchi* (From the Papers of Kamil al-Chadirchi) (Beirut: Dar al-Tali'a, 1971), pp. 101–145; and Fadil Husain, *Ta'rikh al-Hizb al-Watani-l-Dimuqrati* (The History of the National Democratic Party) (Baghdad: Matba'at al-Sha'b, 1963), pp. 29–49, 103–214.

3. For a detailed study of the Iraq Communist Party, see Tareq Ismail, *The Rise and Fall of the Communist Party of Iraq* (Cambridge, UK: Cambridge University Press, 2008); the early period and Fahd's role are contained in chapter 1. Hanna Batatu, *The Old Social Classes and the Revolutionary Movements of Iraq: A Study of Iraq's Old Landed and Commercial Classes and of Its Communists, Ba'thists, and Free Officers* (Princeton, NJ: Princeton University Press, 1978), remains the authoritative study of the rise of the party and its organization. For the early history of the party, see pp. 390–462. For the composition of Fahd's central committee in 1941, see pp. 494–495.

4. For the events of the *wathba*, see Abd al-Razzaq al-Hasani, *Ta'rikh al-Wizarat al-Iraqiyya* (The History of Iraqi Cabinets) (Sidon, Lebanon: Matba'at al-Irfan, 1953–1967), 7:219–233, 253–274; Taufiq al-Suwaidi, *Mudhakkirat* (Memoirs) (n.pl.: Dar al-Kitab al-Arabi, 1969), pp. 473–477; Chadirchi, *Memoirs*, pp. 170–177; Kubba, *My Memoirs*, pp. 223–233; and Akam, *History of the Iraqi Independence Party*, pp. 210–228. In addition, the following material draws on interviews with several Iraqis, including Suwaidi, Taufiq Wahbi, and Yahya Qasim, the editor of *al-Sha'b*, who accompanied the party to Portsmouth.

5. Michael Eppel, *The Palestine Conflict in the History of Modern Iraq* (Devon, UK: Cass, 1994), pp. 187–191; Fred Khoury, *The Arab-Israeli Dilemma* (Syracuse, NY: Syracuse University Press, 1969), pp. 68–109.

6. For the story of this exodus, see Yehouda Shenhov, "The Jews of Iraq," *IJMES* 31 (1999): 605–630.

7. In the 1950s, IPC included the Anglo-Iranian Oil Company (now British Petroleum), Royal Dutch Shell, Compagnie Française des Pétroles (now Total), and the Near East Development Corporation, a U.S. group that included Standard Oil of New Jersey and Mobil. Calouste Gulbenkian, an Armenian entrepreneur, also had a small share.

8. Edith Penrose and E. F. Penrose, *Iraq: International Relations and National Development* (Boulder, CO: Westview Press, 1978), p. 167.

9. Charles Issawi and Muhammed Yeganeh, *The Economics of Middle Eastern Oil* (New York: Praeger, 1962), pp. 143, 147.

10. Abd al-Rahman al-Jalili, *al-I'mar fi-l-Iraq* (Development in Iraq) (Beirut: Dar Maktabat al-Haya, 1968), pp. 239–242.

11. Doreen Warriner, *Land Reform and Development in the Middle East* (London: Royal Institute of International Affairs, 1957), p. 118.

12. John Simmons, "Agricultural Development in Iraq: Planning and Management Failure," *Middle East Journal* 19:2 (1965): 131.

13. Penrose and Penrose, *Iraq*, p. 177.

14. Ferhang Jalal, *The Role of Government in the Industrialization of Iraq, 1950–1965* (London: Cass, 1972), p. 8.

15. Hasani, *The History of Iraqi Cabinets*, 8:276–277.

16. Khalil Kanna, *al-Iraq, Amsuhu wa Ghaduhu* (Iraq: Its Past and Its Future) (Beirut: Dar al-Rihani, 1966), p. 172; Ahmad Mukhtar Baban, interview with author, Beirut, 21 December 1967.

17. *New York Times*, 25 September 1954. For failures of government in this period, see Adeed Dawisha, *Iraq: A Political History from Independence to Occupation* (Princeton, NJ: Princeton University Press, 2009), chap. 7.

18. For the constitution of the federation, see Hasani, *The History of Iraqi Cabinets*, 10:211–223.

19. Suwaidi, *Memoirs*, pp. 594–597.

Chapter 5: The Qasim Era, 1958–1963

1. The members of the committee were Muhyi-l-Din Abd al-Hamid, Naji Talib, Abd al-Wahhab Amin, Muhsin Husain al-Habib, Tahir Yahya, Rajab Abd al-Majid, Abd al-Karim Farhan, Wasfi Tahir, Sabih Ali Ghalib, Muhammad

Sab', Abd al-Karim Qasim, Abd al-Salam Arif, Abd al-Rahman Arif, and Abd al-Wahhab al-Shawwaf. Many went on to play an important role in the revolutionary period.

2. Sabih Ali Ghalib, *Qissat Thaurat 14 Tammuz wa-l Dubbat al-Ahrar* (The Story of the Revolution of 14 July and the Free Officers) (Beirut: Dar al-Tali'a, 1968), pp. 44–45. Testimony of Naji Talib in Iraq, Ministry of Defense, Coordinating Committee for the Special High Military Court, *Muhakamat* (Trials) (Baghdad: Ministry of Defense, 1958–1962), 5:2093.

3. Falih Hanzal, *Asrar Maqtal al-A'ila-l-Malika fi-l-Iraq 14 Tammuz 1958* (Secrets of the Murder of the Royal Family in Iraq, 14 July 1958) (n.pl.: n.p., 1971), pp. 126–130.

4. King Hussein, *Uneasy Lies the Head* (New York: B. Geis, 1962), pp. 197–201.

5. Muhammad Hadid (finance) and Hdaib al-Hajj Hmud (agriculture) represented the National Democrats; Saddiq Shanshal (guidance), the Istiqlal; Fu'ad al-Rikabi (development), the Ba'th; and Ibrahim Kubba (economics), the Communists. The Kurd was Baba Ali, son of Shaikh Mahmud, who took the Ministry of Communications; the Arab nationalist was Abd al-Jabbar Jumard, who became minister of foreign affairs.

6. Majid Khadduri, *Republican Iraq* (London: Oxford University Press, 1969), pp. 100–104. Whatever Rashid Ali's involvement, the real threat came from the Nasserite and Ba'thist army officers.

7. The plot itself was hatched by a number of nationalist groups, including midlevel nationalist officers, Free Officers, and civilian Ba'thists.

8. On the Mosul revolt, see Khadduri, Republican Iraq, pp. 104–112; and Hanna Batatu, *The Old Social Classes and the Revolutionary Movements of Iraq: A Study of Iraq's Old Landed and Commercial Classes and of Its Communists, Ba'thists, and Free Officers* (Princeton, NJ: Princeton University Press, 1978), pp. 866–889. Details of the revolt are to be found in Iraq, *Trials*, vols. 8, 9. A Ba'th view is found in Ali Karim Sa'id, *Iraq 8 Shabat 1963, Min Hiwar al-Mafahim ila Hiwar al-Dam. Muraja'at fi Dhakira Talib Shabib* (Iraq of 8 February 1963: From the Dialogue of Conceptions to the Dialogue of Blood: Reviews on Talib Shabib's Memories) (n.pl.: Dar al-Kunuz al-Arabiyya, 1999), pp. 24–25.

9. Efriam Karsh and Inari Rautsi, *Saddam Hussein: A Political Biography* (New York: Free Press, 1991), pp. 17–18.

10. See Iraq, *Trials*, vols., 20–22.

11. The Ba'th attempt on Qasim came after the Kirkuk events described later in the chapter. For an excellent account of the role of the Communists in the

period after Mosul, see Tareq Ismail, *The Rise and Fall of the Communist Party of Iraq* (Cambridge, UK: Cambridge University Press, 2008), pp. 87–106.

12. Uriel Dann, *Iraq Under Qassem* (New York: Praeger, 1969), pp. 55–56.

13. On the Kirkuk episode, see Batatu, *The Old Social Classes*, pp. 912–921.

14. Batatu, *The Old Social Classes*, p. 704.

15. For a discussion of this subject, see Khaldun al-Husri, *Thaurat 14 Tammuz* (The 14 July Revolution) (Beirut: Dar al-Tali'a, 1963), chap. 7. For a discussion of the USSR's relations with Iraq in this period, see Oles Smolansky with Bette Smolansky, *The USSR and Iraq: The Soviet Quest for Influence* (Durham, NC: Duke University Press, 1991), pp. 13–16.

16. A dunam is equivalent to .618 acres.

17. The text of the law is taken from Muhammad Hasan Salman, *Dirasat fi-l-Iqtisad al-Iraqi* (Studies on the Iraqi Economy) (Beirut: Dar al-Tali'a, 1966), pp. 383–416.

18. For an account of these events and the Communist role in them, see Dann, *Iraq Under Qassem*, pp. 56–61; Rony Gabbay, *Communism and Agrarian Reform in Iraq* (London: Croom Helm, 1978), pp. 108–151. As Gabbay pointed out, the Communists were challenged in the countryside by the National Democratic Party and did not have the field wholly to themselves.

19. Gabbay, *Communism and Agrarian Reform*, p. 134.

20. John Simmons, "Agricultural Development in Iraq: Planning and Management Failure," *Middle East Journal* 19:2 (1965): 131.

21. J. N. D. Anderson, "A Law of Personal Status for Iraq," *International and Comparative Law Quarterly* 9 (1960): 542–563. For a retrospective on this law, see Noga Efrati, "Women Under the Monarchy," in *Iraq Between Occupations: Perspectives from 1920 to the Present*, ed. Amatzia Baram et al. (New York: Palgrave Macmillan, 2010).

22. Office of the Iraqi Cultural Attache, *Education in Iraq* (Washington, DC: Embassy of Iraq, n.d.), p. 2; Arab Information Center, *Education in Iraq* (New York: Arab Information Center, 1966), p. 32.

23. Kathleen Langley, "Iraq: Some Aspects of the Economic Scene," *Middle East Journal* 18 (1964): 184.

24. For an excellent discussion of these negotiations and their outcome, see Edith Penrose and E. F. Penrose, *Iraq: International Relations and National Development* (Boulder, CO: Westview Press, 1978), pp. 257–269, from which the following section has largely been drawn.

25. On the role of Hakim in this revival, see Pierre-Jean Luizard, "The Nature of the Confrontation Between the State and Marja'ism," in *Ayatollahs, Sufis, and Ideologues*, ed. Faleh A. Jabar (London: Saqi Books, 2002), pp. 90–100.

On the role of the *marji'* in Shi'ism, see Faleh A. Jabar, "The Genesis and Development of Marja'ism in the State," in *Ayatollahs*, pp. 61–89.

26. Ali al-Mu'min, *Sanawat al-Jamr: Musira-l-Harakat al-Islamiyya fi-l-Iraq, 1957–1986* (Years of Embers: The Journey of the Islamic Movement in Iraq, 1957–1986) (London: Dar al-Musira, 1993), p. 45; Faleh A. Jabar, *The Shi'ite Movement in Iraq* (London: Saqi, 2003), chap. 6; Amatzia Baram, *State-Mosque Relations in Ba'thist Iraq, 1968–2003* (forthcoming), pt. 3, sec. 2.

27. Jabar, *The Shi'ite Movement*, pp. 95-98; and Baram, *State-Mosque Relations*, pt. 3, sec. 1.

28. Sadr's participation in the party faced opposition from senior clerics as incompatible with his future status as a *marji'*. In 1960 he withdrew from the Da'wa, but he remained its intellectual inspiration (Shaikh Muhammad Rida al-Na'mani, *al-Shahid al-Sadr: Sanawat al-Mihna wa Ayyam al-Hisar* [The Martyr al-Sadr: The Years of His Ordeal and the Days of His Siege], 2nd printing [n.pl.: Isma'iliyyan, 1997], p. 175).

29. The group kept no public records. For various accounts of the founding, see Mu'min, *Years of Embers*, pp. 32–36; Jabar, *The Shi'ite Movement*, pp. 95–104; Baram, *State-Mosque Relations*, pt. 3, sec. 1; Na'mani, *The Martyr al-Sadr*, pp. 145–147; and Abdul-Halim al-Ruhaimi, "The Da'wa Islamic Party: Origins, Actors, and Ideology," in *Ayatollahs*, pp. 149–161. Information is also drawn from Sayyid Muhammad Bahr al-Ulum, interview with author, London, June 1991.

30. On the foundation of the KDP, see Chris Kutschera, *Le Mouvement National Kurde* (The Kurdish National Movement) (Paris: Flammarion, 1979), pp. 191–194; and Gareth Stansfield, *Iraqi Kurdistan: Political Development and Emergent Democracy* (London: Routledge Curzon, 2003), pp. 61–67.

31. For the text of these agreements, see Salman, *Studies on the Iraqi Economy*, pp. 417–440.

32. Roger Pajak, "Soviet Military Aid to Iraq and Syria," *Strategic Review* 4:1 (Winter 1976): 52.

33. They may even have extended some help to Qasim in fending off Egyptian-backed Arab nationalist attempts to overthrow him (Malik Mufti, "The United States and Nasserist Pan-Arabism," in *The Middle East and the United States: A Historical and Political Assessment*, ed. David Lesch, 2nd ed. [Boulder, CO: Westview Press, 1999], p. 169).

34. Jasim Abdulghani, *Iran and Iraq: The Years of Crisis* (Baltimore, MD: Johns Hopkins University Press, 1984), pp. 17–18.

35. Malcolm Kerr, *The Arab Cold War*, 3rd ed. (London: Oxford University Press, 1971), pp. 17–19.

36. The following account has been drawn largely from Richard Schofield, *Kuwait and Iraq: Historical Claims and Territorial Disputes* (London: Royal Institute of International Affairs, 1994); and Majid Khadduri and Edmund Ghareeb, *War in the Gulf, 1990–1991: The Iraq-Kuwait Conflict and Its Implications* (New York: Oxford University Press, 1997), pp. 6–67.

Chapter 6: The Arab Nationalists in Power, 1963–1968

1. One of the most useful records of this coup and its results is to be found in Ali Karim Sa'id, *Iraq 8 Shabat 1963, Min Hiwar al-Mafahim ila Hiwar al-Dam. Muraja'at fi Dhakira Talib Shabib* (Iraq of 8 February 1963: From the Dialogue of Conceptions to the Dialogue of Blood: Reviews on Talib Shabib's Memories) (n.pl.: Dar al-Kunuz al-Arabiyya, 1999). (As this work is both a memoir of Shabib and a commentary by Sa'id, it will henceforth be referred to with both authors' names, as Sa'id/Shabib.)

2. A translation of the party constitution is to be found in Sylvia Haim, *Arab Nationalism: An Anthology* (Berkeley and Los Angeles: University of California Press, 1962), pp. 233–241. An excellent account of the party in this period is found in Hani al-Fukaiki, *Aukar al-Hazima* (Dens of Defeat), 2nd ed. (Beirut: Riad El-Rayyes Books, 1997), pp. 231–235.

3. Hanna Batatu, *The Old Social Classes and the Revolutionary Movements of Iraq: A Study of Iraq's Old Landed and Commercial Classes and of Its Communists, Ba'thists, and Free Officers* (Princeton, NJ: Princeton University Press, 1978), pp. 741–743.

4. For an account of the coup planning, see Majid Khadduri, *Republican Iraq* (London: Oxford University Press, 1969), pp. 188–190; Batatu, *The Old Social Classes*, pp. 968–973; Sa'id/Shabib, *Iraq of 8 February 1963*, pp. 45–59.

5. For an account of this end, see Fukaiki, *Dens of Defeat*, pp. 247–252; and Sa'id/Shabib, *Iraq of 8 February 1963*, pp. 101–109. According to Shabib, who was present, there was no organized body or legal procedure; Qasim and several captured companions, including Fadil Abbas al-Mahdawi, were simply shot in a separate room by soldiers after a rough interrogation by the coup leaders present. A decree was subsequently issued claiming that he was sentenced by a martial law tribunal. Fukaiki, also present, supported this view.

6. Batatu, *The Old Social Classes*, p. 1003; Khadduri, *Republican Iraq*, p. 197.

7. Because of the secrecy, there is some disagreement on the membership. Most sources agree on the following: Ali Salih Sa'di, Hazim Jawad, Talib Shabib, Hamdi Abd al-Majid, Muhsin al-Shaikh Radi, Hamid Khalkhal, Hani

al-Fukaiki, Abd al-Salam Arif, Ahmad Hasan al-Bakr, Salih Mahdi Ammash, Abd al-Sattar Abd al-Latif, Tahir Yahya, Abd al-Karim Nasrat, Abd al-Ghani Rawi, Khalid Makki al-Hashimi, Hardan al-Tikriti, and Abd al-Qadir al-Hadithi (Batatu, *The Old Social Classes*, pp. 1004–1007). Some sources would add Mundhir al-Wandawi, Dhiyab al-Alkawi, and Sa'dun Hammadi; others would omit Karim Shintaf and Abd al-Ghani Rawi (see also Khadduri, *Republican Iraq*, p. 197; and Sa'id/Shabib, *Iraq of 8 February 1963*, p. 177).

8. Fukaiki gave a graphic description of the bitter civilian-military and generational divide in his memoirs. In one meeting, Ammash is reported to have told a young Ba'thist (Fukaiki) "that he did not take orders from secondary students, but his party colleague reminded him that he had obeyed the orders of secondary students when was given the rank of general and appointed minister of defense": Fukaiki, *Dens of Defeat*, p. 275.

9. On the Ba'thist persecution of the Communists and disputes in the party over the killings, see Batatu, *The Old Social Classes*, pp. 982–991; Fukaiki, *Dens of Defeat*, pp. 254–265, and Sa'id/Shabib, *Iraq of 8 February 1963*, pp. 176–194. Between 7,000 and 10,000 Communists were imprisoned, and 149 were officially executed. The unofficial death toll was much higher.

10. Richard Schofield, *Kuwait and Iraq: Historical Claims and Territorial Disputes* (London: Royal Institute of International Affairs, 1994), pp. 110–111; Fukaiki, *Dens of Defeat*, p. 303.

11. For these discussions, see Dana Adams Schmidt, *Journey Among Brave Men* (Boston: Little, Brown, 1964), pp. 253–255, 260–265.

12. Chris Kutschera, *Le Mouvement National Kurde* (The Kurdish National Movement) (Paris: Flammarion, 1979), p. 237.

13. Sa'id/Shabib, *Iraq of 8 February 1963*, pp. 287–289; Malcolm Kerr, *The Arab Cold War*, 3rd ed. (London: Oxford University Press, 1971), pp. 85–86.

14. For this aspect of inter-Arab politics, see Kerr, *The Arab Cold War*, pp. 44–95; Kemal Abu Jaber, *The Arab Ba'th Socialist Party* (Syracuse, NY: Syracuse University Press, 1966), pp. 75–95; and John Devlin, *The Ba'th Party: A History from Its Origins to 1966* (Stanford, CA: Hoover Institute Press, 1966), pp. 239–271.

15. Talib Shabib, interview with author, New York, 13 September 1980.

16. For this historic congress, see Itamar Rabinovich, *Syria Under the Ba'th, 1963–1966* (New York: Halsted Press, 1972), pp. 75–108; and Batatu, *The Old Social Classes*, pp. 1020–1022.

17. The National Command of the Ba'th Party was pan-Arab and included party members from various Arab countries. The Regional Command, in Ba'th parlance, represented the leadership of the party within a single country, like Iraq.

18. Fukaiki, *Dens of Defeat*, pp. 345–357; Sa'id/Shabib, *Iraq of 8 February 1963*, pp. 317–332. Those exiled were Ali Salih al-Sa'di, Hani al-Fukaiki, Hamdi Abd al-Majid, Muhsin al-Shaikh Radi, and Abu Talib al-Hashimi.

19. The assessments of the mistakes made were clearly laid out in the report of the Eighth Regional Congress (engineered by Saddam Husain) in Baghdad in 1974 (Arab Ba'th Socialist Party, *Revolutionary Iraq, 1968–1983* [Baghdad: Arab Ba'th Socialist Party, 1974], pp. 57–61).

20. Pajak, "Soviet Military Aid to Iraq and Syria," *Strategic Review* 4:1 (Winter 1976): 52. The Soviets also constructed an atomic reactor, completed in 1964, and set other projects in motion.

21. Khair al-Din Hasib, *Nata'ij Tatbiq al-Qararat al-Ishtirakiyya fi-l-Sana-l-Ula* (Results of the Application of the Socialist Decisions in the First Year) (Baghdad: Economic Organization, n.d.), pp. 3–5.

22. These included his brother, Abd al-Rahman Arif, as acting commander in chief; Sa'id Slaibi, commander of the Baghdad Garrison; and Abd al-Razzaq al-Nayif, in Military Intelligence.

23. T. A. Aziz, "Muhammad Baqir al-Sadr: Shi'i Activism in Iraq," *IJMES* 25:2 (1993): 211; Ali al-Mu'min, *Sanawat al-Jamr: Musira-l-Harakat al-Islamiyya fi-l-Iraq, 1957–1986* (Years of Embers: The Journey of the Islamic Movement in Iraq, 1957–1986) (London: Dar al-Musira, 1993), p. 68.

24. On sectarianism under the Arif regime, see Abd al-Karim al-Uzri, *Mushkilat al-Hukm fi-l-Iraq* (The Problem of Governance in Iraq) (London: n.p., 1991), pp. 249–261.

25. For the text of the government announcement, see Mahmud al-Durra, *al-Qadiyya-l-Kurdiyya* (The Kurdish Question) (Beirut: Dar al-Tali'a, 1966), pp. 351–353.

26. On this split in the Kurdish movement, see Kutschera, *Le Mouvement National Kurde*, pp. 245–253; and David McDowall, *A Modern History of the Kurds* (London: I. B. Tauris, 1997), pp. 315–317.

27. The government's text of the accord is to be found in Khadduri, *Republican Iraq*, pp. 274–276.

28. The following material has been drawn mainly from Edith Penrose and E. F. Penrose, *Iraq: International Relations and National Development* (Boulder, CO: Westview Press, 1978), pp. 381–390, 394–397; Centre for Global Energy Studies, "Politics, Economics and Oil Policy," sec. 3 of *Iraq*, vol. 4 of *Oil Production Capacity in the Gulf* (unpublished report) (London: Centre for Global Energy Studies, 1997), pp. 74–75.

29. *Middle East Economic Survey* 10 (11 August 1967): 1–5; 10 (24 November 1967): 1–4; 11 (12 April 1968): 1–5.

30. For this movement, see Abbas Kelidar, "Aziz al-Haj: A Communist Radical," in *Integration of Modern Iraq*, ed. Abbas Kelidar (New York: St. Martin's Press, 1979), pp. 183–192; Batatu, *The Old Social Classes*, pp. 1069–1072, 1100–1101 and Tareq Ismail, *The Rise and Fall of the Communist Party in Iraq* (Cambridge, UK: Cambridge University Press, 2006), pp. 125–154. Haj later recanted.

31. *Middle East Record* 4 (1968): 516–517.

Chapter 7: The Era of Ba'th Party Rule, 1968–1979

1. The members of the RCC were Ahmad Hasan al-Bakr, Hardan al-Tikriti, Salih Mahdi Ammash, Hammad Shihab, and Sa'dun Ghaidan.

2. *The Economist* (London), 24–30 June 1978, p. 78.

3. The Central Treaty Organization (CTO) included the former Baghdad Pact countries; the pact was renamed the CTO after Iraq withdrew in 1958.

4. Bazzaz died on 28 June 1973 after an illness resulting from maltreatment during a long prison sentence. He was released from prison before his death.

5. The new members of the RCC were Saddam Husain, Abd al-Karim al-Shaikhli, Abd Allah Sallum al-Samarra'i, Izzat Mustafa, Shafiq al-Kamali, Salah Umar al-Ali, Izzat al-Duri, Murtada-l-Hadithi, and Taha-l-Jazrawi.

6. These included Salah Umar al-Ali, a relative of Bakr; Abd Allah Sallum al-Samarra'i; Shafiq al-Kamali; and Abd al-Karim al-Shaikhli, all removed by 1970. In 1973 Abd al-Khaliq al-Samarra'i was imprisoned.

7. For biographies of Saddam Husain, see Efraim Karsh and Inari Rautsi, *Saddam Hussein: A Political Biography* (New York: Free Press, 1991); and Said Aburish, *Saddam Hussein: The Politics of Revenge* (London: Bloomsbury, 2000); as well as the "semiofficial" biographies: Fuad Matar, *Saddam Hussein: The Man, the Cause, and the Future* (London: Third World Center, 1981); and Amin Iskandar, *Saddam Hussein: The Fighter, the Thinker, and the Man* (Paris: Hachette, 1980).

8. Arms Control and Disarmament Agency, *World Military Expenditures and Arms Transfers, 1970–1979* (Washington, DC: Government Printing Office, 1982), p. 62, cited in Amirav Acharya, *U.S. Military Strategy in the Gulf* (London: Routledge, 1989), p. 29.

9. For this episode, see Richard Schofield, *Kuwait and Iraq: Historical Claims and Territorial Disputes* (London: Royal Institute of International Affairs, 1994), pp. 114–117; and Majid Khadduri, *Socialist Iraq* (Washington, DC: Middle East Institute, 1978), pp. 154–156.

10. The Regional Command now consisted of Ahmad Hasan al-Bakr, Saddam Husain, Izzat al-Duri, Izzat Mustafa, Taha-l-Jazrawi, Na'im Haddad, Tayih Abd al-Karim, Muhammad Mahjub, Adnan al-Hamdani, Ghanim Abd al-Jalil, Tahir Taufiq al-Ani, Abd al-Fattah al-Yasin, and Hasan al-Amiri.

11. For the hierarchical structure of the party, see Falih Abd al-Jabbar, *al-Daula, al-Mujtama' al-Madani wal-Tahawwal al-Dimuqrati fi-l-Iraq* (The State, Civil Society, and Democratic Transformation in Iraq) (Cairo: Ibn Khaldun Center, 1995), p. 82.

12. Abd al-Jabbar, *The State, Civil Society, and Democratic Transformation*, p. 80. *The Economist* (London), 24–30 June 1978, pp. 78–79, claimed that there were 50,000 regular members and 500,000 followers in 1978. Batatu claimed that "active" members, that is, those at the highest level, numbered about 10,000 in 1976 (Hanna Batatu, *The Old Social Classes and the Revolutionary Movements of Iraq: A Study of Iraq's Old Landed and Commercial Classes and of Its Communists, Ba'thists, and Free Officers* [Princeton, NJ: Princeton University Press, 1978], p. 1078).

13. The Albu Nasir tribe, located in the vicinity of Tikrit, was a small group of about 25,000. However, they were able to field about 2,000 to 3,000 males in active politics. Because of their small numbers, the Albu Nasir frequently made political alliances with neighboring tribes and clans, such as the Duris (from Dur) and the Rawis (from Rawa). For a study of this phenomenon, see Faleh A. Jabbar, "The State, Society, Clan, Party, and Army in Iraq," in *From Storm to Thunder*, ed. Faleh A. Jabbar, Ahmand Shikara, and Keiko Sakai (Tokyo: Institute of Developing Economies, 1998), p. 6; Amatzia Baram, *Building Toward Crisis: Saddam Husayn's Strategy for Survival* (Washington, DC: Washington Institute for Near East Policy, 1998), pp. 20–25; Faleh A. Jabar, "Sheikhs and Ideologues," and Hosham Dawood, "The State-ization of the Tribe and the Tribalization of the State: The Case of Iraq," both in *Tribes and Power*, ed. Faleh A. Jabar and Hosham Dawood (London: Saqi, 2003), pp. 61–135.

14. On contacts between Barzani and the Israelis and on Israel's economic and military aid, see Edmond Ghareeb, *The Kurdish Question in Iraq* (Syracuse, NY: Syracuse University Press, 1981), pp. 142–145; and Jonathon Randall, *After Such Knowledge, What Forgiveness?* (New York: Farrar, Straus and Giroux, 1997), chap. 7.

15. For a good discussion on the development of the Fursan, see Martin van Bruinessen, "Kurds, States and Tribes," in *Tribes and Power*, p. 173.

16. Some have argued that the word used in the agreement was *self-rule*, something less than autonomy (Khadduri, *Socialist Iraq*, p. 103). The issue was

not semantics but how much self-rule or autonomy would be granted the Kurds.

17. On these attacks, see David McDowall, *A Modern History of the Kurds* (London: I. B. Tauris, 1997), pp. 330, 342 n26.

18. Chris Kutschera, *Le Mouvement National Kurde* (The Kurdish National Movement) (Paris: Flammarion, 1979), pp. 282–283. On the CIA aid, see the portions of the Pike report (made to Congress) that appeared in the *Village Voice* (New York), 16 February 1976, p. 88.

19. Ghareeb, *The Kurdish Question*, p. 180.

20. McDowall, *A Modern History of the Kurds*, p. 339.

21. Celine Whittleton, "Oil and the Iraqi Economy," in *Saddam's Iraq: Revolution or Reaction?* ed. Committee Against Repression and for Democratic Rights in Iraq (London: Zed Books, 1986), p. 65.

22. World Bank, *World Tables*, 3rd ed., vol. 1: *Economic Data* (Baltimore, MD: Johns Hopkins University Press, 1983), pp. 90–91.

23. Iraq, Ministry of Planning, *Man: The Object of Revolution* (Baghdad: Government Press, 1978), p. 34; *AAS* 1978, p. 135; Iraq, Ministry of Planning, *Statistical Pocketbook, 1982*, pp. 27–28.

24. Iraq, *Man*, p. 87; *AAS* 1980, pp. 225, 228, 240.

25. Iraq, *Man*, p. 98; World Bank, *World Tables*, 3rd ed., vol. 2: *Social Data* (Baltimore, MD: Johns Hopkins University Press, 1983), p. 45.

26. Shakir Moosa Issa, "Distribution of Income in Iraq, 1971" (Ph.D. diss., University of London, 1978), p. 11.

27. Anthony H. Cordesman and Ahmed S. Hashim, *Iraq: Sanctions and Beyond* (Boulder, CO: Westview Press, 1997), pp. 218–221.

28. UN, Economic Commission for West Asia (ECWA), "Industrial Development in Iraq: Prospects and Problems" (unpublished paper) (Beirut: ECWA, 1979), p. 14.

29. These figures are taken from Phebe Marr, *The Modern History of Iraq* (Boulder, CO: Westview Press, 1985), table 9.6, p. 266, and table 9.7, p. 267. Similar trends with even lower figures are cited in Muhammad Ali Zainy, "The Iraqi Economy Between Saddam Hussain and the UN Sanctions," in *Studies on the Iraqi Economy*, ed. Iraqi Economic Forum (London: Iraqi Economic Forum, 2002), pp. 38–40.

30. Nirou Eftekhari, "Le Petrole dans l'Economie et la Societe Irakiennes, 1958–1986," *Peuples Mediterraneens* 40 (July–September, 1987): 53.

31. Batatu, *The Old Social Classes*, p. 1123.

32. *AAS* 1978, p. 26.

33. Petroleum Finance Company, "Iraq: Political and Economic Structures" (Country Report, unpublished) (Washington, DC: Petroleum Finance Company, December 1994), p. 31. Much of the report was authored by Joe Stork.

34. Marr, *The Modern History*, p. 279.

35. Karsh and Rautsi, *Saddam Hussein: A Political Biography*, p. 95.

36. Amatzia Baram, "Qawmiyya and Wataniyya in Ba'thi Iraq: The Search for a New Balance," *Middle East Studies* 19:2 (April 1983): 188–200, cited in Karsh and Rautsi, *Saddam Hussein*, p. 100.

37. Saddam Husain, *Iraqi Politics in Perspective*, 2nd ed. (Baghdad: Dar al-Ma'mun, 1981), pp. 29–30.

38. Arab Ba'th Socialist Party, *Revolutionary Iraq, 1968–1983* (Baghdad: Arab Ba'th Socialist Party, 1974), p. 182.

39. *Al-Thaura* (Baghdad), 8–10 September 1976.

40. Ismet Cheriff Vanley, *Le Kurdistan Irakien Entité Nationale* [Iraqi Kurdistan: A National Entity] (Boudry-Neuchatel, Switzerland: Editions de la Baconniere, 1970), p. 300.

41. The status of native Iraqis of Iranian origin is a controversial issue in Iraq. After the modern Iraqi state was founded, the population of Iraq was registered either as Ottoman or Persian (Iranian) subjects. A number of Arab Shi'i families had previously chosen Persian nationality to avoid the Ottoman draft. The choice then carried over into modern Iraq, giving rise to controversy over citizenship and providing the pretext for the expulsions. Many sources say the numbers expelled reached over 100,000 (Ali al-Mu'min, *Sanawat al-Jamr: Musira-l-Harakat al-Islamiyya fi-l-Iraq, 1957–1986* [Years of Embers: The Journey of the Islamic Movement in Iraq, 1957–1986] [London: Dar al-Musira, 1993], p. 103).

42. Much of the following material has been taken from Faleh A. Jabar, *The Shi'ite Movement in Iraq* (London: Saqi, 2003), pp. 216–224; and Mu'min, *Years of Embers*, pp. 163, 222–223.

Chapter 8: The Saddam Husain Regime, 1979–1989

1. Abd al-Husain was identified as one of those who had openly opposed Bakr's resignation. This disagreement is openly discussed in a semiofficial biography of Saddam, for which the main source was Saddam himself (Fuad Matar, Saddam Hussein, *The Man, the Cause, and the Future* [London: Third World Center, 1981], p. 54). Such opposition also appears in Ali Karim Sa'id, *Iraq 8 Shabat 1963, Min Hiwar al-Mafahim ila Hiwar al-Dam. Muraja'at fi Dhakira Talib Shabib* (Iraq of 8 February 1963: From the Dialogue of Conceptions to

the Dialogue of Blood: Reviews on Talib Shabib's Memories) (n.pl.: Dar al-Kunuz al-Arabiyya, 1999), p. 347.

2. For a good description of the proceedings, see Said Aburish, *Saddam Hussein: The Politics of Revenge* (New York: Bloomsbury, 2000), pp. 171–172.

3. Iraq News Agency (Baghdad) (hereafter, INA), cited in Foreign Broadcast Information Service (Washington, DC) (hereafter, FBIS), 30 July 1979, pp. E1–E4; INA, 7 August 1979, cited in FBIS, 8 August 1979, p. E1.

4. FBIS, 8 October 1980, p. E8.

5. INA, 29 June 1979, cited in FBIS, 2 July 1979, p. E4; INA, 30 June 1979, cited in FBIS, 3 July 1979, p. E1; INA, 4 August 1980, cited in FBIS, 8 August 1980, p. E5.

6. *Middle East Economic Digest* (London) (hereafter, *MEED*), 24 (18 April 1980): 40.

7. Ralph King, *The Iran-Iraq War: The Political Implications*, Adelphi paper 219 (London: International Institute for Strategic Studies, 1987), p. 10.

8. Dilip Hiro, *The Longest War: The Iran-Iraq Military Conflict* (New York: Routledge, 1991), p. 36; Simon Henderson, *Instant Empire: Saddam Hussein's Ambition for Iraq* (San Francisco: Mercury House, 1991), pp. 104–105; Mark Gasiorowski, "The Nuzhih Plot and Iranian Politics," *IJMES* 34:4 (November 2002).

9. Gregory Gause, *The International Relations of the Persian Gulf* (New York: Cambridge University Press, 2010), pp. 63–64. Gause and others have emphasized the defensive nature of the war.

10. Text of Foreign Minister Sa 'dun Hammadi's speech, UN General Assembly, 3 October 1980, cited in FBIS, 7 October 1980, pp. E1–E6.

11. Hiro, *The Longest War*, p. 40.

12. For confirmation of the use of chemical weapons in the war, see Wafiq al-Samarra'i, *Hitam al-Bawaba-l-Sharqiyya* (Shattering the Eastern Gates) (Kuwait: Dar al-Qabas, 1997), p. 41. The best documentation on this use is Joost Hiltermann, *A Poisonous Affair: America, Iraq, and the Gassing of Halabja* (New York: Cambridge University Press, 2007).

13. Hiro, *The Longest War*, p. 185.

14. Amatzia Baram, "Iraq Between East and West," in *The Iran-Iraq War: Impact and Implications*, ed. Efraim Karsh (New York: St. Martin's Press, 1989), p. 86.

15. President Ali Khamenei, in his letter accepting UN Security Council Resolution 598, referred to the airbus tragedy and a war that was engulfing even innocent civilians (*The Times* [London], 19 July 1988, p. 9, cited in

Thomas McNaugher, "Walking Tightropes in the Gulf," in *The Iran-Iraq War*, p. 198 n77).

16. Samarra'i, *Shattering the Eastern Gates*, p. 107.

17. The complex role of the Kurds and Iranians in this affair is carefully examined in Hiltermann, *A Poisonous Affair*, chap. 5.

18. For an excellent analysis of Iraq's foreign policy in this period, see Charles Tripp, "Iraq," in *The Cold War and the Middle East*, ed. Yezid Sayigh and Avi Shlaim (Oxford, UK: Clarendon Press, 1997), pp. 186–215.

19. Relations with Syria had returned to their normal, strained position in 1979 after Saddam had accused Syria of the failed plot that led to the party massacre in Baghdad. Iraq broke relations with Syria in October 1980 because Syria was sending arms to Iran. Syria, for its part, saw Iran as a regional balance against a hostile neighbor.

20. Syria likewise harbored Iraqi oppositionists, including the ICP, elements of the KDP and the PUK, Iraqi members of a pro-Syrian faction of the Ba'th Party, and even members of the Da'wa.

21. Fred Axelgard, "Why Baghdad Is Wooing Washington," *Christian Science Monitor*, 29 July 1983.

22. For a good analysis of Saddam Husain's thinking on the United States, see Hal Brando and David Palkki, "Conspiring Bastards: Saddam Hussein's Strategic View of the United States," *Diplomatic History* (forthcoming). The article is drawn from captured records of the Saddam Husain regime now archived at the Conflict Records Research Center at the National Defense University, Washington, DC.

23. FBIS, 29 June 1982, pp. E1–E2.

24. Shahran Chubin and Charles Tripp, *Iran and Iraq at War* (Boulder, CO: Westview Press, 1988), p. 101.

25. Faleh A. Jabar, *The Shi'ite Movement in Iraq* (London: Saqi, 2003), chap. 14; Amatzia Baram, *State-Mosque Relations in Ba'thist Iraq, 1968–2003* (forthcoming), pt. 3, chap. 1, sec. 3.

26. Jabar, *The Shi'ite Movement*, p. 253.

27. David McDowall, *A Modern History of the Kurds* (London: I. B. Tauris, 1997), p. 346; Shahram Chubin and Charles Tripp, *Iran and Iraq at War* (Boulder, CO: Westview Press, 1988), pp. 105–106; Hussein Tahiri, *The Structure of Kurdish Society and the Struggle for the Kurdish State* (Costa Mesa, CA: Mazda Publications, 2007), pp. 159–164.

28. Much of this section is drawn from McDowall, *A Modern History of the Kurds*, pp. 348–352.

29. The Fursan was heavily drawn from specific tribes. Some, like the Bara-dostis, Khushnaw, Surchis, Harkis, and Zibaris, had long been opposed to the Barzanis. Others, such as the Jaf and Pizhdar, were generally progovernment. Still others joined to avoid having their villages razed or their population displaced. Many also joined to avoid the draft and service on the southern front.

30. The term *anfal,* meaning "spoils," is taken from the eighth *sura* (chapter) of the Qur'an and refers to the great Muslim battle with unbelievers in AD 624. The *sura* claims that the spoils of the battle belong to God and the Messenger (Muhammad).

31. The best accounts of the Anfal and related events are to be found in Middle East Watch, *Genocide in Iraq: The Anfal Campaign Against the Kurds* (New York: Human Rights Watch, 1993): and Joost Hiltermann, *A Poisonous Affair* (New York: Cambridge University Press, 2007).

32. In this first episode in which chemical weapons were used, victims were treated in local hospitals, but a number, estimated between 225 and 400, died (Middle East Watch, *Genocide,* p. 70). There is no way to independently verify these figures, most of which are taken from interviews with survivors and other reputable evidence. Both Middle East Watch, *Genocide;* and Hiltermann, *A Poisonous Affair,* give detailed descriptions of each of these attacks.

33. Middle East Watch, *Genocide,* pp. 73–74.

34. These figures are taken from Middle East Watch, *Genocide,* p. xiv; and McDowall, *A Modern History of the Kurds,* pp. 357, 360.

35. This observation is based on a trip by the author to the area and a visit to three large cities, Arbil, Kirkuk, and Sulaimaniyya, in May 1989. These areas were living on the development of the region in the early 1970s (Gareth Stansfield, *Iraqi Kurdistan: Political Development and Emergent Democracy* [London: Routledge Curzon, 2003], p. 44).

36. Eliyahu Kanovsky, "Economic Implications for the Region and the World Oil Market," in *The Iran-Iraq War: Impact and Implications,* ed. Efraim Karsh (New York: St. Martin's Press, 1989), p. 233.

37. Kanovsky, "Economic Implications," p. 238.

38. "Special Report: Iraq," *MEED,* 26 October 1982, p. 4.

39. Chubin and Tripp, *Iran and Iraq at War,* p. 110.

40. Petroleum Finance Company, "Iraq: Political and Economic Structures" (Country Report, unpublished) (Washington, DC: Petroleum Finance Company, December 1994), p. 15.

41. Zuhair al-Jaza 'iri, "Ba'thist Ideology and Practice," in *Iraq Since the Gulf War,* ed. Fran Hazelton (London: Zed Books, 1994), p. 44.

42. For an excellent study of this Mesopotamian phenomenon and the rewriting of Ba'thist ideology, see Amatzia Baram, *Culture, History, and Ideology in the Formation of Ba'thist Iraq: 1968–1989* (Oxford, UK: Macmillan, 1991).

43. *MEED*, 19 August 1988.

44. *New York Times*, 22 November 1988.

Chapter 9: The Saddam Husain Regime, 1990–2003

1. For an excellent analysis of the decision process, see Gregory Gause, *The International Relations of the Persian Gulf* (New York: Cambridge University Press, 2010), chap. 4; and Gregory Gause, "Iraq's Decision to Go to War, 1980 and 1990," *Middle East Journal* 1:56 (Winter 2002): 47–59.

2. Lawrence Freedman and Efraim Karsh, *The Gulf Conflict, 1990–1991* (Princeton, NJ: Princeton University Press, 1993), p. 39.

3. Sa'd al-Bazzaz, *Harb Tulid Ukhra* (One War Gives Birth to Another) (Amman, Jordan: al-Ahliyya lil-Nashr wal-Tawzi'a, 1992), p. 34.

4. Freedman and Karsh, *The Gulf Conflict*, p. 45. Roland Dannreuther, *The Gulf Conflict: Political and Strategic Analysis*, Adelphi paper 264 (London: International Institute for Strategic Studies, 1991–1992), p. 12.

5. Minutes of the meeting between Tariq Aziz and Secretary of State James Baker, 9 January 1991, FBIS, 14 January 1992.

6. Anthony Cordesman, *Iran and Iraq: The Threat from the Northern Gulf* (Boulder, CO: Westview Press, 1994), pp. 236, 262.

7. Amatzia Baram, "The Invasion of Kuwait: Decision Making in Baghdad," in *Iraq's Road to War*, ed. Amatzia Baram and Barry Rubin (London: Macmillan, 1993), p. 11.

8. Carrying Iraq's debt on the books, even if Kuwait did not call it in, affected Iraq's credit position and its ability to get new loans.

9. Saddam's 30 May speech to the Arab summit, FBIS, 19 July 1990.

10. He is reputed to have remarked to an aide, when departing the meeting, that he had given the ambassador a lesson in diplomacy the United States would not forget (Sa'd al-Bazzaz, *al-Janaralat Akhir Ya'lim* [The Generals Are the Last to Know], 3rd ed. [London: Dar al-Hikma, 1996], p. 67). For a good exposition of this meeting, see Gause, *The International Relations*, pp. 99–101.

11. Shaul Bakkash, "Iran: War Ended, Hostility Continued," in *Iraq's Road to War*, p. 288; Richard Schofield, *Kuwait and Iraq: Historical Claims and Territorial Disputes* (London: Royal Institute of International Affairs, 1994), p. 131.

12. Local time is seven hours ahead of US time. Local time will be indicated where the difference affects the dates of events.

13. Al-Bazzaz, *The Generals*, pp. 94–95.

14. Al-Bazzaz, *The Generals*, pp. 90–94.

15. The best works on this effort are Bob Woodward, *The Commanders* (New York: Simon and Schuster, 1991); George Bush and Brent Scowcroft, *A World Transformed* (New York: Knopf, 1998), chap. 13; and Michael Gordon and General Bernard Trainor, *The Generals' War* (Boston: Little, Brown, 1995).

16. For a view sympathetic to the Arab attempt at a solution, see Majid Khadduri and Edmund Ghareeb, *War in the Gulf, 1990–1991: The Iraq-Kuwait Conflict and Its Implications* (New York: Oxford University Press, 1997).

17. Statement by the Iraqi RCC, 8 August 1990, FBIS, 9 August 1990, p. 27.

18. Baram, "The Invasion of Kuwait", p. 25.

19. Al-Bazzaz, in *One War Gives Birth to Another*, discusses the failure of these attempts. They were extensive, including secret talks between French contacts and Tariq Aziz and efforts by the USSR's main Middle East specialist, Yevgeni Primakov, and King Husain of Jordan. They also included a last-minute meeting between Secretary of State James Baker and Tariq Aziz in Geneva on 9 January. This latter meeting was notable for the veiled warning by the United States that if Iraq used weapons of mass destruction in the war, the regime was unlikely to survive.

20. Al-Bazzaz, *The Generals*, pp. 120–121.

21. Dannreuther, *The Gulf Conflict*, p. 48.

22. Freedman and Karsh, *The Gulf Conflict*, p. 329.

23. These deprivations and the anger and shock they provoked are vividly described by Nuha al-Radi, a well-known painter and sculptor who kept a diary of life under siege. See Nuha al-Radi, *Baghdad Diaries* (London: Saqi Books), 1998.

24. These estimates are taken from Freedman and Karsh, *The Gulf Conflict*, p. 408.

25. United Nations, *The UN and the Iraq-Kuwait Conflict, 1990–1996* (New York: United Nations, 1996), pp. 30–33.

26. For a good analysis of Saddam's strategic perception on the outcome of the war, see Kevin Woods and Mark Stout, "Saddam's Perceptions and Misperceptions: The Case of 'Desert Storm,'" *Journal of Strategic Studies* 33:1 (February 2010): 5–41. The authors draw heavily on the captured Iraqi records of the Saddam Husain regime now archived at the Conflict Records Research Center at the National Defense University, Washington, DC.

27. Much of this account is drawn from five articles written by Fa'iq al-Shaikh Ali on the *intifada* in *al-Hayat* (London), 22–26 March 1996 and from interviews with him and other participants in London and Amman in 1999.

28. Adil Jamil, interview with author, Amman, 26 August 1999. Jamil was a professor at Basra University and an observer of events.

29. Falih Abd al-Jabbar, "Why the Intifada Failed," in *Iraq Since the Gulf War*, ed. Fran Hazelton (London: Zed Books, 1994), p. 106.

30. See Kanan Makiya, *Cruelty and Silence* (New York: Norton, 1993), pp. 65–66; and Najib al-Salihi, *Al-Zalzal* (The Earthquake) (London: Rafid, 1998), p. 273. Some sources claim that Iraqis and especially the Badr Brigade came across the border well before the *intifada* (al-Bazzaz, *One War Gives Birth to Another*, p. 449; Wafiq al-Samarra'i, *Hitam al-Bawaba-l-Sharqiyya* [Shattering the Eastern Gates] [Kuwait: Dar al-Qabas, 1997], p. 413).

31. Abd al-Jabbar, "Why the Intifada Failed," p. 10. How much planning was behind the SCIRI role has been disputed; some apparently did take place in Tehran after the occupation of Kuwait (Makiya, *Cruelty and Silence*, p. 82).

32. In Tehran, President Rafsanjani was busy negotiating with emissaries from Baghdad, trying to improve relations.

33. The reasons for this decision are best stated in Bush and Scowcroft, *A World Transformed*, pp. 484–485, 489.

34. Jonathon Randall, *After Such Knowledge, What Forgiveness?* (New York: Farrar, Straus and Giroux, 1997), p. 47; Hussein Tahiri, *The Structure of Kurdish Society and the Struggle for the Kurdish State* (Costa Mesa, CA: Mazda Publications, 2007), pp. 166–167.

35. Ibrahim al-Nawwar, *al-Mu'arida-l-Iraqiyya wal-Sira'a-l-Isqat Saddam* (The Iraqi Opposition and the Struggle to Remove Saddam) (London: Aurora Press, 1993), p. 94; Salihi, *The Earthquake*, chap. 6; David McDowall, *A Modern History of the Kurds* (London: I. B. Tauris, 1997), pp. 371–372.

36. Ali Allawi, *The Occupation of Iraq: Winning the War, Losing the Peace* (New Haven, CT: Yale University Press, 2007), p. 143.

37. Sarah Graham-Brown, *Sanctioning Saddam: The Politics of Intervention in Iraq* (London: I. B. Tauris, 1999), p. 28.

38. Amatzia Baram, "Neo-Tribalism in Iraq: Saddam Hussein's Tribal Policies, 1991–1996," *IJMES* 20 (1997): 13; Talib Suhail, tribal leader of the Bani Tamim, interview with author, Amman, July 1993; Keiko Sakai, "Tribalization as a Tool of State Control in Iraq," in *Tribes and Power*, ed. Faleh A. Jabbar and Hosham Dawood (London: Saqi, 2003), pp. 141–145.

39. Army Day speech by Saddam Husain, 6 January 1992, FBIS-NES, 6 January 1992. See also Ofra Bengio, *Saddam's Word: Political Discourse in Iraq*

(Oxford, UK: Oxford University Press, 1998), chap. 13. For a good exposition of this shift to religion, see Amatzia Baram, *Iraq 1968–2003: State-Mosque Relations Under the Ba'th* (forthcoming), pt. 2, sec. 2C.

40. Boutros Boutros-Ghali, "Introduction to United Nations," in United Nations, *The UN and the Iraq-Kuwait Conflict*, pp. 30–33. This volume also contains a documentary record of the UN resolutions, reports, and other actions on Iraq.

41. Harry Brown, "The Iraq-Kuwait Boundary Dispute: Historical Background and the UN Decisions of 1992–1993," *IBRU Boundary and Security Bulletin*, October 1994, www.dur.ac.uk/resources/ibru/publications/full/bsb 2–3_brown.PDF.

42. This account draws on reports from IAEA and UNSCOM; numerous interviews with a number of inspectors; Andrew and Patrick Cockburn, *Out of the Ashes* (New York: HarperCollins, 1999), chap. 4; and Scott Ritter, *Endgame* (New York: Simon and Schuster, 1999). Much of the UN documentation on Iraq's disarmament can be found in United Nations, *The UN and the Iraq-Kuwait Conflict*.

43. UNSCOM was tasked with investigating chemical and biological weapons and long-range missile programs. The IAEA was to investigate the nuclear program.

44. Rolf Ekeus, Talk before the Council on Foreign Relations, Washington, DC, 17 June 1997.

45. Anthony H. Cordesman and Ahmed S. Hashim, *Iraq: Sanctions and Beyond* (Boulder, CO: Westview Press, 1997), p. 127.

46. Food and Agriculture Organization/World Food Programme, "Food Supply and Nutritional Assessment Mission to Iraq," Special Report (3 October, 1997); Nutritional Mission to Iraq, "Special Report" (3 October 1997), p. 10, www.fao.org/giews/english/alertes/srirq997.htm.

47. Cordesman and Hashim, *Iraq*, p. 151.

48. EIU, *Iraq 2001*, p. 27.

49. These were Saddam Husain, Ali Hasan al-Majid, Kamil Yasin Rashid, Samir Abd al-Aziz Najm, and Adil Abd Allah Mahdi al-Duri—all Albu Nasir—together with Izzat Ibrahim al-Duri (Harb) and Muhammad Zamam Abd al-Razzaq al-Sa'dun (Sa'dun).

50. Samarra'i admitted he left just as he was about to be apprehended: Samarra'i, *Shattering the Eastern Gates*, pp. 437–449.

51. For a good account of this defection and its denouement, see Amatzia Baram, *Building Toward Crisis: Saddam Husayn's Strategy for Survival* (Washington, DC: Washington Institute for Near East Policy, 1988), pp. 13–16.

52. The upper levels of leadership in 1998 included all of the Regional Command and the RCC. Both bodies were overlapping except for one member of the RCC, the Kurd Muhyi al-Din Ma'ruf, who was not on the Regional Command. They were Saddam Husain, Izzat Ibrahim al-Duri, Ali Hasan al-Majid, Muhammad Hamza al-Zubaidi, Mizban Khadr Hadi, Kamil Yasin Rashid, Abd al-Ghani Abd al-Ghafur, Latif Nsayyif Jasim, Muhammad Zamam Abd al-Razzaq al-Sa'dun, Muhammad Yunis al-Ahmad, al-Radi Hasan Salman, Aziz Salih al-Nu'man, Samir Abd al-Aziz Najm, Fadil Ibrahim al-Mashhadani, Adil Abd Allah Mahdi al-Duri, Taha Yasin Ramadan, Tariq Aziz, and Taha Muhyi al-Din Ma'ruf.

53. Falih Abd al-Jabbar, "Iraq Mutates into a Society of Tribalism," *Gulf News*, 3 August 2000.

54. Ministry of Education, *al-Tarbiyya-l-Wataniyya* (National Education), text for fifth grade elementary (Baghdad: Ministry of Education, 1994).

55. McDowall, *A Modern History of the Kurds*, p. 386; Tahiri, *The Structure of Kurdish Society*, pp. 172–182.

56. McDowall, *A Modern History of the Kurds*, p. 387. For a good discussion of this conflict, see Michael Gunter, "The KDP-PUK Conflict in Northern Iraq," *MEJ* 50:2 (Spring 1996): 225–241.

57. The PKK was established in Turkey in 1979 but came into public view in August 1984 when it began its insurgency campaign against the Turkish government. Led by Abd Allah Ocalon (known as "Apo"), the PKK was devoted to Kurdish independence but also to Marxism-Leninism. In the 1990s, the movement increased its activities in southeastern Turkey; at the same time, it made some progress in developing mass support.

58. Hushyar Zibari, KDP representative, interview with author, Salah al-Din, 24 August 1998; Tahiri, *The Structure of Kurdish Society*, p. 188.

59. The marsh area in question comprised some 6,000 square miles of wetlands and swamp, formed by the waters at the confluence of the Tigris and Euphrates, constituting a triangle stretching roughly from Basra in the south to Nasiriyya in the west and Amara in the east. The two largest marshes were the Haur al-Hawiza, on the Iranian border between Qurna and Amara, and Haur al-Hammar, in the west near Suq al-Shuyukh and Nasiriyya.

60. Cordesman and Hashim, *Iraq*, p. 103.

61. For information on Sadr and his movement see Amatzia Baram, "Sadr the Father, Sadr the Son," in *Iraq Between Occupations*, ed. Amatzia Baram et al. (New York: Palgrave Macmillan, 2010), pp. 143–157; Patrick Cockburn, *Muqtada: Muqtada al-Sadr, the Shia Revival, and the Struggle for Iraq* (New York: Scribner, 2008), chaps. 7–8; and and Baram, *Iraq 1968–2003*, pt. 3, chap. 1.

62. The EIU's *Profile of Iraq, 2002–2003*, gives estimated exile figures at 1 to 2 million, with 500,000 in Iran (London: The Economist, 2003). These are lower than others.

63. Nawwar, *The Iraqi Opposition*, pp. 117–127.

64. For the Shi'i Islamist parties in this period, see Allawi, *The Occupation of Iraq*, pp. 73–76. For SCIRI after the Gulf War, see "Shiite Politics in Iraq: the Role of the Supreme Council," International Crisis Group report 70 (15 November 2007), pp. 5–9.

65. Muhammad al-Shamrani, *Sira'-l-Addad: al-Ma'arida-l-Iraqiyya Ba'd Harb al-Khalij* (The Struggle of the Adversaries: The Iraqi Opposition After the Gulf War) (London: Dar al-Hikma, n.d.). A list of those on the executive committee can be found on pp. 322–323.

66. Shamrani, *The Struggle of the Adversaries*, pp. 395–399.

67. Allawi, *The Occupation of Iraq*, p. 63.

68. David Phillips, *Losing Iraq: Inside the Postwar Reconstruction Fiasco* (Boulder, CO: Westview Press, 2005), p. 73.

Chapter 10: The US Attempt at Nation-Building in Iraq, 2003–2006

1. The best explanation is given in Gregory Gause, *The International Relations of the Persian Gulf* (New York: Cambridge University Press, 2010), chap. 6. See also Bob Woodward, *Plan of Attack* (New York: Simon and Schuster, 2004); George Packer, *The Assassins' Gate: America in Iraq* (New York: Farrar, Straus and Giroux), 2005), chaps. 1–7; Ali Allawi, *The Occupation of Iraq: Winning the War, Losing the Peace* (New Haven, CT: Yale University Press, 2007), Prologue, chaps. 3–5; Todd Purdum, *A Time of Our Choosing: America's War in Iraq* (New York: Times Books, 2003); Ivo Daalder and James M. Lindsay, *America Unbound: The Bush Revolution in Foreign Policy* (Washington, DC: Brookings Institution Press, 2003); Richard Haass, *War of Necessity, War of Choice: A Memoir of Two Iraq Wars* (New York: Simon and Schuster, 2009), chaps. 6–9; and Michael Isikoff and David Corn, *Hubris* (New York: Three Rivers Press, 2006).

2. For this thesis, see Isikoff and Corn, *Hubris*, chaps. 4, 6.

3. The most persuasive proponent of this thesis was Kenneth M. Pollack, *The Threatening Storm: The Case for Invading Iraq* (New York: Random House, 2002).

4. Allawi, *The Occupation of Iraq*, pp. 87–88.

5. Most of this war account is drawn from Michael R. Gordon and General Bernard E. Trainer, *Cobra II: The Inside Story of the Invasion and Occupation of Iraq* (New York: Pantheon Books, 2006), the best and most detailed account of the war to date.

6. These forces included three army divisions, one marine division, and one British division. Gordon and Trainer, *Cobra II*, put the number of ground forces at 183,000 (p. 117); Ricks, at 145,000 (Thomas E. Ricks, *Fiasco: The Military Adventure in Iraq* [New York: Penguin Press, 2006], p. 117).

7. Ansar al-Islam had found a foothold in the eastern portion of Kurdish territory around Halabja, which had been under the control of the IMIK. At the end of the 1990s, the IMIK had been radicalized by militant Kurds returning from *jihad* in Afghanistan. The IMIK fractured, and Ansar al-Islam came to dominate this no-man's-land (Gareth Stansfield, "The Kurdish Dilemma: The Golden Era Threatened," in *Iraq at the Crossroads: State and Society in the Shadow of Regime Change*, ed. Toby Dodge and Steven Simon [London: Oxford University Press, 2003], pp. 142–143).

8. Quil Lawrence, *Invisible Nation: How the Kurds' Quest for Statehood Is Shaping Iraq and the Middle East* (New York: Walker and Company, 2008), pp. 168–169.

9. Gordon and Trainer, *Cobra II*, p. 489.

10. Packer, *Assassin's Gate*, p. 139.

11. Allawi, *The Occupation of Iraq*, p. 91.

12. The Sadrists included a number of those who would assume public positions in 2003, like Riyad al-Nuri, Mustafa-l-Ya'qubi, Qa'id Khazali, and Jabr al-Khafaji (Marisa Cochrane, "The Fragmentation of the Sadrist Movement," Iraq Report No. 12 [Washington, DC: Institute for the Study of War, 2006]. p. 11; Juan Cole, "The United States and Shi'ite Religious Factions in Postwar Iraq," *MEJ* 57:4 [Autumn 2003]: 550–566; International Crisis Group, "Iraq's Shi'ites Under Occupation" [Baghdad/Brussels: ICG, 9 September 2003], pp. 15–20).

13. Patrick Cockburn, *Muqtada: Muqtada al-Sadr, the Shia Revival, and the Struggle for Iraq* (New York: Scribner, 2008), p. 117; International Crisis Group, "Iraq's Shi'ites Under Occupation," p. 17; Rory Steward, *The Prince of the Marshes and Other Occupational Hazards of a Year in Iraq* (London: Harcourt, 2006), p. 240.

14. CPA Order No. 1, www.iraqcoalition.org/regulations/6/18/10.

15. Allawi, *The Occupation of Iraq*, p. 150.

16. The issue and the order were discussed in testimony by Douglas Feith to the House International Relations Committee on 15 May.

17. CPA Order No. 2, www.iraqcoalition.org/regulations/6/18/10.

18. The order apparently blindsided many US officers on the ground, like General David Petraeus (Gordon and Trainer, *Cobra II*, pp. 481–485).

19. Global Security.org, "Iraqi Military Reconstruction," www.globalsecurity.org/military/world/iraq/iraq-corps3.htm. The armed forces grew from 99,000 in October 2003 to 181,000 in October 2004.

20. Robert M. Perito, "The Coalition Provisional Authority's Experience with Public Security in Iraq," Special Report no. 137 (Washington, DC: United States Institute of Peace, April, 2005), p. 10.

21. Gause, *The International Relations*, p. 234.

22. For an excellent assessment of this dilemma, see Anne Henderson, "The Coalition Provisional Authority's Experience with Economic Reconstruction in Iraq," Special Report No. 138 (Washington, DC: United States Institute of Peace, April 2005).

23. CPA Order No. 18, 7 July 7 2003, www.iraqcoalition.org/regulations /6/18/10.

24. CPA Order No. 43, 14 October 2003, www.iraqcoalition.org/regulations /6/18/10; Bathsheba Crocker, "Reconstructing Iraq's Economy," *Washington Quarterly* 27:4 (Autumn 2004): 78.

25. Although Bremer and the CPA have been accused by many Iraqis of introducing the concept of a government based on ethnic and sectarian divisions, this was no innovation; it had been an operating principle of the opposition, especially the INC, for years. In fact, even though Bremer clearly held to Iraq's ethnic and sectarian divisions, his search for diversity was broader and included political parties and gender as well. However, the CPA's explicit recognition of the idea unquestionably helped solidify it.

26. According to one source, Hakim thereby implicitly, though not formally, rejected the Iranian concept of *wilayat al-faqih* (rule of the theological jurist), which he had previously accepted (Allawi, *The Occupation of Iraq*, p. 112).

27. Celeste J. Ward, "The Coalition Provisional Authority's Experience with Governance in Iraq," Special Report No. 139 (Washington, DC: United States Institute of Peace, May 2005), p. 5.

28. Phebe Marr, "Who Are Iraq's Leaders? What Do They Want?" Special Report No. 160 (Washington, DC: United States Institute of Peace, March 2006), p. 11.

29. Chief among these were Chalabi, Allawi, Barzani, Talabani, al-Ja'fari, and Abd al-Aziz al-Hakim. The presidency also included Muhammad Bahr al-Ulum (an independent Shi'i Islamist), Muhsin Abd al-Hamid of the IIP, Ad-

nan Pachachi, Ghazi al-Yawar of the Shammar tribe, and Izz ad-Din al-Salim, head of a Da'wa splinter party who was assassinated in May 2004.

30. Roel Meijer, "The Association of Muslim Scholars in Iraq," *Middle East Report* 237 (Winter 2005): 13.

31. Meijer, "Association of Muslim Scholars," p. 14; Allawi, *The Occupation of Iraq*, pp. 182–183.

32. The term "Wahhabi" refers to the austere practices and strict scriptural interpretation of Islam followed in Saudi Arabia. The word is derived from Ahmad Ibn al-Wahhab, the eighteenth-century founder of the movement.

33. Allawi, *The Occupation of Iraq*, p. 182.

34. In early February 2004, the CPA released a letter sent by Zarqawi to bin Ladin outlining his strategy for inciting a Shi'a-Sunni conflict as a means of galvanizing the Sunni Arab community and the dangers of annihilation they faced at the hands of the Shi'a. The letter can be found on www.globalsecurity.org.

35. Ricks, *Fiasco*, p. 375.

36. Ricks, *Fiasco*, p. 254.

37. For Sistani's political role and outlook, see Babak Rahimi, "Ayatollah Sistani and the Democratization of Post-Ba'athist Iraq," Special Report No. 187 (Washington, DC: United States Institute of Peace, June 2007); and Reidar Visser, "Sistani, the United States, and Politics in Iraq," Paper No. 700 (Oslo: Norwegian Institute of International Affairs, 2006).

38. L. Paul Bremer, *My Year in Iraq* (New York: Threshold Editions, 2006), pp.163–167; Rajav Chandrasekaran, *Imperial Life in the Emerald City* (New York: Knopf, 2006), pp. 79–80, 164, 186–198; Gause, *The International Relations*, pp. 159–160.

39. For a copy of the TAL, see Center for Studies on New Regions, TAL, www.cesnur.org/2004/Iraq_tal.htlm.

40. Ahmad Chalabi, Interview with Ghassan Charbel, *al-Hayat* (London), 31 March 2009.

41. Allawi, *The Occupation of Iraq*, p. 332.

42. Allawi, *The Occupation of Iraq*, p. 337.

43. Ahmed S. Hashim, *Insurgency and Counter-Insurgency in Iraq* (Ithaca, NY: Cornell University Press, 2006), pp. 42–43.

44. Allawi, *The Occupation of Iraq*, p. 339.

45. Hajm al-Hasani, an IIP member who was more secular in orientation, dropped out of the party to remain in the cabinet as minister of industry.

46. Kenneth Katzman, "Iraq Elections, Government and Constitution" (Washington, DC: Congressional Research Service, 24 April 2006), p. 1.

47. Adeed Dawisha and Larry Diamond, "Iraq's Year of Voting Dangerously," *Journal of Democracy* 17:2 (April 2006): 93.

48. The distribution of seats among parties *within* these coalitions is not clear because it was arranged behind closed doors. Within the UIA, it appears that the two Da'wa branches were given 29 seats; so, too, were the Sadrists. SCIRI, which led the ticket, took 20, and Chalabi got 3, reflecting their estimated strength in the body politic. Within the Kurdish alliance, seats were distributed in accordance with the agreement between the KDP and the PUK to have relatively equal participation. There was no such division among the INA.

49. A breakdown of voting patterns shows that about 95 percent of the Kurds voted for the Kurdistan Alliance, 75 percent of the Shi'a for the UIA, and at least 75 percent of the Sunnis for their electoral choice—boycott. There were seventeen Sunnis in the assembly, most on secular and nationalist lists (Dawisha and Diamond, "Iraq's Year of Voting Dangerously," p. 94).

50. Results on the provincial elections have been taken from Michael Knights and Eamon McCarthy, "Provincial Politics in Iraq: Fragmentation or a New Awakening?" Policy Focus No. 81 (Washington, DC: Washington Institute for Near East Policy, April 2008), Annex 5, pp. 9–16. Little has been written about the provincial elections; for a good analysis, see Eric Herring and Glen Rangwala, *Iraq in Fragments: The Occupation and Its Legacy* (Ithaca, NY: Cornell University Press, 2006), chap. 3.

51. International Crisis Group, "Iraq's Provincial Elections: The Stakes," Middle East Report No. 82 (Brussels: ICG, 17 January 2009), p. 7.

52. International Crisis Group, "Iraq's Provincial Elections," p. 3.

53. Allawi, *The Occupation of Iraq*, p. 134.

54. International Crisis Group, "Unmaking Iraq: A Constitutional Process Gone Awry," Report No. 19 (Amman /Brussels: ICG, 26 September 2005), p. 2.

55. Jonathan Morrow, "Iraq's Constitutional Process II: An Opportunity Lost," Special Report No. 155 (Washington, DC: United States Institute of Peace, November 2005), p. 9.

56. Ashley S. Deeks and Matthew D. Burton, "Iraq's Constitution: A Drafting History," *Cornell International Law Journal* 40:1 (2007): 4–5.

57. For more detailed discussion of this drafting process and the differing points of view of those involved, see International Crisis Group, "Unmaking Iraq"; Morrow, "Iraq's Constitutional Process II"; Deeks and Burton, "Iraq's Constitution"; and Peter W. Galbraith, *The End of Iraq: How American Incompetence Created a War Without End* (New York: Simon and Schuster, 2006), chap. 10.

58. Deeks and Burton, "Iraq's Constitution," p. 66.

59. The following has been taken from the draft constitution submitted to the population for vote, translated from Arabic by Associated Press. The text can be found at http://news.bbc.co.uk/2/shared/bsp/hi/pdfs/24_08_05_constit.pdf. For textual commentary and analysis, see Nathan J. Brown, "The Final Draft of the Iraqi Constitution: Analysis and Commentary" (Washington, DC: Carnegie Endowment for International Peace, 2005), www.carnegieendowment.org/files /FinalDraftofIraqiConstitution1.pdf.

60. Tawafuq was an outgrowth of meetings among various Sunni groups, some secular, some religious, early in 2005. They feared exclusion from the constitutional process and decentralization of Iraq. The IIP was an essential component of the group, which began by calling itself Ahl al-Sunna (People of the Sunna, i.e., Sunnis). However, a number of intellectuals objected to the sectarian coloring of the name, and the group took the name Ahl al-Iraq (People of Iraq, i.e., Iraqis), which remained. Ahl al-Iraq then became a component of the Tawafuq coalition.

61. George Packer, "The Lessons of Tal Afar," *New Yorker*, 10 April 2006, p. 60.

62. Packer, "The Lessons of Tal Far," p. 61.

63. Linda Robinson, *Tell Me How This Ends: General Petraeus and the Search for a Way Out of Iraq* (New York: PublicAffairs, 2008), p. 15.

64. By this time, the Sunni insurgency had consolidated into four main groups. One group, AQI, was almost wholly oriented toward a narrow (indeed fanatical) anti-Shi'a Islam and aimed at establishing a Sunni Islamic caliphate in Iraq and other territories. The other three were more Iraqi. One, the Islamic Army of Iraq, was strongly nationalist but had a considerable Islamic flavor to its propaganda and was influenced by Sunni Arab neighbors, especially Saudi Arabia. Another, the 1920s Brigade, was more nationalist and pragmatic in orientation and was uninterested in transnational ties, and, as the name suggests, harked back to the 1920 revolt against the British. The last main group was an offshoot of the ousted Ba'th Party, reportedly functioning under the authority of Izzat Ibrahim al-Duri. There were other, smaller groups, but they were less significant.

Chapter 11: The Stabilization of Iraq, 2007–2011

1. Abu Risha had impeccable nationalist credentials. He was the grandson of a tribal leader who had fought in the 1920 revolt and the son of a commander in the Anglo-Iraq War of 1941. His father and two brothers had been

killed by AQI in a gruesome manner. In addition to this personal motive, Abu Risha, like many *shaikhs*, was involved in construction and the import-export business, with offices in Amman and Dubai. The insurgency and the violence it engendered were extremely bad for business.

2. David Kilcullen, "Anatomy of a Tribal Revolt," *Small Wars Journal*, August 29, 2007, p. 2, http://small warsjournal.com./blog/2007/08/anatomy-of -a-tribal-revolt/.

3. The story of Amiriyya is told in Linda Robinson, *Tell Me How This Ends* (New York: PublicAffairs, 2008), pp. 231–234.

4. Robinson, *Tell Me How This Ends*, p. 234.

5. Sam Dagher, "Iraq's Sadr Uses Lull to Rebuild Army," *Christian Science Monitor*, 11 December 2007, www.csmonitor.com/2007/1211.

6. The move was also undertaken because of Sadr's fear of US influence on the government to activate his arrest warrant, which was still "pending."

7. Marisa Cochrane, "The Fragmentation of the Sadrist Movement," Iraq Report No. 12 (Washington, DC: Institute for the Study of War, 2009), p. 31.

8. Telephone interview, Lt. Colonel Joel D. Rayburn, United States Central Command, 7 October 2009. Colonel Rayburn served in Iraq during this period.

9. United Nations High Commissioner on Refugees (UNHCR), "Iraq Situation Update," August 2008, p. 1; International Organization for Migration (IOM), "Emergency Needs Assessment: Four Years of Post-Samarra Displacement in Iraq," April 2010, p. 1.

10. For an excellent book on this subject, see Joseph Sassoon, *The Iraqi Refugees: The New Crisis in the Middle East* (London: I. B. Tauris, 2009).

11. The Kurds claimed that the federal constitution gave the authority for development of "new" oil and gas fields to the KRG so long as revenue was distributed among all Iraqis on an agreed basis. Already discovered fields, such as those in Kirkuk, had to await settlement of disputed areas. The central government disagreed with this interpretation.

12. DNO (Det Norske Oljesekskop) is a Norwegian oil company listed on Norway's stock exchange.

13. *Hawlati* (Kurdish bi-weekly newspaper), Sulaimaniyya, 3 October 2007, cited in Denise Natali, *The Kurdish Quasi-State: Development and Dependency in Post–Gulf War Iraq* (New York: Syracuse University Press, 2010), p. 82.

14. Natali, *The Kurdish Quasi-State*, p. 91.

15. USAID, "Kurdistan Region: Economic Development Assessment" (Arbil, Iraq: USAID, 2008), cited in Natali, *The Kurdish Quasi-State*, p. 99.

16. USAID, "Kurdistan Region," p. 91.

17. Hayawa Aziz, "Kull Yidrus 'ala Hawa" (Everyone Studies as He Likes), *al-Sharq al-Awsat* (Arabic daily), London, 2 August 2010, p. 11.

18. Hussein Tahiri, *The Structure of Kurdish Society and the Struggle for the Kurdish State* (Costa Mesa, CA: Mazda Publishers, 2007), p. 335.

19. The new KNA itself reflected the Strategic Agreement. Consisting of 111 members, it was overwhelmingly dominated by the KDP and the PUK, which together controlled 74 percent of the seats. The KDP got 41 seats and gave 1 to a smaller party; the PUK got the same number and gave 2 to smaller parties. The Kurdish Islamic Union got 9; the Kurdistan Islamic Group, 6: the Turkmen, 4; and other minorities and smaller parties, the remainder. The Kurdish Assembly did, however, include women (nearly 30 percent) and low-ered membership age to twenty-five, allowing room for the younger generation (Natali, *The Kurdish Quasi-State*, p. 85).

20. Natali, *The Kurdish Quasi-State*, p. 119.

21. Under these circumstances, it was not worth producing for the company

22. For a discussion of this issue, see Natali, *The Kurdish Quasi-State*, p. 106.

23. Political and territorial issues in Kurdish areas only gradually became eth-nicized over time. Up until 1958, the notion of Kirkuk as exclusively part of Kurdistan was not "highly salient." For a good discussion of this issue, see Denise Natali, "The Kirkuk Conundrum," *Ethnopolitics* 7:4 (November 2008): 434.

24. Accurate figures on Kirkuk's shifting population are hard to come by. The last relatively accurate census of Kirkuk province was taken in 1957 under the monarchy. It showed the Kurds as a plurality, but not a majority, in the province and Turkmen predominating in Kirkuk City. In the city there were 45,306 Turkmen, 40,047 Kurds, and 27,127 Arabs; in the province, 187,591 Kurds, 109,620 Arabs, and 83,371 Turkmen. Since 1957, considerable demographic change has occurred, some by natural growth, more by rural to urban migration as Kurds and others flocked to Kirkuk in the wake of a developing oil industry. There is little doubt, however, that with the advent of the Ba'th regime in 1968, purposeful and increasingly forced Arabization took place, accompanied by re-pression of the Kurdish national movement. Many Arabs were brought from poorer Shi'i areas in the south. During the Anfal campaign, mass killings in-volved Kurds from Kirkuk village areas. Even though the censuses taken under Saddam are not considered "legitimate," there is little doubt of major displace-ment of Kurds and Turkmen.

25. International Crisis Group (ICG), "Iraq and the Kurds: The Brewing Battle over Kirkuk," Middle East Report No. 56 (Brussels: ICG, 18 July 2006), p. 11.

26. International Crisis Group, "Iraq's Kurds: Toward an Historic Compromise," Middle East Report No. 26 (Amman/Brussels: ICG, 8 April 2004), p. 11, n66.

27. International Crisis Group, "Iraq and the Kurds," p. 16.

28. International Crisis Group, "Iraq and the Kurds," pp. 4–5.

29. Robinson, *Tell Me How This Ends*, pp. 329–330.

30. Nazar Janabi, "Who Won the Battle of Basra?" Policy Watch No. 1361 (Washington, DC: Washington Institute for Near East Policy, 10 April 2008).

31. Anthony H. Cordesman and Adam Mauser, "Iraqi Force Development, 2008" (Washington, DC: Center for International and Strategic Studies, 2008), pp. 8–10.

32. Cordesman and Mauser, "Iraqi Force Development," p. 16.

33. Toby Dodge, "Iraq and the Next American President," *Survival* 50:5 (October–November 2008): 54.

34. International Crisis Group, "Iraq's Provincial Elections: The Stakes," Middle East Report No. 82 (Amman/Brussels: ICG, 27 January 2009), p. 17.

35. International Crisis Group, "Iraq and the Kurds: Trouble Along the Trigger Line," Middle East Report No. 88 (Washington, DC: ICG, 8 July 2009), p. 12.

36. Speech by Nuri al-Maliki to the Conference on Iraqi Elites and Efficiencies, Baghdad, 11 November 2008, cited in International Crisis Group, "Iraq's Provincial Elections," p. 17n96.

37. Michael Gordon, "The Last Battle," *New York Times Magazine*, 3 August 2008.

38. By this time, the Sons of Iraq had reached about 91,000 (some 78 percent were Sunni) and the US military had decided to put a freeze on recruitment.

39. Reidar Visser, Historiae.org, 27 November 2008, www.historiae.org.

40. The provincial election law provided a compromise between a closed list and an open list. Voters had several choices: They could pick from a preselected party list, they could select an individual candidate, or they could select both a single, individual candidate and a party list. Seats were reserved for minorities in several provinces, and there was a quota of a third for women. There was a threshold for a seat in any given province. This was defined by dividing the number of votes cast by the number of seats assigned to the province. Those not making the threshold (so-called wasted votes) were then reassigned to the winning parties and groups in the order in which they had won votes, obvi-

ously favoring the better-organized parties (International Crisis Group, "Iraq's Provincial Elections," p. 12).

41. Pascale Warda, head of the Hammurabi Human Rights Organization, quoted in International Crisis Group, "Iraq's Provincial Elections," p. 10.

42. Usama al-Musawi, head of the Sadr Office, Diwaniyya, 29 September 2008, quoted in International Crisis Group, "Iraq's Provincial Elections," p. 10.

43. Khalaf al-Thanun, head of the Education Committee, Salah al-Din Provincial Council, 18 September, 2008, quoted in International Crisis Group, "Iraq's Provincial Elections," p. 10.

44. Interviews with students at American University in Iraq-Sulaimaniyya, Sulaimaniyya, 22–25 May 2010.

45. Interviews with Muhammad Tawfiq, a leader of Goran, 23 May 2010, and Denise Natali, 22 May 2010, Sulaimaniyya.

46. Within the Iraqi government there were political repercussions, too. Muhammad al-Shahwani, director of the Iraqi National Intelligence Service (appointed and supported by the CIA), had presented evidence to tie Iran to the attacks, but these were rejected by Maliki. Shahwani was retired and sent packing to London. The service came to an end, leaving Maliki and his own people in charge of Iraqi intelligence and ending another link with the United States.

47. Transparency International, "Corruption Perceptions Index, 2010," www.transparency.org.

48. International Crisis Group, "Iraq's Uncertain Future: Elections and Beyond," Middle East Report No. 94 (Brussels: ICG, 25 February 2010), pp. 20–27.

49. International Crisis Group, "Iraq's Uncertain Future," p. 16.

50. For a good analysis of Maliki's position on "strong leadership," see Anthony Shadid, "Maliki Says Iraq Needs a Strong Leader Like Him," *New York Times*, 10 September 2010.

51. The legal status of the commission itself was questionable because members of the old De-Ba'thification Committee were still in charge, namely, Faisal al-Lami, executive director, and Ahmad Chalabi, president, both running for the CoR on the INA ticket. The movement was spearheaded by Chalabi, charging Ba'thists were returning under the rubric of secular Iraqi nationalists. For a good analysis of these disputes, see a series of commentaries by Reidar Visser in Historiae.org: "The Ruling by the Appeals Court," 5 February 2010; "Back to Work for the Appeals Court," 6 February 2010; "Chalabi and Lami Also Control the Independent Elections Commission," 9 February 2010; "Mutlak and Ani Are Banned," 11 February 2010; "The IHEC Publishes the Names of 6, 127 Approved Candidates," 10 February 2010; and "Governorate

and Party-Level Indicators of De-Ba'thification," 16 February 2010. These commentaries indicate the degree of distrust—and opportunism—of all major groups and political figures running for office.

52. A week before the election, Ali al-Lami, head of the Supreme National Commission for Accountability and Justice, sought to disqualify fifty-two more candidates, in addition to the previous five hundred banned, and he further tried to ban nine more candidates who won after the election. The appeals court eventually overruled these bans. For a good account of this issue, see Marina Ottoway and Danial Kaysi, "Post-Election Maneuvering: Rule of Law Is the Casualty," Carnegie Endowment, 30 April, 2010, http://Carnegieendowment.org /publications/index.cfm?fa=view&id=40722.

53. These included Hummam al-Hammudi and Jalal al-Din al-Saghir (ISCI), Muwwafiq al-Ruba'i and Sami al-Askari (former Da'wa), and Adnan Pachachi, veteran Sunni secularist.

Chapter 12: Economic, Social, and Cultural Change in Iraq, 2007–2011

1. US Department of Energy, Energy Information Administration (EIA), "Country Analysis Briefs Header: Iraq," September 2010, www.eia.doe.gov /cabs/iraq/full.html.

2. EIA, "Country Analysis," p. 1.

3. With the fall of Saddam, the old centralized Iraq National oil Company had broken up into subsidiary state-owned companies responsible for producing the oil: Southern Oil Company in the Basra area, Northern Oil Company for the northern (Kirkuk) fields, Midland Oil Company for the center, and Maysan Oil Company for that province. The State Oil Marketing Organization was responsible for exporting and marketing the oil, but the Oil Ministry in Baghdad would be responsible for managing the process and concluding the contracts.

4. Gina Chon, "Oil Companies Reject Iraq's Contract Terms," *Wall Street Journal*, 1 July 2009.

5. At the end of the bidding process, Exxon-Mobil, partnering with Shell and the government of Iraq, got the huge West Qurna field, while Shell and its Malaysian partner, Petronas, got the enormous Majnun field. France's Total, along with the CNPC and Petronas, captured Halfaya. ENI of Italy, with US Occidental and a Korean company, took Zubair. Lukoil and Gazprom of Russia as well as Statoil of Norway also came away with some fields.

6. Special Inspector General for Iraq Reconstruction, "Quarterly Report to the United States Congress" (Washington, DC: SIGIR, 30 April 2010), p. 92, Figure 2.32, www.sigir.mil/files/quarterlyreports/april2010/report-april_2010.pdf.

7. Erik DeVrijer, Udo Kock, and David Grigorian, "Iraq Makes Progress on Economic Front," *IMF Survey Magazine: Countries and Regions*, 13 February 2008, www.imf.org/external/pubs/ft/survey/S0/2008/car021308b.htm.

8. The ICI presents a clear picture of Iraq's needs and goals. For a detailed matrix of these, see UN Assistance Mission for Iraq, "International Compact with Iraq Fact Sheet," www.uniraq.org/ici.asp.

9. This report, put out on 19 February 2009, is one of the best assessments of Iraq's development and needs issued up to that point: World Bank, "Interim Strategy Note for the Republic of Iraq for the period Mid-FY09–FY11" (Washington, DC: World Bank, 19 February 2009).

10. The government charged customs duties of 5 percent on all goods except food, medicine, and clothing.

11. Economist Intelligence Unit (EIU), *Iraq Country Report* (London: Economist Intelligence Unit, May 2010), p. 16.

12. World Bank, "Interim Strategy," p. 6. The Paris Club is an informal group of financial officials representing the world's largest economies; the group helps negotiate debt relief for heavily indebted nations.

13. EIU, *Iraq Country Report*, p. 17; Joseph Sassoon, "Economic Policy in Iraq, 2003–2009," in *Post-Saddam Iraq: New Realities, Old Identities, Changing Patterns*, ed. Amnon Cohen and Noga Efrati (East Sussex, UK: Sussex Academic Press, 2011).

14. CIA, *The World Factbook: Iraq*, 9 November 2010, www.cia.gov/library/publications/the-world-factbook/geog/iz.html.

15. United Nations Statistics Division, "Country Profile: Iraq" (New York: UN Statistics Division, 2011), http://data.un/org/CountryProfile.aspx?srName=Iraq.

16. Andy Sambidge, "UAE Tops List of Foreign Investors in Iraq in 2009," Arabianbusiness.com, 24 November 2009, www.arabianbusiness.com/574432?tmpl=print&page.

17. Kenneth Katzman, "Iran's Activities and Influence in Iraq" (Washington, DC: Congressional Research Service, 4 June 2009), p. 8.

18. Gina Chon, "Iran's Cheap Goods Stifle Iraq Economy," *Wall Street Journal*, 18 March 2009.

19. Dunia Frontier Consultants, "Private Foreign Investment in Iraq" (Washington, DC/Dubai: Dunia Frontier Consultants, March 2009), p. 7.

20. World Bank, "Interim Strategy," p. i.

21. "Iraq: Key Figures Since the War Began," Associated Press, 2 January 2009, www.huffingtonpost.com/2009/01/02/iraq-key-figures-since-the_n_15 4879.html.

22. SIGIR, "Quarterly Report," p. 79.

23. Ben Lando, "Iraq Races to Avoid Export Collapse," *Iraq Oil Report*, 18 October 2010.

24. Brookings Institution, "Iraq Index," 30 September 2010, p. 35, www.brookings.edu~/media/files/centers/saban/iraq.index/index/index20100 930.pdf. These figures do not include the KRG.

25. Joseph Sassoon, *The Iraqi Refugees and the New Crisis in the Middle East* (London: I. B. Tauris, 2009), p. 146.

26. CIA, *The World Factbook: Iraq 2010*, www.workmall.com/wfb2010 /iraq/index.html; CIA, *The World Factbook: Jordan 2010*, www.cia.gov /library/publications/the-world-factbook/geos/jo.html; CIA, *The World Factbook: Syria 2011*, www.cia.gov/library/publications/the-world-factbook/geos /sy.html.

27. CIA, *The World Factbook: Iraq 2010*.

28. Sassoon, "Economic Policy in Iraq."

29. SIGIR, "Quarterly Report," p. 103.

30. Antoine Blua, "Iraq Tussles with Neighbors over Water," Radio Free Europe/Radio Liberty, 13 October 2009, www.rferl.org/content/Iraq_Tussles _with_Neighbors_over_water/182160.

31. Ma'd Fayadh, "Wazir al-Mawarid al-Ma'iyyah-al-Iraqi: La Nuhasil Hatta ala Ruba' Hissatina min Miyyah al-Farat" (The Iraqi Minister of Water Resources: We Are Not Even Receiving a Quarter of Our Share of Euphrates Water), *Al-Sharq al-Awsat*, 19 August 2010.

32. Blua, "Iraq Tussles."

33. Anthony Cordesman, Charles Loi, and Adam Mausner, "Iraq's Coming National Challenges: Economy, Demography, Budget, and Trade" (Washington, DC: Center for Strategic and International Studies, 5 January 2011), p. 8, http://csis.org/files/publication/110105_iraq_3-economy_budget.pdf.

34. CIA, *The World Factbook: Iraq 2010*, p. 3.

35. Campbell Robertson, "Iraq Government Rolls Soar as the Private Sector Falters," *New York Times*, 11 August 2008.

36. World Bank, "Doing Business 2011: Making a Difference for Entrepreneurs," 4 November 2010, www.doingbusiness.org/report/doing-busines/doing -business-2011.

37. *Lancet*, a well-known medical journal, has put the estimated death toll at the end of 2006 much higher, roughly at 601,000 excess deaths, of which 31 percent were caused by the coalition, 24 percent by others, and 46 percent by unknown sources. These figures are much higher than those given by the Iraqi Ministry of Health, the United Nations, and household surveys such as the Iraq Family Health Survey.

38. Sinan Salaheddin, "Iraq: 85,000 Iraqis Killed from 2004–2008," Baghdad, Associated Press, 14 October 2009; "U.S. Military Tallies Deaths of Iraqi Civilians and Forces," *New York Times*, 15 October 2009.

39. United Nations High Commissioner for Refugees, "Iraq Situation Update—August 2008," www.unhcr.org/491956a02.html; International Organization for Migration, "Emergency Needs Assessment: Four Years of Post-Samarra Displacement in Iraq," 13 April 2010, www.iomiraq.net/library/iom _displacement_monitoring_reports/yearly_and_mid_year_reviews/2010/10m _displacement_reports_four_years_of_post_samarra_displacement.pdf.

40. Estimates were based on refugees registered abroad and extensive canvassing of IDPs inside Iraq, but registration may have been inflated because host governments were given subsidies based on these figures. Not all refugees registered, but those who did not were more apt to be wealthier. For example, in 2009 UNHCR revised the number of refugees registered in Syria by 25 percent; these were the largest concentration.

41. UNHCR, "Iraq Situation Update." See also Deborah Amos, *Eclipse of the Sunnis: Power, Exile, and Upheaval in the Middle East* (New York: PublicAffairs, 2010).

42. Author's interviews with a number of Iraqi businessmen and civil servants, Washington, DC, at various times, 2010.

43. Leila Fadel and Ali al-Qeisy, "Iraqi Christians Flee After Violence," *Washington Post*, 18 November 2010.

44. For an excellent summary of this problem, see Sassoon, *The Iraqi Refugees*, pp. 140–151, from which much of the following is taken.

45. These figures have been taken from Sassoon, *The Iraqi Refugees*, pp. 142–143.

46. Sassoon, *The Iraqi Refugees*, pp. 148–149.

47. Sassoon, *The Iraqi Refugees*, p. 148, reporting on interviews with Iraqi professors in Jordan.

48. Sassoon, *The Iraqi Refugees*, p. 23.

49. Iraq Ministry of Health and the World Health Organization, Iraq Mental Health Survey, 2006–2007, www.emro.who.int/Iraq/surveys.imhs.htm;

A. A. al-Jawadi and S. A. Abdul-Rahman, "Prevalence of Childhood and Early Adolescence Mental Disorders Among Children Attending Primary Health Care Center in Mosul," *BMC Public Health* 7 (2007): 274, cited in Jafar al-Mashat, "Psychological Impact of the Recent Conflict on Iraqi Youth," unpublished paper (Morgantown, WV: West Virginia University School of Medicine, 2010).

50. Author's interview with Denise Natali, Washington, DC, 8 May 2011. Natali taught a mix of Arab and Kurdish university students in Sulaimaniyya and Arbil from 2005 to 2010 and is undertaking a study of their attitudes.

51. Sassoon, *The Iraqi Refugees*, p. 17.

52. United Nations Assistance Mission in Iraq, *Human Rights Report*, 1 April–30 June 2007, pp. 14–17, 222.uniraq.org, cited in Sassoon, *The Iraqi Refugees*, p. 17.

53. Jack Healy, "Families of the Missing Find an Ally on Iraqi TV," *New York Times*, 30 November 2010.

54. With help from UNESCO, a professional committee in higher education revised these texts in 2008 and published them in 2009. The process was extremely sensitive, and the products are still controversial. One means of achieving compromise, as a reading of the texts reveals, was to avoid certain subjects entirely. The books from which this material is drawn include three civics texts (*al-Tarbiyya-l-Wataniyya*) from all three grades of intermediate (junior high school); five texts on Islamic education (*al-Taribyya-l-Islamiyya*) from all three intermediate grades and grades five and six of preparatory (high school); and five history texts, *Arab Islamic History* (second grade intermediate), *Modern History of the Arab Nation* (third grade intermediate), *Arab Islamic Civilization* (fourth grade preparatory), *Modern History of Europe* (fifth grade preparatory), and *Modern History of the Arab Nation* (sixth grade preparatory).

GLOSSARY

Agha. A tribal leader or landowner among the Kurds.

Ahali. "Popular, populist." The name of a reform movement and a newspaper active in the 1930s.

Albu Nasir. A tribal group in the vicinity of Tikrit to which Saddam Husain and his family belonged.

Amn al-Amm. Public Security Directorate. The main Iraqi government organization charged with public security and criminal investigation under Saddam Husain.

Amn al-Khass. Special Security Organization. Was responsible for protecting the regime of Saddam Husain and its WMD program.

AMS. Acronym for Association of Muslim Scholars. Committee of Sunni religious scholars formed following the US invasion in April 2003. Active in promoting insurgency. Led by Shaikh Harith al-Dari.

Ansar al-Islam. "Supporters of Islam." A radical offshoot of the IMIK founded in 2001. Controlled Kurdish territory near the northern Iraqi border with Iran until eliminated by US forces in 2003.

AQI. Acronym for al-Qa'ida in Iraq, or al-Qa'ida in Mesopotamia. Radical Sunni Islamist group formed in 2004 with a declared allegiance to the global al-Qa'ida under Usama bin Ladin. Was active in the insurgency and was led by Abu Mus'ab al-Zarqawi until his 2006 death.

Awakening. Arabic, Sahwa. Alternatively, Sons of Iraq (SOI). Sunni tribal groups that turned against al-Qa'ida and then formed councils to coordinate with US military forces from 2005.

Ayatallah. "Sign of God." A senior clerical rank among Shi'i Muslims. Respected as a *marji'*, an object of emulation for pious Shi'a.

Badr Brigade. Shi'i militia formed as the military arm of SCIRI from Iraqi Shi'i exiles in Iran. Returned to Iraq in 2003 and formed a political organization known as the Badr Organization.

Baghdad Pact. Security agreement made in 1955 by Turkey, Iran, Pakistan, Iraq, and Britain, with headquarters in Baghdad (hence the name). After Iraq dropped out in 1958, became known as the Central Treaty Organization, or CENTO.

Ba'th. "Renaissance," or "rebirth," refers to the Ba'th Party, a pan-Arab party founded in Syria in 1946 that took root in Iraq in the 1950s. Was the power in Iraq from 1968 to 2003.

COIN. Acronym for counterinsurgency. Operations to put down unrest by organized armed groups against a central government. Became an incremental part of US military strategy in Iraq after 2006.

Combined Joint Task Force 7, or Task Force 7. US-commanded multinational military force that occupied Iraq from June 2003 to May 2004. Replaced by MNF-I.

CoR. Acronym for Council of Representatives. The Iraqi parliament created by the 2005 constitution to replace the National Assembly.

CPA. Acronym for Coalition Provisional Authority. Transitional government of Iraq run by the United States and its allies under L. Paul Bremer from May 2003 until June 2004. Appointed the IGC to advise in running Iraq's executive, legislative, and judicial affairs.

Da'wa. "Call," or "summons," in a missionary sense, refers to the Islamic Da'wa Party. A Shi'i religious party established in Iraq in the late 1950s. Supported by Iran during the Saddam Husain years despite differences over clerical rule. Active in the opposition until returning to Iraq in 2003. Since 2004, leaders Ibrahim al-Ja'fari and Nuri al-Maliki Da'wa served as Iraqi prime minister, respectively.

Dunam. A measure of land equal to 0.618 acres.

Fadila. "Virtue," refers to the Islamic Virtue Party. Founded as an offshoot of the Sadrist movement in July 2003 by followers of Ayatallah Muhammad Ya'qubi. More moderate than the Sadrists, with a stronghold in Basra.

Faili. Shi'i Kurds.

Fatwa. Formal legal opinion given by a qualified Islamic scholar, especially important among the Shi'a.

Fida'iyyin. "Those who sacrifice." A special elite militia established to support the Ba'th regime. Fought against the coalition in the 2003 invasion.

Fursan. "Knights," or "cavalry." Kurdish irregular troops, recruited by tribal leaders who supported the government against the militias (*peshmerga*) of the Kurdish population. Manned frontier posts in the Iran-Iraq war.

GCC. Acronym for Gulf Cooperation Council. A regional security organization formed in 1981 of six Arab Gulf states: Saudi Arabia, Kuwait, Bahrain, Qatar, the UAE, and Oman.

Goran. "Change," refers to political reform movement founded in 2009 by some members of the PUK. Primary opposition to the two ruling parties in the KRG.

al-Hadba'. "Bent," refers to the leaning minaret of Mosul's oldest mosque. A local Arab nationalist party that won control of Ninawa Province in 2009.

IAEA. Acronym for International Atomic Energy Agency. The UN agency responsible for inspections of Iraq's nuclear facilities after the Gulf War.

IAO. Acronym for Islamic Action Organization. Radical Shi'i party founded in Karbala in the 1970s.

IDP. Acronym for internally displaced person. An individual who has been forced to leave home but remains within the same country.

IGC. Acronym for Interim Governing Council. An advisory and administrative body of Iraqis appointed by the CPA. Held office from September 2003 until June 2004, when it was replaced by the Interim Iraqi Government (IIG).

IIP. Acronym for Iraqi Islamic Party. The largest Sunni Islamic party in post-2003 Iraq. Founded in 1961 as the Iraqi version of the Muslim Brotherhood. Opposed Saddam Husain's regime, participated in Iraqi governments from April 2003 until November 2004, joined the Tawafuq coalition. Lost influence after 2009 and 2010 elections.

IMIK. Acronym for Islamic Movement of Iraqi Kurdistan. An Islamic movement established in the Kurdish area of Iraq in the early 1980s. Controlled territory near the Iranian border in the 1990s.

INA. Acronym for Iraq National Accord. Main secular Iraqi opposition group founded in 1991 by Ayad Allawi. Played an important role in Iraqi politics after 2003, forming the nucleus of the Iraqiyya coalition led by Allawi.

INA. Acronym for Iraqi National Alliance. See *I'tilaf.*

INC. Acronym for Iraqi National Congress. An umbrella organization of exile Iraqi opposition groups formed in 1992. Headed by Ahmad Chalabi, became a vehicle for US-supported activities against the Saddam Husain regime. Participated in post-2003 Iraqi elections with little success.

Intifada. "Uprising." The disturbances that took place in 1952, as well as the uprisings in the north and south of Iraq in 1991.

IPC. Acronym for the Iraq Petroleum Company. Created after the First World War to operate and manage the Iraqi oil concession granted to several major international oil companies. Was dominated by the British.

Iraqi Front for National Dialogue. Nationalist party formed by ex-Ba'thist Salih al-Mutlak in 2005. Joined Ayad Allawi's Iraqiyya list for the 2010 elections.

Iraqiyya. "Iraqi," refers to two political coalitions, led by Ayad Allawi. The first was the Iraqi National List formed for the December 2005 parliamentary election; the second was the Iraqi Nationalist Movement, which ran for the 2010 parliamentary elections. Advocated secular nonsectarian policies.

Istiqlal. "Independence." A nationalist and pan-Arab political party founded after the Second World War.

I'tilaf. "Coalition," refers to coalition of Shi'i Islamic parties. Originally the United Iraqi Alliance (UIA), won a plurality in both 2005 parliamentary elections. After the Da'wa broke with the coalition in 2009, reformed as the Iraqi National Alliance (INA) for the 2010 elections, in which it placed third behind Iraqiyya and the State of Law.

KDP. Acronym for Kurdistan Democratic Party. Kurdish party founded in 1946. Led by Mustafa Barzani until his death in 1979 and thereafter by his son Mas'ud Barzani.

KDPI. Acronym for Kurdistan Democratic Party of Iran. The leading Iranian Kurdish party until its split in 2006 into factions. Members often taking refuge in Iraqi Kurdistan.

KIU. Acronym for Kurdistan Islamic Union. Sunni Islamist party formed in 1994 among Iraqi Kurds with close ties to the Muslim Brotherhood. Until mid-2005, was a member of the Kurdistan Alliance coalition. Has run independently since the December 2005 elections.

KRG. Acronym for Kurdistan Regional Government. The autonomous regional government controlling the three Kurdish provinces of Dahuk, Arbil, and Sulaimaniyya. Established as a federal region under Iraq's 2005 constitution.

Madinat al-Thaura. "City of the Revolution." Named after the 1958 revolution, a poor urban section of Baghdad housing Shi'i migrants from southern Iraq. Renamed Saddam City in 1982 by Saddam and Sadr City in 2003 after Muqtada al-Sadr's father.

Mahdi Army. Shi'i militia founded by Muqtada al-Sadr in April 2003. Military arm of the Sadrist movement.

Maktab al-Amn al-Qaumi. Bureau of National Security. A higher-security bureau that coordinated the efforts of several intelligence and security services during the Ba'th regime.

Marji'. "Source of emulation" (full title: *marji' al-taqlid*). A senior cleric in Shi'i Islam recognized as an authoritative religious source for questions of faith and practice.

Marji'iyya. The body of Shi'i religious scholars who have reached the position of *marji'.*

MNF-I. Acronym for Multi-National Forces–Iraq. Official name of the US-led military coalition occupying Iraq from May 2004 through the end of 2009. Restructured on 1 January 2010 as the United States Forces–Iraq (USF-I).

Muhassasa. "Allotment," or "sharing," refers to the distribution of cabinet positions across ethno-sectarian and party lines.

Mukhabarat al-Amma. General Intelligience Service. Iraq's secret police under Saddam Husain, responsible for domestic and foreign intelligence on potential threats to the regime.

Mutasarrif. Provincial governor. Head of one of Iraq's eighteen provinces.

National Assembly. Transitional legislature elected in January 2005 to draw up the Iraqi constitution. Replaced by the CoR after ratification of the constitution in October 2005 and the December 2005 parliamentary election.

NDP. Acronym for National Democratic Party. A political party favoring social and democratic change founded after the Second World War.

ORHA. Acronym for Office of Reconstruction and Humanitarian Assistance. Founded in January 2003 by the United States to act as caretaker government in Iraq following the invasion. Headed by Jay Garner, later replaced by the CPA.

Peshmerga. "Those who face death." Militias attached to Kurdish political parties, especially the KDP and PUK. Since 2003, have served as the official security force of the KRG.

PKK. Acronym for Partiya Karkari Kurdistan (Kurdistan Worker's Party). Radical Kurdish nationalist party mainly operating against Turkey. Founded in 1978 by Abd Allah Öcalan, now operating mainly out of Iraqi Kurdistan.

Qa'imakam. Local district administrator. Head of a subdistrict below the provincial level.

Regional Command. The leadership of the Ba'th Party in a specific country (or "region," in Ba'th terminology). In charge of party (and government) affairs in Iraq during the Ba'th regime.

Resolution 661. UNSC resolution passed 6 August 1990 after Iraq's annexation of Kuwait and imposing a severe international sanctions regime on Iraq and Iraq-occupied territory.

Resolution 1483. UNSC resolution passed 22 May 2003 naming the United States and the United Kingdom as occupying powers of Iraq.

Resolution 1546. UNSC resolution passed 8 June 2004 recognizing the handover of authority from the CPA to the Iraqi interim government on 30 June.

Sadr City. See *Madinat al-Thaura.*

Sadrist movement. Populist Shi'i Islamist movement predominant in Sadr City and portions of the south of Iraq and appealing to poorer sectors of the population. Led by Muqtada al-Sadr.

Salafists. From *salaf,* "predecessors," or "ancestors." Conservative fundamentalist groups within Sunni Islam that look back to the founding generations of Islamic civilization for their teachings and rules of behavior. Often used to describe Saudi-based "Wahhabism."

SCIRI. Acronym for Supreme Council for the Islamic Revolution in Iraq. Shi'a Islamist party established in Iran in 1982 in opposition to Saddam Husain regime. Headed by Ayatallah Muhammad Baqir al-Hakim until 2003, then by his brother Abd al-Aziz al-Hakim until 2009, and since by his son, Ammar al-Hakim. Changed name to Islamic Supreme Council of Iraq (ISCI) in 2007.

Shaikh. Head of a tribe among Arabs.

SOFA. Acronym for Status of Forces Agreement. US-Iraq agreement approved in November 2008 that specified US combat forces would withdraw from Iraqi cities at the end of June 2009 and from all Iraq by the end of 2011.

State of Law. Arabic: Daulat al-Qanun. Shi'i political front formed by Nuri al-Maliki. Composed mainly of Da'wa Party members. Ran in the 2009 provincial and 2010 parliamentary elections.

TAL. Acronym for Transitional Administrative Law. The temporary constitution written in March 2004. Governed Iraq from June 2004 until May 2006 when the permanent constitution went into effect.

Tawafuq. "Accord," refers to Iraqi Accord Front. Coalition of Sunni Islamist parties, including primarily the IIP, the General Council for the People of Iraq (Ahl al-Iraq), and the Iraqi Front for National Dialogue Council. Created in October 2005, ran in the 2005 and 2010 parliamentary elections.

Thalweg. Deepwater channel in the center of a river. Used specifically to denote the (disputed) boundary between Iraq and Iran in the Shatt al-Arab.

UAR. Acronym for United Arab Republic. A political union formed by Egypt, Syria, and Yemen in 1958. Lasted only until 1961.

Ulama. Islamic scholars knowledgeable in Islamic law and theology.

UNSCOM. Acronym for United Nations Special Commission. A body created in 1991 to conduct inspections in Iraq for chemical and biological weapons and long-range missiles.

USF-I. Acronym for United States Forces–Iraq. Took over from the MNF-I on 1 January 2010.

Wathba. "Leap," or "attack," refers to the disturbances that broke out in 1948 in protest against the Portsmouth Treaty.

Wilaya. State or province. A unit of government under the Ottoman Empire.

POLITICAL PERSONALITIES

Abd al-Hamid, Muhsin. Leader of the Iraqi Islamic Party, the main Sunni Islamist party, until 2004. Of Kurdish background, was a professor of Islamic studies before the US invasion. Member of the IGC and its president in February 2004.

Abd al-Ilah, Crown Prince. Crown prince and regent of Iraq from the death of King Ghazi in 1939 until 1953, when King Faisal II came of age. Continued to be the dominant influence in the palace until he was brutally killed in the revolution of 1958.

Abd al-Mahdi, Adil. Vice president of Iraq since 2005. The son of a minister to King Faisal I, became an economist while in exile in France. Was previously affiliated with both Ba'thist and Marxist movements; embraced Islamist politics during the Iranian Revolution and joined SCIRI. Returned to Iraq in 2003 and was finance minister in the 2004–2005 interim government and appointed vice president in 2005.

Abu Risha, Abd al-Sattar. Sunni tribal leader in Anbar province, known for mobilizing the Anbar Awakening movement to counter al-Qa'ida insurgents. After participating in the insurgency against the US occupying forces, worked with US military to organize Sunni tribes against foreign al-Qa'ida and other Sunni extremist groups. Was killed by al-Qa'ida near his house in Ramadi in September 2007.

Ahmad, Ibrahim. Secretary general of the KDP from 1953 to 1958 and a leader of its intellectual wing; espoused leftist ideals and split with Mustafa Barzani in 1964. Daughter Hiro married Jalal Talabani. From 1975 until his death in 2000, lived in political exile in London.

al-Bakr, Ahmad Hasan. President of Iraq under the Ba'th regime from 1968 until 1979. An army officer and a Tikriti from the Albu Nasir tribe. Played a role in the Free Officers movement and was prime minister in the Ba'th regime of 1963. Removed from power by Abd al-Salam Arif in 1964. Instrumental in bringing the Ba'th to power in 1968. Gradually overshadowed by Saddam and resigned in 1979. Died in 1982 under mysterious circumstances.

Allawi, Ayad. Prime minister of Iraq from 2004 to 2005. Born to a prominent Shi'i family and a first cousin of Ahmad Chalabi; left Iraq in 1972 to study medicine in Britain. Was a Ba'th Party member in his youth and headed the Ba'th student movement during his studies. Began to organize opposition to Saddam Husain from abroad in 1976 and established links with the CIA and MI6. Founded INA in 1991 and headed the secular nationalist Iraqiyya list in the 2005 and 2010 elections.

Barzani, Masrur. Son of Mas'ud Barzani and leader in the KDP. Director of the security and intelligence services in the Kurdish region since 1999.

Barzani, Mas'ud. President of the KRG since 2005 and leading figure in Kurdish politics. Son of Mustafa Barzani and leader of the KDP from 1979 to the present. Rival of Jalal Talabani for leadership of the Kurdish national movement. In the 1990s, held influence in the Dahuk and Arbil regions in the north. Following the 2003 invasion, was a member and president of the IGC.

Chalabi, Ahmad. Member of a wealthy Shi'i family, lived abroad beginning in 1956 and educated at MIT and the University of Chicago. After lecturing in mathematics in Beirut, founded the Petra Bank in Jordan and was indicted for fraud there following the bank's 1989 collapse. In the 1990s, assumed a leading role among exile Iraqis in the United Kingdom and the United States opposed to the Saddam Husain regime. Headed the opposition umbrella group, the INC, founded in 1992. Returned to Iraq in 2003 and sat on the IGC. Once a close US ally, increasingly fell out of favor with the Bush administration amid accusations of mishandling US secrets to Iran. Has played only a secondary role in Iraqi politics since.

Faisal I, King. King of Iraq from 1921 until his death in 1933. A leading member of the Hashimite family of Mecca and active in the Arab revolt against the Turks in the First World War. Installed as monarch in Iraq under British auspices. Established the Hashimite dynasty there, which lasted until its overthrow in 1958.

Faisal II, King. Song of King Ghazi, grandson of Faisal I, and king of Iraq from 1953 until his murder in the revolution of 1958. Too young to exercise much authority as king. Crown Prince Abd al-Ilah the leading figure in the palace during Faisal's tenure.

Ghazi, King. Son of Faisal I and king of Iraq from 1933 to 1939. Assumed the position at a young age and was inexperienced. British and senior Iraqi officials anxious about his nationalist sentiments. Died in a violent auto crash in 1939 that has been regarded with suspicion by many Iraqis.

al-Hakim, Abd al-Aziz. Son of Muhsin al-Hakim and brother of Muhammad Baqir al-Hakim. A former leader of the Badr Brigade, became leader of SCIRI following his brother's death in 2003. Chaired the UIA parliamentary list in the 2005 elections, but did not take political office. Died in 2009 following a two-year battle with lung cancer.

al-Hakim, Ayatallah Muhammad Baqir. Head of SCIRI, headquartered in Iran until 2003, which drew support from Iraqi exiles in Iran as well as Shi'a inside Iraq. From a dynastic rival to the Sadr clerical family, son of former chief *marji'* Muhsin al-Hakim. Returned to Iraq in May 2003 after the fall of the regime and was killed in a bombing in Najaf in August of that year.

al-Hammudi, Humam. Deputy leader of ISCI and parliamentary leader of the UIA. Served in 2005 as chair of both the Constitutional Drafting Committee and the Constitutional Amendment Committee.

al-Hashimi, Tariq. Vice president of Iraq since 2006. Served in the Iraqi army until 1975 and then joined the IIP. Was secretary general of the IIP from 2004 until 2009. Left the IIP in 2009 to join the Iraqiyya list in the 2010 elections.

Husain, Qusayy. Younger son of Saddam Husain. Played a leading role in security affairs during the 1990s and until the regime's overthrow in 2003. Killed along with his brother Udayy in a raid on their Mosul hideout by US Special Forces in July 2003.

Husain, Saddam. President of Iraq from 1979 until his overthrow in 2003. Vice president of the RCC from 1969 to 1979 and the architect of the Ba'th government and its policies after 1968. A Tikriti, a relative of Ahmad Hasan al-Bakr, and a member of the Albu Nasir tribe, used his tribal connections to get ahead and to maintain himself in power. Was captured by US troops in a bunker near Tikrit on 13 December 2003 and was put on trial by the Iraqi government in 2004. In November 2006 was convicted of crimes against humanity and executed by hanging on 30 December.

Husain, Udayy. Older son of Saddam Husain, known for his brutal, flamboyant, and irresponsible behavior. Head of youth and sports affairs and editor of *Babil* newspaper. Badly wounded in an assassination attempt in 1996. Killed along with his brother Qusayy in a raid on their Mosul hideout by US Special Forces in July 2003.

al-Husri, Sati'. Ottoman-educated Syrian intellectual who adopted Arab nationalism after the First World War. Leading figure in Iraqi education during and after the mandate. Helped shape education curriculum in a secular Arab-nationalist direction, to the consternation of many Shi'a and Kurds.

Jabr, Bayan. Also known as Baqir al-Zubaidi. Minister of finance from 2006 to 2010 and senior member of ISCI. As interior minister from 2005 to 2006, oversaw the integration of the Badr Brigade, the SCIRI-affiliated Shi'i militia, into the security forces. Accused by opponents of encouraging Shi'i militia activity against Sunnis during the height of sectarian strife.

Jabr, Salih. The first Shi'i prime minister in Iraq in 1947–1948 and a leading politician in the post–Second World War period. Responsible for negotiating the unpopular Portsmouth Treaty of 1948, which was repudiated after it generated riots back home.

al-Ja'fari, Ibrahim. Prime minister of Iraq from 2005 to 2006. Joined the underground Shi'i Da'wa Party in 1968 and was forced to leave Iraq for Iran in 1980, where he represented Da'wa in SCIRI. Lived in London beginning in 1989 and returned to Iraq in 2003 as a member of the IGC. Formed the National Reform Trend in 2008 to run against Nuri al-Maliki in 2009 and 2010 elections.

al-Kailani, Rashid Ali. A leading politician under the monarchy. Prime minister in 1941, when he and four officers undertook an anti-British "coup," removing the pro-British regent. Coup caused second British occupation of Iraq.

al-Khu'i, Abd al-Majid. Son of Ayatallah Abu al-Qasim al-Khu'i and a moderate Shi'i cleric. Played an active role in the 1991 uprising against Saddam Husain and was exiled to London, where he administered the Imam Al-Khoei Benevolent Foundation. Was killed by a mob of Muqtada al-Sadr supporters shortly after returning to Iraq in 2003.

Khumaini, Ayatallah Ruhallah. Shi'i cleric; leader of the 1979 Islamic Revolution in Iran and its most important political and religious figure until his death in 1989. As an opponent of the shah, spent thirteen years in exile in Najaf, until his expulsion by Saddam in 1978. Created the religious foundations of the Islamic Republic of Iran.

Kubba, Muhammad Mahdi. A Shi'a and leader of the anti-British, nationalist Istiqlal Party formed in 1946. Minister in the short-lived cabinet formed in 1948 after the *wathba*.

al-Majid, Ali Hasan. A member of Saddam's clan and a leading figure in the Ba'thist regime from the 1980s until its overthrow in 2003. A member of the RCC and the party's Regional Command in the 1990s. Responsible for the Anfal campaign against the Kurds in 1988 and other atrocities. Captured by US troops in August 2003, put on trial by the Iraqis beginning in 2006. Was sentenced to death four times and finally executed in January 2010.

al-Maliki, Nuri. Prime minister of Iraq since 2006 and secretary general of the Da'wa Party. Lived in exile from 1979 until 2003 in Syria and Iran and was active in Da'wa. Returned to Iraq in 2003 and elected to National Assembly in 2005. Succeeded Ibrahim al-Ja'fari as prime minister. Formed the State of Law coalition in 2009 after advocating a more nationalist position.

al-Mashhadani, Mahmud. Chairman of the CoR from 2006 until 2008. A member of the Tawafuq bloc. Was arrested by both Saddam's regime, for protesting the Iran-Iraq war, and the United States, for connections to Sunni terrorist groups.

Mustafa, Naushirwan. Founder and leader of Goran, established in 2009 in opposition to the main Kurdish parties in the KRG. An author and historian, cofounded the PUK with Jalal Talabani and served as its deputy secretary general until 2006.

al-Mutlak, Salih. Deputy prime minister since 2010. Controversial secular Sunni politician and leader of the Iraqi Front for National Dialogue—a Sunni-led nonsectarian bloc. Disbarred from running in 2010 because of his former Ba'thist connections, a decision struck down by the CoR in December 2010.

al-Najaifi, Usama. Chairman of the CoR since November 2010 and a member of the Iraqiyya List. Minister of industry and minerals from 2005 to 2006 and representative of Mosul in the CoR after 2006. Brother, Athil, governor of Ninawa Province since 2009 and founder of an Arab nationalist party called al-Hadba' in Mosul.

Qasim, Abd al-Karim. Army officer and leader of the 1958 revolution that overthrew the monarchy. Prime minister from 1958 to 1963. Undertook substantial social and economic reforms. Overthrown and killed by the Ba'th in 1963.

Pachachi, Adnan. Foreign minister and senior diplomat of Iraq before the rise of the Ba'th Party. After a thirty-five-year exile in London and the UAE, returned to Iraq to become a member and president of the IGC in January 2004. Part of Ayad Allawi's Iraqiyya List in 2005 and the Iraqiyya bloc in 2010.

al-Sadr, Ayatallah Muhammad Baqir. A cleric and leading Shi'i reformer, considered the founder of the Da'wa Party, established in the late 1950s. Author of several works attempting to reconcile traditional Shi'i theology and modern social science. A moving force behind Shi'i opposition to the regime in the late 1970s. Tortured and executed by the Ba'th regime in 1980.

al-Sadr, Ayatallah Muhammad Sadiq. Chief *marji'* for the Shi'a between 1992 and 1999. Cousin to Ayatallah Muhammad Baqir al-Sadr. Developed a populist conservative Shi'i movement advocating a more active role for clerics as opposed to traditional Shi'i quietism. Was assassinated by the Ba'th regime in 1999; supporters later rallied around his son, Muqtada al-Sadr.

al-Sadr, Muqtada. Populist Shi'i leader of the Sadrist movement and its military wing, the Mahdi Army. A junior cleric and son of Muhammad Sadiq al-Sadr and son-in-law of Muhammad Baqir al-Sadr. Inherited his father's following after his death in 1999 and emerged in 2003 as an outspoken and militant opponent of US occupation. Espoused a theocratic platform, led uprising against coalition forces in 2004. In 2007, left for Qum in Iran to further his religious studies. Followers, known as Sadrists, continued to participate in Iraqi politics and achieving positions in the cabinet in 2010.

al-Sa'id, Nuri. The most important politician in Iraq from the end of the mandate period in 1930 to the overthrow of the monarchy in 1958. Repeatedly prime minister and the moving force in numerous cabinets. Held the threads of power through shrewd manipulation of the parliamentary system. Pro-British and pro-monarchy. Steered Iraq's foreign and domestic policies in a pro-Western direction until his violent death during the 1958 revolution.

Salih, Barham. Prime minister of the KRG since 2009 and deputy prime minister of Iraq in the interim government and under Nuri al-Maliki from 2006 until 2009. A member of the PUK since 1976, represented the party in the United States throughout the 1980s and 1990s. Prime minister of the PUK-controlled Kurdish enclave from 2001 until 2004 and served as minister of planning and coordination in the transitional government from 2005 to 2006.

Salman, Yusif (Comrade Fahd). A Christian and founder of the Iraq Communist Party in 1941. Played an important role in organizing the party and spreading Marxist ideas among intellectuals. Executed in 1949.

al-Samarra'i, Ayad. Chairman of CoR from 2009 to 2010 and chairman of Tawafuq. A member of the IIP.

al-Shahristani, Husain. Deputy prime minister for energy since 2010 and minister of oil from 2006 through 2010. A nuclear scientist imprisoned for Shi'i activism by Saddam Husain's regime in 1980, escaping in 1990 first to Iran and then to the United Kingdom. Close to Ayatallah Ali al-Sistani, served as deputy chairman of the National Assembly from 2005 to 2006.

Sidqi, Bakr. A Kurd, an army officer, and a key leader in the first military coup in Iraq in 1936. Also considered responsible for the Assyrian massacre in 1933. Assassinated by Arab nationalist officers in 1937.

al-Sistani, Ayatallah Ali. Regarded as chief *marji'* in Shi'i Islam, based in Najaf. Born in Iran, emerged as the leading *marji'* following the 1992 death of Ayatallah al-Khu'i. Represents the quietist school, but played an active role behind the scenes in post-2003 Iraq, demanding democratic elections and helping form a Shi'i political coalition.

Sulaiman, Hikmat. Ottoman-educated politician of the mandate period. With Bakr Sidqi and a group of liberal-left reformers, participated in the 1936 coup and led the government that followed.

Talabani, Jalal. President of Iraq since 2005. A leading figure in the Kurdish nationalist movement. Left the KDP and established the PUK in 1975. Rivalry with Mas'ud Barzani, which broke into open warfare in the mid-1990s. After a peace accord in 1998, led a government in the Sulaimaniyya region. Worked with the coalition during the 2003 invasion and served in the IGC.

al-Ya'qubi, Muhammad. Senior Shi'i cleric and student of Muhammad Sadiq al-Sadr; formed the Fadila Party in 2003.

al-Yawar, Ghazi. President of Iraq from 2004 to 2005. Leader of the Shammar tribe, lived in Saudi Arabia as a businessman when family was driven into exile by Saddam in 1991. Returned to Iraq in 2003 and served on the IGC before being named interim president.

al-Zarqawi, Abu Mus'ab. Nom de guerre of a Jordanian-born Islamic militant who organized and led AQI. Was killed in a US airstrike in June 2006.

Zibari, Hushyar. Foreign minister of Iraq since 2003. Served previously as a KDP spokesperson and representative in the 1980s and 1990s, mainly in London. Maternal uncle to Mas'ud Barzani.

BIBLIOGRAPHY

The Land and People of Modern Iraq

A good overview is R. I. Lawless, "Iraq: Changing Population Patterns," in *Populations of the Middle East and North Africa*, ed. J. I. Clarke and W. F. Fisher (London, 1972), but this needs to be updated with recent population estimates. The best description of the geography and population of Iraq in the early part of the twentieth century is Great Britain, Naval Intelligence Division, *Iraq and the Persian Gulf* (London, 1944). A good review of how Iraq's boundaries were established is given in Richard Schofield, "Borders, Regions, and Time: Defining the Iraqi Territorial State," in *An Iraq of Its Regions: Cornerstones of a Federal Democracy?* ed. Reidar Visser and Gareth Stansfield (New York, 2010). C. J. Edmonds, *Kurds, Turks and Arabs* (London, 1957), has the best background on the Kurds during the mandate period. For a delightful firsthand account of village life and customs in the south of Iraq, see Elizabeth Warnock Fernea, *Guests of the Sheik* (Garden City, NJ, 1969). Other cultural and anthropological descriptions of groups can be found in Philip Kreyenbroek and Christine Allison, eds., *Kurdish Culture and Identity* (London, 1996); W. Thesiger, *The Marsh Arabs* (New York, 1964); and Shakir Mustafa Salim, *Marsh Dwellers of the Euphrates Delta* (London, 1962). The classic work on Iraqi tribes is still Abbas al-Azzawi, *Asha'ir al-Iraq* (The Tribes of Iraq) (Baghdad, 1956). An updated version, representing tribal structure under the Ba'th, can be found in Thamir Abd al-Hasan al-Amiri, *Mausu'a-l-Asha'ir al-Iraqiyya* (Encyclopedia of Iraqi Tribes), 9 vols. (Baghdad, 1992). For a discussion on tribalism in Ba'thist Iraq, see Faleh Abdul-Jabar, "Sheikhs and Ideologues: Deconstruction and Reconstruction of Tribes Under Patrimonial Totalitarianism in Iraq, 1968–1998," and Hosham Dawood, "The State-ization of the Tribe and the Tribalization of the State: The Case of Iraq," both in *Tribes and Power: Nationalism and Ethnicity in the Middle East*, ed. Faleh A. Jabar and Hosham Dawood (London, 2002). Two good studies of how tribes work in post-2003

445

Iraq are Michael Eisenstadt, "Tribal Engagement: Lessons Learned," *Military Review*, September-October, 2007; and Katherine Blue Carroll, "Tribal Law and Reconciliation in the New Iraq," *Middle East Journal* (*MEJ*), Winter 2011. On the Kurds, three scholarly studies are worth reading: Mehrdad Izadi, *The Kurds: A Concise Handbook* (Washington, DC, 1992); Martin Van Bruinessen, *Agha, Shaikh, and State: On the Social and Political Organization of Kurdistan* (Rijswijk, the Netherlands, 1978); and Martin Van Bruinessen, "Kurds, States, and Tribes," in *Tribes and Power*, ed. Jabar and Dawood. On the Shi'a, the best overview is Moojan Momen, *An Introduction to Shi'i Islam* (New Haven, CT, 1985). In Iraq, the best recent studies on the development of the Shi'i community include Yitzhak Nakash, *The Shi'is of Iraq* (Princeton, NJ, 1994); Yitzhak Nakash, "The Conversion of Iraq's Tribes to Shi'ism," *International Journal of Middle East Studies* (*IJMES*) 26 (1994); and Faleh A. Jabar, *Ayatallahs, Sufis, and Ideologues* (London, 2001). A good study on Iraq's Turkman population is Aziz Qadir al-Samanchi, *al-Ta'rikh al-Siyasi lil-Turkman al-Iraq* (The Political History of the Turkmen of Iraq) (London, 1999).

Iraq Before the British Mandate

This book does not deal with Iraq's ancient or Islamic history, but two classical works can be suggested for these periods: Georges Roux, *Ancient Iraq* (New York, 1964); and Marshall G. S. Hodgson, *The Venture of Islam* (Chicago, 1974), vols. 1–2. The Ottoman period in Iraq has been neglected by scholars until recently. The two standard works are Stephen Longrigg, *Four Centuries of Modern Iraq* (Oxford, UK, 1925); and Abbas al-Azzawi, *Ta'rikh al-Iraq bain Ihtilalain* (The History of Iraq Between Two Occupations), 8 vols. (Baghdad, 1956), but both, even though meticulously detailed, are little more than chronologies. Two more recent studies focus on economic and social life in the nineteenth century: Hala Fattah, *The Politics of Regional Trade in Iraq, Arabia, and the Gulf, 1745–1900* (New York, 1997); and Sarah Shields, *Mosul Before Iraq: Like Bees Making Five-Sided Cells* (New York, 2000). Reidar Visser deals with Basra under the Ottomans in *Basra, the Failed Gulf State: Separatism and Nationalism in Southern Iraq* (Piscataway, NJ, 2005). The classic study on the social aspects of Iraq in this period is Ali al-Wardi, *Lamahat Ijtima'iyya min Ta'rikh al-Iraq al-Hadith* (Social Aspects of the Modern History of Iraq) (Baghdad, 1969–1972), 6 vols., especially vols. 1–4. The Shi'a in this period are well covered in Pierre-Jean Luizard, *La Formation de l'Irak Contemporain* (The Formation of Contemporary Iraq) (Paris, 1991); and a shorter work, Abdul-Hadi Hairi, *Shi'ism and Constitutionalism* (Leiden, the Netherlands, 1977). The section on Iraq in *The Economic History of the Middle East, 1800–1914*, ed. Charles Issawi (Chicago, 1966), has excellent excerpts dealing with economic changes in Iraq in the last century of Ottoman rule. A colorful picture of life at the end of the Ottoman era is contained in several memoirs of Iraqi politicians, chief among them Sulaiman Faidi, *Fi Ghamrat al-Nidal* (In the Heat of the Struggle) (Baghdad, 1952); and Abd al-Aziz Qassab, *Min Dhikrayati* (From My Memories) (Beirut, 1966).

The British Occupation, the Mandate, and the Struggle for Independence

The British occupation and mandate have been dealt with extensively, and only the most important works can be mentioned here. The most essential is Abd al-Razzaq al-Hasani, *Ta'rikh al-Wizarat al-Iraqiyya* (The History of Iraqi Cabinets), 10 vols. (Sidon, Lebanon, 1953–1967); although weak on analysis, it is exhaustive in facts, documents, and statements from participants. In English the classic study is now Hanna Batatu, *The Old Social Classes and the Revolutionary Movements of Iraq* (Princeton, NJ, 1978), mainly a social history but containing a wealth of political data. Two standard older works, still useful, are Stephen Longrigg, *Iraq, 1900 to 1950* (London, 1953); and Philip Ireland, *Iraq: A Study in Political Development* (New York, 1938). The view of the India School can be found in two books by A. T. Wilson: *Loyalties: Mesopotamia, 1914–1917* and *Mesopotamia, 1917–1920: A Clash of Loyalties* (London, 1930). For the opposing view, see Elizabeth Burgoyne, *Gertrude Bell: From Her Personal Papers, 1914–1926* (London, 1961). More recent works on British policy in the region are Aaron S. Klieman, *Foundations of British Policy in the Arab World: The Cairo Conference of 1921* (Baltimore, MD, 1970); David Fromkin, *A Peace to End All Peace* (London, 1989); and Toby Dodge, *Inventing Iraq: The Failure of Nation-Building and History Denied* (New York, 2003). Peter Sluglett has updated his earlier work *Britain in Iraq: Contriving King and Country* (New York, 2007). Official British accounts can be found in records in the India Office and Colonial Office and in the Foreign Office in London. Good published accounts include Great Britain, India Office, *Review of the Civil Administration of Mesopotamia* (London, 1920); and Great Britain, Colonial Office, *Special Report on the Progress of Iraq During the Period 1920–1931* (London, 1931).

The material on the struggle for independence is scarcer, but studies on the 1920 revolt are numerous. In Arabic the most important are Abd al-Razzaq al-Hasani, *al-Thaura-l-Iraqiyya-l-Kubra* (The Great Iraqi Revolt) (Sidon, Lebanon, 1952); Muhammad Mahdi al-Basir, *Ta'rikh al-Qadiyya-l-Iraqiyya* (The

History of the Iraqi Question), 2nd ed. (London, 1990); and Abd Allah al-Nafisi, *Daur al-Shi'a fi Tatawwur al-Iraq al-Siyasi al-Hadith* (The Role of the Shi'a in the Development of the Modern Political History of Iraq) (Beirut, 1973). A good study in English is Ghassan Atiyyah, *Iraq, 1908–1921: A Political Study* (Beirut, 1973). Several memoirs deal with the mandate period. The most important are Sati'-l-Husri, *Mudhakkirati fi-l-Iraq* (My Memoirs in Iraq), 2 vols. (Beirut, 1967); Muhammad Mahdi al-Jawahiri, *Dkhirayati* (My Memories), 2 vols. (Damascus, 1988); and Ali Jaudat, *Dhikrayati* (My Memories) (Beirut, 1968).

The Erosion of the British Legacy, 1932–1945

The best accounts covering this period are found in Majid Khadduri, *Independent Iraq, 1932–1958* (London, 1960); Hanna Batatu, *The Old Social Classes and the Revolutionary Movements of Iraq* (Princeton, NJ, 1978); and Charles Tripp, *A History of Iraq* (Cambridge, UK, 2000), which emphasizes alternative narratives in Iraqi history. The Assyrian affair is dealt with by R. S. Stafford, a British officer who served in Mosul at the time, in *The Tragedy of the Assyrians* (London, 1935). A more nationalist view is found in Khaldun S. Husry, "The Assyrian Affair of 1933," I and II, *IJMES* 5:2 and 5:3 (1974). Two good studies on army politics in this period are Mohammad Tarbush, *The Role of the Military in Politics: A Case Study of Iraq to 1941* (London, 1982); and Reeva Simon, *Iraq Between the Two World Wars: The Creation and Implementation of a Nationalist Ideology* (New York, 1986), which also deals with education and textbooks in this period. On the Rashid Ali movement, there is no dearth of material. German involvement is meticulously presented by Polish scholar Lukasz Hirszowitz in *The Third Reich and the Arab East* (Toronto, 1966). The German point of view is put forth by Fritz Grobba, the German representative in Baghdad, in *Irak* (Berlin, 1941). Iraqi accounts of the movement, mainly from a nationalist point of view, are found in Abd al-Razzaq al-Hasani, *al-Asrar al-Khafiyya* (The Hidden Secrets) (Sidon, Lebanon, 1958); Mahmud al-Durra, *al-Harb al-Iraqiyya-l-Baritaniyya, 1941* (The Iraqi-British War of 1941) (Beirut, 1969); Ahmad Yaghi, *Harakat Rashid Ali al-Kailani* (The Rashid Ali al-Kailani Movement) (Beirut, 1974); and Khairi-l-Umari, *Yunis al-Sab'awi: Sirat Siyasi Isami* (Yunis al-Sab'awi: Biography of a Self-Made Politician) (Baghdad, 1980). Among the memoirs by major participants are those of Salah al-Din al-Sabbagh, *Mudhakkirati* (My Memoirs) (Damascus, 1956); Uthman Haddad, *Harakat Rashid Ali al-Kailani* (The Rashid Ali al-Kailani Movement) (Sidon, Lebanon, n.d.); Naji Shaukat, *Sira wa Dhikrayat Thamanin Amman, 1894–1974* (Biography and

Memoirs Through Eighty Years, 1894–1974) (Beirut, n.d.); and Taha-l-Hashimi, *Mudhakkirati, 1919–1943* (My Memoirs, 1919–1943) (Beirut, 1967). A different view is found in Taufiq al-Suwaidi, *Mudhakkirati* (My Memoirs) (Beirut, 1969). A British perspective from a participant in the aftermath is found in Freya Stark, *Baghdad Sketches* (London, 1946).

The End of the Monarchy, 1946–1958

The best overall view of the period is found in Hanna Batatu, *The Old Social Classes and the Revolutionary Movements of Iraq* (Princeton, NJ, 1978); and Majid Khadduri, *Independent Iraq, 1932–1958* (London, 1960). A critique and review of Batatu's work with several decades of hindsight are found in Robert Fernea and William Louis, eds., *The Iraqi Revolution of 1958: The Old Social Classes Revisited* (London, 1991). Elie Kedourie, "The Kingdom of Iraq: A Retrospect," in *The Chatham House Version and Other Essays* (New York, 1970), has a critical but incisive analysis of the monarchy and its politicians. The main wealth of material for these years, however, is to be found in the memoirs published by leading Iraqi politicians since 1958. Their usefulness varies. Most significant are Taha-l-Hashimi, *Mudhakkirati, 1919–1943* (My Memoirs, 1919–1943) (Beirut, 1967); Taufiq al-Suwaidi, *Mudhakkirati* (My Memoirs) (Beirut, 1969); Ali Jaudat, *Dhikrayat Ali Jaudat* (Beirut, 1968); Khalil Kanna, *al-Iraq, Amsuhui wa Ghaduhu* (Iraq: Its Past and Its Future) (Beirut, 1966); and Abd al-Karim al Uzri, *Ta'rikh fi Dhikrayat al-Iraq, 1930–1958* (History in Memories of Iraq, 1950–1958) (Beirut, 1982).

A number of works, both memoirs and studies, depict the opposition to the monarchy. An excellent overview of the period is found in Orit Bashkin, *The Other Iraq* (Stanford, CA, 2009). On the left, the main works include the memoirs of Kamil al-Chadirchi, *Mudhakkirati* (My Memoirs) (Beirut: 1970); *Min Awraq Kamil al-Chadirchi* (From the Papers of Kamil al-Chadirchi) (Beirut, 1971); Fadil Husain, *Ta'rikh al-Hizb al-Watani al-Dimuqrati* (The History of the National Democratic Party) (Baghdad, 1963); and Ibrahim Abd al-Fattah, *Mutala'a fi-l-Sha'biyya* (A Study in Populism) (Baghdad, 1935). On the nationalist side, there are Muhammad Mahdi Kubba, *Mudhakkirati* (My Memoirs) (Beirut, 1965); Abd al-Amir al-Akam, *Ta'rikh Hizb al-Istiqlal al-Iraqi, 1946–1958* (The History of the Iraqi Independence Party, 1946–1958) (Baghdad, 1980); and Talib Mushtaq, *Awraq Ayyami* (Papers from My Days) (Beirut, 1968). For a Communist version of events, see Abd al-Karim Hassun al-Jar Allah, *Tasaddu'-l-Bashariyya* (The Crackup of Humanity) (Beirut, n.d.). A recent reassessment of this history as a prelude to understanding post-2003 Iraq is

Adeed Dawisha, *Iraq: A Political History from Independence to Occupation* (Princeton, NJ, 2009).

The economic and social conditions that contributed to the overthrow of the regime have received considerable attention. Batatu, *The Old Social Classes*, remains the key study. Others include Doreen Warriner, *Land Reform and Development in the Middle East* (London, 1957); Robert Fernea, *Shaikh and Effendi* (Cambridge, MA, 1970); Muhammad Ali al-Suri, *al-Iqta' fi-l-Liwa' al-Kut* (Feudalism in the Kut *Liwa'*) (Baghdad, 1959); and Abd al Razzaq al-Zahir, *Fi-l-Islah al-Zira'i wa-l-Siyasi* (Toward Agrarian and Political Reform) (Baghdad, 1959). The classic document on which land policy was based is Ernest Dowson, *An Inquiry into Land Tenure and Related Questions* (Letchworth, UK, 1932). On the overall economy and the development of oil, the best general study is Edith Penrose and E. F. Penrose, *Iraq: International Relations and National Development* (Boulder, CO, 1978). For the development program, see Abd al-Rahman al-Jalili, *al-I'mar fi-l-Iraq* (Development in Iraq) (Beirut, 1968); and James Salter, *The Development of Iraq* (Baghdad, 1955). More detailed monographs include Khair al-Din Haseeb, *The National Income of Iraq, 1953–1961* (London, 1964); Ferhang Jalal, *The Role of Government in the Industrialization of Iraq, 1950–1965* (London, 1972); Kathleen Langley, *The Industrialization of Iraq* (Cambridge, MA, 1961); and Abbas al-Nasrawi, *Financing Economic Development in Iraq: The Role of Oil in a Middle Eastern Economy* (New York, 1967). A work that puts this development into theoretical context is Samira Haj, *The Making of Iraq, 1900–1963* (Albany, NY, 1997). Fairly accurate statistical data are available in statistical abstracts published by the Iraqi Ministry of Economics in this period.

Revolutionary Regimes of the Military Era

The causes of the 1958 revolt and the Free Officers movement are well set forth in several histories of this period: Majid Khadduri, *Republican Iraq* (London, 1969); Hanna Batatu, *The Old Social Classes and the Revolutionary Movements of Iraq* (Princeton, NJ, 1978); Edith Penrose and E. F. Penrose, *Iraq: International Relations and National Development* (Boulder, CO, 1978); and Marion Farouk-Sluglett and Peter Sluglett, *Iraq Since 1958: From Revolution to Dictatorship* (London, 1987); as well as in an account by an unidentified Englishman, Caractacus (a pseudonym) in *Revolution in Iraq: An Essay in Comparative Public Opinion* (London, 1959). The Free Officers movement is dealt with in several works, including that of an insider, Sabih Ali Ghalib, *Qissat Thaurat 14 Tammuz wa-l-Dubbat al-Ahrar* (The Story of the Revolution of 14 July and the Free Officers) (Beirut, 1968); and a good historical account by Laith Abd al-Hasan al-Zubaidi, *Thaurat 14 Tammuz 1958 fi-l-Iraq* (The Revolution of 14 July 1958 in Iraq) (Baghdad, 1981). The best account of the end of the royal family is found in Falih Hanzal (a member of the Royal Guard), *Asrar Maqtal al-A'ila-l-Malika fi-l-Iraq 14 Tammuz 1958* (Secrets of the Murder of the Royal Family in Iraq, 14 July 1958), 2nd ed. (n.pl., 1992). Although it has to be dealt with carefully, the trial of Abd al-Salam Arif is recorded in Iraq, Ministry of Defense, *Muhakamat* (Trials), vol. 5 (Baghdad, 1958–1962); this volume has fascinating material on the Free Officers movement as well as the later split between Arif and Qasim. The Qasim era has received the most attention in this period. The standard account is Uriel Dann, *Iraq Under Qassem* (New York, 1969). The role of the Communist Party is dealt with extensively in Batatu, *The Old Social Classes*; Tareq Ismael, *The Rise and Fall of the Communist Party in Iraq* (Cambridge, UK, 2008); and Rony Gabbay, *Communism and Agrarian Reform in Iraq* (London, 1978). Ibrahim Kubba, *Hadha Huwa Tariq 14 Tammuz* (This Is the Way of July 14) (Beirut, 1969), represents the left-wing view of this period, whereas Jasim Mukhlis, *Mudhakkirat al-Tabaqchali wa Dhikrayat Jasim Mukhlis, al-Muhami* (Memoirs of al-Tabaqchali and Memories of Jasim Mukhlis the Lawyer) (Sidon, Lebanon, 1969), expresses the nationalist opposition to Qasim. The 14 Ramadan coup and the short-lived Ba'th regime of 1963 need to be put in the perspective of regional Ba'th politics in this period. Several good books do this, among them, Kemal Abu Jaber, *The Arab Ba'th Socialist Party* (Syracuse, NY, 1966); John Devlin, *The Ba'th Party: A History from Its Origins to 1966* (Stanford, CA, 1976); and Malcolm Kerr, *The Arab Cold War* (London, 1971). Ba'thists themselves have written voluminously on their party. The Ba'th Party National Command has published a multivolume work, *Nidal al-Ba'th* (The Ba'th Struggle) (Beirut, 1964); volume 4 includes the important proceedings of the sixth Ba'th congress in 1963, which contributed to the downfall of the Ba'th regime in Iraq in that year. Also useful in shedding light on this experience is Munif al-Razzaz, *Al-Tajriba-l-Murra* (The Bitter Experience) (Beirut, 1967); and a Ba'thist who later defected, Fu'ad al-Rikabi, *al-Hall al-Awhad* (The Sole Solution) (Cairo, 1963). Among the most penetrating criticisms of the 1963 Ba'th regime is that of one of its main participants, Hani al-Fukaiki, *al-Aukar al-Hazima Tajribati fi Hizb al-Ba'thi al-Iraqi* (Dens of Defeat: My Experience in the Iraqi Ba'th Party) (Beirut, 1993). Another semimemoir comes from Talib Shabib, written down just before his death and edited with careful footnotes by Ali Karim Sa'id: *Iraq 8 Shabat 1963. Min Hawar al-Maghahim ila Hawar al-Dam. Maraja'at Dhakirat Talib Shabib* (Iraq of 8 February 1963: From the Dialogue of Conceptions to the Dialogue of Blood, Reviews in Talib Shabib's Memory) (Beirut, 1999). The Arif regime has received little scholarly attention. Arif's own views, as told to Ali Munir, are represented in "Mudhakkirat Abd al-Salam Arif" (The Memoirs of Abd al-Salam Arif), *Ruz al-Yusuf,* 30 May 1966, but these must be used with caution. Also interesting are a series of articles by Abd al-Rahim Mu'adh, a participant in events who was close to Arif, in "Dhikrayati wa Intaba'at" (My Memoirs and Impressions), *al-Ittihad* (Amman), 9 October 1989–May 8, 1990. For an analysis of changes in the structure of political elites in this period, see Phebe Marr, "Iraq's Leadership Dilemma: A Study in Leadership Trends, 1948–1968," *MEJ* 24 (1970).

The Ba'th Regime to 1990

The Ba'th regime has generated a plethora of journalistic accounts but few good, in-depth studies. Hanna Batatu, *The Old Social Classes and the Revolutionary Movements of Iraq* (Princeton, NJ, 1978), covers the onset of the regime but stops in the mid-1970s. Charles Tripp, *A History of Iraq* (Cambridge, UK, 2000) does bring the regime up to the end of the century. Christine Moss Helms, *Iraq: Eastern Flank of the Arab World* (Washington, DC, 1984); and Majid Khadduri, *Socialist Iraq* (Washington, DC, 1978), are early accounts, both close to the regime's own view. Among the best analyses of the political structure of the regime are Falih Abd al-Jabbar, *al-Daula; al-Mujtama' wa al-Tahawwal al-Dimuqrati fi-l-Iraq* (State, Society, and the Democratic Transition in Iraq) (Cairo, 1995); and Faleh A. Jabar, "The State, Society, Clan, Party, and Army in Iraq," in *From Storm to Thunder,* ed. Faleh A. Jabar, Ahmad Shikara, and Keiki Sakai (Tokyo, 1998). Keiko Sakai has an excellent contribution, "Tribalization as a Tool of State Control in Iraq," in *Tribes and Power: Nationalism and Ethnicity in the Middle East,* ed. Faleh A. Jabar and Hosham Dawood (London, 2002). Amatzia Baram has analyzed the ethnic and social background of the elite in "The Ruling Political Elite in Ba'thi Iraq, 1968–1986," *IJMES* 21 (1989); and in "La 'Maison' de Saddam Husayn," in *Emirs et Presidents,* ed. Pierre Bonte, Edouard Conte, and Paul Dresch (Paris, 2001). Trenchant but accurate critiques of the regime are to be found in Samir al-Khalil (Kanan Makiya), *Republic of Fear* (Berkeley, CA, 1989); and Hasan al-Alawi, *al-Iraq: Daulat al-Munadhima-l-Sirriyya* (Iraq: A State of Secret Organization) (London, 1990). The opposition group the Campaign Against Repression and for Democratic Rights in Iraq has assembled some good essays by scholars of the regime in *Saddam's Iraq: Revolution and Reaction* (London, 1986). An interesting analysis of political dynamics is to be found in Abbas Kelidar, *Iraq: The Search for Stability* (London, 1975). The ideological factor has been dealt with by Amatzia Baram, "Qawmiyya and Wataniyya in Iraq," *Middle East Studies* 19 (1983); Amatzia Baram, *Culture, History, and Ideology in the Formation of Ba'thist Iraq, 1968–1989* (New York: 1990), and Amatzia Baram, *State-Mosque Relations in Ba'thist Iraq, 1968–2003* (forthcoming), a major study of the role of religion under the Ba'th. Other works on the role of ideas and identity in Ba'thist Iraq include Ofra Bengio, *Saddam's Word: Political Discourse in Iraq* (New York, 2002); and Eric Davis, *Memories of State: Politics, History, and Collective Identity in Modern Iraq* (Berkeley, CA, 2005). There are four biographies of Saddam Husain. Two are semiofficial but nonetheless reflect Saddam's thinking in the late 1970s: Amir Iskandar, *Saddam Husain: Munadilan, Mufakkiran wa Insanan* (Saddam Husain: The Fighter, the Thinker, and the Man) (Paris, 1980); and Fuad Matar, *Saddam Hussein: The Man, the Cause, and the Future* (London, n.d.) More objective are Efraim Karsh and Inari Rautsi, *Saddam Hussein: A Political Biography* (New York, 1991); and Said Aburish, *Saddam Hussein: The Politics of Revenge* (London, 2000). For the Ba'th's own perspective, there are party reports, most important of which is the report of the eighth party congress, published as *Revolutionary Iraq, 1968–1973* (Baghdad, 1974), reflecting the policy it was to take thenceforth. Saddam's writings and speeches have been published as pamphlets but also collected in *al-Mu'allafat al-Kamila* (The Complete Works) (Baghdad, 1987–1990). Iraq's foreign policy has been analyzed in several works. Eberhard Kienle looks at the conflict with Syria in *Ba'th vs. Ba'th: The Conflict Between Syria and Iraq, 1968–1989* (New York, 1990). Soviet relations have been dealt with in Oles Smolansky with Bettie Smolansky, *The USSR and Iraq: The Soviet Quest for Influence* (Durham, NC, 1991); and Haim Shemesh, *Soviet-Iraqi Relations, 1968–1988* (Boulder, CO, 1992). Two good analytical chapters on Iraq's foreign policy by Charles Tripp are to be found in "Iraq," in *The Cold War and the Middle East*, ed. Yezid Sayigh and Avi Shlaim (Oxford, UK, 1997); and "The Foreign Policy of Iraq," in *The Foreign Policies of Middle East States*, ed. Raymond Hinnebusch and Enoushiravan Ehteshami (Boulder, CO, 2002). For a general overview of Iraq's foreign policy, see Phebe Marr, "Iraq: Balancing Foreign and Domestic Realities," in *Diplomacy in the Middle East*, ed. L. Carl Brown (New York, 2003).

The Iran-Iraq war has been well covered in a number of works. A valuable insider view of the war is to be found in Wafiq al-Samarra'i, *Hitam al-Bawaba-l-Sharqiyya* (Shattering the Eastern Gates) (Kuwait, 1997). Samarra'i was in charge of the Iraqi military intelligence division responsible for Iran during the war, and he later defected. The causes of the war are dealt with in several works, including Ralph King, *The Iran-Iraq War: The Political Implications* (London,

1987); Efraim Karsh, "Geopolitical Determinism—the Iran-Iraq War," *MEJ* 44 (1990); Majid Khadduri, *The Gulf War: Origins and Implications* (New York: 1988); and Tareq Ismael, *Iraq and Iran: Roots of Conflict* (Syracuse, NY, 1982), which has a useful appendix of documents relating to the crisis. The latter two works present the Iraqi case. A blow-by-blow account of the war is given in Dilip Hiro, *The Longest War* (New York, 1991). The military side is examined in Anthony Cordesman and Abraham Wagner, *The Lessons of Modern War*, vol. 2: *The Iran-Iraq War* (Boulder, CO, 1990).

The way the war affected domestic political dynamics is dealt with in Charles Tripp and Shahram Chubin, *Iran and Iraq at War* (Boulder, CO, 1988). The consequences are examined in Efraim Karsh, ed., *The Iran-Iraq War: Impact and Implications* (New York, 1989); and Christopher Joyner, ed., *The Persian Gulf War* (New York, 1990). A treasure trove of primary source materials based on the regime's own records, captured by American forces in 2003 and now stored in digital form at the Conflict Records Research Center at the National Defense University in Washington, DC, is available to scholars. Two additional collections, mainly composed of Ba'th Party records, are housed at the Hoover Institute at Stanford University and at the Archives at the University of Colorado, Boulder. Interested scholars can contact these institutions. An excellent article on Saddam's motives and views on the United States during this war, drawn from these sources, is Hal Brands and David Palkki, "'Conspiring Bastards': Saddam's Strategic View of the United States" (forthcoming, 2011).

The Gulf War and Its Aftermath

The Gulf War and the events leading up to it have generated an enormous amount of material, much of it uneven. On the Iraqi side are three good accounts: Sa'd al-Bazzaz, *Harb Tulid Ukhra* (One War Gives Birth to Another) (Amman, 1992); Sa'd al-Bazzaz, *al-Janaralat Akhar min Ya'lim* (The Generals Are the Last to Know) (London, 1996); and Wafiq al-Samarra'i, *Hitam al-Bawaba-l-Sharqiyya* (Shattering the Eastern Gates) (Kuwait, 1997). Other good accounts are found in Gregory Gause, "Iraq's Decision to Go to War, 1980 and 1990," *MEJ* 56:1 (Winter 2002); Gregory Gause, *International Relations of the Persian Gulf* (Cambridge, UK, 2010), chap. 4; and Amatzia Baram and Barry Rubin, eds., *Iraq's Road to War* (London, 1993) (especially the chapter by Baram on decisionmaking in Baghdad). Kevin Woods and Mark Stout, "Saddam's Perceptions and Misperceptions: The Case of 'Desert Storm,'" *Journal of Strategic Studies* 33:1 (February 2010), draw on the documents available in the Conflict Records Research Center. Also recommended are Roland Dannreuther,

The Gulf Conflict: The Political and Strategic Analysis (London, 1991–1992); Charles Tripp, "Symbol and Strategy: Iraq and the War for Kuwait," in *The Iraqi Aggression Against Kuwait*, ed. Wolfgang F. Danspeckgruber with Charles Tripp (Boulder, CO, 1996); and Ofra Bengio, "Iraq," *Middle East Contemporary Survey*, 1990. Two accounts from an Arab perspective are Majid Khadduri and Edmond Ghareeb, *War in the Gulf: The Iraq-Kuwait Conflict and Its Implications* (New York, 1997); and Mohamed Heikal, *Illusions of Triumph: An Arab View of the Gulf War* (London, 1993). On the American decision, the two best sources are George H. W. Bush and Brent Scowcroft, *A World Transformed* (New York, 1998), chaps. 13–19; and Bob Woodward, *The Commanders* (New York, 1991). On the war itself, two works stand out: Lawrence Freedman and Efraim Karsh, *The Gulf Conflict, 1990–1991* (Princeton, NJ, 1993); and Michael Gordon and Bernard Trainor, *The General's War* (Boston, 1995). On the background to the tangled Iraq-Kuwait border dispute, the best historical study is Richard Schofield, *Kuwait and Iraq: Historical Claims and Territorial Disputes* (London, 1991). Two worthwhile pieces on the impact of the war on Iraq are John Heidenrich, "The Gulf War: How Many Iraqis Died?" *Foreign Policy* 90 (Spring 1993); and Nuha al-Radi, *Baghdad Diaries* (London, 1998).

The *intifada* has been more difficult to research because of its nature and the difficulty of getting accurate information. A number of participants have written accounts, and a few studies have been attempted, but most should be treated with some caution. Among the best is a series of five articles written by Fa'iq al-Shaikh Ali, "al-Intifada-l-Iraqiyya fi Dhikraha al-Khamisa" (The Iraqi Uprising in Its Fifth Anniversary), *al-Hayat* (London), 22–26 March 1996. Also important are Majid al-Majid, *Intifadat al-Sha'b al-Iraqi* (The Uprising of the Iraqi People) (Beirut, 1991), which traces the *intifada's* background and how the uprising unfolded in different places. Najib al-Salihi, *al-Zalzal* (The Earthquake) (London, 1998), tells the story of the uprising as seen by a retreating officer, with considerable detail on the north and the south. Good accounts in English are Faleh Abd al-Jabbar, "Why the Uprisings Failed," *Middle East Report* 22 (May–June 1992); and Kanan Makiya, *Cruelty and Silence* (New York, 1993). The outside opposition in this period is dealt with in Ibrahim Nawwar, *al-Ma'arida-l-Iraqiyya wal-Sira'a-l-Isqat Saddam* (The Iraqi Opposition and the Struggle to Remove Saddam) (London, 1993), which has lengthy interviews with opposition leaders; and Ali Muhammad al-Shamrani, *Sira' al-Adhdad: al-Ma'arida-l-'Iraqiyya ba'd Harb al-Khaliji* (The Struggle of the Contestants: The Iraqi Opposition After the Gulf War) (London, n.d.).

On the last decade of the regime, especially the sanctions regime and the conflict over weapons inspections, there is much good material in English. The best record of the dispute is the UN volume *The United Nations and the Iraq-Kuwait Conflict, 1990–1996* (New York, 1996), containing a good narrative summary by Boutros Boutros-Ghali of UN involvement, together with all relevant documents and reports. On the issue of arms control and inspections, the main sources are the UN reports of the International Atomic Energy Agency and the UN Special Commission. Also recommended are Scott Ritter, *Endgame: Solving the Iraq Problem Once and for All* (New York, 1999), which details his confrontation with Iraqis as an inspector; and Seymour Hersh, "Saddam's Best Friend," *New Yorker*, 5 April 1999, which discloses CIA involvement in the inspections process. Important in understanding Saddam's motives are works published after 2003 that draw on interviews with Saddam Husain, notably Charles Duelfer, *Hide and Seek: The Search for Truth in Iraq* (New York, 2009).

On the impact of sanctions and the politics involved, see Sarah Graham-Brown, *Sanctioning Saddam: The Politics of Intervention in Iraq* (London, 1999). The economic impact of sanctions on Iraq has been controversial but can be traced in voluminous reports from the UN secretary general, the Food and Agriculture Organization, the World Food Programme, UNICEF, the UN Human Rights Commission, and various nongovernmental organizations, mainly on their Web sites. A good corrective to some of these reports is to be found in Amatzia Baram, "The Effect of Iraqi Sanctions: Statistical Pitfalls and Responsibility," *MEJ* 54 (Spring 2000). Studies on Iraq's economy after the Gulf War are sparse owing to greatly reduced access to materials by scholars and Iraq's isolation. Assessment of the damage done by sanctions only slowly came to light after the occupation by coalition forces in 2003, and much scholarly study needs to be undertaken on Iraq's economy. The Iraqi government published statistical abstracts each year, *Annual Abstract of Statistics (AAS)*, but in the decade of the 1990s these were difficult to obtain, and since the early 1980s Iraqi statistics have been increasingly viewed as suspect.

The restructuring of Iraq's political system after the Gulf War and the *intifada* has been more difficult to document because of Iraq's isolation. Among the most reliable works on this subject are several by Amatzia Baram: *Building Toward Crisis: Saddam Husayn's Strategy for Survival* (Washington, DC, 1998); "Saddam's Power Structure: The Tikritis Before, During, and After the War," in *Iraq at the Crossroads: State and Society in the Shadow of Regime Change*, ed. Toby Dodge and Steven Simon (London, 2003); "Neo-Tribalism in Iraq: Saddam Hussein's Tribal Policies, 1991–1996," *IJMES* 29 (1997), and by Faleh Abdul Jabar: "Sheikhs and Ideologues," in *Tribes and Power: Nationalism and Ethnicity in the Middle East*, ed. Faleh A. Jabar and Hosham Dawood (London, 2002); "The State, Society, Clan, Party, and Army in Iraq," in *From Storm to Thunder*,

ed. Faleh A. Jabar, Ahmad Shikara, and Keiki Sakai (Tokyo, 1998). A good journalistic account is Andrew Cockburn and Patrick Cockburn, *Out of the Ashes:*
The Resurrection of Saddam Hussein (New York, 1999). Two collections of essays
by scholars have varied content: D. Hopwood, H. Ishaw, and T. Koszinowski,
eds., *Iraq: Power and Society* (Reading, PA, 1993), tends to be favorably disposed
to Iraq; Fran Hazelton, ed., *Iraq Since the Gulf War: Prospects for Democracy*
(London, 1994), is opposed to the regime. An excellent article by Isam al-
Khafaji, "The Myth of Iraqi Exceptionalism," *Middle East Policy* 7:4 (October
2000), outlines Iraq's unfavorable development. Good analyses of the reorganization of the military and the security systems can be found in Anthony Cordes-
man and Ahmed Hashim, *Iraq: Sanctions and Beyond* (Boulder, CO, 1997);
Michael Eisenstadt, "Like a Phoenix from the Ashes: The Future of Iraqi Mili-
tary Power," Policy Paper No. 36 (Washington, DC, 1993); and Sean Boyne,
"Inside Iraq's Security Network," part 2, *Jane's Intelligence Review*, August 1997.
The regime's own view can be found in Saddam Husain's collected works and in
Arab Ba'th Socialist Party, *al-Bayan al-Siyasi an al-Mu'tamar al-Qutri al-Ashir*
(Political Report of the Tenth Regional Congress) (Baghdad, 1991). A collection
of high-quality journalistic articles from a variety of Western, Iraqi, and Middle
Eastern sources on Iraq in the period is contained in *al-Malaf al-Iraqiyya* (The
Iraqi File), published monthly by Ghassan Atiyya in London. Thabit Abdulla
gives a history of Iraq from this period to the present from an Iraqi perspective
in *Dictatorship, Imperialism, and Chaos: Iraq Since 1989* (London, 2006). For a
good retrospect of Iraqi history by leading scholars, see an edited volume by
Amatzia Baram, Achin Rohde, and Ronen Zeidel, eds., *Iraq Between Occupa-*
tions: Perspectives from 1920 to the Present (New York, 2010).

Iraq After 2003

Iraq's evolution since 2003 is still under way; hence, there is as yet no overar-
ching study of this critical period, but practitioners, journalists, and scholars
have produced books, articles, and memoirs on specific periods or aspects of
the period. The opening of Iraq has also produced or made available documents and reports now accessible on the Internet. These vary in quality, and
only the most useful and significant can be mentioned here.

The occupation and its immediate aftermath in Iraq have generated reams
of material, including journalistic accounts and memoirs by some of the main
participants. On the controversial U.S. decision to invade, Bob Woodward,
Plan of Attack (New York, 2004); Iva Daalder and James Lindsey, *America Un-*
bound: The Bush Revolution in Foreign Policy (Washington, DC, 2003); and

Michael Isikoff and David Corn, *Hubris* (New York, 2006) are among the best. Among the memoirs, Richard Clarke, *Against All Enemies: Inside America's War on Terror* (London, 2004); and Douglas Feith, *War and Decision* (New York, 2008), both with differing views, are worth reading. David Phillips, *Losing Iraq: Inside the Postwar Reconstruction Fiasco* (Boulder, CO, 2005), details the failure of political planning beforehand; the failed State Department effort on the Future of Iraq Project can be downloaded from the National Security Archive. Gregory Gause, *International Relations of the Persian Gulf* (Cambridge, UK, 2010), chap. 6, gives the best short assessment of how and why the decision was made. On the conduct of the war itself, the best book is Michael Gordon and General Bernard Trainor, *Cobra II: The Inside Story of the Invasion and Occupation of Iraq* (New York, 2006). Saddam's motives and reactions can be found in Kevin Woods et al., *The Iraqi Perspectives Report* (Annapolis, MD, 2006), based on captured Iraqi documents.

On the aftermath of the war and the attempt to remake Iraq, the essential work is Ali Allawi, *The Occupation of Iraq: Winning the War, Losing the Peace* (New Haven, CT, 2007). Written by an Iraqi participant in events and meticulous in scholarship, it is the single best book on this period. Among the best of the rest are George Packer, *The Assassin's Gate: America in Iraq* (New York, 2005), an insightful journalist's analysis; Eric Herring and Glen Rangwala, *Iraq in Fragments: The Occupation and Its Legacy* (Ithaca, NY, 2006), an excellent academic study; Rajiv Chandrasekaran, *Imperial Life in the Emerald City* (New York, 2006); and Thomas Ricks, *Fiasco: The American Military Adventure in Iraq* (New York, 2006). Firsthand accounts are given by Larry Diamond, *Squandered Victory* (New York, 2005), a scholar who served briefly in Iraq; and Rory Stewart, *The Prince of the Marshes and Other Occupational Hazards of a Year in Iraq* (London, 2006), an administrator on the ground in southern Iraq. L. Paul Bremer III, *My Year in Iraq* (New York, 2006), gives his own account as chief of the Coalition Provisional Authority. Several "think tanks" have published trenchant assessments of the CPA's activities and outcomes, including several special reports from the United States Institute of Peace (USIP): Celeste J. Ward, *The Coalition Provisional Authority's Experience with Governance in Iraq* (no. 139, 2005); Anne Ellen Henderson, *The Coalition Provisional Authority's Experience with Economic Reconstruction in Iraq* (no. 138, 2005); and Robert Perito, *The Coalition Provisional Authority's Experience with Public Security in Iraq* (no. 137, 2005). Rand has published a later assessment: James Dobbins et al., *Occupying Iraq: A History of the Coalition Provisional Authority* (Santa Monica, CA, 2009). A good economic analysis is Bathsheba Crocker, "Reconstructing Iraq's Economy, *Washington Quarterly*

27:4 (2004). CPA documents and decrees can be accessed through the CPA Web site: www.iraqcoalition.org.

The emergence of the new political order in Iraq from the 15 November agreement until the end of the 2005 elections has also been well covered in several of the books mentioned previously, especially Allawi, *The Occupation of Iraq*; Herring and Rangwala, *Iraq in Fragments*; Ricks, *Fiasco*; and Bremmer, *My Year in Iraq*. More detailed analysis can be found in a number of papers and studies. Among the best and most detailed are those published by the International Crisis Group (ICG) Middle East Reports, in particular: "Iraq's Kurds: Toward an Historic Compromise" (no. 26, 2004); "Iraq's Transition: On a Knife's Edge" (no. 27, 2004); and "Iraq: Can Local Governance Save the Central Government?" (no. 33, 2004). Peter Galbraith deals with his role during the negotiations for the Transitional Administrative Law and the constitution in a work that is otherwise a thorough critique of US policy toward Iraq: *The End of Iraq: How American Incompetence Created a War Without End* (New York, 2006). Sistani's role is dealt with by Reidar Visser, *Sistani, the United States, and Politics in Iraq*, Norwegian Institute of International Affairs, No. 700 (2006); and by Babak Rahimi, *Ayatallah Sistani and the Democratization of post-Ba'thist Iraq*, USIP Special Report No. 187 (2007). Ahmad Chalabi presents his largely self-serving view in several interviews with *al-Hayat* serialized from 21 March to 1 April 2004. Good articles on the drafting of the constitution include Jonathan Morrow, *Iraq's Constitutional Process II, an Opportunity Lost*, USIP Special Report No. 155 (2005); and Ashley S. Deeks and Matthew D. Burton, "Iraq's Constitution: A Drafting History," *Cornell International Law Journal* 40:1 (2007). On the 2005 elections, the best article is Adeed Dawisha and Larry Diamond, "Iraq's Year of Voting Dangerously," *Journal of Democracy* 17:2 (2006). On provincial politics, see Michael Knights and Eamon McCarthy, "Provincial Politics in Iraq: Fragmentation or a New Awakening?" Washington Institute for Near East Policy, No. 81 (2008). A good summary of the year's events is found in Kenneth Katzman, "Iraq: Post-Saddam Governance and Security," Congressional Research Service Report, April 2006. The election process and the results can be found on the Website of the Independent Election Commission of Iraq: www.ieciraq.org.

The insurgencies (both Sunni and Sadrist) and the sectarian war of 2006–2007 have been dealt with in several books but mainly in journal articles. The best account of the Sunni insurgency, especially its motives and background, is Ahmed Hashim, *Insurgency and Counter-insurgency in Iraq* (Ithaca, NY, 2006). Hashim was on the ground at the time. Good accounts are also given in Amatzia Baram, *Who Are the Insurgents? Sunni Arab Rebels in Iraq*, USIP Special

Report No. 134 (2005); Roel Meijer, "The Association of Muslim Scholars in Iraq," *Middle East Report*, no. 237 (2005); and ICG, "In their Own Words: Reading the Iraqi Insurgency" (no. 50, 2006). David Kilcullen, "Anatomy of a Tribal Revolt," *Small Wars Journal*, 2007, www.smallwarsjournal.com, discusses the Sunni tribal awakening.

A good journalistic account of the Sadr phenomemon and the background to his movement is found in Patrick Cockburn, *Muqtada: Muqtada al-Sadr, the Shia Revival, and the Struggle for Iraq* (New York, 2008), but good studies on the movement from a ground-level perspective are scarce. Among the best available are Juan Cole, "The United States and the Shi'ite Religious Factions in Postwar Iraq," *MEJ* 57:4 (2003); Amatzia Baram, "Sadr the Father, Sadr the Son, the 'Revolution in Shi'ism,' and the Struggle for Power in the Hawzah of Najaf," in *Iraq Between Occupations: Perspectives from 1920 to the Present*, ed. Amatzia Baram, Ronen Zeidel, and Achim Rohde (New York, 2010); Marissa Cochrane, "The Fragmentation of the Sadrist Movement," Institute for the Study of War, Iraq Report No. 12 (2009); and ICG, "Iraq's Muqtada al-Sadr: Spoiler or Stabilizer?" (no. 55, 2006). The sectarian war and the surge are discussed in Linda Robinson, *Tell Me How This Ends* (New York, 2008), a good journalistic account. George Packer has a vivid article on Tal Afar in "The Lesson of Tal Afar," *New Yorker*, 10 April 2006. A good ground-level account of the war in Baghdad is found in Michael Comstock, "The Battle for Saydia," *Small Wars Journal*, 2008. Deborah Amos deals with the fallout from the struggle in *The Eclipse of the Sunnis: Power, Exile, and Upheaval in the Middle East* (New York, 2010).

For the period since 2007, good in-depth analysis is still hard to come by. Even though press accounts and online blogs are voluminous, in Arabic and in English, access to sources on the ground is still difficult, even for Iraqis. Interpretations of events often vary according to the eye of the beholder and the sources available; hence, most accounts must be considered tentative at best—a first draft of the history that will, of necessity, be written later. The best on-the-ground reporting of events in this period can be found in ICG reports, especially "Oil for Soil" (no. 80, 2008); "Iraq and the Kurds: Trouble Along the Trigger Line" (no. 88, 2009); "Iraq's New Battlefront: The Struggle over Ninewa" (no. 90, 2009); and "Iraq's Uncertain Future: Elections and Beyond" (no. 94, 2010). Two excellent blog accounts of events in this period are those of Reidar Visser, www.historiae.org; and Juan Cole, Informed Comment, www.juancole.com.

Bob Woodward, *The War Within* (New York, 2008), gives a good account of the debates within the U.S. administration that led to the surge and a change of policy on Iraq. On Iraq itself, Reidar Visser and Gareth Stansfield, eds., *An*

Iraq of Its Regions: Cornerstones of a Federal Democracy? (New York, 2010), have good assessments by experienced scholars of Iraq's regions and groups since 2003. Reidar Visser, *A Responsible End? The United States and the Iraqi Transition, 2005–2010* (Charlottesville, VA, 2010), contains detailed and useful analysis of political events since 2007 from his blog, embedded in large quantities of political advice. An edited volume by Amnon Cohen and Noga Efrati, *Post-Saddam Iraq: New Realities, Old Identities, Changing Patterns* (East Sussex, UK, 2011), has a number of very good studies on the new Iraq. An analysis of Iraq's new political leaders is found in two studies by Phebe Marr: *Who Are Iraq's Leaders? What Do They Want?* USIP Special Report No. 160 (2006); and *Iraq's New Political Map*, USIP Special Report No. 179 (2007). Denise Natali has authored an excellent study on Kurdistan, *The Kurdish Quasi-State* (Syracuse, NY, 2010), based on ground-level research. For good data and analysis of the security situation, see Anthony Cordesman, *Iraq: The Realities of US "Withdrawal" of Combat Forces and the Challenges of Strategic Partnership* (Washington, DC, 30 August 2010), http://csis.org/publications/iraq-realities-US-withdrawal-combat -forces-and-challenges-strategic-partnership. Further updates are available in an online report by Anthony Cordesman, "Iraq and the United States," http://csis .org/publications/Iraq-and-the-United States.

The economic and social impact of events since 2003 is best followed through institutional reports, such as those of the World Bank and various UN organizations, as well as scholars and journalists reporting for more specialized professional organizations, all available on the Web. A good overview of the economy can be found in Joseph Sassoon, "Economic Policy in Iraq, 2003–2009," in Cohen and Efrati, *Post-Saddam Iraq*; and in SIGIR (Special Inspector General for Iraq Reconstruction), *Hard Lessons: The Iraq Reconstruction Experience* (Washington, DC, 2009). Among the best sources on oil developments are the U.S. Department of Energy, Energy Information Administration, "Country Analysis Briefs: Iraq," periodically updated, and the reporting done by Ben Lando for the *Iraq Oil Report*, at benlando@iraqoilreport.com. The London Economist, Economist Intelligence Unit, *Country Reports on Iraq*; and SIGIR's "Quarterly Reports," www.sigir.org, are also very good sources on the economy and its development. On social and demographic change and the refugee crisis, the best books are Joseph Sassoon, *The Iraqi Refugees: The New Crisis in the Middle East* (New York, 2009); and Amos, *The Eclipse of the Sunnis*. Detailed accounts of Iraqi displacement and returnees are published periodically by the UN High Commissioner for Refugees and the International Organization for Migration– Iraq, the latter at www.iomiraq.net. Several good studies on women are available: Noga Efrati, "Women in Post-Saddam Iraq: Hopes and Disappointments," in

Post-Saddam Iraq, ed. Cohen and Efrati; Yasmin Husein al-Jawaheri, *Women in Iraq: The Gender Impact of International Sanctions* (Boulder, CO, 2008); and Nadje Sadig al-Ali, *Iraqi Women* (London, 2007).

Shi'a Since the Gulf War

In the past two decades more attention has been given to the Shi'a of Iraq and their recent history. Two general works are useful: Graham Fuller and Rend Rahim Franke, *The Arab Shi'a: The Forgotten Muslims* (New York, 1999); and Vali Nasr, *The Shia Revival: How Conflicts Within Islam Will Shape the Future* (New York, 2006). On relations between Shi'a and Sunnis in Iraq from the Shi'i point of view, two books stand out: Abd al-Karim al-Uzri (a former minister), *Mushkilat al-Hukm fi-l-Iraq* (The Problem of Governance in Iraq) (London, 1991); and Hasan al-Alawi (a former Ba'th Party member), *al-Shi'a wal-Daula-l-Qaumiyya fil-Iraq* (The Shi'a and the Nationalist State in Iraq) (France, 1989). On the rise of the Shi'i Islamic movements, see Faleh A. Jabar, *The Shi'ite Movement in Iraq* (London, 2003); and Joyce Wiley, *The Islamic Movement of Iraqi Shias* (Boulder, CO, 1992). On Muhammad Baqir al-Sadr, the founder of the movement, there are numerous studies; among the best are Shaikh Muhammad Rida al-Na'mani, *al-Shahid al-Sadr: Sanawat al-Mihna wal-Ayyam al-Hisar* (The Martyr Sadr: Years of Tribulation, Days of Blockade) (n.pl., 1997); Ali al-Mu'min, *Sanawat al-Jumar: Musirat al-Harakat al-Islamiyya fi-l-Iraq, 1958–1986* (Years of Embers: The Journey of the Islamic Movement in Iraq, 1958–1986) (London, 1993); T. M. Aziz, "The Role of Muhammad Baqir al-Sadr," *IJMES* 25 (1993); and Chibli Mallat, "Religious Militancy in Contemporary Iraq: Muhammad Baqer as-Sadr and the Sunni/Shia Paradigm," *Third World Quarterly* 10:2 (April 1988). The best example of Sadr's own work is to be found in *Falsafatuna* (Our Philosophy) (Beirut, 1982); and *Iqtisaduna* (Our Economics) (Beirut, 1982). On Muhammad Sadiq al-Sadr, see Amatzia Baram, "Sadr the Father, Sadr the Son, the 'Revolution in Shi'ism,' and the Struggle for Power in the Hawzah of Najaf," in *Iraq Between Occupations: Perspectives from 1920 to the Present*, ed. Amatzia Baram, Ronen Zeidel, and Achim Rohde (New York, 2010); and Amatzia Baram, *State-Mosque Relations in Ba'thist Iraq, 1968–2003* (forthcoming). On the death of Muhammad Sadiq al-Sadr and interesting material on the politics of the *hauza*, see Fa'iq al-Shaikh Ali, *Aghsal Sha'b* (The Assassination of a People) (London, 2000). For current Shi'i leaders, see the works cited previously on Sistani and Muqtada al-Sadr. The best material on the current leaders and movements are Patrick Cockburn, *Muqtada: Muqtada al-Sadr, the Shia Revival, and the Struggle for Iraq* (New York, 2008); Baram,

"Sadr the Father, Sadr the Son"; and ICG reports "Iraq's Muqtada al-Sadr: Spoiler or Stabilizer?" (no. 55, 2006); and "Shiite Politics in Iraq: The Role of the Supreme Council" (no. 70, 2007).

The Kurds

The Iraqi Kurds have received considerable attention in a number of recent works. The best general history of the Kurds is David McDowall, *A Modern History of the Kurds* (London, 1997). On the early phases of the Kurdish nationalist movement, there are numerous good studies, some scholarly, some journalistic, drawing on interviews with the main participants. These include Chris Kutschera, *le Mouvement national Kurde* (The Kurdish National Movement) (Paris, 1979); Sa'ad Jawad, *Iraq and the Kurdish Question, 1958–1970* (London, 1981); and Edmond Ghareeb, *The Kurdish Question in Iraq* (Syracuse, NY, 1981). The Kurdish point of view is well represented by Ismet Cheriff Vanley in *le Kurdistan Irakien Entité Nationale* (Iraqi Kurdistan, a National Entity) (Boudry-Neuchatel, Switzerland, 1970); and Ismet Cheriff Vanley, "Le Kurdistan d'Irak" (Iraqi Kurdistan) in *Les Kurdes et le Kurdistan* (The Kurds and Kurdistan), ed. Gerard Challiand (Paris, 1978). There are also works by some of the main participants, including Jalal Talabani, in *Kurdistan wal-Haraka-l-Qaumiyya-l-Kurdiyya* (Kurdistan and the Kurdish National Movement (Beirut, 1971); Naushirwan Mustafa Amin in *Al-Akrad wal-Barliman* (The Kurds and Parliament) (Arbil, Iraq, 1993); Naushirwan Mustafa Amin, *Hukumat Kurdistan: Kurd la Gama Soviet da* (The Government of Kurdistan: The Kurds in the Soviet Game) (Utrecht, the Netherlands, 1993); Naushirwan Mustafa Amin, *Fingers That Crush Each Other: Iraqi Kurdistan from 1979 to 1983* (in Kurdish) (Sulaimaniyya, Iraq, 1998); and Naushirwan Mustafa Amin, *Going Around in Circles: Events in Kurdistan, 1984–1988* (in Kurdish) (Berlin, 1999). The parties have published records: KDP, *Kurdistan Democratic Party Congresses, 1946–1993* (Arbil, Iraq, 1993); and PUK, *Revolution in Kurdistan: The Essential Documents of the Patriotic Union of Kurdistan* (New York, 1977). A number of good studies have dealt with the Kurdish uprising of 1991 and subsequent events in Iraqi Kurdistan. The best scholarly study is Gareth Stansfield, *Iraqi Kurdistan: Political Development and Emergent Democracy* (London: 2003). On the civil strife between the parties, see Michael Gunter, "The KDP-PUK Conflict in Northern Iraq," *MEJ* 50:2 (Spring 1996); and two white papers put out by both parties: KDP, "What Happened in Iraqi Kurdistan in May 1994" (June 1994); and PUK, "Iraqi Kurdistan: A Situation Report on Recent Events" (February 1995). Jonathan Randall gives a sympathetic but thorough journalistic account of these years in *After Such Knowledge, What Forgiveness? My Encounters with Kurdistan* (New York, 1997); and Michael Gunter has dealt with them in *The Kurdish Predicament in Iraq* (New York, 1999). The Anfal campaign against the Kurds is best dealt with in Middle East Watch, *Genocide in Iraq: The Anfal Campaign Against the Kurds* (New York, 1993); and a major study by Joost Hiltermann, *A Poisonous Affair: America, Iraq, and the Gassing of Halabja* (New York, 2007). The post-2003 situation has generated numerous books, many openly supportive of Kurdish national aims. These include several edited volumes, among them Mohammed M. A. Ahmed and Michael Gunter, eds., *The Kurdish Question and the 2003 Iraqi War* (Costa Mesa, CA, 2005); and Mohammed M. A. Ahmed and Michael Gunter, eds., *The Evolution of Kurdish Nationalism* (Costa Mesa, CA, 2007). Hussein Tahiri, *The Structure of Kurdish Society and the Struggle for a Kurdish State* (Costa Mesa, CA, 2007); and Denise Natali, *The Kurdish Quasi-State* (Syracuse, NY, 2010), provide more critical analyses. A good account of post-2003 Kurdish political dynamics is found in Michel Eppel, "Kurdish Leadership in Post-Saddam Iraq," in *Iraq Between Occupations: Perspectives from 1920 to the Present*, ed. Amatzia Baram, Ronen Zeidel, and Achim Rohde (New York, 2010).

INDEX